BIBLICAL PREACHING
AN EXPOSITOR'S TREASURY

EDITED BY
JAMES W. COX

THE WESTMINSTER PRESS
Philadelphia

ACKNOWLEDGMENTS
National Council of Churches, for Scripture quotations from the Revised Standard Version of the Bible, copyright 1946, 1952, © 1971, 1973.

Oxford University Press, Inc., and Cambridge University Press, for Scripture quotations from *The New English Bible,* copyright © the Delegates of the Oxford University Press and the Syndics of the Cambridge University Press 1961, 1970.

BOOK DESIGN BY ALICE DERR

First edition

Published by The Westminster Press ®
Philadelphia, Pennsylvania

PRINTED IN THE UNITED STATES OF AMERICA
9 8 7 6 5 4 3 2 1

Dedicated to the Memory

of

CLYDE TAYLOR FRANCISCO

1916–1981

Library of Congress Cataloging in Publication Data

Main entry under title:

Biblical preaching.

Includes bibliographies and index.
1. Bible—Homiletical use. I. Cox, James William,
1923–   .
BS534.5.B5 1983   251   83-10518
ISBN 0-664-21397-9

CONTENTS

CONTRIBUTORS

ELIZABETH ACHTEMEIER, Visiting Professor of Homiletics and Old Testament, Union Theological Seminary, Richmond, Va. B.A., Stanford University; M.Div., Union Theological Seminary, New York City; Ph.D., Columbia University. Author: *Preaching as Theology and Art; Creative Preaching; The Old Testament and the Proclamation of the Gospel; The Community and Message of Isaiah 56–66*. Editor: *Proclamation 2; Proclamation 3*.

GEORGE R. BEASLEY-MURRAY, Professor of New Testament Interpretation, Southern Baptist Theological Seminary (Retired). Principal, Spurgeon's College, London, 1958–1973. B.D., Spurgeon's College, London University; Th.M., Ph.D., King's College, London University; B.A., M.A., Jesus College Cambridge University; D.D., London University. Author: *Preaching the Gospel from the Gospels; Baptism in the New Testament; The Book of Revelation*.

RONALD E. CLEMENTS, University Lecturer in Divinity and Fellow of Fitzwilliam College, Cambridge University. B.D., Spurgeon's College; B.A., M.A., Christ's College, Cambridge University; Ph.D., Sheffield University. Author: *God and Temple; Abraham and David; God's Chosen People; Prophecy and Covenant; Prophecy and Tradition; One Hundred Years of Old Testament Interpretation*.

JAMES W. COX, Victor and Louise Lester Professor of Christian Preaching, Southern Baptist Theological Seminary. B.A., Carson-Newman College; M.Div., Ph.D., Southern Baptist Theological Seminary. Author: *A Guide to Biblical Preaching; The Twentieth Century Pulpit*, Vols. I and II. Editor: *Pulpit Digest* and *The Minister's Manual* (an annual volume).

CLYDE T. FRANCISCO, John R. Sampey Professor of Old Testament Interpretation until his death in 1981, Southern Baptist Theological Seminary. A.B., University of Richmond; Th.M., Th.D., Southern Baptist Theological Seminary. Author: *Introducing the Old Testament; Studies in Jeremiah; Book of Deuteronomy.* Translator: *Proverbs,* Berkeley Version of the Bible.

REGINALD H. FULLER, Professor of New Testament, Virginia Theological Seminary. B.A., M.A., Cambridge University; S.T.D., General Theological Seminary, Philadelphia Theological Seminary. Translator of Bonhoeffer. Author: *Interpreting the Miracles; The Foundations of New Testament Christology; The Use of the Bible in Preaching.*

WILLIAM E. HULL, Pastor of the First Baptist Church, Shreveport, La. Professor, Dean of the School of Theology, and Provost, Southern Baptist Theological Seminary, 1955–1975. B.A., Samford University; M.Div., Ph.D., Southern Baptist Theological Seminary. Author: *The Gospel of John; Beyond the Barriers;* and *Love in Four Dimensions.*

DONALD MACLEOD, Frances L. Patton Professor of Preaching and Worship, Princeton Theological Seminary. A.B., M.A., LL.D., Dalhousie University, Nova Scotia; M.Div., D.D., Pine Hill Seminary, Nova Scotia; Th.D., University of Toronto. Author: seven titles, including *Presbyterian Worship.* Editor: *Princeton Seminary Bulletin,* 1955–1982.

JAMES EARL MASSEY, Professor of New Testament and Homiletics, Anderson School of Theology. Founding pastor, Metropolitan Church of God of Detroit, 1954–1976. Radio preacher, Christian Brotherhood Hour, 1977–1981. B.R.E., B.Th., Detroit Bible College; M.A., Oberlin College; University of Michigan. Author: *The Sermon in Perspective; Designing the Sermon.*

HENRY H. MITCHELL, Dean, School of Theology of Virginia Union University and Professor of Homiletics. B.A., Lincoln University; M.A. (Linguistics), California State University at Fresno; M.Div., Union Theological Seminary, New York City; Th.D., Southern California School of Theology at Claremont. Author: *Black Belief; Black Preaching; The Recovery of Preaching* (Beecher Lectures).

ERIC C. RUST, Professor Emeritus of Christian Philosophy, Southern Baptist Theological Seminary. B.Sc., M.Sc., London University; B.A., M.A., B.D, Oxford University; Litt.D., University of Richmond.

Author: *Christian Understanding of History; Salvation History; Science and Faith; Religion, Revelation, and Reason; The Word and Words: Towards a Theology of Preaching.*

LEO R. SANDS, C.S.B., Associate Professor of Preaching and Communications, University of St. Michael's College, Toronto School of Theology, Ontario. B.A., University of Ottawa; S.T.B., University of St. Michael's College; M.A., University of Michigan; M.A., Catholic University of America; Ph.D., Pennsylvania State University. Author: "Preaching Since the Council" (article).

EDUARD SCHWEIZER, Professor of New Testament, University of Zurich, Switzerland; Rector, 1964–1966. Visiting professor in numerous countries. D. Theol., University of Zurich. Author: EGO EIMI; *Jesus; The Good News According to Mark; The Good News According to Matthew; The Letter to the Colossians; Luke: A Challenge to Present Theology; God's Inescapable Nearness.*

FRANK STAGG, Emeritus Professor of New Testament Interpretation, Southern Baptist Theological Seminary. B.A., Louisiana College; Th.M. and Ph.D., Southern Baptist Theological Seminary; LL.D., Louisiana College. Author: *Polarities of Man's Existence in Biblical Perspective;* coauthored with wife, *Woman in the World of Jesus.*

KRISTER STENDAHL is the Andrew W. Mellon Professor of Divinity at the Harvard Divinity School, where he teaches New Testament and the Arts of Preaching and Worship. He was educated at the Uppsala University, Sweden, and is a pastor in the Lutheran Church in America. Some of his publications are *The School of St. Matthew; The Bible and the Role of Women; Holy Week;* and *Paul Among Jesus and Gentiles.*

DWIGHT E. STEVENSON, Dean Emeritus and Professor of Homiletics Emeritus, Lexington Theological Seminary. A.B., Bethany College; B.D., Yale University; D.D., Bethany College. Recently, coordinator, Theological Education Association of Mid-America; currently, visiting professor of Old Testament, Episcopal Theological Seminary in Kentucky.

WILLIAM P. TUCK, Professor of Christian Preaching, Southern Baptist Theological Seminary. B.A., D.D., University of Richmond; B.D., Th.M., Southeastern Baptist Theological Seminary; Th.D., New

Orleans Baptist Theological Seminary. Pastor for twenty years of churches in Virginia and Louisiana. Author: *Facing Grief and Death.* Editor: *The Struggle for Meaning.*

JOHN D. W. WATTS, Professor of Old Testament, Southern Baptist Theological Seminary. Former President and Dean of Baptist Theological Seminary, Ruschlikon, Switzerland; Professor of Old Testament, Fuller Theological Seminary. B.A., Mississippi College; Th.M., New Orleans Baptist Theological Seminary; Ph.D., Southern Baptist Theological Seminary. Author: *The Books of Joel . . . Zephaniah,* Cambridge Bible Commentaries on the New English Bible. Old Testament Editor for *Word Biblical Commentary.*

INTRODUCTION
JAMES W. COX

These chapters have been prepared under the influence of several assumptions:

The Bible speaks a message that is crucial for our lives today;

The Scriptures have decisive value as instruments of God's continuing disclosure of his nature and ongoing purpose;

The historical-critical method is essential to a thorough understanding of the text in its present significance;

It is possible to present the biblical message in ways that effectively expose its credibility, its timely relevance, and its urgent authority.

It is the editor's hope that preaching ministers, students for the ministry, and teachers of religion will find here a comprehensive reference tool for biblical exposition, that is, for preaching that "gives diligence" to let the timely Word of God come to expression with clear reference to the text. Those who wish to make a further study of principles and methods of biblical preaching can find guidance in a number of books on this subject, and a brief selection of these is listed at the end of this introduction.

While the authors of the chapters follow the same general approach, their contributions reflect their personal convictions as to the nature and significance of the biblical text. Each author has final control over the content of his or her chapter. Though individual authors have differently structured their chapters, each chapter can be divided roughly into two parts: (1) general exegetical/hermeneutical matters related to the biblical writer's theme(s), and (2) homiletical studies of pivotal texts. The purpose of these studies is twofold: (1) to give examples of how to work through a biblical text toward a homiletical interpretation; (2) to provide material that can be reminted, expanded, and/or applied in developing sermons or Bible lessons, studies that will enhance the preacher's ability to move responsibly from "then" to "now."

The impact of the Bible on preaching should result in making its words and themes increasingly accessible to the needs of people living today. If this does not happen, something is amiss in our preaching and must be set right.

Two esteemed colleagues, whose contributions appear in this work and whose books are well known in the scholarly world, have been my consultants in the editorial phase of this project. Eric C. Rust has carefully read the Old Testament chapters, and Frank Stagg the New Testament chapters. To them I wish to express hearty thanks.

In addition, I gratefully acknowledge the helpful suggestions made at an early stage of the project by my late, lamented colleague, Clyde T. Francisco, and by a former colleague, Peter Rhea Jones, pastor of the First Baptist Church of Decatur, Georgia. These friends shared with me in the joyful venture of a team-taught class in biblical preaching and exemplified the ability to do superbly what they taught.

FOR FURTHER READING

Achtemeier, Elizabeth. *The Old Testament and the Proclamation of the Gospel.* Westminster Press, 1973. Proper methods of preaching from Old Testament texts presented by discussion and example.

Best, Ernest. *From Text to Sermon: Responsible Use of the New Testament in Preaching.* John Knox Press, 1978.

Cox, James W. *A Guide to Biblical Preaching.* Abingdon Press, 1976. A presentation of homiletical method, including content, strategy, structure, illustration, and style.

Robinson, Haddon W. *Biblical Preaching: The Development and Delivery of Expository Messages.* Baker Book House, 1980. A step-by-step procedure for the development and delivery of expository messages.

Sanders, James A. *God Has a Story Too.* Fortress Press, 1979. Examples and explanations of the movement from Scripture to sermon.

Schweizer, Eduard. *God's Inescapable Nearness.* Tr. James W. Cox. Word Books, 1971. Thirteen sermons by a well-known New Testament scholar, prefaced by an essay analyzing Schweizer's preaching.

Smart, James D. *The Strange Silence of the Bible in the Church.* Westminster Press, 1970. Addressed to "the problem of how to translate the full content of an ancient text into the language and life-context of late twentieth-century persons."

Thompson, William D. *Preaching Biblically: Exegesis and Interpretation.* Abingdon Press, 1981. Sets forth basic principles and a simple methodology.

1. PREACHING FROM THE PRIMEVAL NARRATIVES OF GENESIS

CLYDE T. FRANCISCO

It is not wise to force a choice between modern science and Genesis, for not only does it tend to polarize people, it is not necessary. The principal point of tension between Genesis and science is in the area of the time element in creation. The Bible says that the earth was created in six days, and science opts for billions of years.

One way to approach the matter is superbly presented in an unforgettable scene in *The King and I*. Anna is summoned late one night to the king's audience hall, where she finds the Siamese monarch engrossed in the reading of a large book. "Why, your majesty," she exclaims, "you are reading the Bible!"

His response was to the effect that Moses was surely an ill-informed man if he thought the world was created in six days. Anna's reply was informed and accurate: "Your majesty, Moses was not a man of science; he was a man of faith."

However, the writer of Scripture may not be as much at fault as his interpreters are in error. A close scrutiny of Genesis 1 and 2 reveals that the term "day" is used in three different ways. It is used of light over against darkness (Gen. 1:5a); a combination of light and darkness ("evening" and "morning," Gen. 1:5b); and the whole period of creation ("In the day the LORD God made the earth and the heavens," Gen. 2:4b).

The terms "evening" and "morning" are literally "twilight" and "dawn" and do not so much describe a twenty-four-hour day as they do prolonged periods of darkness followed by the dawning of light. Furthermore, the sun was not created until the fourth day and it is the earth's position in reference to the sun that is responsible for the twenty-four-hour day.

The end of each day is marked by the formula "evening and morning." However, the seventh day does not have this phrase applied to it. It is the opinion of the writer of The Letter to the Hebrews that we are still in the seventh day, the day of God's rest. If the seventh day is of indeterminate length, why should the others be arbitrarily limited to twenty-four hours?

There is yet a better way to resolve the tension. This becomes apparent when we are aware that there are two accounts of creation in the book of Genesis itself.[1] Instead of one biblical perspective on creation, there are two. Genesis 1:1–2:4a is generally regarded as Priestly material and Gen. 2:4b–4:26 as a Judean source. The Priestly source was completed by 500 B.C. (in the Babylonian exile) and the Judean material by 950 B.C. (during Solomon's reign). This earlier source is anthropomorphic and does not attempt to approach creation chronologically, whereas the writer of the more sophisticated source is chronological and meticulous. They do not have the same order of creation. In Genesis 1, the order is earth, plants, fish, birds, animals, and man (male and female). In ch. 2, it is earth, man, plants, animals, and woman. Which order is correct? Are their accounts in contradiction?

The proper approach to this question aids us in the science-Genesis problem. The simple story in ch. 2 met the needs of the Hebrews in 950 B.C., but a more advanced account was needed in 500 B.C. They are not to be seen in contradiction, but as serving different needs. They both begin from the same conviction: that God made man in his own image to serve him. For the earlier writer, man's responsibility was to till the soil of the garden; for the later one, "to be fruitful and multiply, fill up the earth and subdue it." Different writers brought all the skills available to the task of communicating God's intention for the man he created. In order to do so, they used the cultural materials of their own day to communicate with an audience to whom those concepts were familiar. It becomes clear, then, that we should be free to use our own cultural expressions to declare to our generation the same truth proclaimed by the biblical writers.

There is still another helpful approach to the science-Genesis tension. Not only do we have two Old Testament accounts of creation and flood but also accounts from ancient Sumer and Babylonia. These accounts are remarkably similar to those in the Old Testament, particularly the Gilgamesh Epic's account of the Flood.[2]

Some scholars contend that the Hebrews borrowed from the Babylonians; others, that both the Hebrews and the Babylonians were dependent upon an earlier account; but what is obvious is that the materials found in the Old Testament had been handed down for many years. It is obvious that, instead of the account being dictated by God to Moses, the commonly shared materials are derived from ancient sources. Thus the stories must be viewed as basically tradition materials. They are neither eyewitness accounts nor parables created for homiletical purposes. They are ancient stories being used by writers of Scripture to teach the great truths that God has laid upon their hearts.

These tradition stories naturally bear the marks of both their origin in history and their transmission through the centuries. The most important point to be recognized, however, is that the biblical writers received their stories in their tradition and used them in their witness. They did not change them to suit their times or concepts. Having received their revelation from God, they used the ancient stories as vehicles to express the truth that God had placed upon their hearts. Valid interpretation of Genesis must distinguish between the original revelation and the tradition story used to express it. The writer does not invent a Garden of Eden; it is in his tradition. He does not arbitrarily make the patriarchs before the Flood live longer to stress the toll of sin upon the race; his tradition has already told him that Methuselah lived 969 years.

The longevity of the antediluvian patriarchs is not an invention of the biblical writer. Rather, he used these old accounts to show that their long lives had little meaning: "they lived, they had children, and they died." Enoch, who lived only about one third as long as the average man, had a quality of life that resulted in a shattering of the monotony of being merely a link between the generations. Thus we should not so much concern ourselves with explaining how the patriarchs could or could not live so long as with the reason why the inspired writer has used the old accounts in his proclamation. The preacher is far more concerned with *Geschichte* (interpreted, preached history) than with *Historie* (actual event).

It is not that the event itself is not important. If there had been no creation event, an actual fall of man, or the outpouring of God's wrath on sinful man, then Genesis would join the company of folklore and fairy tales. Our problem is that although the stories of Genesis are clearly based upon a primeval event to which they give witness, we do not have the critical tools to get behind the form of the tradition as we have it. We too must preach it in faith, even as the original writers.

What the preacher must understand is that the reliability of the truth of a passage does not depend upon the exactness with which the details of the original have been preserved. If we are conservatives, we will accept the entire biblical account without question. If we are of a different persuasion, we may have real reservations about some of the historical statements. It is helpful, therefore, to distinguish between the vehicle and the thrust of the passage.

The truths of Genesis 1–11 are not to be found so much in the exactness with which the original event has been preserved as in the witness to that event. Witnesses in court give clues to the judge concerning the actual event; they cannot reproduce it. Rather, they point to it. Even so, the biblical accounts, regardless of their condition in transmission, give authentic witness to the redemptive acts of God which are both before and beyond their words.

Theologians will continue to argue concerning the historical and the scientific accuracy of the Bible, but the preacher's task is elsewhere. Regardless of the outcome of debate upon the meaning of Scripture, of one thing we can be confident: the basic thrust of each passage is from God and can be preached with confidence.

Within the believing Christian community the teaching of Jesus concerning the authority of Scripture (Matt. 5:17–18; John 10:35) will always be binding. Such a stance cannot be scientifically proved or disproved, but is a faith stance without which Christianity cannot endure. When scholars fail to agree, preachers need to take their stand squarely on the scriptures, not on their brittle edges but at the center. Scholarly chipping at their edges will never reach their heart.

To preach on creation, preachers do not need to be technical scientists or learned philosophers. After studying what they can, and appropriating what they understand and can accept, they must get to the task of proclamation, which goes at once to the heart of the issue. There they must stand. Scientific theory and theological systems are constantly revised, and our understanding of the Bible enlightened, but the essential message is still the same. It is upon that ground that preachers move. They point out the unchanging God to mortal man, and cannot afford to play academic games. It is their task to keep the ship on course while the storms of conflict are raging.

In addition to the science-Genesis issue, another major dilemma confronts the interpreter of Genesis 1–11. How much of the material should be interpreted symbolically and how much is to be taken literally? There is no simple answer to this question in spite of the fact that some interpreters insist upon interpreting all of it literally and others just as firmly demand a universal symbolical approach.

In ch. 1 Adam seems to be symbolic of man himself (the Hebrew word *'ādām* means "mankind").[3] Yet the same Priestly source continues in Genesis 5, where we are told about Adam's sons and daughters, and his age at the time of his death. There Adam is not *symbolical* man but *representative* man. In Hebrew tradition he is regarded as the first man; yet he is described as like us, for we are the children of a common ancestor. Thus the description of Adam is characteristically symbolic of us all; yet at the same time he is regarded as the first of our fallen race.

The Garden of Eden pericope clearly contains symbolism, for we find no such arrangement of rivers in the ancient Near East. Admitting that the rivers may have been rearranged after the Flood, but acknowledging that we have no evidence of such an occurrence, it is most likely that the rivers represent the four great cultures that arose on their banks in ancient times. The notation that they came from one source is cultural memory concerning their common ancestry. Thus the story is both historical and symbolic.

The account of the Fall of man (Gen. 2–3) is most clearly symbolic and can accurately be classified as a parable if it is assumed that it is derived from old traditions about the beginning of man. In other words, it is a parable based upon traditions out of which it is woven. The serpent is clearly symbolic of the power of evil within creation. He is one of God's creatures, but it is beside the point to ask whether he crawled or flew, for in regard to God's description of the warfare between his seed and that of the woman, no interpretation is likely to conclude that the words merely picture hostility between snakes and people. Rather, they anticipate the war to the death between the human race and the evil forces seeking to destroy it. It is just as obvious that the tree of life is representative of meaningful life after death and the tree of knowledge symbolic of knowledge that can be obtained by man's reason.

Just as Jesus used parables to describe his great truths, the Genesis writer uses a symbolic story to tell of the historical event of the Fall. In this way he can describe both what happened originally and how it continues to happen. Only symbolic truth can be so all inclusive, for mere history can only describe a bare event. It cannot declare its meaning. "I must first understand that I am Adam, made in God's likeness, rebelling against his purpose, desiring to be 'as God.' "[4]

Some scholars find examples of myth in the Old Testament, but the term is increasingly avoided in recent scholarship. Different writers define the term differently, and readers have different connotations of the word. The average person thinks that a myth is something that is not true, but ancient myths often contained more truth than bare event ever could. If God has led a writer to use a myth, then that form of symbolic literature should be recognized and honored for what it is. However, the presence of a myth should be determined by scientific criteria. Such a study reveals that in the sense in which myths were used in the ancient Near East, the Old Testament contains none. A myth was the *spoken* part of a ritual that was performed to guarantee the return of the events described in the myths.

Old Testament writers always opposed the use of such magical formulas. Their stories of the past were told to preserve what had really happened and as lessons to be learned from the past. They were not recited to guarantee the favor of God. The Old Testament does reveal an awareness of the mythical literature of Israel's neighbors, both in Canaan (Ras Shamra literature) and in Babylonia (creation and Flood accounts). Hebrew writers reflect the material in this literature, but they never endorse their presuppositions or encourage the practices of their neighbors. The Jews believed that their God actually moved in history and that he could not be induced to further activity simply by a liturgical rite. His future acts would be as personal as his past deeds. Because the past was real, the future was certain.

No myth as such occurs in the Old Testament, for myth is basically foreign to the Hebrew concept of history. A writer would refer to myths or use figures of speech derived from them, but he would not accept them unchanged or base his faith upon them. He had faith in what had actually happened in creation, exodus, conquest, exile, and restoration.

The purpose of the preacher should be the discovery of the use that is being made of ancient tradition in declaring the revelation of God. Thus we must always distinguish between the tradition and the message. There are stories about a great flood recalled by all peoples, and even verbal correspondence between the Hebrew account and the Babylonian. The quest of the interpreter is to discover what is the writer's purpose in telling the story in the Bible.

One does not read Shakespeare's *Hamlet* just to find out what happened to Hamlet. For that information we can go to the same source consulted by Shakespeare. We study *Hamlet* in order to see how Shakespeare understands the personal crises confronted by the tragic prince. In like manner we read the biblical account of the Flood, not so much to discover what happened as how our God was related to that event.

The Hebrews already knew about a great deluge. The message proclaimed by the writers is that the Flood not only came because of man's sin but was followed by the promise of God's grace. Never again would he send a flood. Without this assurance the ancient Hebrews lived in constant fear of another deluge, for they knew that mankind was just as sinful as before. Would the present heavy rains be a prelude to another worldwide devastation? Now man is reassured that in spite of his depravity God will spare him from such a second calamity.

Another ancient conclusion that could be drawn from the Flood tradition was that human life was of minimal value. If God could destroy all mankind with one blow, human life must be of little concern. If God could kill multitudes, why cannot we kill a few? To prevent this convenient supposition, God gave Noah the covenant of life, warning man that he cannot take life without facing the wrath of God, for, unlikely as it may sometimes seem, man is made in the image of God. We must recognize that image in every man. Thus a Flood tradition that was simply a story out of the past about the wrath of God became the vehicle of his grace and concern.

The task of the preacher has just begun when the thrust of a biblical passage has been determined. The world of the Bible was so different from ours that we are frequently perplexed about how a word to that world could be a word to us. How do we move from "what it meant" to "what it means"? There are many ways to do this, but the simplest and most reliable one is suggested by Jesus in the introduction to the Sermon on the Mount (Matt. 5:17–20). Some may object to the use of such a passage, since it probably does not contain the *ipsissima verba* (exact words) of Jesus but is Matthew's understanding of what Jesus meant by what he said. As such it may simply be one man's opinion. The fact that the Gospel of Matthew is in the New Testament canon is witness that the early church was convinced that Matthew's understanding was correct. Whether or not these are the exact words of Jesus is not important. The church confirmed the witness.

Besides, there is an overwhelming probability that the key that unlocks the door is the proper one. If we follow the method suggested by Matt. 5:17–20, we will be satisfied that we have discovered a valid hermeneutic when his word is confirmed in the life of the church today.

Jesus was about to preach the Sermon on the Mount, and there was the likelihood that he might be misunderstood on his view of the authority of the Old Testament Scriptures. Especially would eyebrows lift when he declared, "You have heard that it was said to the men of old [a reference to the Scriptures], . . . but I say to you" (Matt. 5:21).

Quickly Jesus assured his listeners that the smallest letter in the Torah
had a place in the purpose of God. He then proceeded to warn the
interpreter concerning two wrong approaches to interpretation:

1. Relaxing even a minor commandment of the Old Testament,
   saying it is no longer a word of God for man (v. 19a);
2. Limiting the interpretation of a passage to the literal meaning,
   then ignoring the true spirit of it (v. 20).

The first error results in a person being the most immature in the
kingdom, for that one cannot profit at all from what went before. The
second prevents the interpreter from even getting into the kingdom
because of adherence to a deadly legalism.

The interpretative method of Jesus was neither of these. He came
to fulfill the Old Testament, to complete it, "to take it farther in the
same direction." When he had determined the thrust of a passage, he
sought to continue its living word in a creative way. He did not
hesitate to ask the question Why? of the Old Testament, an approach
that a typical Pharisee would never use. The Pharisee simply accepted
the law as it was, and obeyed it meticulously. The question Why? is the
clue to the thrust. Why is it wrong to kill? The answer comes quickly
in Gen. 9:6: Because man is made in the image of God. If all men are
made in the image of God, then other conclusions follow, Jesus
taught. None of us can put another down (call him or her a fool)
without breaking the spirit of the commandment "Thou shalt not
kill." Thus Jesus fulfilled that commandment.

The religious leaders of the day conscientiously kept the letter of
the Sabbath laws without seeking to understand the reason for those
laws. Jesus wanted to know why the Sabbath laws were given. Are they
for the benefit of the Sabbath or for the welfare of man? Whatever
failed to benefit man did not belong there, however time-honored it
might be. Man fulfills the Sabbath by keeping its spirit, which may be
utterly quenched by the letter.

Not only did Jesus fulfill the law, he expected his followers to take
his own teachings farther in the same direction: "When the Spirit of
truth comes, he will guide you into all the truth; for he will not speak
on his own authority, but whatever he hears he will speak, and he will
declare to you the things that are to come" (John 16:13). The Holy
Spirit will take what Jesus has said and help the believer to work out
the implication for other times. Not even the teachings of Christ are
to be limited to their letter, for their spirit always breaks the
boundaries of the literal. Only in this way can the word be a living
word for every time.

GENESIS 1:1–2:25. WHAT LIFE IS ALL ABOUT

The interpreter of the creation passages in Genesis 1 and 2 finds the most obvious thrust to be in what the two accounts have in common. When there are two versions of an event, the essential points are their common witness.

1. They both insist that God has created man, that he is not the consequence of chance.

2. They both agree that man is more than an animal and partakes of the nature of deity. The earlier Judean source simply says God "breathed into his nostrils the breath of life" (2:7), but this is not said in reference to animals. Man receives the very breath of God into his own body. The Priestly source is more definite: man shares God's image and likeness.

3. They both teach that God has work for man to do. In the earlier source, his task is confined to the garden. In the later source his responsibilities encompass the earth.

How can we fulfill this thrust? By respecting the image of God in all persons, and especially in ourselves, and in seeing that our life is not our own, but must be lived under God and in his will. This not only includes our little garden and the four corners of the earth but now also applies as we race into space. Our responsibilities are already cosmic.

The Priestly account of creation reaches its climax in the divine charge given to man: "Be fruitful and multiply, and fill the earth and subdue it; and have dominion over the fish of the sea and over the birds of the air and over every living thing that moves upon the earth" (Gen. 1:28).

It is the common experience of parents that their offspring ask, "Who made me?" Then they reply, "Why, God made you." Then comes the response, "Who made God?" If they survive that, then comes the query, "Why did God make me?" Genesis 1 proposes to answer that question. God made man like himself in order that he might continue his work of creation. It should be noted that man is told "to subdue," which implies that much of the natural world is yet to be brought under God's dominion. This wild streak in creation was there before the Fall and marks the incompleteness of creation when man appeared. It is also apparent that man's multiplying is the means by which he is to attain dominion on the earth, for he cannot subdue it until he has first occupied it. However, in the modern world the dynamics have changed. Uncontrolled multiplying is one of the worst hindrances in our attempt to master our environment, and will eventually make the earth virtually uninhabitable. Thus the literal interpretation of "Be fruitful and multiply" could result in the defeat of the very end for which it was first intended.

It was formerly thought that the directive gave man the right to exploit the natural world for his own benefit. Modern environmental devastation has forced us to face the disastrous results of such a conclusion. Man has been given dominion in order to assist the natural world in becoming what it was intended to be. Thus man's responsibility is not only to reach his own potential but to participate in the ongoing program of all the life around him. In fact, his very life is dependent upon how well life goes on among those other creatures so lovingly created by God. Could we say it more clearly than Paul: "We know that the whole creation has been groaning in travail together until now" (Rom. 8:22). The present universe is in the "bondage to decay" (Rom. 8:21), not because man's sin caused it, but rather because man has been so depraved that he could not contribute to its freedom. In Jesus Christ we can now join in the noble task of creating a new universe, which will one day be complete when history as we know it comes to an end (Rev. 21:1). Meanwhile we are a sort of firstfruit of God's creatures (James 1:18). What God had intended Adam to be was not achieved until Jesus lived and died, that he might live in us; begetting us in his likeness as Adam passed on his nature to his descendants.

The thrust of Genesis 2 is quite different. While Genesis 1 stresses man's role under God, the Judean writer moves toward emphasizing man's social needs. While every day ends in ch. 1 with "and God saw that it was good," in ch. 2 God looks at Adam and sees that "it is not good." (2:18). Man is not complete without adequate earthly companionship. It is not said, "It is not good that man should lack a wife" but, "It is not good that man should be alone." It is not the intention of the passage to say that single persons are incomplete, for then Jesus would not have been a complete person. The passage teaches that man needs the companionship of other persons. The way in which this was provided originally was by giving Adam a wife. The need for companionship can be met in other ways today, but the emphasis here is upon the significance of marriage. There is no hint of inferiority for the woman as she is created from Adam's rib. She is taken from a part of him because only those who were originally one could become one again. Genesis 2:24 is hardly etiological, for neither was it the usual custom then nor is it now for the husband to leave home, but rather for the wife to do so. It is of major importance that it be translated, "Therefore *shall* a man leave his mother and father and cleave to his wife." It was expected that the woman do so, but now it is declared that the man should do the same.

A new marriage is like a new colony, where one's first loyalty no longer belongs to the original country from which one came. No sound marriage can be built upon any other foundation. Priority must be given to the home being established. Frequently husbands and wives cannot agree on belonging to the same church. This is usually not due to religious scruples, but is due to loyalty to the families from which they came. Real concern for one's marriage demands that priority be given to the dynamics of that home in both religious and secular concerns.

It is significant that the Priestly writer corrects any misconception about the relative rank of man and woman because of the secondary creation of Eve in the Judean story. He makes it clear that both male and female are made in the image of God (1:27).

Not only are the social needs of men and women recognized in Genesis 2 but there is also the implication that just as we need others to be mature socially, we also need companionship to mature spiritually. It is not good for a Christian to be alone as a child of God. We need the company of other Christians. Jesus told his disciples to pray *"Our* Father," not just *"My* Father." The writer of Hebrews warns his readers not to neglect meeting together, where they "stir up one another to love and good works" and are concerned about "encouraging one another" (Heb. 10:24–25).

GENESIS 3:1–24. THE "DO IT YOURSELF" DEBACLE OF HISTORY

The Fall of man is more a failure than a fall. It was a fall, for mankind lost ground; but the biblical writer clearly shows that man never became what God intended. There were no faults in the original Adam; yet he never attained God's objective for him. The tree of life symbolized meaningful afterlife, which was not given to man in creation. Man could eat of that tree only after he demonstrated that he could be trusted. The Hebrews never believed, as did the Greeks, in natural immortality of the soul. They believed that all men lived on in Sheol after death, but this shadowy existence had no positive meaning.

Many people think that God's only purpose in Jesus Christ is to get believers into heaven. If everlasting life were the only purpose of

God, that could have been arranged by allowing sinful Adam to eat of the tree of life. However, God had no intention of letting man live forever until he developed the character that would enable him to live the life of his Creator. There was no point in continuing the trauma of this life into the world to come.

The primary purpose of Christ is to change the believer into the kind of person who can live the life of the righteous forever. In Christ we are not only declared to be righteous, we are becoming righteous. We are being changed into his ways. If this is not taking place, the nominal Christian is possessed by a grand delusion.

"The tree of knowledge: good and evil" (literal Hebrew) symbolizes that knowledge which a man can acquire by his own intelligence. Such knowledge can be either good or evil, depending upon how it is used. Some interpreters find here an opposition to learning and philosophy, but this is not true. One's interpretation of the crisis must include the teaching of both the Judean and the Priestly account. Lest men suppose that God is opposed to man's learning all that he can, the Priestly source, edited with the Judean source in hand, stresses the fact that God told man he could eat of *every* tree (1:29).

Taken together, the two sources teach that although God intended that men should eat of the tree of knowledge, he forbade it at first. Until man developed his trust in God, he would not be able to handle the knowledge. Knowledge without faith is a deadly thing. Faith is both a test and a directive of knowledge. Without faith we may know how to perceive knowledge but not what to do with it. For knowledge to be beneficial it must be the servant of faith. It may lead to faith or away from it. Faith always opens avenues to knowledge that one has not known before. The Priestly writer believed that if Adam had resisted the tree of knowledge he would eventually have been permitted to eat of it. Surely the tree was not put in the garden just to test Adam. One does not put something before a child and warn the child against it just to see if he will obey. He is warned because there is danger to him. The tree of knowledge was there for Adam to eat of, but he was not to touch the flame. Later he would know what to do with it. The child who avoids the fire may one day use it to fabricate steel.

What connection does the Fall have with sex? The verb "to know" (4:1) is used for sexual intercourse. After Adam and Eve sinned, they covered their sexual organs (3:7). The popular view is that the original sin of the first pair was sexual intercourse. Nothing could be farther from the truth. There are several reasons why sexual intercourse cannot be the sin: (1) In Genesis 1, God told them to be fruitful and multiply. Surely he would not blame them for doing what was necessary to fulfill the command! (2) Eve committed the sin when she was alone. (3) God is said to have the kind of knowledge that they would derive from the tree (3:22). The most plausible explanation is that when they ate of the tree they became aware of the otherness of man and woman. What before had been natural and wholesome had now become a source of conflict and shame.

The basic temptation, therefore, was to forsake God's word of warning and follow their own judgment. In this respect we are truly their children. The results of the yielding to temptation are worth noting:

1. At first there was only enjoyment. They expected to be struck dead (whatever that meant), but Satan seemed to be right. God was depriving them of what was rightfully and joyously theirs.

2. Then came the guilt feelings. They were neither understood nor dealt with realistically. They covered their bodies, when in reality their sinful hearts were exposed. How irrational is the transfer of guilt in humans!

3. God seeks out man in his sin. To wait for man to come to him is to wait forever. The church seldom grasps that. The church keeps expecting the world to come to it.

4. Adam and Eve refuse to accept responsibility for their sin.

5. God's wrath falls upon the sinners: *Upon the serpent.* He is doomed, his head crushed, but only after mortal conflict with mankind. *Upon the woman.* A threefold curse falls: bearing more children than she can manage; the pain of travail; subjection to her husband. *Upon the man.* A twofold curse comes: struggle with a hostile environment, unlike the Garden of Eden; the removal of any hope for life after death.

6. There is a faint glimmer of hope. Two acts of God keep man from total despair: *(a)* He covers the bodies of Adam and Eve, which probably symbolizes the covering of their sins, a familiar theme in the Old Testament; *(b)* the gate to the garden is guarded by the cherubim, but is not locked, nor is the garden destroyed. The gate awaits the arrival of someone concerning whom God will say to the cherubim: "Put aside your flaming swords and let him in." Such a man appears in Genesis 5, Enoch. If he walked with God and God took him, then there is a hope for others who do the same.

The Judean source shows remarkable insight in the description of the consequences upon the woman. This has been woman's threefold plight. The tragedy is that some think it is ordained to remain

continually so. Yet Jesus died not only for the sins of men but also for
those of women. He has set us all free. It is in cultures most
influenced by Christianity that women have been freed from these
consequences.

It is significant that the church has often been the powerful
opponent of women's freedom from these misfortunes. The use of
anesthetics in childbirth was opposed because it was contended that
women were supposed to have travail. The struggle for equality
before law is often opposed by those who contend that a woman is
supposed to be subject to her husband. Birth control is opposed
because women are supposed to multiply through conception, "have
as many children as possible." Is the new freedom in Christ only for
men? Even Paul declared that in Christ there is neither male nor
female. In doing so, he was suggesting more than he realized. Later
generations must work out its implications through the guidance of
the Holy Spirit.

GENESIS 4:1–16. PAGAN VERSUS PROPER WORSHIP

In spite of the curse upon the ground, Cain became a farmer, but
Abel became a shepherd (Gen. 4:1ff.). Then each man voluntarily
brought an offering to God, but it was not commanded. Cain
appropriately brought his produce, while Abel presented sheep. Yet
God accepted both Abel and his offering and rejected Cain and his
gift. What went wrong? They were both sincere. They brought their
presents out of their own desire. Neither then nor now is sincerity
enough. Was the difference in the materials offered? Did God reject
Cain because he brought produce instead of a blood offering? This
could hardly have been true, for the produce offering ("meat offering," Lev. 2:1, KJV) was a principal offering in the later sacrificial
system. Obviously God was more pleased with the blood offering,
which was the primary one in the Old Testament, but he would not
have rejected the produce except as a sin offering. There is no
indication here that a sin offering is the issue.

A valuable clue is seen in the mention of "firstlings" in Abel's
offering. There is a corresponding "firstfruits" used of produce in the
Old Testament. Just as the firstlings were the most precious among
the animals, so were the firstfruits among the produce. The absence
of the corresponding term in reference to Cain is conspicuous. In
spite of the view of Gunkel and most modern commentators that the
context implies that Cain brought the "choicest thereof," or the view
of the Talmud that his offering was of the poorest quality, the passage

obviously implies that in contrast to Abel's best, Cain simply brought God something. It was not that it was poor quality; it was not his *best*.

Cain was grateful to God for a successful year of farming. He wanted to thank him for his help, so he brought him a present. Abel in giving God his best, as men would later do before human rulers, witnessed to his total dependence upon God, his indebtedness to him. Cain thanked God for serving him. Abel confessed himself to be a servant of God.

Cain represents pagan religion of all the ages, especially Canaanite religion. The major purpose of such worship was to persuade the gods to help man achieve his ends, and to thank them when they were cooperative. Biblical faith, represented by Abel, is the opposite. Man sees himself as the servant of God. It is the purpose of life to do the will of God rather than to have him perform ours. When Cain did not bring God his best, God would accept nothing at all. His ways with men have not changed.

GENESIS 4:17–26. THE SECULAR VERSUS THE SPIRITUAL LIFE-STYLE

Genesis 4:17–26 was originally independent of 4:1–16. It was placed here to describe the development of Cain's line in contrast to that of Seth. Cain's descendants began all the major advances of material civilization—cities, domestication of cattle, music, and metal-working. Thus secular culture is rooted in Cain and must always be regarded with suspicion by godly persons, for in spite of its possible use by them, it will always tend to return to its beginnings.

The tragedy was that the material progress of Cain's line was not matched by moral and religious gain. Not only did those of Cain's line initiate polygamy, but Lamech represents the end of the line, a man who no longer needs God's protection, who boasts that with his own manufactured weapons he can defend himself against a "young boy" (Heb. *yeledh*). In this context the word may mean a youth in his prime, but it is not the usual sense. The song may be ironically exposing the empty boast of a hollow man. Jesus reverses the Lamech boast of seventy-seven-fold revenge to teach the corresponding amount of forgiveness (Matt. 18:22).

In contrast to the Cain line, a new direction is begun with the birth of Seth to Adam and Eve. This time, Eve's joy is mixed with sorrow and she uses the more impersonal term for God. When a son was born to Seth, he named him Enosh ("weakness"). Then man began to call upon the name Yahweh. In their strength Cain's line felt no need for God; in his weakness Enosh knew his need of him. Cain's strength would ultimately avail him nothing. Enosh would establish a line that would never end. Yet the struggle between the two life-styles still continues.

GENESIS 9:18–29. EXPOSING ANOTHER'S SHAME

There is hardly an Old Testament passage more difficult to interpret than Gen. 9:18–29. (See my article in *Christianity Today*, April 24, 1964, pp. 8–10). This Scripture was the favorite text of Southern preachers during the Civil War, as they asserted the right of white men to enslave the Negro. Sometimes used even today to defend segregation, it is the unrecognized source of the saying, "A Negro is all right in his place," by which is meant that his proper position is secondary to that of the white man. Since the curse fell on Canaan rather than on Ham, this must be seen as a passage explaining the servitude of the Canaanites, who were not black. There is no indication that all Ham's descendants experienced this curse (which was more of a prediction than a curse). The curse upon Canaan has no direct bearing upon the vexing black-white problem of our time.

The scene that unfolds is a familiar one. Righteous Noah had been the means of God's triumph over the forces of evil in the world. The wicked had been destroyed, and Noah and his family had been spared to build a new world. But the man who had weathered the ridicule of his neighbors and every storm of the Flood could not meet the challenge of the time of peace. With the opportunity to start an ideal new society, Noah was found drunk in his tent.

Some commentators note that there is not a word of condemnation of Noah for his drunkenness. Yet it is stated that "he died" in spite of the fact that he walked with God (Gen. 6:9) even as Enoch had done. Thus he did not escape the consequences of his sins.

What did Ham do to his father? He disgraced him by exposing his shame to the world. Ham could not have been blamed for stumbling on his drunken father, but he was blamed for reporting on his father's condition. What his brothers did he should have done: he should have covered his father and said nothing about it. Although Noah did not escape the wrath of God for his sin, it is obvious that of the sins, Ham's sin is taken more seriously. Sins of pride are worse than sins of the flesh, which are committed because of weakness. There is no excuse for pride. Ham found perverse satisfaction in seeing his father in a compromising position. He inflated his own ego by putting him down. Is this not a temptation to us all?

GENESIS 11:1–9. THE FIELD IS THE WORLD

The central event in the Babel story is the building of the "tower with its top in the heavens." Similar expressions were actually used by Babylonians concerning their temples, particularly the one dedicated to Marduk in Babylon. At the time of the writing of 11:1–9, the ziggurat at Babylon, built probably in the Hammurabi period (eighteenth to seventeenth century B.C.), was in massive ruins that spoke eloquently of its former glory. The reference here, however, is not to a catastrophe that occurred so close to the time of Abraham, but to a more ancient one. Speiser is correct in assuming that the account is more dependent upon the Babylonian creation story than upon the actual ziggurat of Babylon.[5] Doubtless the Hebrews had their own traditions concerning an attempt, before the site was even called Babel, to build a temple there, which preceded the Hammurabi effort. The latter was an attempt to rebuild the previous ruins in the light of the *Enuma Elish*.

What went wrong at Babel? A traditional interpretation is that the people were attempting to work their way into heaven. The Babylonians really believed that their temple was "the gate of heaven," for the word "Babel" means "gate of God" in their language. If they had been realistic, as were the Hebrews, however, they would have perceived that as they laid one brick upon another they were getting little closer to the sky.

Others suggest that it was an attempt to provide a place of refuge in case of another flood. If that had been true, there was little likelihood of their building it as high as the mountains of Ararat! The idiom should not be taken literally. "A tower to heaven" (literal Hebrew) means a tall tower, a "skyscraper."

What was wrong with building a "tower to heaven"? Nothing, in itself. To the writers of Genesis the sin was in their motivation. "Let us make a name for ourselves, lest we be scattered abroad." Man was made to live to the glory of God, and his legitimate search for a good and permanent name must be carried out in that context. God appealed to Abraham on the basis of making his name great (12:1–3), but it was to be achieved in the service of God. From the very beginning God had told man to be fruitful and multiply and fill up the earth, and the order was reiterated to Noah. Man was to fill the whole earth, not just one corner of it. Until this day the population problem is not essentially a lack of room on the earth for all its people, but the fact that the people want to live in the same place (the cities) and are not concerned about the less fortunate parts of the world.

Although to the Babylonians the word "Babel" meant the "gate of God," to the inspired writer it had come to have a Hebrew meaning, "a place of confusion." All utopian schemes where men are concerned only for their own selves and their personal fortunes end in such chaos. Selfish men will always be insensitive to the thoughts and needs of others, and their attempts at building will ultimately fail.

How did the confusion of tongues happen? The writer does not say. He is more concerned with the reason for it, who brought it about, and the end result. God uses various means to effect his will, but he consistently reacts in a similar way to men's behavior, with comparable results. It is the intention of the writer to teach that whenever men are concerned only with their own attempts at fame, those efforts are doomed to failure. What God expects is a generation dedicated to goodwill for all men. Until men go voluntarily, he will scatter them by force, employing the diverse means available to him to achieve his final purposes. Thus he scattered the New Testament church (Acts 11:19), and he has continued to act in our day.

NOTES

1. D. N. Freedman, "Documents," and B. W. Anderson, "Creation," *The Interpreter's Dictionary of the Bible*, Vol. 1 (Abingdon Press, 1962), pp. 860, 725ff.

2. J. B. Pritchard (ed.), *Ancient Near Eastern Texts Relating to the Old Testament*, 3d ed. (Princeton University Press, 1969).

3. Cf. Alan Richardson, *Genesis 1–11*, Torch Bible Commentaries (London: SCM Press, 1963), p. 30.

4. Ibid., p. 31.

5. E. A. Speiser, *Genesis*, The Anchor Bible, Vol. 1 (Doubleday & Co., 1964), p. 75.

FOR FURTHER READING

Commentaries

Cassuto, Umberto. *A Commentary on the Book of Genesis.* 2 vols. Tr. Israel Abrahams. Jerusalem: Magnes Press, 1961, 1964. A creative and unique approach to the book of Genesis from the viewpoint of an Israeli scholar who knows both historical research and rabbinic tradition.

Kidner, F. Derek. *Genesis*. The Tyndale Old Testament Commentaries. Inter-Varsity Press, 1968. Genesis approached from an evangelical position by an able British scholar.

Rad, Gerhard von. *Genesis, A Commentary*. Tr. John H. Marks. The Old Testament Library. Westminster Press, 1961. The definitive commentary on Genesis of our time. Provocative and rewarding.

Interpretive and Expositional Works

Bonhoeffer, Dietrich. *Creation and Fall*. Macmillan Co., 1959. A remarkable theological study of Genesis 1–3.

Hanson, Richard S. *The Serpent Was Wiser*. Augsburg Publishing House, 1972. A fresh, imaginative engagement with the biblical text by an able scholar.

Thielicke, Helmut. *How the World Began*. Tr. John W. Doberstein. Muhlenberg Press, 1961. The inspiring kind of book that could be expected from a German scholar who is devoted to Spurgeon.

2. PREACHING ON THE PATRIARCHS

HENRY H. MITCHELL

I. HERMENEUTICAL BACKGROUND

Preaching on the patriarchs could hardly be assessed as very popular in the 1980s, yet the early fathers' potential as a basis for both spiritually fruitful and utterly interesting preaching is virtually unlimited. To sense the relevance of these Scriptures for today, one needs only to take the trouble to find out what God was doing with his people then. And one needs only to understand and experience the Genesis process of oral tradition and its impact on the world to want to recover some of that "primitive" but life-shaping power. The early cultures used such tales for *living* far more than for entertainment, and the soul-searching sagas of the patriarchs gave guidance and stamina to a peculiar people and all their progeny throughout most of known history.

I welcomed this assignment because of my deep interest in the dynamics of oral tradition and narrative. In fact, I have already published what I consider to be the principles for resurrecting such a tale-telling, soul-saving tradition in our times, based on observation of the lively art of America's black pulpit.[1] In the providence of God, within my world, these oral tradition processes are alive and well, and the patriarchs survive unscathed. One writes out of a kind of living contact, concretely rather than in mere theory. But this powerful folk art form is as available to all the family of God as the universally imitated music of "Soul" is to the entertainment world, and for far more important goals.

Let us, then, turn first to a brief rationale for the recovery of folk narrative in the pulpit. We then address the issues of the text, its facticity, and the uses of history, since authentic narration demands wholehearted telling. (There can be no inhibition or reservation about the tale in the mind of the teller.) Then the reader will be ready for the question of what God was doing with his people, and for the final exploration of the preaching themes and gospel messages of the patriarchs.

THE REASON AND ROLE OF FOLK NARRATION

Today's electronic church thrives, while prestigious pulpits languish, because, at least in part, the "boob tube" is entertaining. This hardly constitutes a valid model, because of the all-too-often simplistic messages, and motives clearly suspect of selfishness. But the viable alternatives do not include the right to be boring; liveliness has no inescapable tie with oversimplification. The dullness of most mainline preaching is due to its being conceived of as argument rather than art—as syllogism rather than symbol. The preacher as inspired artist can easily compel attention to the most profound themes of the gospel, once they are made to live in narrative, picture, and poetry. It has always been so.

The Genesis accounts of the patriarchs are loaded with theological interpretations and irrefutable logic, but the medium is the folk tale. Their track record includes influence spanning worldwide Christianity, Judaism, and Islam. Obviously God used and uses this supposedly primitive stuff a lot better than he does our profound proclamations. We need to find out how and why.

The answer lies in how tales impinge upon consciousness. As compared to essays, which type reaches which sector of the mind? The abstract argument reaches rational consciousness, but this is neither the seat of faith nor the source of commitment. Reason is a synonym for what the Bible calls sight, which by very definition is *not* faith. Paul refers to it (Eph. 3:19) as abstract knowledge surpassed by the personal, experiential impact of the love of Christ. On the other hand, tales have an impact upon the total person, and especially the intuitive sector of consciousness, wherein dwells faith. So this is the "secret" of the Genesis narrative and other narratives: they provide a vicarious *experience* of the truth to be taught, and thus they move persons to identify with and live by that truth.

The immediate cry arises, of course, "What about our cherished faculty of reason, the crowning gift of *Homo sapiens?*" It can never be jettisoned; it is always indispensable for safety and sanity. But the monitoring and screening of insights and experiences is a negative necessity utterly incapable of *begetting* faith in the first place. It can remove the intellectual obstacles and fit the parts coherently together, but it cannot produce faith. This is the task of the foolishness of tale-telling, and that task has been performed magnificently for millennia before the advent of modern methods.

We now know why this is true and can state it in the very terms of those modern scientific insights. In the first place, the intuitions and emotions of faith are not predictable or subject to human control, but they are born in response to experience. What psychiatrists call levels of trust cannot be argued up; they are planted and watered by a vast and complicated array of experiences, both conscious and unconscious, actual and vicarious. We may refer to them in transactional terms as "tapes," and they are being made all the time. However, actual experience is diffuse and unfocused, while vicarious experience can be quite purposeful. When I identify with the prodigal son well told, I may learn/experience as much in twenty minutes as might have taken twenty months or many years to "walk out" on the ground. This, in a nutshell, is the genius and function of the folk narrative, the reason "primitives" succeeded in achieving stable, godly ways, many of them into the present decade. The tales of the patriarchs are a part of that foundational heritage.

RECORD, SAGA, AND SALVATION HISTORY

Of course, these tales have to be told as authentically and enthusiastically as ever, which for modern minds poses a few problems. However, these are not insurmountable.

The first problem is mislabeled "historicity." One wants to know if it "really happened," since one cannot sincerely wax dramatic over fabrications. At this point, the easy way out would be to call attention to the new digs at 4,500-year-old Ebla, in the north of Syria (*Time* magazine, Sept. 21, 1981). With this, one can close in on what may prove to be amazingly hard data on Abraham, Ur, and Haran. But this is not the issue. After old Father Abraham's historicity is as solid as that of Lenin (under glass in Moscow), the real issue will still be *why* these tales were preserved through centuries of tale-telling (oral tradition), and then why they were finally recorded, edited, and chosen as canon in the way that produced our cherished Scripture. For this preacher, the answer is, "Yes, Virginia, there surely was a man named Abraham, with a son called Isaac . . ." But there is much more to establishing a firm footing for telling their tales.

It might help here to unmask the fiction called objectivity. Even the best newspaper reporters are incapable of the "simple facts," simply because *all* recorders of history are limited to her or his story. They select as significant the details that support the truth they seek to project. And that is as it should be, since "complete objectivity" is as impossible as it is useless. Thus these Genesis tales are preserved to avoid the necessity for reinventing the wheel, spiritually speaking. The patriarchs are the characters of a kind of kerygma.

Saga is far less intent on facticity than, say, on periodical reportage, simply because its purpose is to express what a people think of their own history and its meaning.[2] This lively Genesis curriculum was formed by the inspiration of God, and I have always known this. However, it has been only in recent years that I have been able to explain it cogently and allay the doubts and inhibitions of friends not so blessed with a long and living oral tradition right in their home churches. The Yahwist editor and later the Priestly editor wrote to teach, and they had every right and reason to continue and to enlarge on the cultic function and vision of the original sources.

Recently I sensed suddenly how naturally all of us do this sort of thing. While attempting to give hope to a cigarette fiend who wanted to kick the habit, I described my own providential liberation over thirty-six years ago. I mentioned having used as many as two packs a day, and that is a fact. However, it is not a true representation of my habit, since it happened only twice, on a transcontinental train ride. At other times it was more like two packs a week. So the selected "fact" was a misrepresentation of truth.

When one is aware of such possibilities, the spiritual truth may demand a more and more corrected telling of factual but misrepresentational detail. It is like the Hollywood producer who rejected my documentary script. It was not that the details were each inaccurate; it was just that, in the time frame available, my *facts* presented a garbled and inaccurate image. Again, it is like the painter's brush, which must emphasize the painter's vision and ignore irrelevant detail. The written record of the patriarchs reflects generations of oral retelling and then the written editing. All of this is characterized by ever sparser background and ever more vivid spiritual concerns.

Thus Abraham's dishonesty about his pretty wife being his sister is mentioned in chs. 12; 20; and 26. It is so very important to portray his inability to trust God to protect him long enough to fulfill the promise of progeny. Whatever some editors' views of such redundancy, this editor is inspired, and his product is instructive salvation history.

Therefore, the contemporary homiletic tale-teller must shed her or his partially misguided self-image as "exact" historian and enter into the spirit of the saga. Early peoples used cultic saga not as entertaining fantasy or fairy tale, but to re-present actual events of historical significance in ever greater waves of profound understanding of what that history means. In the patriarchal tradition, these waves were linked with and shed light on the then contemporary issues. Yet whatever the emerging increase in spiritual insight, they "preserve a mood, a spiritually religious atmosphere . . . that was obviously a characteristic of the pre-Mosaic period, and the restriction of all to a single independent family or clan is a sign of its antiquity."[3] So the preacher/narrator of today is unchallenged to a different but no less worthy style of "intellectual integrity," an artistic creativity synthesizing compelling narrative and theological commentary.

For instance, the chief character in any of the patriarchal tales is not, in fact, one of the fathers but *the* Father. The characters of Germanic saga are used to model loyalty, courage, and readiness to die. But the patriarchs are never important for their own sake. Thus "warts and all" are vividly portrayed, giving *God* a better canvas on which to work. "The nobleness of these figures consists in the fact that they conquer in the strength of the grace granted to them, and when defeated, they arise again and again."[4] Only a very few of the tales are meant to encourage imitation. So one could readily say that the chief character is a God of promise, providence, and self-revelation.

The power of the art by which this great theological theme is advanced is to be found in the details of personalities, the description of subjective response (such as Jacob's surprise that God was there, Gen. 28:16), and, above all, meaningful conversations. Nowhere is the richness of folk narrative greater, or its value more obvious, than in the great dialogic give-and-take of the patriarchs.[5] Effective use of these resources today consists of elaboration of details in harmony with the source, and of rendition or performance which amounts to a "rerun" of the experience. This requires an "eyewitness" type of account. The teller relives the tale in all its vividness, and makes available to the audience a vicarious *experience* of the theological theme projected by the inspired editor's use of the sources.

Some further suggestions about the style appropriate to saga may be helpful here:

1. Avoid stepping out of the tale to give interpretative or technical asides, not even chapter and verse. It breaks the experience. The teller must be unreservedly committed to or "inside" the tale. He or she must be willing, through this foolishness of identification with the ancients, to maintain the audience's flow of profound experience. Most necessary data, details, or explanations can be included in the "script." If scholarly commentary is deemed absolutely essential to a serious hearing, such should precede the opening "curtain."

2. Take special care to preselect the lesson to be taught, and to identify the character who learns it. Then be sure so to present that person that the audience will be drawn to identify with her or him and so experience its way through that saving truth. As stated, the narrative must be entertaining, but this high art has reason to be performed as gospel only if the artist has some clear notion of how the Holy Spirit might use it to generate growth in the hearers. They must be moved from point A to point B along a lived path whose ultimate end and model is Jesus Christ. For instance, the tale of Jacob wrestling with God is a gold mine for teaching folks who have unresolved interpersonal conflicts and guilt. But they will presume that the message is given to "somebody else," unless Jacob is so introduced that they like him and identify with him, so as to live out his lesson and go through his change from cheater to chosen vessel.

3. This ancient saga and salvation history will be profitably relived, however, only if the *details* attract the listener to move into the stream of experience of the tale. They must be sufficiently vivid and must represent the tiny commonalities between ancient and modern life which, in sum, cause the hearer to recognize the persons and actions as "next-door neighbors." For instance, parental partiality, sibling rivalry, cheating, and conscience-stricken insomnia are timeless. Today's teller needs only to dress these up in modern vocabulary, while sticking faithfully to the *idea* in the Genesis account. Where there are no details, one must use inspired imagination to put back into the record what was dropped out as unessential to the main issue. It took too long to write, and would have made the scroll too bulky, but it is needed now to create an experience in oral rendition. Like the water removed from dried milk to make it portable, the color of a robe or the taste of a hunter's stew must be put back in to make the story look or taste like the real thing.

4. To vivid detail must be added effective timing. Whatever the constraints of paper and quill, it is unthinkable that the original tales were rendered with less than exquisite timing. That is to say, the tension or suspense was carefully and patiently built, with clear awareness of the exact conflict. Asides to cinch the application would have been a no-no, and one would not have dared to "telegraph" the "punch" by supplying premature previews of the resolution. However, once that denouement was arrived at, it was *celebrated*. This may be called good showmanship and held suspect on that account, but its main purpose is the powerful ecstatic reinforcement of the lesson. In my home church and parishes, it would be held criminal to fail to get

as emotional as Jacob when one says (28:16), "Surely the LORD is in this place; and I did not know it."

Much, much more could be said, but like the author of the books of Kings, I must refer the reader to the other "chronicles" of narrative preaching, of which there seem to be quite a few these days.[6]

THEOLOGY, OR WHAT GOD WAS DOING

While "theology" is usually tied to the abstract, the tales of the patriarchs are theology "on the hoof." Before we delve into what this may mean, however, we must register one overarching point of reference. There is wide scholarly agreement pointing to the idea that, as Eric Rust puts it, "the Old Testament without the New is like a torso without a head." He goes on to say, "Our final standard of what is significant must therefore be the Christological, what points to and is fulfilled in the New Testament faith."[7]

The first doctrine of the patriarchs and the whole Old Testament is hardly new to anybody: "God works *in* history." The uniqueness of the patriarchs lies in the fact that this belief is set forth in appealing narratives of high literary quality about personalities and their conversations and experiences. This results from a sense of the wholeness of reality, so that one's experience in life is one's experience with God—in family, nature, and everywhere else. The tales of the patriarchs constitute, in their present form, a highly theological treatment of their whole experience as a people.

Further, this God goes so far as to reveal his plans, and has chosen Abraham and his descendants as his third beginning (after Adam and Noah) in the effort to spawn a more perfect humanity. The whole Abraham sequel is concerned with his ups and downs in anticipation of this promised son, without whom the other offspring promised to him would be impossible. Whether the chief character is Abraham or Sarah (a distinct possibility at points), the issue of faith in God's promise is the same and unquestionably dominant. The point is that God does what he says or reveals that he will do.[8]

The instant corollary to the premise that God acts inside history is that God reveals himself directly in human encounters. Because it is different from general history, it is apt to be missed. Modern thinkers are not comfortable saying, "God said, or spoke, or commanded, or promised," but the Genesis editor has no problem with it. There is no inhibition or suspended judgment while he sends out teams to see if that really is God. God speaks and sticks to his word.

The writer's purpose is to motivate faith in Yahweh and faithfulness to him. Although there are many subthemes and interesting highlights, the "Acts of God" in the life of the patriarchs is history with a purpose. The need for such a purpose is a major subtheme also. The growth of evil was rampant. The history served as an enticement to godliness *and* as a prophetic announcement of judgment on cities, etc., that refused to hear. So God is the omnicompetent punisher of wickedness, as well as the extravagant promiser of numberless descendants. He is able also to stop all threats to his people before they go too far. He is not yet seen as the God of love, but he is headed in that direction, consistent with the New Testament criteria. In fact, he may already be caught in the act of redeeming his people. The ponderous promises of ch. 15 include the pledge to be a shield (v. 1) and to deliver his people from Egypt after four hundred years (v. 13). Whatever one may rightfully say about all this accuracy as formulated after the exodus deliverance,[9] the meaning given to Hebrew life by this "theological reflection" was indeed inspired and used of God. It motivated faith, and it still does.

II. PATRIARCHAL TRADITION: NARRATIVE FOR TODAY

In the pages that follow, the purpose is to give more specific assistance toward the recovery of oral tradition, focusing especially on vivid narration. Forms are given that suggest the essential categories or elements of preparation, and model answers are supplied for as many sermon themes as space permits. The first model is preceded by a transcript of a sermon tale rendition that uses such preparation.

It should be evident from these forms that folk narrative is no shortcut to good preaching, bypassing exegetical research and intensive preparation. Living stories demand hours of searching for good detail, and then days of living one's way into the roles. All this after a basically convincing script has been dreamed up, and the lines have been learned. Crucial transitions also need designing and memorization. This must have been what old preachers in my boyhood were doing when they seemed to sit for so long doing "nothing." It takes quite an effort to get the knack of it and to shed inhibitions, and quite a while to generate a repertoire. My one consolation for those for whom this seems so demanding is that it is equally rewarding.

A note should be added concerning a sound rule about purposes: Make them affective, not cognitive; behavioral, not intellectual. Jesus spoke of those who hear his sayings and *do* them (Matt. 7:24), not just know or believe. "Do" is the bottom line, and thus the ultimate purpose of every sermon, although each will include some ideas and reasons en route to the behavioral goal. Beware of sermons designed to "show" or "inform": they don't go deep enough to change life, which is the goal always. It may be hard to develop this discipline, but its mastery pays off. If even the preacher does not know what the hearer is supposed to do, how will anybody else? But if the text is properly wedded to a purpose, the sermon will almost preach itself.

The first story is the celebration from a sermon on Providence preached by this writer on NBC's "National Radio Pulpit," July 30, 1978, under the unfortunate title "All Things Work Together."

Very often we are tempted to feel that trusting is useless and morality in vain. However, we are *guaranteed* that the forces of good will win the game of life. In everything God is at work for good, to them that love him.

Perhaps the best illustration I know is a testimony that comes very early in the Old Testament from the words of Joseph. You will remember that after the burial of their father, Joseph and his brothers returned to Egypt, to their flocks and their families, whom they had left behind. As their father, Jacob, had advised the other brothers, they wrote a message to their younger brother, Joseph, asking for an appointment to beg forgiveness. This was followed up with a well-planned appeal when they stood before him in his office. The speech went something like this: "Brother Joseph, we stand before you today painfully aware that we have treated you most cruelly. Daddy was also aware of it, and he told us before he died to come to see you and make a clean breast of it. We admire you much. We sold you into slavery, and we feel bad about this, and yet you yourself have borne it with a calm and even pleasant spirit. We understand that you were badly dealt with because of the tricks of Potiphar's wife, but you stayed as fine a person as ever. Unjustly you were made to serve time in Pharaoh's prison, but even this did not break your spirit, and you made good things come out of your stretch there. Now, of course, you have been in this high office these few years, and even here your head has not turned. When we came to you for help during the big food shortage, you were gracious, and we are most grateful. But we feel kinda like Daddy did; you were nice out of respect for him. He would have known that we deserved whatever you might have given, but he would have grieved about it. And now that he's gone, we're scared and on our own. And we feel like chickens running before a hawk in a wide-open field. It's only a matter of time until you will get us. So we've come to beg forgiveness and to be at your feet as servants. Please! little brother, have mercy on us!"

Joseph had been crying almost from the start. He raised his head slowly and wiped his eyes, and said with great feeling: "Please don't be afraid of me. I am not God, and I have no ambitions to exercise his powers. Now, of course, I know that you thought great evils against me; I have no illusions there. I know that you meant to get rid of me. There is no hatred like that which sometimes occurs between brothers. I know the shocking dimensions of your cruelty, but I also know the Lord God, and his providence. I know he'll never let you go but so far. I have learned that he always leaves enough for me to make it. I know that if I just wait on the Lord, he'll make everything all right. You see, he lets you run your games, but *he* decided what the end will be. *You* meant it for evil, but *God* meant it for good." For we *know* that in all things God works for good to those that love him and accept the call to follow his will and purpose in the world. (The constraints of radio scheduling kept this last paragraph from being elaborated upon considerably in celebration.)

The work that leads up to this sort of rendition (much better heard than read) can be summed up in the following categories:

Title (do last): The Providence of God
Text: Genesis 50:20 and Romans 8:28
Lesson (to be read in the service): Genesis 50:14–21
Purpose (for personal discipline, not public announcement): To move persons to trust the providence of God regardless of the always temporary hardships
Protagonist/Chief Character: Joseph
Conflict/Point of Tension: Will Joseph take revenge on his brothers, now that his father is gone?
Resolution of Conflict: Joseph's declaration of confidence in providence
Celebration Material: Imaginative, poetic expansion of Joseph's affirmation
Crucial Details (for audience identification with the action)
50:17 Joseph *wept* when his brothers spoke to him.
16 "Daddy *told* us to throw ourselves on your mercy and hope for your complete pardon."
15 It is implied that Joseph withheld vengeance so it would not grieve his father during his life. Yet his father knew how richly it was deserved.
20 "But god meant it unto good" is an affirmation already so powerful and road-tested by Joseph that it offers a basis for marvelous imaginative elaboration.

Title: Blind Faith
Text: Genesis 12:4 and Hebrews 11:8, 10

Lesson: Genesis 12:1–5 and Hebrews 11:8–16
Purpose: To generate adventurous faith and help persons to maintain
it, even when security and barest necessities are threatened, as
this world sees it
Protagonist: Abraham
Conflict: Although the apparent conflict is that of leaving comfort and
kindred to seek a godly community, the more interesting
conflict is the struggle to maintain the high level of faith so
readily manifest when he left.
Resolution: God's *acceptance of Abraham's imperfect effort,* while sticking
to his own promise
Celebration Material: Imaginative elaboration on the amazing idea in
which Abraham's two major bursts of faith are "reckoned . . .
to him as righteousness" (Gen. 15:6) despite numerous failings. Use with Heb. 11:16: God is not ashamed to be called his
God (cf. Rom. 4:9). The preacher celebrates that ultimate
acceptance.
Special Angle: The whole of the Abraham saga is dominated by
Abraham's inability to maintain his trust in the promise. In
addition to three accounts of lies to protect the proposed
mother of the unborn progeny, he also gets anxious and
accepts a concubine to guarantee offspring. He even goes so
far as to express doubt in the form of laughter about his age.
The going out not knowing whither he is going and the
sacrifice of Isaac are the glorious *exceptions.*
Crucial Details: Abraham left home *sixty years* before his father's death,
a breach of culturally accepted obligation (Gen. 11:26, 32).

12:3   Victory includes literalness of "all the earth" blessed by
Abraham, exactly as promised.
The story line goes from the magnificent faith described in
Heb. 11:8, spelled out in great detail against its background of
"loftier than average" idolatry. Thus were wives sought in this
setting. For God's new humanity, this wasn't good enough,
and so the powerful yearning for "a city" that motivated
Abraham.

12:2   It is proper to *sympathize* with Abraham's failures, since the
"great nation" promise is so very "far out." Avoid being
judgmental about the lapses, since God wasn't. But faith is
motivated by the celebration of God's *grace.*

15:5   Can *you* imagine having descendants as numerous as the stars,
22:17   or the grains of sand on the beach? That's a bit much for a
serious promise from *God!*

NOTE: On the face of it, the *three* accounts of lies told in a moment of disbelief might seem to merit a story. But the thrust is basically negative, and all good preaching has to have a positive thrust. Celebration demands affirmation.

Title: On Praying for Folks

Text: Genesis 19:29 and James 5:16

Lesson: Genesis 18:20–33

Purpose: To move persons to deep human compassion, irrepressibly expressed in intercessory prayer. A subtheme might be that of comforting persons with wayward offspring.

Protagonist: Abraham

Conflict: Will God consider Abraham's intercessions?

Resolution: Angels are sent to warn Lot and drag him and his family out of the condemned city.

Celebration Material: It is dangerous to make room for the inference that some folks' children are lost because they didn't have enough prayerful parental concern. However, the message here is plain that somehow, in his own way, God's answer is Yes! to *some* of the intercessions of loved ones. And the "odds" are well worth the prayers of all of us. So the heart of every believer joins Abraham, again and again (Gen. 18:30, 32), crying: "O Lord, please don't be angry with me and think me a pest at the seat of mercy. Just once again may I lay before you the concern, the plea, the tear-stained petition of my heart: *Please* protect my child." "God remembered Abraham, and sent Lot out of the midst of the overthrow" (19:29).

Special Angle: Abraham's permissive and generous division of the land, as well as his repeated intercession, is plausible as an expression of *fatherly* love. Thus he becomes prototypical of parents who have done all they can, and have left to themselves only the role of intercessor. There is nothing else to be done until Lot steps back into the arc of safety and blessedness which God has guaranteed to Abraham's kin. (It all seems so like the attitude of the father of the so-called prodigal son in Jesus' parable.)

Crucial Details: Lot has no business leaving his father to go

12:4   with his uncle unless his father is gone already and Abraham is acting *in loco parentis*.

13:10   In a land where water was desperately short and ancestral seniority was acquiesced to at all times, it is amazingly gen-

erous of Uncle Abe to let Lot have a goodie like the Jordan
Valley. He must have loved Lot more like a son, and that in a
setting where he had no other son whatever.

13:6   The fact that they were so rich (possibly from commerce) that
available land would not support the flocks and other hold-
ings of both Lot and Abraham may be used to justify
Abraham's generosity, but there is a complicated issue about
this seeming to nullify the very promise of God. So, again, the
love of peace and great generosity must surely be coupled
here with *love of Lot.*

Title: On Being in the Way. (Introduction might play on two mean-
        ings.)
Text: Genesis 24:27 (KJV)
Purpose: To motivate hearers to get off dead center and take the first
        steps toward the fulfillment of their cherished goals
*Protagonist:*Abraham's slave
Conflict: Will the slave really be able to find an acceptable wife for
        Isaac before Abraham dies, and will she be willing to go back
        with the slave?
Resolution: The answer to well-conceived prayer is immediate.
Celebration Material: The word of thanks uttered so spontaneously and
        with such deep feeling is a perfect celebration. One needs
        only to move into it slowly, with careful, detailed buildup, and
        to perform/render it with elaboration.
Special Angle: Many versions of the Bible use the phrase "in the way,"
        but the KJV says it in a manner that highlights the basic angle:
        that none of this would have happened if the slave had not
        taken the initiative to start out, even though he had so little to
        go on. Yes, this helps fulfill God's promise to Abraham, but
        the slave's *loyalty* and *movement* forward in faith are crucial.
Crucial Details
24:10   Despite the camels and other evidence of fantastic wealth, this
        servant is under no illusions: he has not the faintest idea how
        to succeed in so delicate a matter. He had already voiced the
24:5   fear that the lady would not agree to return with him, a
        stranger taking her *to* a stranger to live in a strange land.
24:7   Sure, the faith of a spiritual giant like Abraham guarantees an
        angel escort, but even so, a matter as complicated as this
24:12   requires *prayer* and the guidance of God. But here, again, the
 —14   initiative taken to start is matched by the design of a way to

screen possibilities. The watering of camels demands a girl who is gracious, generous, and hardworking. (It will be hard not to break the story and do an aside on using such criteria for a wife today.)

NOTE: There are many scholars who assume that there was at work a means of being sure that either a girl would be dressed as a member of the kinship clan, or that any person going to that particular well was already a kinsperson. Even so, it was overwhelming to see a girl so hospitable, hardworking, and also attractive, doing the exact things asked for in the prayer.

24:33   This servant is a man of tremendous ability, as well as of loyalty to his master. He refuses politely even to accept food until he has explained his mission. Unlike the man in Jesus' parable, he has all this wealth with him and uses every bit for the purpose for which it was sent.

24:27   Then, after masterminding all this, he gives the credit to his boss's faith and his boss's God.

Title: Room for God's People
Text: Genesis 26:22 and Matthew 5:5
Lesson: Genesis 24:14–22
Purpose: To motivate meekness among God's people, in the midst of a chronically aggressive and competitive culture
Protagonist: Isaac
Conflict: Will poor, undistinguished Isaac ever get a place where he can settle down and be at peace?
Resolution: Somehow the herdsmen ceased contention, and there was finally room, as stated in the text. Yet done in peace.
Celebration Material: Everybody has his or her Eseks and Sitnahs, but, thank God, everybody has Rehoboths. They that live by the sword die by the sword, and anything taken by violence can be taken again. But the meek shall inherit the earth, because God has promised it to them, even as he promised the land to Abraham and his seed.
Special Angle: Isaac shows no bitterness or pain when leaving the first two wells. He seems a monumentally secure person, despite the usual problems of the sons of great men. There is an African proverb that says that great heroes always have cowards for sons, but this man is no coward. He is calm and poised in the security of the promises of God.
Crucial Details: Only one chapter is devoted to Isaac's life. But he is an indispensable link in the chain of providence.

26:17 Isaac was obviously not in rebellion against his dad's strength
 –22   or reputation. He was not trying to compete with him either.
       His respect for his father is seen in his digging of his father's
       wells and restoring the names his father gave them.

NOTE: The Philistines have an interesting cultural possibility here.
       They may be of a more northern European stock, which has
       interesting implications, as one sees their competitive and
       aggressive ways. Why else should they resent the prosperity of
       a good neighbor, or seize the very wells they had stopped up
       themselves? There is a reverse to keeping up with the Joneses.
       It is like making sure they don't keep up with you. But God
       blesses whom he will, and cruel envy cannot stop the promises
       of God.

NOTE: Isaac is all the more admirable in that the water rights he was
       denied were more important in his world than land rights or
       real estate. Even when dealing with so critical a concern for
       his day, he was calm. And this narrative is doubtless from the
       most ancient of the sources.

Title: The Price of a Clear Conscience
Text: Genesis 32:26, 30
Lesson: Genesis 32:22–30
Protagonist: Jacob/Israel
Conflict: Jacob's fear for his life as he approached Esau, which
       triggered an even greater need to get in tune with God before
       having to meet him that last time
Resolution: Jacob wrestles with God without knowing it, and by his
       strength and persistence, he prevails. God forgives and re-
       stores him and makes of him a new person with a new name.
Celebration Material: Jacob's great relief and joy when he realizes that
32:30 he has seen God face-to-face and is still living is an experience
       to be re-created and enjoyed. From the dread born of the
       awareness that one is wrestling with a being from another
       realm to the victory of being allowed to prevail and being
       given a blessing is a long and now overwhelmingly joyous
       journey. The relief of a clear conscience, a factor never
       expressly mentioned, is like a load from the shoulders of one
       chosen of God.
Special Angle: The new name given Jacob signifies a total rebirth and
       new acceptability with God. This is the greatest blessing

possible. This new person can now be admitted to the Promised Land and to the inheritance promised.

Crucial Details: While Jacob left home relatively lightheartedly and

28:10 dreamed pleasant dreams en route, he did not feel so on his
−17 return, even though he was ordered by God to go back.

32:9 Thus he prayed for deliverance from Esau in great humility
−12 (v. 10) even before he sent his family two separate ways for protection. So conscience is never the issue openly, but it is.

32:25 That "touch" was really a *hit* that God gave him, before he gave the blessing and the new name.

28:13 Jacob could easily have blamed all his evil on his scheming mother, who started out as an innocent answer to prayer, and ended up in the same role with her evil genius brother, Laban.

32:25 The insistence on a blessing suggests a much higher level of spiritual goals than those held when he cooperated with Mom to steal his brother's blessing and birthright.

NOTES

1. Henry H. Mitchell, *The Recovery of Preaching* (Harper & Row, 1977). An elaboration of the 1974 Lyman Beecher Lectures at Yale.

2. Gerhard von Rad, *Genesis, A Commentary*, rev. ed., tr. by John H. Marks, The Old Testament Library (Westminster Press, 1973), p. 33.

3. Ibid., p. 35.

4. Ibid., p. 37 (Delitzsch quoted here).

5. Ibid., pp. 36–37.

6. Some of the recent titles that focus on narrative preaching: Fred B. Craddock, *Overhearing the Gospel* (Abingdon Press, 1978); Richard A. Jensen, *Telling the Story* (Augsburg Publishing House, 1980); Eugene L. Lowry, *The Homiletical Plot* (John Knox Press, 1980); James A. Sanders, *God Has a Story Too* (Fortress Press, 1979).

7. Eric C. Rust, "The Theology of the Old Testament," in *General Articles; Genesis-Exodus* The Broadman Bible Commentary, Vol. 1 (Broadman Press, 1969), p. 71.

8. E. A. Speiser, *Genesis*, The Anchor Bible, Vol. 1 (Doubleday & Co., 1964), *passim;* G. Henton Davies, "Introduction," in *General Articles; Genesis-Exodus*, The Broadman Bible Commentary, Vol. 1, p. 102.

9. Claus Westermann, *The Promises to the Fathers*, tr. by David E. Green (Fortress Press, 1980), p. 162.

FOR FURTHER READING

The Broadman Bible Commentary. Broadman Press. A resource that com-
bines a hospitable attitude to the latest and best of scholarship, while
holding to a theological stance close to the narrative-loving folk of the
congregation.

Jensen, Richard A. *Telling the Story.* Augsburg Publishing House, 1980. A
serious and suggestive analysis of the whole concept of gospel as story, with
a special section on story preaching.

Mitchell, Henry H. *The Recovery of Preaching.* Harper & Row, 1977. An earlier
elaboration of much of the material in this chapter, originally presented as
the Lyman Beecher Lectures at Yale, 1974.

Rad, Gerhard von. *Genesis, A Commentary.* Tr. John H. Marks. Rev. ed. The
Old Testament Library. Westminster Press, 1973. Probably the richest
single commentary of scholarly standing.

Speiser, E. A. *Genesis.* The Anchor Bible, Vol. 1. Doubleday & Co., 1964. Less
detailed but an excellent adjunct to the von Rad material.

3. PREACHING FROM THE HISTORY OF THE EXODUS WANDERINGS AND THE SETTLEMENT

ERIC C. RUST AND JAMES W. COX

PART I. THEOLOGICAL HERMENEUTICS AND PREACHING VALUES
Eric C. Rust

Our concern with the biblical material in this chapter concentrates on the early history of the Hebrew people as the "people of God." Biblical scholarship with its analysis of the sources and traditions involved will be taken for granted. We shall concentrate more upon the historical context and theological meanings that characterize such traditions. The introductory analyses are valuable tools for arriving at a sound exegesis and for understanding the subtle differences which the biblical text exposes because of the different traditions and memories which are blended in it. Such traditions embody the memories of a particular group and these memories will be selective in accordance with the theological beliefs and cultural concerns of that group. All this is important as we examine the relevance of our material to the homiletical task.

LIBERATION AND THE CREATION OF A COVENANT PEOPLE

The first four of the books we are studying offer us the history of a slave people released from bondage and learning in their wilderness wanderings what it meant to be the people of God. The record is basically compiled from the already blended JE traditions, but the Priestly editor of the postexilic period has skillfully provided a framework from his own priestly traditions as well as editing and refining the earlier JE material. The result is a continuous story which brings us in the book of Numbers to the borders of Canaan. The different emphases in the traditions are still present, and we need to note their presence. This helps us often to understand the way in which certain events are described. The J traditions are generally associated with the southern section of Israel and probably were preserved in a shrine like Hebron. Their association with Judah, which seems to have invaded Canaan from the south and which included groups or clans like the Kenites, would account for the generally accepted fact that these traditions do not regard Yahweh as a new name for God but use it in the book of Genesis and associate it with Abraham. The E traditions seem to be employed more as a supplement to J in the blended JE story. They belong more to the northern section of Israel, were probably preserved in shrines like Shechem, and regard the name Yahweh as a new divine revelation to Moses. They are particularly associated with the Josephite nucleus of the tribes that invaded Canaan across Jordan.

These traditions before and after they were blended take us back much nearer to the events they record, whereas the Priestly traditions were shaped and selectively remembered across the long period of Solomon's Temple, the exile, and the early days of the rebuilt Temple of the postexilic period. This explains the concern of the P sections and additions with the status and services of the priest, with the Temple and its sacrifices. P adds little to the basic story of the liberation and the wilderness wanderings. Indeed, it breaks into the continuity of that story with the long sections which offer a Priestly corpus of laws—Exodus 25–40; Leviticus; Num. 1:1–10:10. We shall find that this body of laws offers little homiletical material.

It is the JE story of the pilgrim people of God which speaks to our own lives and experience (Ex. 1–20; 24; 32; 34; Num. 10–36). In this story, the central actor is God, not Moses or Aaron. Divine election and promise dominate. In the traditions, the figure of Abraham and God's dealing with him provide the hidden agenda. Both the J and P traditions preserve a divine covenant with Abraham in which God calls Abraham to venture out under his guidance to possess a land for him and his descendants (Gen. 12:1f.; 17:1ff.). To this is added in J the promise that his descendants shall be a blessing to the world. The JE story is concerned to show how the divine promise was fulfilled in certain historic acts. It is God who acts, who guides the Hebrew people, who delivers them from bondage, provides a leader in Moses, makes a covenant with them, and leads them to the borders of Canaan. In the second part of the story from Deuteronomy through Joshua and Judges, it is still God who acts. It is Yahweh who gives them the land.

The second aspect of the divine promise in J—that Abraham's descendants would bring blessing to the world—finds little reference in the story of the settlement. One fragmentary reference to it is Balaam's oracle (Num. 24:3–9). It remained for the prophets with their hopes to look forward to the fulfillment of that dimension of God's promise. Meantime, God was bringing and did bring them into the land. This is the story with which we are concerned.

The highlights of this story offer homiletical insights. They point always to God and his revelatory and redemptive activity; they find relevance to where our listeners are. The JEP narrative begins in Genesis with the myths of the Garden of Eden and the Tower of Babel. History is there symbolized as rebellious man's life in the wilderness and as subject to a process of divine judgment in which society is torn asunder. The story of the pilgrim people is the record of how God set about restoring the creative process which man's sin had misdirected. He began to create a people through whom all the people of the earth would be blessed. A loose group of tribes with a common ancestry back to Abraham found itself down in Egypt, making bricks without straw. They stand, indeed, as a reminder that sinful man lives in a divided and oppressive world. He lives in a wilderness where he both exploits and is exploited by his fellows. His basic sin against his Creator is his self-centered arrogance. Thus the Hebrews, like so many people in our modern world, belonged to the exploited and the oppressed, the ranks of those who are the concern of contemporary "liberation theology." This emphasis on slavery and the yearning for liberation forms a good background for the preacher's picture of Moses.

Moses is often an obscure figure. His kinship with the oppressed Hebrews and an innate humane concern finally led to the flight to Midian. Here the divine call came to him as he tended the flock. The phenomenon of the burning bush, however susceptible it may be to natural explanation, became for him the medium of an encounter with the living God. He is the God of the fathers, the God of promise. Still more, he is a God who sees the suffering and hears the cry of the exploited. Is this not true still of the God whom we proclaim? God acts by choosing a human instrument for the accomplishing of his purpose. But again, that is the way he always works. We think of those who have been used across social history, sometimes without acknowledged religious motivation, to fight injustice and deal with oppression.

The divine call to Moses accepted the reality of human freedom. Moses could enter into a dialogue with God. Serious doubts about his adequacy for the special task he was to perform were conjoined to ignorance of the nature of the divine mystery which was constraining his consent. God gives him his name in a phrase which is best rendered "I will be who I will be." This is an explanatory paraphrase of the actual name YHWH, the sacred Tetragrammaton which pious Jews have never pronounced, replacing it with the word *'adonai*, Lord. It is rendered as Yahweh by Old Testament scholarship, but it remains a mystery. It is a personal name, and the paraphrase might suggest that the hiddenness of God will be unveiled in what he does. He is the God who acts and his nature will be disclosed in his activity in history and in the inspired words of his prophets. God never calls us, preachers or laypersons, without the giving of himself, sufficient to inspire us and adequate to meet our need. Furthermore, he respects our freedom.

What happened in God's relationship to Moses also holds of the Hebrew people. They were chosen by God, who renewed his promise to their fathers (Ex. 3:17). The people are to affirm Moses' message, however. They must believe (Ex. 4:31). God was entering into a real partnership with his people. Deuteronomy emphasizes this "election" all over again. In Moses' final address, they are told that God did not choose them because they were great in number, for they were not (Deut. 7:6ff.), nor were they chosen because of their righteousness, for they were a stubborn and rebellious people (Deut. 9:4ff.). The sole basis of their election was that God loved them. He is faithful who promised! God set his love on Israel as in Jesus he has set his love on us. That will preach! So God renews his promise to Moses in Ex. 6:2ff., even though the oppression continues and the people begin to doubt the divine promise (Ex. 5; 6:9). Even Moses has complained and made accusations against God (Ex. 5:22–23). Do not we sometimes wonder where God is?

The successive plagues that smite the people, can most of them be accounted for as natural occurrences associated with an abnormal Nile flood? What made them a miracle was the time of their occurrence and the presence of Moses to point to the divine activity behind them. These people had no modern scientific sense of secondary causes. What mattered was the divine presence. These "wonders" confirmed their belief in Yahweh's promise. This still holds. Perfectly normal events occurring when they are especially effective may become disclosures of the divine presence, and we can describe them as miracles.

The Passover, whatever its original and earlier associations, was celebrated (Ex. 12; 13). Its close association with the flight from Egypt gave it a new significance. Its future celebration reminded the Hebrews of how "by strength of hand the LORD brought us out of Egypt" (Ex. 13:11–15). Its later association with the Last Supper and our Lord's crucifixion is not in doubt, although the nature of that association is a matter of dispute. It does, however, provide a basis for a pre-Communion sermon. Our Lord's Supper is associated with a greater and more effective redemptive event than the exodus from Egypt. It too is a commemorative feast. It too is a sacrificial feast, for it points to Him through whose sacrifice there came the new Israel of God. The old feast pointed to the Sinai covenant, and the new feast points to the new covenant in Christ's outpoured life. This also preaches.

The climactic miracle was the crossing of the sea of reeds (Ex. 14:10–15:22). The guardian pillars of cloud and fire might suggest a sermon on God's reinforcing and protecting presence in life's dark times. Once more the miracle was an unusual but natural occurrence. A strong wind piled up the shallow waters of the marshy sea and ceased in time for the pursuing Egyptians to be engulfed (Ex. 15:8). The miracle was the coincidence of the arrival of the people and the wind together with the prophetic voice of Moses to declare the presence of Yahweh in the event. Here was the crucial event, the final moment of deliverance which made possible the creation of the people of God. No wonder that it should become a type for that greater exodus—the death and resurrection of the Lord Jesus and its subsequent reenactment in the life of the Christian believer, symbolized in the baptismal waters (I Cor. 10:1–5).

Deliverance and grumbling is a repetitive story of the wilderness journey. But then even the modern Bedouin faces the same hazards in the desert sand. Thirst, hunger, and weariness might well cause grumbling, despite the shadow of a great deliverance. God kept faith with his people despite their fickleness (Ex. 15:22–26). First bitter water! Then came lack of food, and God provided the quails and the manna. Then came thirst, and God provided the water from the flinty rock. Again, we need to remember the absence of any understanding of secondary causes. Every such event leaned back directly on God, however much we may interpose natural factors and causes. After all, the Creator of nature can use and direct natural forces, especially in days when science regards scientific laws as statistical and descriptive, not regulative. Here is material for a consideration of divine providence. Is it not also true that when we come to the end of our tether, when we touch rock bottom, God intervenes?

So we come to Sinai and the covenant that sealed the redemptive event and brought God's people into being. Moses' call in the encounter of the burning bush now reached its consummation in the thunder and lightning on the mountaintop. In the sounds of the thunder, he heard God's voice deep down in his inner being. His prophetic consciousness was fed with divine insights and moral convictions. He came down from the cloud-covered mount to seal a covenant between Yahweh and the chosen people. Yahweh's electing love set the conditions by obedience to which they could truly be his people, "a kingdom of priests and a holy nation" (Ex. 19:6). In the shadow of a great deliverance and in the awesome experience of the storm-enveloped mount, the people heard the prophetic words of Moses and declared: "All that the LORD has spoken we will do" (Ex. 19:8). The mark of any covenant is the faithfulness, the steadfast love, of the two parties involved. Israel could not bargain with God. He imposed the conditions and in the light of a great liberation, they accepted. God's election and promise, sealed in the Sinai covenant, held despite Israel's subsequent waywardness. He would not allow Israel to be overthrown.

The conditions of the covenant are contained in the Decalogue (Ex. 20:1–17). They involve an implicit monotheism with an affirmation, often to be repeated through Israel's history (e.g., Hos. 11:1; Amos 2:10; 3:1, 2: Jer. 31:32), that Yahweh has brought them up out of the house of bondage in Egypt. There is the assurance that God will show his steadfast love to them. There follows a series of moral injunctions concerning family relationships and social obligations.

Such good material for moral teaching and preaching is amplified by the later Covenant Code which the editors have inserted at this point (Ex. 20:22–23:19). This evidently reflects settled life in an agricultural community, and so includes both moral and ceremonial rules, going back to prophetic voices, and also the criminal and civil injunctions (Ex. 21:1–22:17) which would arise out of decisions made by judges at the gate. We need to note how all such laws gather under the extended personality of Moses and are regarded as divinely given. This was a theocratic community—not a democracy, least of all a secular society. A basis for some prophetic preaching about the lifting up of a divine standard in our permissive structures! Here is the possibility of awakening moral consciousness and of making the church the conscience of the community.

Immediately the pattern of the garden myth repeats itself. No sooner had they participated in the covenant sacrifice, and been united with one another and with God by the outpoured life of a third party, than they fell into their old ways. Their leaders had seen God and eaten and drunk in his presence (Ex. 24:11)—a great communion text! This is very relevant to our own celebration of the Lord's Supper, where we remember the new covenant in Christ, our Lord, and renew our commitment. Moses goes back up the mountain, and they, weary with waiting, break the prophetic injunction, and make graven images (Ex. 32). How like us! For we too so easily move from the sacrament back to our world with its material values and false gods. It is so easy to be secular in a secular order, even for the Christian. But God's redemption and promise still hold in Christ.

The wilderness narrative is now interrupted by a second and much later legal code, bearing all the marks of priestly concern, and evidently belonging to Solomon's Temple and its later rebuilding after the exile in Babylon (Ex. 25–31; Lev.; Num. 1–10). This interruption has little real homiletic material, except for the wonderful passage, quoted by our Lord as the summation of all the law: "You shall love your neighbor as yourself" (Lev. 19:18). We need to remind our people that the Christian motivation is not legal sanction and duty but a love for Christ which is expressed in love for our neighbor. So our Lord bids us to go beyond the law and to fulfill its injunctions by love, a love that walks the extra mile and goes beyond legal injunctions and requirements.

The small Holiness Code (Lev. 17–26), which is probably exilic, forms the basis for a sermon later in this chapter. A preacher might find homiletical material in the sacrificial legislation by combining it with the insights of The Letter to the Hebrews and by remembering that a true understanding of the verb "to atone" is not to propitiate an angry God but to expiate or cover up man's sin.

Numbers 10–32 brings us back to the wilderness journey. The ingratitude of the people comes all over again. The manna is not good enough for them. A part of the cross that Moses bore is disclosed in his prayer to Yahweh. The burden of leadership is too heavy. He did not father this people, and yet he has to feed them. Let Yahweh kill him and relieve him of his misery (Num. 11:11–15). Here the prophet becomes intercessor, a man of prayer, and the prayer avails with Yahweh—Yahweh brings the quails from the sea.

During this incident, the spirit of Yahweh came on the seventy elders and they prophesied. Two men who remained in the camp also shared in this experience, and Joshua, jealous for Moses' prophetic status, asked his leader to silence them. Moses' magnanimity shone through as he wished that all the Lord's people might be prophets and share in the Spirit. This hope is echoed in Joel, and fulfilled in

the new people of God through the sacrifice of one greater than
Moses, Jesus the Christ. Moses' cross, the price he paid for serving
Yahweh, as all God's servants pay a price, comes out in the pathos of
the vision from Pisgah's height (Deut. 34:1–6). So Moses the servant
of God points forward to that greater servant upon whom was the
chastisement that makes us whole (Isa. 53:5).

The plague of serpents (Num. 21) affords another picture of Moses
as the great interceder, pleading for his people. The bronze serpent
was a symbol of God's presence. He did not act by direct healing, but
through the victims viewing the symbol and believing in the divine
power which it represented. No wonder the New Testament men saw
the bronze serpent as pointing to the lifting up of the Son of Man
(John 3:14).

In Numbers 22–34, the outstanding theme is not the fear of Moab
but the prophetic testimony of the mysterious Balaam with the
emphasis on Yahweh's choice of Israel and with its vision of a future
in which Israel shall both prevail and bring blessing to the nations.
The incredible behavior of the donkey need not be stressed. Here the
other dimension of the promise to Abraham becomes evident, a
dimension that waited upon the new people of God, the body of
Christ, for fulfillment.

THE CONQUEST AND THE SETTLEMENT

With Deuteronomy there comes another interruption in the wilderness narrative. The book of Deuteronomy offers a new perspective,
and becomes the basic editorial position of the books that follow—
Joshua, Judges, I and II Samuel, I and II Kings. The J and E
traditions are still present, and the preacher will find the evidence in
any standard commentary or Old Testament introduction. For example, two crossings of the Jordan (Josh. 3:17; 14:11). Yet these
traditions have been set, along with Priestly material especially chs. 13
through 22, within a Deuteronomic framework. This framework is
still more evident in The Book of Judges. Thus the story of the
exodus and its "salvation history" is continued with new emphases, of
which the preacher should be aware. For these we must turn to the
book of Deuteronomy itself.

The central portion of this book consists of a law code (Deut. 12–
36) which begins with the stipulation that the worship of Israel shall
be centralized in one sanctuary (Deut. 12:5ff.). This had led scholars
to identify the code with the law book discovered in the Temple,
which initiated the Josianic reformation in the seventh century B.C. (II
Kings 22–23), when many of the shrines outside Jerusalem were

destroyed. The code certainly enshrines the teaching of the great eighth-century prophets—Isaiah, Hosea, Micah, especially Hosea. There is the declaration of the oneness of Yahweh, as contrasted with the multiplicity of the fertility gods, with their many shrines (Deut. 6:4ff.). The command to love Yahweh with the whole man reflects the teaching of Hosea. The understanding of Israel's election was not grounded on any merit on its part but solely on God's love (Deut. 7:6ff.). Here is the gospel!

Because of the great prophets, Deuteronomy enshrines many great moral and humanitarian concerns. More important, however, for the historical books that follow is the emphasis on divine judgment and retribution (e.g., Deut. 28:15–68; 31:16–22). In the Song of Moses there is a passage that likens God's treatment of his pilgrim people to an eagle stirring up her nest and teaching her young to fly—a good description of the salvation history of the Hebrew people and also of our own pilgrimage (Deut. 32:10–14). The process of divine judgment is also described in this song (vs. 19–35), but it is tempered by mercy (vs. 36–43). This alternation of divine judgment and mercy is a recurrent pattern in The Book of Judges.

One other emphasis in the Deuteronomic code is one that today we find repugnant—the theme of "Holy War" (Deut. 20:1–20). Central in this theme is the "ban," according to which all the inhabitants of the land and their animals are to be completely destroyed (vs. 16–18). This was justified by the code on the grounds that the practices of the Canaanites and others would infect the religion and social life of the invading Hebrew people. Joshua and Judges show how this policy was carried out. The Israelites went to battle in the name of Yahweh, taking with them their sacred Ark, which was a visible sign of his presence. Such ideas and practices are repugnant to us and we find it difficult to believe that they had divine sanction. Undoubtedly their employment in the early days helped in the Hebrew settlement. Other nations employed the same techniques with their gods. The Hebrews had to learn, and also we today, that the Lord does not bless war and is not on the side of the big battalions. It is part of his cross, and it constitutes one of mankind's greatest collective sins. This makes parts of Joshua and Judges difficult material for the homiletician.

What really matters in these books is that the story moves to the fulfillment of one aspect of the divine promise, the possession of the land. However we may view their brutal and often bloodthirsty ways, somehow God overruled their sin and inhumanity, bringing them to deeper and nobler visions of himself and his purpose. "Holy War" was a passing theme in the education of the people of God, a wrong understanding from which they had to be emancipated. But then we too seek to justify war and even link it with our faith in Him who rather taught us that God's way is that of suffering, redeeming love.

The closing words of Deuteronomy offer a fitting epitaph on Moses, as he dies on Pisgah's height, viewing the Promised Land from afar (Deut. 34:9ff.). Joshua, his appointed successor, had a divine gift of wisdom and led the people through the parted water of Jordan into the Land of Canaan. We note the emphasis on the Ark of Yahweh's covenant, the symbol of the divine presence. This led their procession through Jordan and around the walls of the besieged city of Jericho. One might here point to the guiding and reinforcing presence of God as we face spiritual obstacles and besiege the citadels of evil, but the analogy might become farfetched. It would be best to leave the story, but to remember that, whatever may be God's relation to these events, the divine suffering and redeeming love was an overruling presence.

The picture presented by Joshua is very idealistic. The conquest is pictured as completed, a war in which the inhabitants were exterminated without mercy and at the Lord's command (Josh. 11:20). D's "ban" was carried into effect with Yahweh's help! The actual picture is much more realistic (see Judg. 1:1–2:5). Extermination was not the sole weapon, as the Deuteronomic editors suggest (e.g., Deut. 20). Intermarriage was much more a possibility, and the result was that the fertility cults and the Baalism of the Canaanites existed side by side with and infiltrated into the Yahwistic faith and cult.

This is evident in The Book of Judges. Apart from Deborah and Barak, the stories deal, not with war against the Canaanite inhabitants, but with war against invaders like "the king of Mesopotamia" (Judg. 3:7–11), the Edomites, the Philistines, the Ammonites, and the Midianites. The Deuteronomic editing sets these successive battles into a framework of divine retribution. This is stated in Judg. 2:11–23. There is a repetitive cycle of the worship of fertility gods and rebellion against Yahweh, followed by divine wrath and foreign oppression. Then came the cry to Yahweh for deliverance and God provided a deliverer. The cycle was repeated by another relapse into Baalism when such a hero had passed from the scene. The judges appear actually to have been local characters leading various groups of tribes. The whole nation does not appear to have been involved except in the case of Deborah. There was thus no final unification of the tribes into a nation.

The call of these "judges" or "deliverers" varies. What is significant is the charismatic aspect of their leadership. They were all, in various ways, possessed by the spirit of God. We need to remember that, at this stage, "spirit" was not the inner aspect of human personality but was wholly a divine invasive force with purposive direction. Indeed, the Hebrew word for "spirit" is the same as for "wind." Since it came from God, no explanation of it was possible. It came upon some individual whom Yahweh called and endowed with special gifts and powers. Such an individual could claim no personal responsibility for such powers. He recognized them as of divine origin. A divine force was operating in and through him, so that the tribes or groups acknowledged his leadership and were set free from the oppressing power. We may think in different ways of such a divine presence, but the emphasis on God's invasive presence is still a necessity. The Spirit of God made history, then, through inspired persons, and his presence can still be effective in the contemporary scene. Inspired persons can still be the media of God's activity.

The Book of Joshua points to a tribal amphictyony and covenant-renewal ceremony of Shechem (Josh. 23:1–26:28), so that a movement toward national unity was beginning. We should note the confession of faith which accompanied this ceremony. Joshua records the mighty acts of God in their pilgrimage, and the people respond with a confession that reiterates the liberation from Egypt and Yahweh's fulfillment of his promise. So this phase of Israel's history comes to an end. "Not one of all the good promises which Yahweh had made to the house of Israel had failed: all came to pass" (Josh. 21:45). God is still a God of promise, his faithfulness endures, and we are still in salvation history as Christ's church.

PART II. SERMONIC STUDIES
James W. Cox

EXODUS 20:1–17. GOD AND HIS COVENANT

The stabilizing factor in all the ups and downs of Israel was the covenant. Walther Eichrodt has asserted that the concept of covenant "gave definitive expression to the binding of the people to God" and that the covenant "established firmly from the start the particularity of this knowledge of him."[1] It did not matter that this or that prophet did not mention the covenant as such—the reality was always present. Though it was for the moment out of sight, it was never out of mind. This text testifies to the nature of that covenant—what it implied on God's part and what it implied on the part of the people. Karl Barth has said, "It seems as though world history is ordained always to be the framework for the history of this people."[2] The meaning of the text extends to us today. We are its contemporary beneficiaries. God has taken the initiative in establishing a relationship to us, a new covenant in the blood of Jesus Christ; he has thus made it possible for us to live in such a manner as to carry forward his purpose.

The apostle Paul opposed efforts to earn salvation by the works of the law. He discovered that salvation could not be based on human striving. In fact, placing one's confidence in works righteousness as the way to a right relationship to God actually nullifies the true experience of salvation by faith (Gal. 5:2–6). But it is wrong to suppose that the kind of life-style God sought in the Ten Commandments is therefore contradictory to what Paul sought. Exodus 20:2 speaks of God's electing love, the very soil from which all ethical behavior is to spring. God establishes himself as the God of these people, demonstrating the fact clearly in his delivering them "out of the land of Egypt, out of the house of bondage." This is not because of any merit they possess, "but it is because the LORD loves you," they are told, "and is keeping the oath which he swore to your fathers, that the LORD has brought you out with a mighty hand, and redeemed you" (Deut. 7:8). It is in this context that the commandments come— imperatives born of the mighty indicative of God's grace. This agrees with Paul when he says, "Love is the fulfilling of the law" (Rom. 13:10), for what does the "first and greatest commandment" mean if it does not mean a hearty and sincere commitment to God in obedience to whatever he requires?

The words "I am the LORD your God" (Ex. 20:2) are the crucial words of the text. To these words we may respond in the words of the psalmist with trust: "The LORD is my shepherd" (Ps. 23:1). The former is what makes the latter possible. The text does contain and bind us to the Ten Commandments. "*Thou* shalt! means, *Israel* shall! and everything that Israel shall is only an imperative transcription of what Israel *is,* repeating in some sense only what Israel has become by God, and what it must always be with God."[3] What we find there has not basically changed. God still commands us—*now* in terms of our own life situation and needs.

It is important to add that the decisive act of God in the exodus experience did not remain for Israel a datum of history which would gradually fade away. The recital of those events became a regular feature of the ongoing life of the people. As memory was refreshed and hope renewed, sustaining grace poured into their life in changed and changing circumstances. In the same way, the Christ—full of grace and truth—becomes a part of everyday life. Memory plays an indispensable role in our devotion and obedience. It tells us who we are and reminds us of the ethical implications of our identity. Hope makes the enterprise worthwhile. We are on the way to a future filled with God. Again and again the Eucharist brings the history and hope together in a renewing experience of God's grace.

LEVITICUS 19:1–2, 17–18. HOW TO BE HOLY

Jonathan Edwards wrote of an early experience:

> Holiness appeared to me to be of a sweet, pleasant, charming, serene, calm nature. It seemed to me, it brought an inexpressible purity, brightness, peacefulness, and ravishment to the soul.[4]

How close to the biblical view of holiness was Edwards' view, we shall see.

God has revealed himself as holy and has declared that because of his nature as holy his people must be holy. What does this word "holy" mean? It means separate, set apart, reserved for special use. Basically it does not have moral connotations, but in actual use it does.

If I have placed my faith in God and acknowledge his Lordship, then I am obligated to order my life in such a way as to reflect the very character and purpose of God. It is a "like father, like son" proposition.

The exegetical issues here are few. They have to do mainly with the meaning of "holy." J. Hänel has characterized the entire religion of the Old Testament as a "religion of holiness," leading Walther Eichrodt to say that it does occupy a position of unique importance, in virtue of the frequency and emphasis of its use.[5]

Even so, the idea of the holy did not originate in Israel. Other religions had their concepts of the holy—holy places, holy persons, holy things. Wherever the holy was believed to be focused, the people regarded it with a mixture of admiration and dread. It represented a world beyond the ordinary, a world of mystery. Thus a cultus with rituals and ceremonies developed to facilitate intercourse with this transcendent world.[6]

Eichrodt, however, has pointed out that from the time of Moses the personal element was introduced into the theory of holiness. This raised the concept to a higher spiritual plane. It was God who was holy—God first of all! The heathen religions rarely applied the word "holy" to their god. "That which transfers men or things to the sphere of the holy is the operation of God's own activity."[7]

It remained for Hosea to show that a quality in God's holiness is love, which, of course, the New Testament in I John emphasizes as the distinguishing characteristic of his nature: "God is love" (I John 4:8).

Nevertheless, there was an ethical dimension to God's holiness, so that he required of his people a certain quality of behavior in personal and social life. This is echoed in Leviticus 17–26, the so-called Holiness Code, and we find it in the New Testament in Hebrews: "Follow peace with all men, and holiness, without which no man shall see the Lord" (Heb. 12:14). I Peter admonishes Christians: "The One who called you is holy; like him, be holy in all your behavior, because Scripture says, 'You shall be holy, for I am holy' " (I Peter 1:15–16; cf. II Peter 3:11).

We cannot overlook some instances of apparent unethical action by God himself (see Gen. 12; 20; 27f.; Ex. 3:22; 11:2; 12:35f.; 17:14). But in these cases Israel's faith reflected a crude stage of understanding and spiritual growth as a people and should not be judged today on the basis of our fuller understanding of God's ethical nature.

The call to holiness is likely to fall on deaf ears today. The word is so covered with barnacles of misunderstanding that it would sink. It conjures up pictures of Pharisaical piety, separation from real life, and oddities of speech, dress, or custom. It does not, therefore, appeal to most persons as it did to Jonathan Edwards.

Harry Emerson Fosdick argued for the thesis that "the sacred and the secular are inseparable."[8] Yet, like it or not, any of us who truly belong to God are, in a genuine sense, holy—that is, special and set apart to express something of our God and to achieve his purposes. In fact, this is a rich experience. Rightly regarded, it should strike a responsive chord in our hearts. I Peter sounds the depths of its meaning: "But you are a chosen race, a royal priesthood, a dedicated nation [RSV reads, "holy nation"], and a people claimed by God for his own, to proclaim the triumphs of him who has called you out of darkness into his marvellous light. You are now the people of God, who once were not his people; outside his mercy once, you have now received his mercy" (2:9–10).

The status called "holy" has implications. Jesus said, "There must be no limit to your goodness, as your heavenly Father's goodness knows no bounds" (Matt. 5:48). These ethical expressions of our status with God or our likeness to him have to be lived out where life is hard, ethical decisions difficult, and dedicated living sometimes dangerous. The efforts of the Jewish people to fulfill such a role are well known, as are the problems and consequences. Jesus' prayer for us is this:

> I pray not that thou shouldest take them out of the world, but that thou shouldest keep them from the evil. They are not of the world, even as I am not of the world. Sanctify them through thy truth: thy word is truth. (John 17:15–17)

We could hardly begin to measure the consequences for family, church, community, nation, and world if just those of us who are presumably holy began in every respect to act in accord with who and what we are. As Dag Hammarskjöld said, "In our age, the road to holiness necessarily passes through the world of action."[9] The words of Martin Luther also are memorable: "When God purifies the heart by faith, the market is sacred as well as the sanctuary; neither remaineth there any work or place which is profane."[10]

DEUTERONOMY 12:1–12. THE PLACE FOR WORSHIP

This text on worship signifies that God may be worshiped at whatever place he designates. He determines what is true worship and how it is to be done.

The references (Deut. 12:5, 11, 14, 18) to "the place" that God would choose would, in Josiah's time, be interpreted to refer to the centralization of worship at Jerusalem. However, worship did take place at many altars, as Ex. 20:24 reminds us. Deuteronomy recognizes this: "You shall not do according to all that we are doing here this day, every man doing whatever is right in his own eyes" (Deut. 12:8). This suggests that rules for the place of worship were lax. Yet the names of the places—Shechem, Shiloh, and Mizpah—come to mind as providing centers for worship that offered tribal unity (see Josh. 24:26; Josh. 22:9, 12, 29; I Macc. 3:44–46). The Josianic reformation was based on the idea that the Temple in Jerusalem was alone legitimate and our text was so interpreted.

This place of worship would be where God chose for his name to dwell. Von Rad says that "in Deuteronomy a more precise distinction is made between Yahweh and the sanctuary. The name dwells on earth in the sanctuary; Yahweh himself is in heaven" (Deut. 26:15).[11] This is an important distinction. It protects the freedom of God. He is not localized, though he may still manifest himself in a place and bless those who worship there. Solomon's long prayer in I Kings 8:22–53 graphically reflects this distinction.

In Jesus Christ, God has caused his name to dwell—to tabernacle! The incarnation brings God near. It makes him accessible. For those who worship God through Jesus Christ it bestows blessing. Even *one* place, though it offers remarkable unity among worshipers, may become a less than adequate center for worship. In the Fourth Gospel, Jesus tells the Samaritan woman, "The hour is coming, and now is, when the true worshipers will worship the Father in spirit and truth" (John 4:23a). Thus Mt. Gerizim and Jerusalem are anachronisms. They have been surpassed by something greater, something that bears finality.

God is free and can cause his name to dwell where he pleases. To a limited degree there are persons and places in whom and where we have touched "the near end" of God. But nowhere has God so manifested himself as in Jesus Christ. "In him the whole fulness of deity dwells bodily" (Col. 2:9).

This text is not without its problems. Deuteronomy 12:2 and 3 raise the specter of bigotry and religious persecution. However, the instructions have to do mainly with the Israelites getting rid of idolatries that they have assimilated after taking the land. It was not so much a matter of their regulating the religious practices of outsiders as it was of purifying their own. Yet there are at least vestiges here of the holy war concept, which is abhorrent to the Christian conscience. Eduard Schweizer says:

> What astonishes us about the Old Testament is that it in no way tries to gloss over the wrong. Everything happened in a very human way—even in Israel's military campaigns. And yet, the Old Testament recognizes that God was with Israel in the midst of all this utter humanness—in suffering, war, and wrong.[12]

Verses 6, 7, and 11 assume that worship includes burnt offerings, etc. Of course, our worship today, even that of Orthodox Jews, does not employ burnt offerings. But we offer our sacrifices of prayer and praise, and, as the apostle Paul entreated, we present our bodies as a living sacrifice (Rom. 12:1).

Now that our worship as Christians finds its focus in Jesus Christ, there are many places hallowed by tradition and sanctified by divine surprise, where God may be truly worshiped. Jesus said, "Where two or three are gathered in my name, there am I in the midst of them" (Matt. 18:20).

Everything that could be expected ethically from Israel or from us is predicated on genuine worship. This must stem from a recognition of the supreme Lordship of God and from a will to love him. "Hear, O Israel: The LORD our God is one LORD; and you shall love the LORD your God with all your heart, and with all your soul, and with all your might" (Deut. 6:4–5). It is this truth that led Augustine to say, "Love God, and do as you will."

Joshua 24:14–28. Religion as Personal Choice

The time comes when each of us must decide whether our religion is to be a relic of past commitments by others or a fresh and vital personal commitment. II Timothy 3:5 speaks of those "who preserve the outward form of religion, but are a standing denial of its reality."

The problem confronting the tribes of Israel was what to do, at a critical juncture, about their religious fealty. Would it be offered to the heathen gods whom their ancestors had served? Would it be the gods of the Amorites among whom they now lived? Or would it be the God of Abraham, Isaac, and Jacob; the God of Moses and Aaron; the God who had led them into the land of promise? The Lord said through Joshua, "I gave you a land on which you had not labored, and cities which you had not built, and you dwell therein; you eat the fruit of vineyards and oliveyards which you did not plant" (Josh. 24:13). The challenge was to "fear the Lord, and serve him in sincerity and in faithfulness" (v. 14a).

Although we read of Joshua's death in this final chapter of the book that bears his name, it does not mean that the incident reported here happened immediately before his death. Rather, this occurred during the period of the conquest (cf. 8:30–35). It was a time of choice for the tribes. Ancient devotions of others were not sustaining spiritual capital. Joshua recited the signal acts of God on their behalf across the years, and then he asked them where their loyalties lay.

The twelve disciples faced a similar choice. When the curious and superficially committed followers of Jesus drifted away because of what he was and what he taught, Jesus turned to the Twelve and compelled them to decide about him one way or the other (John 7:67–68).

The point of immediacy in the text is the last clause of v. 15: "As for me and my house, we will serve the Lord." Joshua's decision had obviously been made already. He was well aware of all the options available to him as well as to all the people. But God's promises—first to Abraham and then to others down the years—and God's actions for his people were so burned into his memory that nothing made sense but to serve this redeemer God. The question of perennial importance is not, What will I have to give up if I serve the true God? rather, What will I have to give up if I refuse to serve him? What will I lose? What will my family lose? Compounded with the disobedience of all the others, what will the world lose?

The lure of idolatry is always present in various modern forms. Whenever some aspect of reality is elevated to supremacy in our lives, we have surrendered to our god, whether that be sex, money, fame, power, beauty, youth, or whatnot. We today have to choose just as decisively as the ancient Israelites. It is simply a matter of our willingness to let God be Lord of all, so that we permit no aspect of our existence to attempt the usurpation of his supremacy.

The Israelites declared their willingness to join Joshua in a solidarity of commitment (vs. 16–18). But Joshua was skeptical. He well knew the difficulty of resisting temptation, and he warned them (vs. 19–20). Enthusiastic would-be disciples of Jesus were treated to a glimpse of what they would be up against (see Matt. 8:19–20). How the truth was betrayed when a pastor eager for a new member told an inquirer, "There are no obligations"!

We are only deceiving ourselves if we believe radical commitment to be a snap. Dietrich Bonhoeffer said that the call to discipleship is a call to die. That may not be literally true, yet something has to die— some old loves, old idolatries, old preoccupations, old loyalties. As uncertain as our performance in the future may be, we nevertheless have to decide and declare our position. In answer to Joshua's skeptical remark, the Israelites said: "Nay; but we will serve the LORD" (v. 21). That is the only way—the journey has to begin in faith and continue in faith.

NOTES

1. Walther Eichrodt, *Theology of the Old Testament*, Vol. 1, tr. by J. A. Baker, The Old Testament Library (Westminster Press, 1961), p. 36.
2. Karl Barth, *Church Dogmatics*, Vol. IV, Pt. 3, tr. by G. W. Bromiley (Edinburgh: T. & T. Clark, 1961), p. 690.
3. Ibid., Vol. II, Pt. 2, tr. by G. W. Bromiley et al. (Edinburgh: T. & T. Clark, 1957), p. 572.
4. Jonathan Edwards, quoted in Mary Wilder Tileston (ed.), *Daily Strength for Daily Needs* (Little, Brown & Co., 1945), p. 123.
5. Eichrodt, op. cit., p. 270.
6. Ibid.
7. Ibid., pp. 271, 272.
8. From a sermon in James W. Cox (ed.), *The Twentieth-Century Pulpit* (Abingdon Press, 1978), p. 57.
9. Dag Hammarskjöld, *Markings*, tr. by Leif Sjöberg and W. H. Auden (London: Faber & Faber, 1964), p. 23.
10. Martin Luther, quoted in Frank S. Mead (ed.), *The Encyclopedia of Religious Quotations* (Fleming H. Revell Co., 1976), p. 340.

11. Gerhard von Rad, *Deuteronomy,* tr. by Dorothea Barton, The Old Testament Library (Westminster Press, 1966), p. 90.

12. Eduard Schweizer, *God's Inescapable Nearness,* tr. by James W. Cox (Word Books, 1971), p. 105.

FOR FURTHER READING

Buttrick, George A., et al., eds. *The Interpreter's Bible,* Vols. 1 and 2. Abingdon Press, 1952, 1953.

Childs, Brevard S. *The Book of Exodus, A Critical, Theological Commentary.* The Old Testament Library. Westminster Press, 1974.

————. *Memory and Tradition in Israel.* London: SCM Press, 1962.

Rad, Gerhard von. *Old Testament Theology,* Vol. 1. Tr. D. M. G. Stalker. Harper & Row, 1962.

Rendtorff, Rolf. *God's History: A Way Through the Old Testament.* Tr. Gordon C. Winsor. Westminster Press, 1969.

Rust, Eric C. *Judges, Ruth, I and II Samuel.* The Layman's Bible Commentary, Vol. 6. John Knox Press, 1961.

————. *Salvation History.* John Knox Press, 1964.

Westermann, Claus. *A Thousand Years and a Day.* Tr. S. Rudman. Muhlenberg Press, 1962.

4. PREACHING ON THE NARRATIVES OF THE MONARCHY

JOHN D. W. WATTS

I. EXEGETICAL APPROACH

Traditionally, the magnificent stories about prophets, judges, and kings found in the books of Samuel and Kings have provided the texts for great sermons. More recently the art of telling the story from the pulpit has fallen into decline. Hans W. Frei has sketched the reasons for this in his masterful book on eighteenth- and nineteenth-century hermeneutics, *The Eclipse of Biblical Narrative* (Yale University Press, 1974).

There now appears to be a favorable climate for the revival of the storytelling art and for sermons based on these biblical classics. A great deal of scholarly work has been done in the last decade to aid the understanding of the narratives of the Old Testament. A useful book to aid in the general understanding is that by Klaus Koch, *The Growth of the Biblical Tradition* (Charles Scribner's Sons, 1969).

A solid commentary can help in arranging the facts. John Gray's *I & II Kings* (2d ed., Westminster Press, 1970) and P. Kyle McCarter's *I Samuel,* Vol. 8 in The Anchor Bible series (Doubleday & Co., 1980), fill the bill very well in this regard with up-to-date information. But reading the commentary is a long way from seeing or exploiting the homiletical potential in the narratives.

One needs a good translation. We are blessed with a variety of good translations today. It is better to stay with the translations proper: the New International Version, the Revised Standard Version, the New American Standard Bible, the Jerusalem Bible, or the New English Bible, rather than with the paraphrases. Preachers can do their own paraphrasing after using the standard text. Sometimes reading the passages in several translations will reveal potential meaning in the stories.

A starting point in understanding the books of Samuel and Kings is the recognition that they are part of a long, connected and continuous account of Israel's history in the Land of Canaan that begins in Deuteronomy and goes through II Kings (from the entry into Canaan to the fall of Jerusalem to Babylon's armies in 587 b.c.). This is not a simple telling of what happened. It is a theological statement which explains why God's people in God's land did not find that experience one of accomplished salvation, a land of milk and honey; why they were buffeted by enemies; why God allowed them the final indignity of exile. This "history" begins with the sermons of Deuteronomy and is continued throughout by short homilies or interpretations that relate various portions to the major theme. A little practice will allow the reader to identify readily the comments of the so-called "Deuter-onomist" who edited the grand work.

The preacher may find it good to use the Deuteronomist's com-ments for the sermon. They are already sermonic in style and illustrate the major points in the masterful book of sermons, Deuter-onomy. Their points are clear, and application is direct.

However, the interpreter also needs to recognize that the great work has incorporated smaller "histories" that were written and gathered to serve other purposes. They are rich in meanings that go far beyond that of the Deuteronomist's one-theme sermon. In Samuel there is the cycle of stories dealing with the Ark of the Covenant, the marvelous accounts of Samuel, the tragic story of Saul as Israel's first king, and the story of David's rise and the establishment of his dynasty. Each of these is rich in theological insights and often deals with issues of pastoral concern.

The books of Kings contain many stories of kings and prophets, often of the interaction between them. Two major cycles of prophetic stories are those which center in Elijah and Elisha. These cycles have their own reasons for being which are different from those of the Deuteronomists who absorbed them into the larger work.

Then the interpreter must note that each of the stories has an independent existence in its own right apart from that of the cycle or series in which it is now found. Each has its own identity which is partly determined by its "genre" (the classification of the kind of story it is) and partly established in its own unique identity. Often the outline of the story will fit that of its genre, while the specifics of the story it tells are uniquely its own.

Claus Westermann's book *Basic Forms of Prophetic Speech* (Westmin-ster Press, 1967) describes the genre and characteristics of many prophetic stories. Westermann thinks that the earliest and most basic one tells how a prophet brings a message of judgment to an individual. This study of that genre helps to define the real nature of the prophet's calling and work.

Klaus Koch's book *The Growth of the Biblical Tradition* is also helpful at this point. Koch gives several illustrations of this method. Two chapters are appropriate for the books dealt with here. In Ch. 12 he deals with the stories of "Saul and David in the Wilderness" (pp. 132–142). In Ch. 15 he deals with "Ahaziah's Fall" (pp. 183–194). The interested interpreter should not be put off by his use of "legend" and "saga" before he has read Koch's definitions and descriptions of what he means (Ch. 12, pp. 148–158, and Ch. 16, pp. 195–199), although one may be well advised not to carry over that terminology into the pulpit. However, the point made that these stories are told to convey a meaning, to teach something, not just to relay information, will be of inestimable help to the person who is looking for meaning in these stories which can teach and inspire the people. One is likely to discover that the same pastoral and pedagogical concerns that motivated the teller and writer millennia ago are relevant to our needs today.

Biblical illiteracy is rife in our congregations today. So the first thing the preacher must do is to tell the story. It can be read in a good translation, read with emphasis and in an interesting way, as a good storyteller would do. Or it can be retold in paraphrase. But it must be told in a way that informs the people of the facts of the story. If done well, it will send many back to the Bible to reread it for themselves.

Then the interpreter must find the essential purpose that the storyteller had in telling the story. The more the interpreter's reason for using the story coincides with the original reason for telling it, the stronger will be the effect. The sermon gains in credibility to the extent that it is obviously pressing the same claims to truth which the text is doing.

The interpreter's discovery and use of the inherent outline of the story which the original storyteller had assure even closer identity with the original. It is at this point that works like those of Westermann and Koch are useful. In identifying the genre, they make one sensitive to the inherent outline usually found in such stories. Sometimes it will appear only as a fragment, not complete. But it is an aid in seeing the skeleton that holds the telling of the story together and prevents us from imposing an alien, arbitrary outline on the classic. We should beware of thinking that we can improve on a classic story.

The essential element in interpretation then turns on sensing for oneself the relevance of the story's purpose to our own life and needs. If the story, in itself, does not speak to the interpreter, the interpreter can hardly make it speak to others.

Then the presentation of the narrative becomes, in essence, an attempt to lead the hearers along the same paths of discovery that the preacher or teacher has already found. We will tell the story. We will provide background material that makes it intelligible. We will help the congregation to enter into the lives and the experiences of the personalities in the story. We will help them to get a "you were there" feeling in which they will be led to feel some of the same reaction to the events that principals or observers felt. And we will allow them to draw the conclusion from the story which the storyteller intended them to draw.

Every one of these stories is in the Bible because it had spiritual and theological meaning. Sometimes we do not see this immediately. We should not press the point. Certainly we should not press our own meaning on a story by "spiritualizing" it or seeing it simply as a "type" of truth from another place. Let it be itself. If it does not speak to us now, put it aside for another day. Find another story that does speak.

II. HOMILETICAL EXAMPLES

To illustrate the suggested approach, let us look at the stories about Elijah and Elisha found in I Kings 17–II Kings 13. They represent independent pieces of literature that were incorporated into the great history. But they clearly were originally written (and told) with much more complex purposes in mind than the narrow thesis of the Deuteronomist. These studies will look for those theological issues as a basis for exposition and preaching.

THE PROPHET OF GOD AND THE WORD OF GOD

I Kings 17 is a literary unity and should be treated as such. It is clearly separated at the beginning from the Deuteronomist's sermon in ch. 16 and from the continuation of the story about the drought in ch. 18.

The chapter is composed of four parts which demonstrate an intricate development of a theme. All of them deal with "the man of God" and the "word of God." Part One is the basis for Parts Two, Three, and Four.

Part One (I Kings 17:1) recounts the strange and abrupt appearance of the Tishbite before King Ahab. He was probably unknown to the king or the public at this time. His clothes and manner identified him as a countryman from beyond the river. His uncouth manner and unusual style of speaking would have shocked a proper prophet. (No prophecy in the Old Testament is presented as a personal oath.)

Elijah means "Yahweh is God." The name may identify him as a member of a group intent on putting Baal worship aside, as ch. 18 will show.

Elijah's appearing is abrupt and his announcement is unequivocal: "I swear by Yahweh, my God, there will be neither dew nor rain until I say so." The message is strange and unorthodox. A real prophet does not talk like that. What is Ahab or his people to make of this man and this message? They probably thought he was just a crank. In any case he fades from their sight and attention—until the rainy season passes without rain, and especially until a second rainy season (perhaps also a third) goes by without rain.

I Kings 17:1 announces an important development for the stories that follow—the drought. But it also poses the issue which ch. 17 develops: Is Elijah credible as a prophet of God? Is his word believable as a word from God?

Part Two (I Kings 17:2–6), in contrast to v. 1, follows a conventional form of telling a story about a prophet. A word from God comes to the prophet. It contains a command: "Go to Kerith," and a promise: "You shall eat and drink there." The prophet obeys the command and the promise is fulfilled. A story in this form teaches that God does give commands and promises. The way of faith is one of obedience and dependence. The story confirms that God keeps his word. It also confirms his protecting care for his prophet and his support of the prophet's message. In the background looms the reality that the drought is taking effect.

Part Three (I Kings 17:7–16) uses a similar pattern to tell another stage of the story. The essential elements are the same: God commands and promises. Elijah obeys and witnesses the promise fulfilled. But the internal development of the story is more complicated. The widow, the obvious one to fulfill God's promise, appears to be unlikely to be able to do it. This tests Elijah's faith. He in turn puts *her* faith to the test in a similar manner with command and promise. She obeys in faith and all are rewarded. Elijah has become a mediator of God's word as well as its recipient.

Part Four (IKings 17:17–24) takes the theme one step farther. It provides an illustration of the prophet of God as one mighty in prayer. It tells of a word directed to God rather than a word from

God. Being a prophet of God includes identification with the hurts and losses for which God is sometimes blamed. It involves the prophet in the hurts of this world.

When the prophet's prayer is answered, the relieved mother blurts out her relief in words that express the achievement of credibility for both the man and his message: "Now I know that you are a man of God and that the word of the Lord in your mouth is truth." The cycle of the chapter is complete.

Homiletical treatment may deal with any one of the stories. In the first or the second the major theme is the Word of God, including demand and promise, and response, including obedience and blessing. The third story is one of answer to persistent prayer. Or the sermon may deal with the entire chapter on the theme of how God's message gains attention and credibility.

BETWEEN TWO OPINIONS

I Kings 18 is a central and climactic chapter in the Elijah story. It picks up the theme of the drought. God has made Elijah's issue (17:1) his own (18:1). The oath of 17:1 is heightened with the effect of the third year of the drought in confrontations with Obadiah (18:3–15) and with Ahab (18:16–19). Then, God keeps his promise to Elijah to send rain (18:41–46). This is a dramatic and meaningful story in itself.

But ch. 18 has, at its heart, another scene that is one of the most gripping and powerful in all Scripture. Verses 18–40 tell the story that grows out of Elijah's confrontation with Ahab but that turns into a contest with the prophets of Baal for the allegiance of Israel. The issues in the contest are complex. They include the problem of whether Yahweh, the Lord, or Baal will be considered the official god of Israel. But the immediate issue concerns the control of the weather. Can Baal bring back the rain? After all, he was considered to be a "weather God." Or can only Yahweh, the Lord of all, bring rain? These background issues are subordinated in the event by a symbol— a bolt of lightning-like fire that is to fall on the altar. The people by their silence give consent. The god who answers by fire will be considered God in Israel. The biblical story is so vivid and complete that it needs only to be told to gain effect. Baal cannot answer. Yahweh does answer. The people hail the victory: "Yahweh, the LORD, is God!" The Baal priests are slaughtered, the first of several actions against Baal worshipers that are climaxed in Jehu's infamous slaughter after the house of Ahab is assassinated (II Kings 10:18–26).

The summary, "So Jehu destroyed Baal worship in Israel," is accurate, for overt national worship of Baal never rose again, although idolatry in other forms continued to be a threat to true faith. The contest on Carmel is a classic picture of faith as an "either-or" choice.

The broader story in the chapter also has meaning. Elijah's cry of outrage against Samaria's ruler and his policies which led to his oath in 17:1 was presented as his own word. But 18:1 shows that the Lord has assumed full responsibility for it and directed the final scenes of the drama. God's word to Elijah again contains a command and a promise. It calls for the prophet to confront Ahab personally. This identifies Ahab and his apostasy to Baal as the source of Israel's troubles (18:18) and regards Yahweh as the indispensable sustainer of life in Israel. Israel's recognition of the Lord as God opened the way for the return of rain.

I Kings 17 showed Elijah's growth in spiritual stature. Chapter 18 demonstrated his heroic dimension in challenging the king and the royal cult of Baal. Chapter 19 will show how human and vunerable he was and how God revealed himself to him in that situation.

WHAT ARE YOU DOING HERE?

I Kings 19 continues the series that deals with the drought. Jezebel hears of the events on Carmel and reacts with a terrible vow to take Elijah's "life." This word, "life," becomes the thread that ties vs. 1–12 together. The intrepid and fearless champion of ch. 18 now panics before the threats of the queen. He runs "for his life." He prays for the Lord to take away "his life." He complains to the Lord on Horeb that his "life" is being threatened. The great man is human after all. Jezebel's bluster hurls him into what Bunyan called "the slough of despond." He runs through Judah deep into the desert. Then, mercifully, his flight takes him to "the mount of God." The tender and understanding words of the angel stand in interesting counterpoint to the Lord's interrogation: "What are you doing here, Elijah?" Elijah is "absent without leave" from his post of duty. His whining complaint opens the way to the magnificent theophany (revelation of God) in which God's presence is not found in the wind, the earthquake, or the fire—but in the stillness of silence. A repetition of the complaint is answered by orders to perform a series of tasks that will bring new kings to the thrones in Damascus and Samaria, and provide for Elijah's successor. God was alive, present, and very much at work in Israel. Elijah's despair was unwarranted.

This chapter, like the preceding one, is very complex. Homiletical treatment may choose to emphasize any one of several layers of meaning in the story. It may stress the story of the prophet's humiliating flight which was finally met by a reassuring vision of God's presence, even the silence (vs. 1–12). Many sermons have been preached on v. 12 alone, stressing the revelation of the nature of God and the assurance of God's presence, even without the spectacular signs that sometimes identify him. A third treatment may concentrate on the great plan of God which is revealed in vs. 15–18 and the assurance that God's work moves on despite the threats of opponents, the discouragement of his leaders, or even the necessity of replacing a great leader like Elijah. (It is pertinent to note that Elijah did not personally fulfill two of the points in this plan. Elisha was appointed. He participated in the other two projects.) No one is indispensable to God's work. Elijah's despair tended to identify his own vulnerability as God's own vunerability. This was a mistake.

HAVE YOU MURDERED AND POSSESSED?

The next chapter of Elijah's story is found in I Kings 21. The first sixteen verses tell a story of conspiracy in high places that led to an act of blatant injustice and violence. This part of the story involves neither God nor Elijah. It is told on a flat historical level, as a newspaper would write the event.

With v. 17, God becomes involved by sending Elijah to confront Ahab. This is a classic narrative of judgment spoken against an individual by a prophet (cf. Westermann, *Basic Forms of Prophetic Speech*, pp. 130–136). As in all such stories, a wrong has been committed that is not (or cannot be) brought to judgment in the ordinary way through the courts. The speech of judgment contains an accusation and an announcement. Here the accusation comes in a question. The brief statement of judgment announces a catastrophic future for Ahab. Note that a messenger is sent (the prophet) to announce judgment—not to enforce it. The sentence is carried out at a later time.

Ahab has broken the divine law in two ways. He has committed murder and theft. No normal court would accuse the king. But he stands accused by God, nonetheless. The appearance of God's messenger with the word of judgment witnesses to God's involvement and to God's judgment. But the messenger is not one to execute God's justice, only to announce it and witness to it.

Homiletical treatment may deal with the issue of God's relation to blatant, unpunished injustice. He neither condones nor allows injustice. It may also be relevant in defining the role of the one who speaks for God in dealing with such a crime.

IF I AM A MAN OF GOD

II Kings 1 contains the next story about Elijah. He is commissioned to confront the king who has broken the First Commandment ("You shall have no other gods beside me") by sending to Baal-zebub of Ekron for an oracular word about his health. As in I Kings 21, the accusation is couched in a question. The sentence is an announcement of death from his illness (II Kings 1:3–4). Elijah stops the messengers and sends them back to the king with the question and announcement.

But then the story turns into a test of status and authority.

The king asserts his authority by sending a contingent of troops with orders to bring Elijah to him. Elijah refuses the order on the grounds that he represents a higher authority ("If I am a man of God"). Two companies of soldiers are consumed by fire before the military, if not the king, are convinced. The third captain "begged" rather than "ordered." The point has been made, so Elijah is allowed to accompany them and deliver his message in person. The story ends with the laconic observation: "So he died, according to the word of the Lord that Elijah had spoken."

Homiletical treatment may deal with ways in which we insult God. Respect for God is the foundation for worship and for faith. Ahaziah lacked this elementary respect for the Lord and showed it in sending to Baal-zebub. He and his captains lacked basic respect for the Lord and his representative by attempting to arrest Elijah and by ordering him to appear. Elijah deserved no such respect in his own right. But as the messenger of God, he represented God's authority. God supported him in his demand for such respect.

THE CHARIOTS AND HORSEMEN OF ISRAEL

The last story in the cycle appears in II Kings 2. It joins the account in I Kings 19:19–21 about the call of Elisha. It relates the passing of the prophetic mantle from Elijah to Elisha. It tells of Elijah's being taken up to heaven in a whirlwind (II Kings 2:1) with a chariot and horses of fire (2:11). The story is full of symbolism. A glimpse of the extent of the prophetic movement in that time is gained from the groups of prophets who are met in the towns visited. Elijah works alone. Elisha is gregarious. This is shown in the story. Their trip together stops in Gilgal, Bethel, and Jericho before crossing the River Jordan to the desert. The towns were significant for their role in Israel's entry into Canaan and continued to be important sanctuaries for Israel's worship. The miraculous crossing of the Jordan under

Joshua was especially meaningful to Israel as the fulfillment of God's promise to Abraham to give to Israel the Land of Canaan. Elijah's role in representing Yahweh, the Lord who had covenanted with the twelve tribes for the Land of Canaan, had already been emphasized in the Carmel story. This is the role that Elisha is now called to fill.

The core of the story (2:7–18) recounts a miraculous crossing of the Jordan, the mysterious disappearance of Elijah into heaven in a whirlwind and a fiery chariot, and the miraculous recrossing of the Jordan which demonstrated that Elijah's powers had now fallen upon Elisha. The immediate intent of the story is to introduce the new prophet, as the retracing of their journey from Jericho to Bethel and on to Carmel and Samaria shows. But the story of Elijah's apparent translation without death made a profound impression on readers of Scripture as traditions about Elijah show. He joins Enoch as a mortal who did not die.

Elijah is the epitome of what a prophet was supposed to be. He is correctly identified as the figure who best represented the ideal of the prophetic movement. The stories in this cycle illustrate the functions of such a prophet of God. As such, they have much to tell us about ministry, especially prophetic ministry, even today.

Elisha's biography is different. It has more small stories. It is clearly dependent on Elijah's story and is concerned to duplicate it in several ways.

The Prophet's Call

I Kings 19:19–21 tells how Elijah, fulfilling God's promise to provide a successor (v. 16), put the mantle of prophetic succession on this farmer's son. The account is brief. Despite Elijah's apparent denial, Elisha understood the gesture and acted upon it.

Elisha owes his calling first to the Lord's long-range plan (v. 16) and to Elijah's search (v. 19). His background is different from Elijah's, though we know nothing of his previous religious experience. His request to bid his parents farewell has parallels in the New Testament (Matt. 8:21–22; Luke 9:59–60). Elijah seems to brush him off, but he persists, preparing for an inaugural sacrifice.

The Prophet's Apprenticeship

The sequel to the call comes in II Kings 2:1–18. Elisha follows his master closely on a farewell tour of cities where groups of prophets live. Rumor has it that Elijah will not be there much longer. Elisha sticks closely to him through the miraculous crossing of the river, only to be separated from him by a chariot of fire and horses. Elijah disappears in a whirlwind. Only his mantle remains. Elisha picks it up and begins to retrace the journey to the prophetic cities to demonstrate that he is the heir apparent to Elijah.

Significant moments are the request for the "double portion" of Elijah's spirit, that is, the heir's part of the inheritance (vs. 9–10); and the recognition of Elijah's significance: "The chariots of Israel and its horsemen" (v. 12). Elisha will earn the same accolade later from King Joash (13:14).

The stories about Elisha appear to parallel consciously those about Elijah. Three stories (II Kings 3:1–4:37) are parallel to I Kings 17:1–18:45. II Kings 2:23–25 is very similar in purpose to II Kings 1.

Other stories trace the ways in which Elisha fulfills God's promises to Elijah. II Kings 8:7–15 recites the fulfillment of I Kings 19:15. II Kings 9:1–13 recounts the fulfillment in Elisha of I Kings 19:16a. II Kings 9:14–10:35 tells of the fulfillment of the judgment on Ahab spoken in I Kings 21:20–26 by Elijah (see II Kings 9:36). And the story of the corpse that touches Elisha's bones (II Kings 13:14–21) seems a parallel to the miracle of Elijah's transportation in II Kings 2.

Apart from these there are several minor stories and three major stories that are independent and powerful.

If Only!—The Maid's Witness

The first major story is the unforgettable narrative in II Kings 5. It answers the question, How can a heathen come to know the Lord, God of Israel? The little maid's testimony in v. 3 speaks of the prophet and healing. The prophet's invitation in v. 8 promises knowledge "that there is a prophet in Israel." But Naaman's testimony goes beyond either to confess in v. 15: "Now I know that there is no God except in Israel." The prophet's instructions to Naaman follow the usual challenge to faith and obedience couched in a command and promise (v. 10).

The second and third stories tell of Elisha's role in the Syro-Israelite wars.

Those with Us Are More

The second story, in II Kings 6:8–23, tells of Elisha's advice to the king of Israel which allowed him to evade the raids into his land by the Syrians. This led the Syrian king to try to capture Elisha with a large force of horsemen and chariots. They approached by night.

The story turns upon "seeing" and "blindness." Elisha's servant has to have his eyes opened to God's protecting forces (vs. 15–17). Then Elisha prays that blindness fall on the Syrian army, which is then led unknowingly into the very heart of Samaria (vs. 18–20). Then Elisha intervenes with Israel's king to spare their lives, feed them, and send them home (v. 23). The result of this successful peacemaking effort not only avoids battle but wins a respite from Syrian raids on Israelite territory. The prophet achieves more in this way than any direct victory over them could do.

THIS IS A DAY OF GOOD NEWS

The third story is found in II Kings 6:24–7:20. War has resumed and Syria has laid siege to Samaria. The king is desperate. He blames Elishah, perhaps because he has advised that the Syrian army be sent home unharmed (6:31). He knows that advice has come from God, but his desperation leads him to feel that God himself is responsible for his present plight. So he cannot be trusted to rescue them (6:33).

The prophet's response is to announce that the siege will be lifted overnight (7:1).

Four starving lepers decide they have nothing to lose, so they go over to the Syrian camp (7:3). They find it empty. The army has panicked when a fantasy of sounds from an approaching army was reported. They loot and eat their fill. But their consciences prompt them not to keep this to themselves: "This is a day of good news and we are keeping it to ourselves" (7:9).

The prophet's prediction is fulfilled, while the skeptical officer dies in the press of hungry people to get through the gate to the waiting food.

Elijah's vision (I Kings 19:15–17) and Elisha's participation in its fulfillment presage the prophetic teaching about God's rule over history, his judgment of nations, and the ways by which pagans may come to worship him.

5. PREACHING FROM THE WISDOM LITERATURE

RONALD E. CLEMENTS

I. HERMENEUTICAL BACKGROUND

Preachers who begin their exposition of the Bible from the New Testament quickly discover that at a number of points they are faced with references to a feature of life called "Wisdom." So Matthew's Gospel can present us with a saying that is almost proverbial in its breadth: "Yet wisdom is justified by her deeds" (Matt. 11:19). Sometimes this reality called wisdom is looked upon rather negatively as a human attainment (cf. I Cor. 2:1–5), whereas at other times it is presented as the highest intellectual gift (cf. Col. 2:2–3). The roots of this concern with wisdom are to be found in the Old Testament, and through this they can be traced even farther back in the ancient Near East. Overall, therefore, the pursuit of wisdom can be seen to be one of the oldest, greatest, and most passionately prized quests of mankind. Who, after all, would not wish to be wise if wisdom can bring success, happiness, and mastery of life with all the demands that life makes upon us (cf. Gen. 3:5)?

So far as the Old Testament is concerned, there are three books that can be clearly classed as books of wisdom, since they were quite evidently written out of a desire to collect the sayings of wise men and to explore the mysteries and possibilities of thought, aided by the skills, methods, and insights of their wisdom. These are the books of Proverbs, Job, and Ecclesiastes. In the Apocrypha of the Old Testament, however, there are two further very rich and extensive books of wisdom: Ecclesiasticus and the Wisdom of Solomon, which are among the richest gems that the Apocrypha offers to the inquiring Bible student. Besides these books we can recognize that the type of thinking and learning developed in Israel's circles of wise men has influenced other parts of the Bible, not least in the Prophets and in the writing and reporting of history. By New Testament times it is abundantly clear that, by using the manner and techniques of the wisdom teachers, devout Jewish scribes, in presenting their faith and spiritual heritage to the Gentile readers, had found a way that could be readily grasped for its practical worth. The teaching of wisdom, therefore, became an important means of commending the riches of Jewish faith to Gentiles, and there is every reason to see why Paul has been profoundly influenced by this in the formulation of his thinking and in his letter writing.

Wisdom, as it is found in the Old Testament, is not a very firmly defined and easily isolated entity. In a formal sense it refers to a literature, and it is not difficult to see that the books of Proverbs, Job, and Ecclesiastes have a number of features in common. They are concerned to teach others, both in a practical sense of imparting sound doctrine that has been gleaned from the observation of life and in encouraging reflection and a more speculative concern with the meaning of life and the explanation of its many complexities and mysteries. For such, it made use of distinctive teaching aids, such as the form of proverbs and parables. It constantly resorted also to certain basic distinctions, as for instance the difference between the wise man and the fool.

The Wisdom Writings, however, are simply the biblical deposit of a way of thinking that must have been quite widely pursued and highly valued in Old Testament times. This was designed to be practical and useful, so that those who were willing to listen to, and follow, the teachings of the wise could expect to be successful and highly respected figures in society. In general, however, it is important to recognize that wisdom did not pretend to set forth a rounded and complete system of teaching, but rather to apply certain principles and fundamental insights, by means of which the wise could determine for themselves their own course of action. In one direction this could lead to a rather skeptical, and almost cynical, attitude toward the world and man's destiny within it. At other times it could lead to a frank facing up to some of the most profound questions concerning the nature of God and his providential regard for mankind. So we have among the wisdom books such very different products as the book of Ecclesiastes on the one side, with its pessimism and resignation, and The Book of Job on the other, with its searching questions regarding the experience of suffering and God's control over human destiny. A strongly doubting and irreligious stream of thought could find a place in wisdom alongside a more profoundly committed sense that the more we learn to think honestly and responsibly, the more are we driven to contemplate the frontiers of eternity and the majesty of the wisdom in which God has fashioned the world.

At many points we can discover valuable signs of contact between Israel's developing traditions of wisdom and those of surrounding peoples. Most strikingly has this come to light in a remarkable series of similarities and connections between chs. 22 and 23 of the book of Proverbs and a significant Egyptian text called the Teaching of Amenemope. This latter composition is of uncertain date, although most probably it should be assigned to approximately 900 B.C. The precise details which a comparison of the two texts brings to light should surprise us less, however, than the realization that, in its formative stages, there must have been a considerable range of borrowing and mutual interaction between Israel's traditions of wisdom and those of the surrounding peoples. The fact that the Old Testament points us to various non-Israelite, possibly Arabian, collectors of wisdom sayings further bears this out (cf. Prov. 25:1; 30:1; 31:1).

That the writings which offer the reader wisdom represent a special category is borne out by the way in which Solomon appears as its special author and patron (Prov. 1:1; 25:1; cf. Eccl. 1:1). Even a very late Jewish writing, such as the Wisdom of Solomon, which shows a number of interesting influences from Greek ideas and ways of thinking, maintains this tradition of a link with Solomon himself. Just as Israel's law belonged to the tradition of Moses, and the psalms belonged to the tradition of David, so did wisdom have its special patron and founder figure in the person of Solomon. This is in some ways rather unexpected, since Solomon is not the most attractive of the Old Testament kings, and in a number of respects the way he exploited the kingdom established by his father proved ultimately ruinous, as I King 12 shows. Even the Old Testament writers expressed strong disapproval of many of Solomon's actions (I Kings 3:3; 11:1–13). Why, then, has he come to be so intimately associated with the growth and development of Israel's wisdom? One tradition points back to Solomon's own personal fondness for the form and intellectual stimulus provided by wisdom (I Kings 4:29–34) and it is by no means impossible that a genuine feature of Solomon's character has given rise to this.

More probably, however, a wider cultural feature of Solomon's reign has contributed to this picture of the king as the patron-author of wisdom. This lay in Solomon's marriage alliance with an Egyptian princess, which reflects a period of close political, social, and cultural contacts between Israel and Egypt. With the high regard for the pursuit of a type of wisdom instruction in Egypt, it is highly probable that this brought into Israel writings of the kind that we now know from the Teaching of Amenemope. It would also have brought to Jerusalem men who were competent in the Egyptian language and who could thereby have produced their own adaptations and translations of wisdom from that and other countries.

There is, too, a further point regarding Solomon's reign which has a bearing upon the development of wisdom in Israel. This king set up the basic administrative organization for the control of his kingdom, the collection of taxes, and the exchange of property. Besides this, his own extensive building developments in Jerusalem led to the setting up of a large palace administration. All of this would have called for trained scribes, secretaries, and district officials for whom the skills of wisdom were especially appropriate. The Egyptian Amenemope himself was an important regional governor, and we find in the Old Testament book of Proverbs a distinctly "middle-class" ethos. The consequences of this are full of interest, even amounting to advice, rather sardonically given, to a diplomat, or nobleman, invited to a royal banquet (Prov. 23:1–3). This "middle-class" atmosphere which pervades many of the sayings of the wise men gives to them a very pertinent and sometimes amusing modern ring. So we learn more about the acquisition and use of wealth in the book of Proverbs than anywhere else in the Bible. Much of it is sound common sense, as for instance the advice not to act as surety for a stranger (Prov. 11:15), and there is a noticeable delight in the strange paradoxes to which money and wealth can give rise (Prov. 11:24; 13:7). Alongside any personal reputation that Solomon may have enjoyed for his wise sayings (cf. I Kings 10:1–10), therefore, we can see that both his links with Egypt and his extensive administrative developments must have contributed greatly to his association with wisdom.

Yet the roots of wisdom lie farther back even than the time of Solomon, since even ancient Sumeria had a type of wisdom instruction. In fact, it is reasonable to accept that the very elements of wisdom teaching are to be found in all human societies. The need for practical advice begins in childhood, in the home itself, with the need to know the difference between safe and harmful actions, healthy and unhealthy behavior, and the need to listen attentively to sound advice (cf. Prov. 13:1). At first, wisdom was essentially practical and clearly defined. Only later did it give rise to more imaginative and speculative features. So even the military commander-in-chief, Joab, could make use of the special skill of the wise woman from the little Judean village of Tekoa (II Sam. 14:1–20).

The story of the wise woman from Tekoa, with her pretense at mourning and her accompanying tale designed to persuade an unwilling King David to allow Absalom back to Jerusalem, introduces us to the two most prominent features of wisdom teaching. Already we have seen that a primary purpose was to say something useful and practical, based on sound experience. Alongside this, however, and frequently interwoven into such an aim was a fondness for saying something clever and for expressing this in a very apt and unforgettable way. So all kinds of artistic devices came to be employed: the proverb, the parable, the riddle, the fable, and various types of subject or word association. Hence it is in wisdom that we encounter the most elaborate forms of rhetoric, with a fascinating use of irony, paronomasia (puns), and hyperbole (exaggeration), which can even now raise a wry smile on the part of the reader. So, "The lazy man says, 'There is a lion outside! I shall be killed in the streets!' " (Prov. 22:13). Or, "Like a madman who throws firebrands, arrows, and death, is the man who deceives his neighbor and says, 'I am only joking!' " (Prov. 26:18–19).

It is not difficult to see why these two sides of wisdom, the practical and the artistic, belong together. The shrewd teacher was very conscious that many of the more fundamental of his admonitions, against laziness, rowdiness, and loose living, will encounter a good deal of resistance on the part of his pupils. Hence he saw the need to use his rhetorical skills so as to slip through the defenses of those he was most concerned to instruct. Even today the artistic skill of the writer succeeds in teasing the ingenuity of the reader to discover to what precisely he is referring under his imagery.

In another direction also we can see that considerations of good taste influenced the way in which teachers of wisdom went about their task. Any concern with right behavior in society must inevitably deal with matters of sexual conduct and with the preservation of family life and unity. Yet instruction in such concerns can easily be counterproductive in arousing a rather crude preoccupation with the opposite sex, and even titillating the imagination in an unhealthy way. Thus we find in the book of Proverbs that exhortations to marital fidelity are set out with a notable delicacy and care (Prov. 5:15–23; 6:20–35; 7:1–27). From the meaningful imagery of "Drink water from your own cistern" (Prov. 5:15) a telling range of metaphors is used to get the main point across with a memorable emphasis. Perhaps even more striking, when it came to warning against the temptations of the flesh, the wise man could describe the home of the loose woman as "the way to Sheol, . . . the chambers of death" (Prov. 7:27). Even more graphically the wisdom teacher knew the value of concentrating upon positive themes rather than resorting to an intimidating string of negative admonitions. So, in contrast to the dangers and misfortunes that come to those who pursued women of no moral virtue were set the inestimable gifts of happiness that came to those who eagerly pursued wisdom (Prov. 8:1–36).

This image of wisdom as a woman of exquisite beauty and attractiveness has occasioned a great deal of scholarly discussion in the attempt to trace its origin. Both Egyptian and Babylonian religious mythology have been explored in order to find a comparable figure of one who is a veritable goddess of wisdom. So too, in its subsequent development, the idea of wisdom as a personalized intermediary between God and his creation became immensely important in Jewish thinking. Yet, however we trace back the varied influences that have contributed to the biblical imagery, we can see the central importance of the techniques and artistic forms devised by the teachers of wisdom. Once the possibilities have been opened up for the use of complex metaphors and imagery in order to convey the truths of wisdom instruction, then it is not at all difficult to see how such a very imaginative and speculative portrayal of the role of wisdom in creation, such as we find in Proverbs 8, could arise.

The combination of the practical and useful with the artistic and imaginative, which represent two aspects, or directions, in which the instructions of the wisdom teachers moved, provided a surprising range of didactic interests. We have already noted the strength of the admonitions against laziness and rowdiness, which make good sense in any human society. So we read:

> The lazy man does not plow in the autumn;
> he will seek at harvest and have nothing.
> (Prov. 20:4;
> RSV's "sluggard" is archaic)

and:

> He who loves pleasure will be a poor man;
> he who loves wine and oil will not be rich.
> (Prov. 21:17)

In fact, the warnings against overeating, and even more emphatically, drinking too much, serve further to give to the advice of the wisdom teachers a very modern ring. The fact that those who were most in need of such warnings were frequently those who were least willing to pay attention to them has led the teachers to inject a delicious touch of humor and exaggeration to make sure that the point goes home and is well remembered. So the warnings against too great a fondness for wine, set out in Prov. 23:29–35, achieve their effect by wit rather than a paternalistic authoritarianism.

These pragmatic aspects of wisdom give it a note of realism and make it an interesting guide to our understanding of the way in which the people of biblical times learned to cope with their world and its temptations. At the same time, this very note of realism occasioned a certain caution, and urged a measure of respect not only for authority in society but for the ultimate authority of God (cf. Prov. 24:21). In large measure the teachers of wisdom were full of confidence in what they were doing, and display a remarkable assurance that those who listen to them can achieve success in life (cf. Prov. 24:3–4). So we read of the legitimate self-interest to which the teachers of wisdom can appeal:

> He who gets wisdom loves himself;
>   he who keeps understanding will prosper.
>   (Prov. 19:8)

Yet there were evident limits to this, and life was not so smoothly and conveniently ordered as to ensure that everyone received what he deserved. There was need for patience, because God's way was not one that always brought swift retribution, nor necessarily quick returns to the obedient pupil:

> Wealth hastily gotten will dwindle,
>   but he who gathers little by little
>   will increase it.
>   (Prov. 13:11)

It is as a consequence of this awareness of the need for patience, and the realization that all things in life are subject to the overarching purposes of God, that we find some of the most significant teachings of the wise. For all men the ultimate frontiers of knowledge, success, and happiness appear to lie beyond man's own power to control:

> Many are the plans in the mind of man,
>   but it is the purpose of the LORD that will be established.
>   (Prov. 19:21)

Here the limitations imposed upon man by his inadequate knowledge are seen to demand a proper humility toward God. That this affects deeply the personal aspects of life is shown by the recognition that a happy marriage is a divine gift rather than the result of careful human planning and decisions:

> House and wealth are inherited from fathers,
> but a prudent wife is from the LORD.
>
> (Prov. 19:14)

Such an openness to the mysterious and incalculable aspects of life, the suddenness with which misfortune may strike, and the awareness that even the most carefully considered of human plans may prove ultimately to be mistaken and ruinous, give to the teachers of wisdom a marked note of humility:

> The fear of the LORD is instruction in wisdom,
> and humility goes before honor.
>
> (Prov. 15:33)

In this way the apparently self-interested and pragmatic aspects of instruction in wisdom gave way before a wider, and more truly religious, spirit of trust. It is this that has led to the profoundly religious emphasis upon reverence for God as the fountainhead from which all true wisdom springs:

> The fear of the LORD is the beginning of wisdom,
> and the knowledge of the Holy One is insight.
>
> (Prov. 9:10)

In many respects, although this submission to the divinely appointed limits of human learning has a place in the earliest wisdom, it was only in its later developments that it came to play a prominent role. Once again, however, it further illustrates the many-sided nature of biblical wisdom. It represented an attitude to life, combined with a number of tried and venerated ways of acquiring knowledge, rather than any rounded set of teachings. In consequence it could readily accommodate ideas and admonitions that were paradoxical in their nature, and certainly it felt no necessity for removing all contradictions. The very fact that its school was provided by life itself meant that it was willing to question and test all things.

This willingness to examine everything, even the deeply held convictions and prejudices of men, pervades the instructions of the wise:

> There is a way which seems right to a man,
> but its end is the way to death.
>
> (Prov. 16:25)

Contrary to its popular evangelical application, this saying is not a condemnation of human wisdom as such, but rather a condemnation of prejudice and a belief that it takes more than a single mind to find out the whole truth. So:

> He who states his case first seems right,
> until the other comes and examines him.
> (Prov. 18:17)

Hence it comes about that it is better to rely on the shared wisdom of many than to hasten into reckless action:

> Without counsel plans go wrong,
> but with many advisers they succeed.
> (Prov. 15:22)

So far we have looked almost exclusively at the teaching of wisdom as it is preserved for us in the book of Proverbs. The primary reason is that it has become an increasingly held conviction among scholars that the earliest forms and teaching of the wise men of ancient Israel are to be found here. The proverb itself was, according to its Hebrew title, a "likeness" (Heb. *mashal*), indicating that the basic feature of this kind of instruction was the establishing of some striking connection, or comparison, in different orders of life (Prov. 25:14, 28).

Yet it would be wrong to suppose that the main interest and importance of ancient wisdom lay in its poetry and literary artistry. Its genuine concern to know the secrets of life, and to explore the frontiers of human experience and understanding, gave to it a powerful note of drama and seriousness. Sometimes a basic conviction has exerted such a profound influence upon a teacher of wisdom that he has developed a most daring and wide-ranging poetic reflection in order to impress its importance upon others. This is evidently the case in Job 28, where there is an extensive reflection upon the theme "Where shall wisdom be found?" (Job 28:12). The final answer that is arrived at (vs. 23–28) is very simple, but it does not lack profundity for all this: "Behold, the fear of the LORD, that is wisdom" (v. 28).

We may, in fact, regard The Book of Job as a very searching reflection upon the question of human suffering. To some, it appears not to have any true answer to its problem of why entirely innocent and noble people should suffer. Yet it affirms (chs. 38–39) the infinite grandeur and beneficent wonder of the universe, and thereby strongly hints that experiences which appear terrifying and mysterious to men do not lie beyond the range of the divine providence. God's wisdom reaches far beyond the little that man can know.

We have already pointed to a similar extended reflection, remarkable for its poetic quality, in Eccl. 12:1–8. A rather similar reflection upon the many-sided face that life presents to us all, and upon the multiplicity of experiences that go to make up human existence is to be found in Eccl. 3:1–9, with its theme "For everything there is a season" (v. 1). Later, in the apocryphal book the Wisdom of Solomon, there is a profoundly moving reflection on the hope of life after death, which is certainly among the most impressive and forthright treatments of the subject to be found anywhere in the Bible (Wisd. of Sol. 3:1–9).

There are evident dangers which the preacher who turns to the Wisdom Literature of the Bible will encounter. It presupposes a willingness to reflect upon and to look into the deeper implications of experience than can be found in any straightforward set of theological answers. Even the very pessimism which it could arouse (cf. Eccl. 8:16–17) is, however, not entirely without a touch of reverent awe and wonder before the seeming infinity of the varied manifestations of trust which we all encounter. Ultimately everything leads us out to mystery, so that the Christian could later find that only Jesus Christ had finally drawn aside the veil of this mystery for us (cf. I Cor. 1:24).

II. HOMILETICAL EXAMPLES

Individual verses appear seldom to be related to their contexts by subject, so that it is generally better to use the single verse, upon which the sermon is to be based, and to find a narrative passage from elsewhere which illustrates the main point. Even The Book of Job, which has a narrative story framework, requires to be understood as a whole if any of the individual speeches, or sayings, of which it is made up are to be properly understood. Most worshiping congregations expect the reading of sacred Scripture and its subsequent exposition to take the form of narrative stories, preferably of an edifying kind, or to focus upon some biblical command or advice. The Old Testament history books, together with the Gospels and the Pauline epistles, are so central to the Bible as to provide most worshipers with a guideline as to what to expect to hear from it as a whole. They are reasonably "tuned in" to this style of writing. The wisdom books are very different in their character, with their obvious call for reflection and the kind of "What do you make of this?" response which they are

looking for. Many of the "proverbs of paradox" are clearly intended
to be heard in this way:

> One man gives freely, yet grows all the richer;
> another withholds what he should give,
> and only suffers want.
>
> (Prov. 11:24)

At first this kind of comment appears not to be saying anything at
all, yet when thought about carefully, it is by no means inappropriate
as a reflection upon the whole commitment to giving in Christian
service.

This introductory note about the character of the biblical wisdom
writings points to the need for planning some form of broad
explanation to the congregation about wisdom in general. This is
obviously all the more necessary if a reading from the Old Testament
Apocrypha is to be used, since many will undoubtedly feel that this
does not properly belong in the Bible at all. Yet, if properly and
sensitively handled, as we shall suggest further, it is no bad thing to
have a few uplifting surprises in store for those who listen to sermons.

EXAMPLE 1

We may begin by suggesting a very basic text from which a useful
introduction to the character of biblical wisdom and its presuppositions can be gleaned:

> The fear of the LORD is the beginning of wisdom,
> and the knowledge of the Holy One is insight.
>
> (Prov. 9:10)

Here is a case for hastening slowly, since to rush toward such a
conclusion does no justice to the long experience which lies behind
such a saying and pays no attention to the proper context of wisdom
instruction in which it has arisen. This, after all, was still in the Old
Testament, so that the author was certainly not thinking, in a Pauline
fashion, of Christian conversion as the basic road to the fear of the
LORD! More practically also, it is clear that an overstressing of this
aspect can lead to a very damaging and misguided anti-intellectualism, urging a simple Christian faith as the antidote to the world's
search for more and more knowledge. Are all our great libraries, with
their millions of books, really unnecessary, so long as we keep the
Bible? This is an obvious extreme position, but it highlights the
dilemmas facing Christian parents, contemplating the cost of sending
their children to college, and quite genuinely anxious that, in gaining

a wider experience of life and in being exposed to many new, and alien, views, they should not abandon their Christian commitment.

Yet here is an opportunity to say something about the role of wisdom in biblical times, with its honest search for truth and its concern for success and happiness. Perhaps too often Christians appear to have closed minds on these issues, so that there is much to be gained by introducing some awareness of biblical interest in the wisdom of Egypt and Solomon's quest for a knowledge of "beasts, birds and reptiles" (I Kings 4:33). More widely there is a real need to combat a rather superficial anti-intellectualism which all too easily slips into Christian faith, leading to a misguided complacency.

Yet it can lead us on to notice many of the limitations of knowledge and wisdom which the biblical teachers had encountered in their experience. Proverbs 19:21 is an obvious pointer here, but so also, in its own way, is the whole history of Solomon's reign. I Kings 3:3 highlights the ambiguity attached to this king's reputation for wisdom. On the one hand there was a wealth, bordering on extravagance, together with all the openness to human culture and art, which previously had had little place in Israel. Can this not quite fairly be presented as an indication of Solomon's confidence in the sufficiency of human learning and wisdom? There are many ways in which this can be illustrated, either from the history of Solomon's kingdom, with its subsequent breakup after his death, or from the teachings of the wise. The fact that a simple doctrine of retribution may serve as a useful guide (cf. Prov. 26:27), but cannot be taken as a universal truth, is relevant here. So also are the evident experiences of illness and suffering. We do not have an answer for everything. Even in the world of the physical sciences it is clear that new discoveries and new knowledge almost invariably raise as many new questions as they answer.

This may bring us back to our main text, with its assertion, "The fear of the Lord is the beginning of wisdom." In so many ways our understanding of who God is and what he requires of us begins with our awareness of mystery and our sense of not knowing all we should wish. God, in his infinite love, has taken pity on our ignorance by giving a full disclosure of himself in Jesus Christ. This Wisdom of God has become personal, knowable, and accessible through his Son. Far from this rendering all other human learning needless and futile, it has had the opposite effect. Only a commitment to Jesus Christ can provide the sure goal and sound principles in which other truths have their place.

EXAMPLE 2

We might take as a second example another very popular theme
from the teaching of the wise men in the book of Proverbs: "All the
ways of a man are pure in his own eyes, but the LORD weighs the
spirit" (Prov. 16:2). It might not be inappropriate to link this with
another saying in the same chapter of the book of Proverbs (16:25)
concerning the way which seems to be right, but in the end proves to
be ruinous. The theme of such a sermon should probably be that of
"The Blind Spot," and it might be useful to introduce such an idea by
citing another saying from Proverbs:

> Like the glaze covering an earthen vessel
> are smooth lips with an evil heart.
> (Prov. 26:23)

Just as not everything is as beautiful as it may at first appear to be,
so not everyone is as inwardly attractive a person as a brief encounter
may suggest. This is a popular theme with the wise men, but it is not
the real aim of our text, which is rather that we may even be deceiving
ourselves. We do not look into our own hearts with sufficient
seriousness, nor with the degree of necessary impartiality, to see the
kind of person that we really are. Perhaps sometimes we surprise
ourselves with a sudden fit of anger, or an outburst of emotion, which
catches us totally off balance.

Obviously psychiatrists know all about such experiences, and the
very fact that we might find ourselves in need of their assistance arises
precisely from the fact that we each possess a hidden "self" deep
inside our being. Only God sees into our inner spirit, and knows the
kind of person we really are.

The special interest of this text in Prov. 16:2 lies in its great stress
upon the fact of self-justification: "All the ways of a man are pure in
his own eyes." We feel we know why we acted badly on a particular
occasion; we can resort to an almost limitless range of excuses to cover
up for ourselves. Anyone who has tried to counsel those involved in a
marriage breakdown will recognize how futile and unhelpful are the
attempts to apportion blame (which the letter of the law may often
want to do). We simply do not see ourselves as others see us.

The third point of our sermon can then turn to consider the
antidote to this condition of the "blind spot": The LORD weighs the
spirit." There is One who sees us as we really are, and who judges with
a complete and total impartiality. So far as the wisdom teachers of Old
Testament times were concerned this was an encouragement to seek
the counsel and guidance of older and more experienced persons.

Yet more than this, even beyond the limits of what men knew to be wise and right, they never lost their faith in the absolute righteousness of God. No doubt this fact in itself has some salutary lessons for those who may feel "let down" by Christians who behave badly. Failure in Christian behavior does not imply that God's standards have in any way been lowered. Yet in the end is not the imperative message of such a text as this a basis for an appeal to the justification which God offers in Christ? Over against all the half-truths of our human self-assessments there stands the saving gift of God in Jesus Christ!

EXAMPLE 3

Job 1:8: "Have you considered my servant Job . . . ?" At first consideration The Book of Job might appear to be a welcome gift to a preacher looking for something that is a bit different but that has an obvious practical bearing. Its message concerning human suffering, with its firm insistence that wholly innocent people may suffer and that this in no sense implies a divine punishment upon them, is very relevant to a recurrent human need. Yet it has problems. It is a relatively long book, yet one must really read and grasp the whole if the individual speeches are to be appreciated. In fact, a dramatic "reading" of The Book of Job can be a very effective way of presenting the story, with individual readers presenting the speeches of Job's friends.

It is important therefore that the preacher think about The Book of Job as a whole rather than make a hurried start on one memorable verse, such as Job 19:25. Most listeners will almost certainly think of the meaning attached to this verse in G. F. Handel's *The Messiah* rather than in its proper biblical setting. If possible, the preacher should aim to read through a modern discussion of the question of human suffering and its significance, such as John Hick's *Evil and the God of Love*, in order to be fully aware of the main issues. Then it would seem entirely practicable to plan a series of four sermons on The Book of Job, which would deal with the main themes found there. It could be handled by a variety of techniques, possibly using each of Job's three friends as a spokesman for one way of looking at the problem. In his study "The Cross of Job" (in *The Cross in the Old Testament*), H. Wheeler Robinson follows such a path, focusing upon Eliphaz the Mystic, Bildad the Traditionalist, and Zophar the Dogmatist. The final sermon could then deal with God's answer to Job (in chs. 38–41), with its theme set out in Job 38:2.

Another and perhaps a more straightforward way of treating The Book of Job from a preaching point of view would be to break it up

rather differently. The first sermon could well be entirely taken up
with the story itself. Passages might be read, together with readings
from sample speeches of each of the three friends, with the main aim
of introducing the story and theme of the book to the congregation.
At this stage the main purpose would be to let the book speak for
itself. The second sermon on the subject could then concern itself
with the answers to the problem of suffering set out in the speeches of
Job's friends. Its main basis could be provided by the speech of
Eliphaz in Job 4:1–5:27. Possibly the text could be provided by Job
5:1, "Call now; is there any one who will answer you?" It would be
important to show that Job's friends are not false comforters but are
doing their best to help in a difficult situation. The fault does not lie in
their lack of concern or sensitivity but in the limitations of the answers
that they have to offer. So it is quite natural that anyone faced with
personal grief and disappointment should look for an answer. Such
answers are not altogether wrong—they are simply insufficient to
cover the whole range of the problem. The preacher can therefore
quite properly use the ideas raised by Eliphaz: there is a just process
which brings retribution to the wrongdoer at work in the world (so
Job 4:8); none of us is wholly innocent before God (Job 4:17–21).
Perhaps most of all, we have to learn that there is an inbuilt factor of
pain and suffering which belongs to the very essence of our human
situation. So "man is born to trouble as the sparks fly upward" (Job
5:7). What it is important to show here, in the context of The Book of
Job as a whole, is that these answers are right up to a point, but they
fail to cover the issue as it may present itself in all its fullness. The very
element of exaggeration in the extent of Job's misfortunes serves to
bring out this point.

   The next sermon on Job might look more freely at other issues that
are raised in the book. The first of these might be that of Job's
outburst of suicidal depression (cf. Job 6:8), and the alerting of
people to the danger and possibility of such feelings. A further point
might then be that of "What is the use of arguing?" as raised by
Eliphaz' speech, especially in Job 15:7–9. All too easily the difficulty of
the problem can lead to an almost cynical indifference to whether or
not we find an answer. The third point could then be concerned with
the Christian belief in life after death (Job 14:14), but taking care to
point out that it is dangerously misleading, and damaging to any
worthy sense of divine providence, to use such a belief as an antidote,
or cure-all, for the problems of living. It would be a sad misrepresentation of God to think of life after death as a compensation for this
life's injustices.

So far such a treatment of Job has concerned itself with the various guidelines that present a partial answer to the problems of and reasons for human suffering. The last sermon could then look at God's response to Job's questions (chs. 38–41). In a sense it does not provide an answer in the formal sense, but it does offer some important help. It shows, first of all, that God's power and concerns embrace far more than the needs of one individual life. It also hints at the importance of the trust that pain and suffering do not hide God's presence from us, but may rather draw it nearer. Finally it shows that, in passing through the turmoil of suffering, we can discover deeper and richer aspects of our own selves. Suffering can make this world "a vale of soul-making," so that it is not irrelevant to suggest that the tragedy lies not in the fact that we all suffer to some extent through pain and loss, but that we waste so much suffering. We fail to let it open our eyes and hearts to the frontiers of experience in which God's presence is more profoundly felt.

EXAMPLE 4

We might turn our attention now to a series of wisdom sayings of a very different texture in Eccl. 3:1–9, and focus upon the text in Eccl. 3:11, "He has made everything beautiful in its time." The aim of the sermon needs to be clarified from the start, since Ecclesiastes is a far from easy book for the casual Bible reader to understand. It is to show that there are many sides to life and a great variety of ways by which our eyes can be opened to discover God. Most of all, the concern should be to show that God has not "written off" either the people or the aspects of life which may not appear to be particularly welcome. We are used to the catchphrases, "Small is beautiful," "Black is beautiful," etc., so there is a valuable challenge in the scriptural assertion that "everything is beautiful in its time."

The opening of the sermon will certainly have to occupy itself with some general comments about the book of Ecclesiastes. A start might well lie in the commonplace experience of people that, for the most part, we are so busy living and enjoying life that there is little time, and little need, to pause over the question of what life is all about. Then there comes a time, as advancing years catch up on individuals and as opportunities begin to become more limited, for time and need to stop and think. This is what the author of Ecclesiastes has done, and he has left out some features that a Christian would certainly need to take more fully into account. Nevertheless his attempt at an overview of the business of living is not without interest and has, for more than one person, provided a basis for reflection. This, in any case, is very much a part of the style of wisdom instruction—that it should have forced us to think seriously about important questions rather than that we should obtain from such instruction a ready-made set of answers. There is no uniform set of rules that we can apply to everybody.

This might lead us on to look at the extraordinary range of experiences that the author includes in his list of "times"—death, killing, weeping and war, as well as birth, healing, dancing, laughter, and love. He is not asserting, in a cynical fashion, that any one such time is as good as any other. Rather, he is insisting that, in the average life, there are times when these experiences happen to all. Surely it is important therefore that we should learn, individually, to be ready for all and not to be thrown off balance by them. Even more, it is important that we should develop a faith which can embrace all these things, and widen our understanding of God, so that we do not suppose that he is only to be encountered in one side of life. There is a great danger in the "I know I shall be happy" syndrome in the implications it makes that, if I am unhappy, somehow God is not there.

This can then lead on to a third, and even more daring, aspect of what the author of Ecclesiastes has to say. The whole sum of life's experiences has something to teach us, and each of them provides us with something essential to our grasp of God's ordering of the world. We learn through being children, just as we can also learn through being parents. We learn as pupils, but can also learn much as teachers. Is there not, hidden in this exceptional passage, some valuable and much-needed encouragement in exploring the possibilities of Christian living. At how many stages in life does the feeling of no longer having any useful task to do, and even of no longer really being needed, come into play: after retirement, after children have left home, after the loss of a partner or of parents? It can open a very fruitful path of exploration to see what new opportunities arise with each change in life's pattern. As a challenge and antidote to the cynicism of which the book of Ecclesiastes has often been accused we can set the discovery of what is beautiful in those times of life which we may have come to fear.

EXAMPLE 5

We might lastly look at the possibility of preaching from the splendid soliloquy on the hope of immortality in Wisdom of Solomon 1–5, especially concentrating on 3:1–9. Perhaps the text, if this is needed, can best be provided by Wisd. of Sol. 2:23, "But God created

man for immortality and made him the image of his own eternal self."
In many respects the great attraction of this passage is less directly
concerned with the understanding of biblical wisdom and more with
the need for firm and positive expressions of hope for use on special
occasions—at memorial services and such like. Yet it is not difficult to
see that the interest in the belief in a life after death has arisen directly
out of certain recurrent features of wisdom thought and instruction.
These concern the question of justice and retribution in this life, the
frontiers of knowledge, and not least the blessedness of establishing in
this life a true and lasting relationship with the eternal God. What is
so appealing in the manner in which the author has expressed his
faith and ideas in this chapter is its insistent clarity and assurance. To
a very mixed audience there is nothing which the writer asserts which
is not directly related to human experience itself, so that, in making
an address from this passage, preachers can base their words of
comfort and assurance on the very feelings and anxieties which their
hearers will feel.

FOR FURTHER READING

McKane, William. *Prophets and Wise Men.* London: SCM Press, 1966. An
interesting, if at times questionable, thesis.
————. *Proverbs: A New Approach.* Westminster Press, 1970. Technical, but it
nevertheless contains one of the fullest treatments.
Rad, Gerhard von. *Wisdom in Israel.* Tr. James D. Martin. Abingdon Press,
1972. The most extensive exploration of its subject.
Scott, R. B. Y. *Proverbs—Ecclesiastes.* The Anchor Bible, Vol. 18. Doubleday &
Co., 1965. Discussion of the rather complex text of these books and
consideration of the many rare words.
————. *The Way of Wisdom in the Old Testament.* Macmillan Co., 1971. A good
general introduction.
Snaith, John G. *Ecclesiasticus.* Cambridge Bible Commentary. Cambridge
University Press, 1974.

6. PREACHING FROM THE PSALMS

DONALD MACLEOD

I. HISTORICAL CONTEXT OF THE PSALMS

At the beginning of a discussion of the book of Psalms, the opinion of Samuel Terrien is an acceptable thesis: "The Psalter is an anthology of hymns and prayers which were composed from the tenth to the third or second century B.C. It grew from the aspirations, vicissitudes, humiliations, and hopes of a people who adored God with music and song even in time of distress."[1] These writings are the product of postexilic Hebrew history, but most scholars will agree with Lawrence E. Toombs that the originals of certain pieces belong to earlier times.[2] No one would imagine preexilic Temple worship without its songs of praise. As W. O. E. Oesterley remarks, "The *fact* of the Temple worship demands that there should have been the element of praise."[3] What we have, therefore, in the Psalter is a collection of poems representing the religious and literary activity of the Jewish church. It is "a hymnbook and a prayer book combined."[4]

The story of the Jewish people covers a period of twelve hundred years during which, halfway, occurred the disastrous exile when the nation was carried off into Babylonian slavery. Before the exile, there had been two kingdoms—Judah and Israel; afterward, there emerged a small community with its center in Jerusalem, resembling less a nation than a church. To the earlier literary period belong the great narratives, the myths, the biographies of the supermen and superwomen of the race; to the second, such stylistic literature as the psalms.

As with other nations of world history, the ruinous conquest of the Jewish people by a foreign power, Babylon under Nebuchadnezzar, did not snuff out their spiritual life. Theirs was a religion which was deeply rooted in their national soul, as was true of no other people in history, and the shock of exile did not destroy it. "It is to this more spiritual side of Old Testament religion," writes W. Stewart McCullough, "that the Psalms bear eloquent witness."[5] In the absence of their ancient and traditional festivals, the Temple services and altar sacrifices, this community in exile did two things: (1) They gathered together those precious documents which preserved their identity with the past; and (2) they turned somewhat in upon themselves with deeper thoughts about God and the world.[6]

With the gradual domination of the Babylonian empire by Cyrus, the Persian era began, and with it a new day of hope dawned temporarily for the Jewish people. A measure of religious and political freedom provided for them a greater sense of identity. However, this new climate created an ambiguous order of things. On the one hand, the absence of any need for political responsibility led to a narrow individualism with a strong focus upon their religious life; and, on the other hand, it allowed to foster a culture that would maintain its identity in future generations.

Then, about 333 B.C., something new appeared: a stream of influence from the west came with Alexander's defeat of the Persian empire and the gradual change of focus toward Alexandria in Egypt whither many Jews had immigrated. The Hebrew Bible was translated into Greek for the sake of these Alexandrian Jews. Although the result was the emergence of a Greek party and a Hebrew party, yet those in the latter remained the custodians of the Jewish heritage with its pride in former history and its resolve to preserve the teachings of its prophets. Even when Syria overcame the Egyptian hold on Palestine, the fierce loyalty of the Jews remained unabated, and in the aftermath of the Maccabean revolt the free exercise of their religion was secured. This new community ought to have thrived in the stability of national and religious cohesion, yet in time it became the victim of inner decadence caused by sectarian factions, class struggle, and partisan interests (overly zealous parties such as Pharisees Sadducees, Herodians, etc.). On account of this general disarray, the Jewish kingdom was in no position to withstand the encroachment of the Roman Empire.

Out of these five hundred years of ferment came the book of Psalms; or, we might say, the Psalter survived. As W. G. Jordan commented:

It is a testimony that in this age of national decline and dreary disappointment, of fierce intolerant struggles and pedantic legalism, there was at the heart of the Jewish nation and religion a living piety, a growing spirituality, a fervent devotion, a sense of sin and sorrow—in other words a hunger of the soul that no mere ritual splendor of dogmatic external rule can satisfy.[7]

II. FORM AND CHARACTER OF THE PSALTER

Our legacy of sacred literature from the Jews falls under three classifications: Law, Prophets, and Writings. These are broken down and sorted further as follows: (1) "The five books of Moses"; (2) the prophets and early histories; and (3) a miscellaneous collection that comprises later histories (Ezra, Nehemiah, Chronicles), Wisdom Literature (Proverbs, Job, Ecclesiastes), and the Psalter. The latter is best described as a collection of "poems," the product of a historical and cultic process and reflecting various points of view. Both generally and distinctively the psalms incorporate "an awareness of the deeper values of the Hebrew faith."[8]

The word "psalm" comes from the Greek word *psalmos*, which is a translation of the Hebrew term *mizmor*, a heading for some fifty-seven psalms, meaning "to play upon the harp" or "sung to the accompaniment of a stringed instrument."[9] A valid assumption, then, is that the collection was regarded early as a hymnbook or book of praise used in various experiences of communal worship. Hebrew religious festivals were marked by music and the singing was known for its extraordinary quality and dimensions.

The question of authorship of the psalms has given rise to much discussion and brought about some debatable conclusions, although the basic position traditionally among scholars is that the ancient theory of Davidic origin cannot definitely be maintained. The Chronicler of the third century B.C. does attribute to David the beginnings of Temple music, but not the authorship of the psalms. A century later, however, in the song of Sirach (Ecclus. 47:9) this sentence occurs: "He set singers also before the altar and their voices made sweet melodies." This view persisted and in time David was considered to be the author of a number of psalms and finally his name was prefaced to the entire collection. John Paterson, in his *The Praises of Israel*, points out that the expression "a psalm of David" in the Hebrew tradition does not necessarily denote actual authorship. The form *le-David*, for example, can be rendered "to David" or "after the style of

David." Hence the Psalms can be denoted more likely as "a collection of songs in the style and manner of David."[10]

What would be regarded, moreover, as spurious authorship today was an accepted literary device in ancient times. With us the focus or emphasis is upon process. Critics and researchers explore a story or literary product for origins. But, as Paterson comments, "The Hebrew does not think as we do. . . . He does not co-ordinate and relate things into a system as does the Greek. . . . The Hebrew thinks with the eye: the connection is optical rather than logical."[11] These ancient writers and recorders took human experiences and literary odysseys that had required centuries to produce and accumulate and subsumed them under the name of one person or generation; e.g., the law of Moses, the wisdom of Solomon, the psalms of David, and the Greek translation of the Seventy. Davidic tradition, therefore, must be the accepted position or terminology rather than authorship; it is safe to assume, however, that "David was a stimulating influence on Israel's sacred poetry."[12]

Biblical scholars have divided the Psalter into five books: Psalms 3–41; 42–72; 73–89; 90–106; and 107–150, with a doxology at the end of each book. Psalm 150 is something of a doxology to the whole collection. As in every compilation, there is bound to be some overlapping: Psalms 53 and 14; 70 and 40 (vs. 13ff.); 71 (vs. 1–3) and 31 (vs. 1–3); 57 (vs. 7–11) and 108 (vs. 1–5); 60 (vs. 6–12) and 108 (vs. 7–13). Another item of interest: in Book I, the name Yahweh predominates; in Book II, Elohim occurs mostly. Paterson ventures an explanation: "In post-exilic Judaism the name *Yahwe* or Jehovah was regarded as ineffable, too sacred to be spoken. Various substitutes were employed in its stead, of which the most common was *Adonay*." Since the name of God was never spoken or pronounced by the Jews, in the Hebrew text "the word YHWH (*Yahwe*, which had no vowels originally) was supplied with the vowels of *Adonay* and is so read in the Jewish service. . . . The form Jehovah is impossible in Hebrew, but it is too deeply embedded in popular usage to be changed."[13]

The foregoing data and observations suggest and indeed indicate not only the composite literary character of the Psalter but also the likelihood of even a separate and independent existence of some of these collections; for example, Psalms 120–134, the so-called pilgrim psalms, were once undoubtedly a separate book. Titles and superscriptions have not been trustworthy guides or indices and have led to much confusion and researchers' dead ends. Prior to the conclusive evidences advanced by scholars such as Hermann Gunkel and Sigmund Mowinckel, efforts to understand the Psalter and label its contents had been developed according to historical frames of reference, and in the majority of cases the results were "quite arbitrary and fanciful" (Paterson). More recently a healthy corrective has come from the research and position of Artur Weiser, who urges a more appropriate frame of reference, namely, "the fixed framework of a common tradition of worship," the preexilic cult of the Covenant. These poems, in his opinion, are "rooted in the cultic tradition of the Covenant" and this factor "dominated the basic ideas of the Psalter."[14]

III. STYLISTIC FEATURES OF THE PSALTER

Our discussion thus far has been by way of general introduction and is intentionally brief because its substance is available generally and readily in most biblical commentaries. The average preacher, projecting a sermon or pulpit series on the psalms, will allow his or her general perspective to be taken from this broader context which is always preliminary to a more pointed focus upon the actual text or pericope. However, the peculiar features of the Psalter as a piece of biblical literature take on homiletical significance because an adequate appreciation and understanding of these phenomena are prerequisite to any honest treatment of a psalm in a sermon. Indeed it can be said that this is more true of the Psalter because its peculiar stylistic features are more varied and pronounced than all the other literary types throughout the Bible.

Let us examine some of these characteristics seriatim and assess their significance for the preacher's craft.

1. *Parallelism.* The most distinctive feature of Hebrew poetry is its parallelism, a literary device or technique in which "a single thought is expressed in one line of a poem; then the same or a related idea is expressed in the next line in a different way. The second line is like an echo of the first, but it is an echo of the *idea* rather than of the sound."[15] For example, in Ps. 95:1 we have:

> O come, let us sing unto the LORD;
>   let us make a joyful noise to the rock of our salvation!
>
>   (Ps. 95:1)

This parallelism is not always a synonymity of thought or idea; sometimes there are the elements of contrast and comparison:

> For the LORD knows the way of the righteous
>   but the way of the wicked will perish.
>
>   (Ps. 1:6)

> As a hart longs for flowing streams,
> so longs my soul for thee, O God.
> (Ps. 42:1)

"Hebrew poetry," writes Dorothea W. Harvey, "makes almost no use of rhyme and no direct use of meter in the sense of regularly recurring accents. Its formal characteristic is a balance of ideas, with the units of thought in each line of the poem enhanced, compared, or emphasized by their relationship to those in a parallel line. . . . The meter in Hebrew poetry is relatively free. Such rhythmic patterns as occur grow out of the parallelism, which requires that each line be a thought unit of approximately the same weight."[16]

Preachers in their approach to the psalms must not forget that these biblical materials are poetry. Moreoever, this is poetry of a definite and particular kind. The advantage of parallelism is its expansion of subtle shades of thought which can enrich, if taken seriously, the preacher's grasp of the semantic secret, the psalmist's original notion or meaning. Also, in both the writing of the sermon and its delivery, the Hebrew poetic technique of the "thought unit," so ably employed by preachers such as F. W. Robertson and Harry Emerson Fosdick, is a corrective of unnecessary wordiness in composition and of a mechanical and academic delivery by the preacher who is unwittingly a reader of words. A hidden danger, however, is the one-liner, the contemporary fondness for sloganizing everything, including the gospel, by which cleverness becomes the enemy of adequate proclamation.

2. *Logic.* The composite nature of the Psalter as a book appears again and again in the thought sequences of individual psalms. Systematic persons, forgetting that they are reading poetry, may be puzzled by the frequent lack of a logical sequence of ideas in any one psalm, because he or she does not realize that the Hebrew mind in its thought processes did not operate as does ours. Theirs was the intuitive mind; ours is pragmatic, syllogistic, and rational. As someone has well said, there is a difference between David and Socrates. In Hebrew there are no "howevers," "moreovers," "on the one hands," or "indeeds"—those handy particles which afford and supply transitions of thought. To repeat, as John Paterson has remarked, "The Hebrew thinks with the eye; the connection is optical rather than logical."[17] For example, to read Psalm 23 with the logic of the mind is to run into a hiatus of ideas, but with the eye one sees an expansive and integral image of the hospitality of God. The preacher who handles the psalms with the canons of logic will end up in a muddle of

frustration. But when preachers seek out truths that surpass logic, they come upon wholesome religious lessons for living that already the inner eye of the poet has perceived.

3. *Figures of Speech.* Hebrew poetry, especially the Psalter, abounds in vivid imagery. Sometimes it is a metaphor from common domestic life; other times it is a picture of a moving entourage of regal splendor or some terrible fracture in the world of nature. Always, however, in the most stirring word picture there is an element of restraint and propriety, and even when there is a sudden hyperbole it does not turn us off like the "purple patches" of the Victorian literary era. Merely a cursory reading of the psalms gives us a travelogue of images: the rocky hills, the fortress walls, the stormy sea, the hot and dusty days of summer, the quiet pool, the flocks and herds on the hillsides, the musician and the chorister, the marching soldier, the royal processions, the lights at evening, and so forth. Only when the dimensions of the world of time were too narrow to contain the writer's concept (e.g., his attempt to indicate the greatness of Solomon) did he launch into hyperbole:

> His name shall endure for ever:
> His name shall be continued as long as the sun:
> And men shall be blessed in him:
> All nations shall call him blessed.
>
> (Ps. 72:17)

Nevertheless, there was a restraining factor; in these word pictures nothing and no one usurped the attributes that belonged to God. The religion of the psalmist kept his perspective inviolate even when similes and metaphors abounded. "His land might be small," wrote Paterson, "but his God was a great God above all gods."

4. *Types of Psalms.* A critical breakthrough regarding the classification of the psalms occurred with the publication of Hermann Gunkel's *Die Psalmen* in 1926. His method was to arrange the psalms according to literary types *(Gattungen),* and for this the criteria were definitely literary rather than considerations of content or idea. For the purpose of interpretation Gunkel assigned a psalm to a type and explained it in the light of others of similar genre. In agreement with him, Oesterley asserts, "Nothing can be understood apart from its *milieu.*" According to this principle, the following classification has won acceptance: hymns, laments of community, royal psalms, individual laments, individual songs of thanksgiving, and miscellaneous minor types (enthronement songs, psalms of confidence, wisdom poetry, etc.) generally referred to as *Mischgattungen.* This sorting out

and tabulation wrested the study of individual psalms from any attempt to establish rigid historical identification (in which always the major flaw could be the occurrence in any one psalm of materials new and old) and, for the advantage of the preacher, uncovered what particular groups of psalms reflected the human need. A more appropriate question is: What is the mood of the psalm? The preacher's answer would indicate the germaneness of the psalmist's message for our day, because certainly some religious, civic, or personal mood or crisis inspired the psalm originally, and none of this is ever alien to the human struggle.

Earlier we referred to Weiser's position and theory regarding the cultic nature of the Psalter. His point of view, more so than that of other scholars who share his opinion, makes the context of each psalm or pericope all the more critical for the preacher; moreover, the stylistic features described above are helpful for and indeed indispensable to any competent interpretation. The cultic nature of the Psalter, however, is a basic prerequisite for its understanding by the preacher. It is the cultic principle, which is a method of operation, but its essence is the Word of God. This is the larger context. Weiser sets forth the cultic principle and its essence admirably as follows:

> The cultic act falls into two parts: the primary one, which according to the general idea dominating the whole of the Old Testament is also the decisive one, is the *actio Dei,* the action of God and the Word of God; that of the congregation is therefore to be understood only as a *reactio hominum,* as something which has been determined by something else; the words offered by the congregation in prayer and in praise have the quality of "response" in that they somehow presuppose the *actio Dei ad salutem.*[18]

These contexts the preacher must consider responsibly as he or she stands within the third, the human context, as interpreter and herald of the message of salvation.

IV. SERMONIC METHOD WITH THE PSALTER

The sermon does not begin with the study of the pericope or text. It begins with the preacher's own understanding of the meaning and purpose of the act of worship. These matters, however, can be discerned only when certain forerunners are clearly in mind: the preacher's own concept of revelation; the meaning and the claim upon him or her of the Word of God; the integrity of preaching in the liturgical act; and the goal of the interpreter who speaks for God to humankind. No basic work on a scriptural text is likely to be honest and fruitful unless the perspective of the preacher upon it is taken clearly from the foundation of these matters of belief.

A modest bibliography is essential at the outset, and in the case of the Psalter the following names are accredited: Paterson, Terrien, Anderson, Toombs, Oesterley, and Weiser especially

The text for the particular sermon may be suggested by the lectionary, or it could be a pericope that has arrested the preacher's attention and, as Spurgeon once said, "demands to be dealt with." On the other hand, a series of sermons may be in the preacher's mind and if so, the psalms or texts will be chosen according to types or congregational needs.

If a single text or short pericope is chosen, it must be seen initially within the larger context (suggested above and in sections I, II, and III) of the preacher's own conception of the nature of Scripture and then within the narrower context of the Psalter itself. Every available version will be read carefully and maybe supplemented by the preacher's own translation from the original Hebrew. All this done, the preacher takes a clean sheet of notepaper and engages in a period of mental brooding upon the text, jotting down everything that comes by way of association: fragmentary recollections, literary tidbits, germinal ideas, contemporary parallels, and so forth.

The next step is research in the commentaries, which must *not* precede the firsthand, original brooding upon the text. From the commentary the preacher learns the answers to five contextual questions: Who wrote it? When was it written? Where? To whom? and Why? These are implements of exegesis and they lead the preacher to an answer to the question, What? All these findings are jotted down on another sheet of the preacher's note pad.

Then follows another period of brooding over both sheets of miscellaneous jottings. Suddenly there comes the moment of illumination—the "Aha!" juncture—when the preacher is arrested by the single message arising out of the miscellany of collected materials. This word is written down immediately in one succinct sentence. This will be the sermon's central idea. This is the Word of God to you and me from this text or pericope of Scripture.

Eduard Schweizer has said that exegesis is what the writer said and hermeneutics is what the writer meant. The preacher must now interpret the meaning and significance of this "word" for the congregation. The next step involves the point of immediacy: Where does this central idea strike what or whom in the parish or community? What moral, social, or political ill does it speak to or judge? After this point has been decided, there is need now for focus. This can be secured through choosing as a single text the verse or verses that will epitomize most pertinently the central idea and by fashioning an engaging topic that brings into sharp focus the message and implications for our life situation of both the idea and text. A skillfully phrased topic can be an excellent channel toward cogency and coherence in the sermon. Then, with these matters in hand, the preacher considers the important question: What is my purpose? This for Dr. Fosdick was more important than a sermon subject. Now the preacher is ready to sketch the outline. Central idea, point of immediacy, text, topic, and purpose are brooded over simultaneously until a pattern of thought begins to emerge. This is what H. Grady Davis called "the extension of the idea." Through reflection, selection, and intuition relating to the mass of material now on hand, the outline of the sermon takes shape. Items, quotations, and illustrations from a well-stocked and up-to-date filing system will flesh out the framework, and the arrangement of the whole according to principles of logic, emotion, and personal rapport will assure impact and lasting effectiveness.

V. SERMONIC STUDIES IN THE PSALMS

PSALM 23

Some psalms are creations of poetic art and hence defy rational analysis. Psalm 23 is one of these. Some others that approach this prototype are Psalms 46; 61; 100; 121; 122; and 150. Here, in our preliminary exploration, we do not employ logic, nor do we look for systematic outlining of a religious doctrine. In these we have a thought unit which cannot be unpacked. Our approach as preachers, therefore, must be with openness of ear and eye, allowing the reflection of its sound and imagery to play upon our human senses. No axiomatic lessons can be extracted. The inner appeal lies in the area of faith and trust. Hence, all the preacher can or really need do is to explore the deeper meaning, the thought unit, and verbalize, if possible, the aspirations behind the metaphor and the mood giving rise to the shout of praise or doom. And having isolated such, then, like Mark Antony, he or she will say, "Now let it work."

The preacher may open the sermon with a striking statement regarding the nature of Psalm 23—for example, Weiser's comment about the psalmist, "A serene soul enjoying perfect peace of mind . . . that flows from an undoubting trust in God."[19] Other remarks to bring the preacher onto a wavelength congenial with the congregation may point to the familiarity of this psalm, its appeal to both Jewish and Christian children, its place as "a song of the martyrs" (Augustine) in religious history, and its beauty in verse in the Scottish paraphrases.

Since the Eastern idiom predominates, preachers must examine at an initial stage the pastoral scene with the shepherd image of God and the grateful and satisfying response the psalmist feels ("I shall not want"). In vs. 2 and 3, according to Hebrew tradition, the psalmist reflects upon what God has done and how in these actions his glory is seen and hailed. Dividends accrue from his closeness to God, and the intimacy of prayer is suggested by the use of the pronoun "thou." Verse 5 portrays the tent in the sheepfold where safety is assured, and in v. 6 the psalmist seemingly backs off for a moment and in something of a doxology he revels in the security of God's loving-kindness and its protection following him forever.

To bring the thrust of the message into the people's world of today, the topic helps to provide focus: "What God means to me." The introduction may discuss, for example, the place and role in the church of the formal creeds. These have been necessarily theologically objective and factually biblical. But both church and people have lived more often by the personal confessions of average men and women. The Old and New Testaments are full of them. Examples may be cited here. Terrien comments: "The whole of faith is contained in this first line."[20] Here we find no doctrinal or philosophical concept. Here is a simple soul "telling it like it is." Or, "This is how it appears to me." And because of this understanding and relationship, four blessings are realized by the child of faith:

1. Satisfaction: "I shall not *want*." Note also the "my" and "me" denoting "belongingness" (antidote to loneliness). Nearness is the key and preliminary to being heard and understood. The shepherd concept implies that the psalmist is the object of another's concern.

2. Renewal: Note the livingness of the phrases "green pastures," "still waters," "restores soul." Also, the intimations of a God who is active for human benefit: "He maketh" (an enabler); "he leadeth" (in the vanguard always). Our acceptance of this relationship brings us into accord with God's way and will.

3. Realism: There is no escapism in Psalm 23. Life's unpleasant things are real. There must of necessity be light and shadow, dark

cloud and hospitality, peril of enemies and safety, but among all these realities there is a presence which is more real.

4. Optimism: Shadow and death are real and inevitable, but "goodness and mercy" are the confidence of the person whose trust is strong.

In the foregoing discussion and example, we see a sermonic method rising out of the nature of the psalm itself. A sequence of images or facets portrays in a thought unit a picture of what Terrien calls "the undiscouraged God." This is the unifying factor, and as the preacher turns its facets around, its fullness and relevance are caught by sight rather than by reason.

PSALM 112

Just as the hymnody of the church has taught congregations much of their basic theology, so the psalms have been mentors of religious ethics. Again and again, either in a single psalm or two psalms in sequence, the nature of the God of Israel is the reason for praise, and then close upon it is a hallelujah for the life and kind of living of the person who worships, serves, and partakes of the will and purpose of this God. Psalm 112 is the counterpart of Psalm 111. Both are hymns of praise composed for some festival occasion of the worshiping covenant community. Psalm 111 acclaims God's role and rule in nature and history. As Weiser comments, "In the Old Testament God is always the God who acts."[21] And since his actions are always redemptive, the person (Ps. 112) who commits himself or herself to God shares his nature and is therefore a re-creative factor in the common events of everyday life.

Psalm 112, then, can be the basis for a teaching sermon on the conduct or behavior of the moral person in an immoral society, or on how to live "a balanced life in an unbalanced world." We find here the element of contrast which is determinative in the sermonic method and emphasizes how the person who accepts God's blessing can be a blessing to some (v. 4) and to others a source of judgment (v. 10).

The beginning of the sermon ought to find the people where they are. Within the average congregation are three types: the worldly-minded, the spiritually-minded, and the ones who exercise a proper balance between the two extremes. The worldly-minded must get everything, although there seems to be no purpose in all that acquiring. They have no objective frame of reference outside or beyond themselves. They are like the rich fool in Jesus' parable (Luke 12). The spiritually-minded are of little earthly use; they stand off from the human situation; their hands are unsoiled. Their focus is upon "pie in the sky when they die." Neither type is steady in unsteady times. One shock can undo them. The third type is the only one that can endure in this naughty and convulsive world.

To bring our approach into focus, v. 7 is useful and pivotal as a text. The psalmist describes the above-suggested third type: "He shall not be afraid of evil tidings: his heart is fixed, trusting in the LORD." The psalm spells out by way of contrast how this person, who is claimed by God's way and will, is both human and religious; he or she is not absorbed exclusively by either worldliness or otherworldliness. The humanness of this person is described as follows: builds up an estate (v. 3), lends to those who ask (v. 5a), is discreet in personal affairs (v. 5b), is sympathetic and kind (v. 9); in other words, is an all-around citizen (v. 6). But this person is also religious: fears God and trusts (v. 1), accepts inner and outer benefits (vs. 2 and 3), takes a stand on the side of right (v. 4), establishes a good name (v. 6).

Now, the preacher brings all these together, and they form a composite picture of the truly good person whose spiritual posture and genuine actions make him or her unflappable in a world in constant crisis. Theirs is no ivory tower; they are not afraid of evil tidings; their hearts are fixed, trusting in the Lord.

How, then, do we spell out their secret?

1. Complete trust ("trusting in the LORD"). See Kittel for a study of the real meaning of "trust" in the biblical sense.

2. Fixed heart ("his heart is fixed"). Such people are not driven by every breeze that blows.

3. Above fear ("not be afraid of evil tidings"). Events or crises plus God make a difference.

"Trust in God," comments Weiser, "gives a person a firm and confident heart, so that there is no need to be afraid."[22]

PSALM 103

Psalm 103 is both a song and a definition of thanksgiving. It is a celebration, and in the course of praise it describes the nature and character of the subject it celebrates. In this psalm, as Toombs comments, "God is praised, not so much for what he gives to his people, as for what he is and for what, out of his nature, he does."[23] Qualitatively speaking, Weiser regards this psalm as "one of the finest blossoms on the tree of biblical faith."[24]

Again, as in the two foregoing examples, the nature of this psalm prescribes the preacher's homiletical and interpretative strategy. Its substance is a thought unit; it sings of the "what, why, and wherefore" of true thanksgiving. It is poetic, yet at the same time it differs from

Psalm 23 in that it is logical. The preacher's purpose can be modeled upon what the psalmist himself does: he takes a secular term and identifies what can be its more deeply spiritual meaning within a religious frame of reference. Moreover, he spells out the moral claim upon the human will that the focus of genuine thanksgiving exercises.

Following our general strategy (see section IV above), the preacher's initial step will be a brooding session on the psalm itself and concurrent reading of the various versions and translations, including the preacher's own. By exercising seriously free mental association, a note page or two of firsthand reflections will be accumulated. Research in commentaries will follow; maybe a textual focus will be vs. 1 and 2. The central idea is stated: thanksgiving is real and effective only when it is a celebration of life, life redeemed by God's grace and nourished by our constant response to the claim of his will. Moreover, real thanksgiving includes faith, and faith involves decision; our gratitude is genuine only insofar as we fulfill the conditions of faith. The topic might be "Bringing God Into Thanksgiving."

In dealing with a theme that has become "worn smooth" through constant use and abuse, the delineation of the point of immediacy is crucial. The psalmist's focus is on God's nature and attributes, but also upon his own spiritual experience and the effects of his own apprehension of this God. The psalm celebrates the wonderful grace of God made manifest in and through his dealings with humankind. Herein lies our hope: God's concern for us.

Now, where does this idea grab us? The preacher must close in upon the contemporary human situation and gather data regarding common attitudes to an understanding of thanksgiving. He or she will note the dearth of gratitude today. Thanksgiving is a lost note even in our worship. Moreover, much of the thanksgiving we engage in is unreal. Our day of national thanksgiving in America lacks a religious focus. Thanksgiving is response, but for the average person the unresolved question is: to what and to whom? The eclipse of genuine thanksgiving is due partly to a contemporary eclipse of human wonder and reverence. "Amazing grace" does not excite an overwhelming sense of human reverence. Hence for many people Thanksgiving never gets beyond the secular dimension, and its annual observance is a pointless routine. The biblical idea of thanksgiving is dialogical: God supplies his grace and we respond. Response, however, must be more than merely a blasé "Thank you." Our "whole being" ("all that is within me") is involved and claimed; only thereby can our thanksgiving have worthwhile effect.

Psalm 103 falls into five distinct parts. (1) Verses 1–2: a call to bless the Lord is directed by the psalmist to himself. He appeals to the whole person to remember God's gracious benefits. His focus is on God and on himself and here sublimity and intimacy meet. (2) Verses 3–5: the psalmist's personal experience of God constrains him to spell out who and what God is and does. His is a God who transforms. The result is a new vitality akin to the New Testament's "being born again." (3) Verses 6–13: the psalmist sketches with broad strokes the evidences of God's care in the world and in history, especially with Israel, and chides us thereby for our lack of comprehension of the dimensions of his grace. (4) Verses 14–17: despite our poor spiritual condition God grants to us to share in his mercy; however, there is a condition: "to such as keep his covenant" (v. 18). (5) Verses 19–22: here is a closing hymn; all barriers of time and space fall, and the psalmist joins with the heavenly host in a magnificent overture of praise.

The foregoing are ideas preliminary to the "body of the sermon." They will be sorted out, arranged in useful sequence, and illustrated by contemporary names and references. The preacher will exercise strict selection, using only those ideas needed as bases for the expansion of the thanksgiving thought unit. From a final session of careful brooding over accumulated materials, three facets of the real nature of thanksgiving emerge and these can form the homiletical framework for the sermon.

1. Real thanksgiving involves our whole being. Thanksgiving is more than a wave of superficial emotionalism or the notion that God has somehow blessed only the Anglo-Saxon race. It embraces and emerges from the exercise of mind and will. "Thou shalt love the Lord thy God with . . . heart, . . . soul, strength, and mind." This is a needed emphasis, for example, in our prayers which degenerate so often into mere petitions for our own selfish ends. Praise and thanksgiving lift us above self. The psalmist attempts to raise us to this higher level where we see not merely what God has done *for* man but chiefly *in* man. This involves more than statistics about crops, but forgiveness, healing, redemption, and satisfaction—the fruits of new life.

2. Real thanksgiving begins with what God is rather than what humankind is. The psalmist does not thank God for what he himself is, but for what God is and for what he has done for his people. Verses 6–13 and 17 give us the psalmist's catalog of "gracious benefits." Then, by implication, he refers to the relationship of the heathen to their gods and by contrast indicates that our genuine sense of wonder

and reverence in God's presence is tempered by a downward reach of a fatherly mercy and concern.

3. Real thanksgiving depends, therefore, upon the extent to which we do God's will. This psalm echoes with calls to responsibility: "to such as keep his covenant"; "hearkening unto his voice"; "them that fear him." Thanksgiving cannot be a duty to be legislated; it is the joyous satisfaction that comes from doing what is right and good through the enabling will of him who wants to make us what we ought to be. It involves, then, surrender and subsequent freedom; surrender to God and freedom from self. Edwin Arlington Robinson wrote:

> Two kinds of gratitude: the sudden kind
> We feel for what we take; the larger kind
> We feel for what we give.

In the New Testament, whenever Jesus offered thanks to God, it was with relation to the giving of himself in the doing of the Father's will and the spiritual satisfaction this relationship supplied. If we bring God honestly into our thanksgiving, we shall still bless his name for what he is and does, but with a difference—we shall appropriate his will as we do his commandments and become ourselves a blessing to others in our time.

NOTES

1. Samuel L. Terrien, *The Psalms and Their Meaning for Today* (Bobbs-Merrill Co., 1952), p. 19.

2. Lawrence E. Toombs, "The Psalms," *The Interpreter's One-Volume Commentary on the Bible*, ed. by Charles M. Laymon (Abingdon Press, 1971), p. 253.

3. W. O. E. Oesterley, *A Fresh Approach to the Psalms* (Charles Scribner's Sons, 1937), p. 38.

4. R. B. Y. Scott, *The Psalms as Christian Praise* (Association Press, 1958), p. 15.

5. W. Stewart McCullough, "Psalms, Introduction," *The Interpreter's Bible*, ed. by George A. Buttrick et al., Vol. 4 (Abingdon Press, 1955), p. 4.

6. Terrien, op. cit., p. 24.

7. W. G. Jordan, *Religion in Song: Studies in the Psalter* (London: James Clarke & Co., 1920), p. 20. Cf. also John Paterson, *The Praises of Israel* (Charles Scribner's Sons, 1950), Ch. 2.

8. McCullough, loc. cit., p. 24.

9. Artur Weiser, *The Psalms, A Commentary*, tr. by Herbert Hartwell, The Old Testament Library (Westminster Press, 1962), p. 20.

10. Paterson, op. cit., p. 19.
11. Ibid., p. 24.
12. McCullough, loc. cit., p. 10.
13. Paterson, op. cit., p. 16.
14. Weiser, op. cit., p. 52.
15. Scott, op. cit., p. 16.
16. Dorothea Ward Harvey, "The Literary Forms of the Old Testament," *The Interpreter's One-Volume Commentary on the Bible*, p. 1077.
17. Paterson, op. cit., p. 24.
18. Weiser, op. cit., p. 29.
19. Ibid., p. 227.
20. Terrien, op. cit., p. 230.
21. Weiser, op. cit., p. 699.
22. Ibid., p. 704.
23. Toombs, op. cit., p. 256.
24. Weiser, op. cit., p. 657.

FOR FURTHER READING

Anderson, Bernhard W. *Out of the Depths: The Psalms Speak for Us Today.* Westminster Press, 1974.

Calvin, John. *Commentary on the Book of Psalms.* 5 vols. Tr. James Anderson. Wm. B. Eerdmans Publishing Co., 1949.

Driver, S. R.; Plummer, A.; Briggs C. A. *Psalms, I & II.* Edinburgh: T. & T. Clark, 1969.

Jordan, W. G. *Religion in Song: Studies in the Psalter.* London: James Clarke & Co., 1920.

Kalt, Edmund, ed. *Herder's Commentary on the Psalms.* Tr. Bernard Fritz. Newman Press, 1961.

Kirkpatrick, A. F. *The Book of Psalms.* Cambridge University Press, 1902.

Mowinckel, Sigmund. *The Psalms in Israel's Worship.* 2 vols. Tr. D. R. Ap-Thomas. Oxford: Basil Blackwell, 1963.

Oesterley, W. E. O. *A Fresh Approach to the Psalms.* Charles Scribner's Sons, 1937.

———, ed. *The Psalms.* 2 vols. London: S.P.C.K., 1939.

Scott, R. B. Y. *The Psalms as Christian Praise.* Association Press, 1958.

Terrien, Samuel L. *The Psalms and Their Meaning for Today.* Bobbs-Merrill Co., 1952.

Weiser, Artur. *The Psalms, A Commentary.* Tr. Herbert Hartwell. The Old Testament Library. Westminster Press, 1962.

Westermann, Claus. *The Praise of God in the Psalms.* Tr. Keith R. Crim. John Knox Press, 1965.

Yates, Kyle M. *Preaching from the Psalms.* Harper & Brothers, 1948.

7. PREACHING FROM ISAIAH, JEREMIAH, AND EZEKIEL

ELIZABETH ACHTEMEIER

I. THE BASIC APPROACH

In order to preach from the first three prophetic books, perhaps we have first of all to lay aside our popular stereotypes of them. Prophetic preaching has most frequently been equated with judgmental preaching, and the Old Testament prophets have been regarded as social critics and reformers who condemned the ways of Israelite society on the basis of absolutized standards of justice and righteousness. Many preachers, therefore, who have leveled criticism against their congregations have comforted themselves with the thought that they were being "prophetic," and the prophetic message has repeatedly been claimed as identical with the ideology of one or another social, political, or economic protests and movements. Such stereotypical uses of the prophetic books badly distort their message and intention.

Like all the prophets, Proto-Isaiah, Deutero-Isaiah, and Trito-Isaiah, Jeremiah and Ezekiel are primarily heralds of a new action of God. As he broke into Israel's life in the promise to the patriarchs and to David, so once again he is breaking into Israel's life in the eighth through the sixth centuries B.C. to create new events that will set Israel and Judah in entirely new situations. It is the prophets who announce that coming action and who give the reasons for it. Indeed, in the understanding of the Old Testament, it is the prophets' words which mark the beginning of God's action and which are then fulfilled when he completes the action.

This movement forward on the part of Israel's God is clearly seen in the prophetic call narratives. Always the emphasis in Isaiah, Jeremiah, and Ezekiel is on the activity of God, and the conception is that the prophets have been allowed to stand in the divine council in heaven where that activity was planned (cf. Jer. 23:18; Isa. 6; 40). They then become the messengers of the divine council, to announce the imminent fulfillment of the plan (cf. Isa. 22:11) to their people and to interpret the reasons why Yahweh is carrying out such a plan. Their words will therefore necessarily be fulfilled (cf. Isa. 40:8; 55:10–11; Ezek. 12:25, 28), whether their people heed them or not (cf. Ezek. 2:4–7).

This function of the prophets is mirrored in the standard form of the prophetic oracle, found, for example, in Isa. 8:6–8 or Jer. 5:10–15. The reason for Yahweh's action is analyzed (Isa. 8:6; Jer. 5:10–13), the messenger formula is stated ("therefore," Isa. 8:7; "therefore thus says the LORD, the God of hosts," Jer. 5:14), and Yahweh's coming action is announced (Isa. 8:7–8; Jer. 5:14–15). This form undergoes wide variations in the Major Prophets and is almost dissipated in Ezekiel, but the emphasis on God's activity remains, and is present in all the principal genres of prophetic literature. Whether the form is that of woe oracle pronounced over the dead (Isa. 5:8–10), legal procedure (Isa. 41:21–24), parable (Isa. 5:1–7), lamenting dirge (Jer. 9:17–22), prophetic torah or teaching (Isa. 1:10–17), salvation oracle (Jer. 35:18–19), priestly oracle of salvation (Isa. 41:8–13), or allegory (Ezek. 17:1–21), the principal reference is to the activity of God among his people or among the nations as a whole, and no sermon from the prophetic literature truly deals with those oracles unless it deals with that dynamic of Yahweh's activity.

It is clear, then, that the prophetic message cannot be reduced to a static ethic. It deals not with rules and regulations, not with a fixed moral code—only once is the law quoted in the major prophetic books (Jer. 7:9)—but with the attitudes and intentions and activities of a living Lord, who is restlessly, ceaselessly, jealously working out his purpose among his people. We are dealing with a living relationship between God and his people Israel in the prophetic writings, a relationship that can never be reduced to fixed formulas or ideals. To try to equate the prophetic message with some present-day ideological movement, therefore, is to maintain that a vital fellowship had about it a fixity which it never had.

Moreover, the fellowship of God with his people Israel was one of overwhelming grace. His judgment on his sinful folk was a work "alien" to his nature (cf. Isa. 28:21), and he carried it out in the grief of a Father over his rebellious son, of a Husband over his faithless wife (cf. Jer. 3:19–20). Even in the midst of judging his beloved, he planned a future and a hope for them (cf. Jer. 31:15–20). None of the Major Prophets considered judgment the last word from God, and they all held out before the eyes of their sinful society the vision, on the other side of the judgment, of that society forgiven, cleansed, and restored by the mercy of God to a new and permanent relationship with him. Indeed, when it became clear to the prophets that Israel was enslaved by sin and incapable of reform (cf. Jer. 13:23), they nevertheless promised a new life for her (cf. Ezek. 37:1–14, 15–28) or for her remnant (cf. Isa. 65:8–16) on the basis of Yahweh's transformation of her inner character (cf. Jer. 31:31–34; Ezek. 36:26–27; Isa. 42:1–4). So radical would such transformation be that Trito-Isaiah finally described it in terms of Yahweh's creation of new heavens and a new earth (Isa. 65:17–25).

In a similar vein, the prophets never saw themselves as set apart from their sinful contemporaries, and there was never any thought that they and God were on one side and Israel was on the other. They included themselves in Israelite society and acknowledged their part in that society's sin (cf. Isa. 6:5; 63:15–19; 64:5–7, 9). To be sure, Jeremiah heard that he was set against the whole people, who would fight him (Jer. 1:18–19) and persecute him (cf. Jer. 11:18–23; 12:5–6). But he, above all other prophets, wept over the destruction of his people (Jer. 8:18–21), and so persistent was his intercession on their behalf that Yahweh finally had to tell him to be silent (Jer. 7:16; 11:14; 14:11; 14:17–15:2, 10–12).

This function of intercession was given to all the prophets (cf. Isa. 62:1, 6–7), so that Ezekiel can characterize a false prophet as one who has "not gone up into the breaches, or built up a wall for the house of Israel, that it might stand in battle in the day of the LORD" (Ezek. 13:5; 22:30). Further, as intercessors for their people before God, the prophets themselves must first suffer, in their own lives and bodies, the judgment of God upon their people. To symbolize the withdrawal of Yahweh's steadfast love and mercy from Judah, Jeremiah is forbidden to marry, or even to attend a party or wedding or funeral (Jer. 16:1–9)—all institutions and functions of community life invested with the grace of God. Ezekiel's wife must die as symbol of the coming destruction of the Temple (Ezek. 24:15–24), and he physically acts out the coming siege and destruction of Jerusalem and the captivity of the exile (Ezek. 4:4–8, 9–17; 12:1–16, 17–20), in an Old Testament foreshadowing of the incarnation of the Word.

To equate prophetic preaching, therefore, solely with judgmental preaching is to distort both the content of the prophetic message and the understanding of the prophet's role among his people. As Martin

Luther King, Jr., once said, "Whom you would change, you must first love." The prophets' love for their sinful people is born of God's love for that people, and apart from that love, God's spokesmen are unable truly to speak his word.

Because the prophets deal in their oracles with the living relationship of Israel to her God of love, it is further clear that their thought moves within the context of the covenant bond. To be sure, they each conceive that bond differently. Proto-Isaiah envisions the relation between God and Israel in terms of the Davidic covenant. Deutero-Isaiah and Trito-Isaiah and Jeremiah mirror the election traditions of the exodus and tribal federation. Ezekiel's thought—perhaps the most sophisticated in the Old Testament—encompasses the whole range of Israel's theological traditions, set within a distinctly cultic and priestly milieu. Any preacher who preaches from a passage in one of these books must therefore acquaint himself or herself with the overall thought of the prophet in order to know the theological context of that which is being announced. For example, the promise to Ahaz, in Isaiah 7, that "a young woman shall conceive and bear a son, and shall call his name Immanuel," is a sign to Ahaz that he can rely on Yahweh's promise to the house of David.

By the same token, the context of the covenant relationship militates against drawing direct parallels between Israel's life as a nation and the life of any present-day secular state, including the United States. The words of the prophets are directed to the covenant people of God, and the only modern analogies to that chosen people are the religious congregations of Judaism and the Christian church.

The covenant relationship between God and Israel further dictates the hermeneutical or interpretative context of preaching from the Major Prophets. If we ask what it was that Yahweh required of Israel in the covenant, according to the Isaiah school and Jeremiah and Ezekiel, then it is clear that each of the Major Prophets gives a distinctive answer to that question.

For Proto-Isaiah, Judah's primary response to the grace of the Davidic covenant is to be *trust*—reliance on the working of the Holy One of Israel, the Lord of Hosts, who is sovereign over the nations and who has entered into covenant with Israel through David (cf. Isa. 7:9; 30:15; 31:1–3). In Jeremiah's preaching, which is so consonant with that of Deuteronomy, the covenant demand is for *love* and *knowledge*—love for God the divine Father and Husband, which issues in intimate knowledge of his gracious Person and leads to thankful obedience to his will as expressed in the Code of Deuteronomy. In the new covenant, Jeremiah therefore proclaims, all will "know" the Lord

(Jer. 31:34). In Ezekiel's oracles, once again the covenant relationship requires the *knowledge* of God; repeatedly it is stated that when Yahweh acts in judgment or salvation, "Then you will know that I am the LORD." But that knowledge is, for Ezekiel, interior realization of Yahweh's kingship (cf. Ezek. 20:33) and obedient response to his statutes and ordinances in both cultic and moral life (cf. Ezek. 22). Deutero-Isaiah, the supreme prophet of God's saving activity, calls for *trust* in that imminent salvation, basing his appeal on Yahweh's past faithfulness to his word and his power in creation, and bidding Israel "wait" for the new word of salvation to come to pass (cf. Isa. 40:31). Trito-Isaiah renews Deutero-Isaiah's promise of salvation (cf. Isa. 56:1), but he is the first prophet to declare that Yahweh will no longer deal with Israel as a unit: members of the postexilic community will be judged or saved on the basis of whether or not they rely in *humble repentance and dependence and obedience* on the Holy One of Israel (cf. Isa. 57:15, 19–21; 65:13–14).

In one's preaching from any pericope within these writings, it is clear then that the demand or exhortation or judgment or promise expressed in the single pericope must be interpreted in the context of the primary demand that the prophet saw imposed upon Israel's life by the covenant relationship. And that primary demand was always one having to do with the most intimate, interior, ongoing relationship with God.

For example, all the Major Prophets condemned Israel's worship life (cf. Isa. 1:10–17; Jer. 7:1–15; Ezek. 8; Isa. 44:9–20; 46; 66:1–4), not because they opposed cultic and sacrificial worship in principle, or thought the Temple was unnecessary, or favored social action over prayer. To interpret Isa. 1:10–17 or Isa. 66:1–2 or Jer. 7:1–4 in such fashion is to lift them out of their context. Rather, Israel's worship was condemned because it was not an expression of Israel's heart. It was mere lip service (cf. Isa. 29:13), or magical incantation (Jer. 7:4), or entertainment (Ezek. 33:30–33), or divorced from day-to-day action (cf. Isa. 1:15–16), or dedicated to false gods (Ezek. 8). Jeremiah's Temple sermon, which Jesus quoted during the Temple cleansing, pointed out that the people were using the Temple as a "den of robbers," that is, as a hiding place, where they imagined themselves safe from the consequences of their own sin (Jer. 7:8–11; Mark 11:17 and pars.). In short, Israel's worship life was divorced from that intimate, interior love and knowledge and obedience of God demanded by him in the covenant relationship.

The Major Prophets are dealing with Israel's heart. "Circumcise yourselves to the LORD" is Jeremiah's cry; "Remove the foreskin of your hearts, O men of Judah and inhabitants of Jerusalem" (Jer. 4:4). "Get yourselves a new heart and a new spirit!" proclaims Ezekiel. "Why will you die, O house of Israel?" (Ezek. 18:31). Israel's difficulty is that she has "removed her heart far from" Yahweh (Isa. 29:13), that she has not taken his judgment "to heart" (Isa. 42:25; Hebrew reading of 57:11), that she has not returned to God "with her whole heart" (Jer. 3:10). And so in Yahweh's salvation of his people, he deals with their hearts. He "speaks to the heart of Jerusalem" (Hebrew reading of Isa. 40:2); he writes the words of his new covenant "upon their hearts" (Jer. 31:33); he gives his people "a new heart" and "a new spirit" (Ezek. 36:26); he revives "the heart of the contrite" (Isa. 57:15). In short, he restores his people to that intimate relationship with himself that he desired in the covenant fellowship in the beginning.

This interior, vital, covenant relationship, which is symbolized by the figure of the "heart," is really an indispensable hermeneutical key to preaching from the prophets. Apart from that living relationship, the preacher will turn the prophetic message into sterile moralism or powerless ethical admonition or unattainable ideology. "Apart from me you can do nothing," our Lord taught (John 15:5). That applies also to preaching from the Major Prophets.

Finally, in this overview of the preacher's approach to the Major Prophets, it must be borne in mind, when the message of any prophetic oracle is applied to the life of a modern congregation, that that prophetic message is firmly rooted in a historical situation and should not be divorced from it. For example, in the reign of Hezekiah, Proto-Isaiah condemns Judah's alliance with Egypt (Isa. 30:1–5; 31:1–3), just as earlier he condemned her alliance with Assyria (Isa. 7). He opposes trust in such alliances and in military weapons, in the strongest terms, calling instead for faith in Yahweh's protective action as the basis of Judah's defense and foreign policy (cf. Isa. 30:15–17). The preacher who wishes to apply such oracles to modern international affairs should not simply lift them out of their historical context and impose them, willy-nilly, upon the twentieth century as eternal principles. They cannot be used to give absolute divine sanction to modern pacifism or isolationism. Or to give another example, when Jerusalem is under Babylonian siege in 588 B.C., Jeremiah counsels his countrymen on the basis of the Word of God to surrender to the Babylonians (Jer. 38:2–3). Had we lifted that out of its historical context and applied it to the Second World War, Russia would have surrendered to Hitler's armies, and England would have capitulated and saved herself from Goering's bombers. Yet such misuse of the Scriptures has been frequent in our time and has turned them into tools of one or another ideological group.

Any prophetic oracle must be understood within its own particular historical context, as the Word of God for that particular situation. But then in order to apply the oracle to the life of his or her congregation, the preacher can ask several legitimate questions:

1. If the oracle is promissory, were its words fulfilled, and if so, when and how? The Old Testament finds some concrete fulfillments of prophetic announcements within the history of Israel itself. For example, Israel does in fact fall victim to Assyria and Judah to Babylonia, as Proto-Isaiah and Jeremiah and Ezekiel had announced they would. But in the New Testament's view, those were partial fulfillments, and the final reinterpretation and fulfillment of the prophetic preaching is understood as having been accomplished in the life, death, and resurrection of Jesus Christ (cf. Luke 22:37; 24:27, 44–45; John 1:45; Acts 13:27; 28:23; I Peter 1:10–11; II Cor. 1:20; Matt. 1:23; 2:15, 17–18; 3:3 *et passim*). The Christian church is therefore heir of that fulfillment and the partaker of it, and the prophetic message is indispensable to us for knowing what we have received and who this Lord is whom we have believed. On this basis, the preacher can therefore show how a prophetic oracle has been fulfilled in Jesus Christ, what that fulfillment means for our lives, and how we should respond to it.

2. What does the prophetic oracle reveal to us about the nature and activity of God? That revelation belongs as much to the church as to Israel, because we are the New Israel in Christ (cf. Gal. 6:16; Heb. 4:9), the true sons of Abraham (Gal. 3:7; cf. Rom. 4; 9:6–9), the "true circumcision" (Phil. 3:3). Because the Old Testament belongs to us only through Christ, we necessarily must finally interpret it in the light of Jesus Christ, but that does not mean that we read Christ back into the Old Testament. Rather, we can allow the prophetic oracle to aid us in illumining the nature and activity of the God revealed in Jesus Christ. For example, Ezekiel 34 forms the background of Jesus' sayings concerning the Good Shepherd in John 10, and makes it very clear that the shepherd image is a royal Davidic figure (Ezek. 34:23). That prophetic oracle therefore prevents the preacher from sentimentalizing Jesus as the Good Shepherd, and reveals to us that we have instead to do with God's chosen King. Or to give another example, the seriousness with which God takes Israel's sin and yet Israel's inability to rid herself of it, in passages such as Jer. 2:4–13, 20–28, 29–32, or Isa. 1:2–3, 4–8, do much to illumine what Paul means when he says we are slaves of sin, who have been freed by

God's payment of the very expensive redemption price of his beloved Son (cf. Rom. 6:12ff.).

3. How is our situation as the New Israel in Christ analogous to Israel's situation before God in the prophetic oracle? We cannot impose Israel's historical situation on ours, but because we in the church are also Israel, our life before God is analogous to hers. For example, we Christians are, in our modern urban life, often as guilty of injustice and dishonest business practices and corrupt government and courts and sometimes even murder as was the city of Jerusalem (Isa. 1:21–23). And we have to do with the same God. We can therefore expect that God's wrath burns as hotly against us as it did against Jerusalem. How he will manifest that wrath against us must be carefully formulated in the light of the New Testament. But Isaiah shows us both our sin and God's anger over it, because our lives as Christians are so analogous to the life of Israel.

To give another example, King Ahaz is given the promise of the birth of Immanuel in Isaiah 7, as a sign that he can trust God's promise in a time of international upheaval and warfare. It must have seemed like a rather ridiculous guarantee to the harassed king, because what Ahaz needed was not a baby but an army! Certainly our own international scene exhibits similar turbulence and danger. And as ridiculous as it may seem to us also, we Christians too are given by way of guaranteed security only the birth of a child in Bethlehem. Our situation before God is quite similar to that of Judah's in 734–733 b.c.! By pointing out such analogies, the preacher can bring the prophetic oracles very much alive for the congregation.

II. SOME TEXTS TO USE

If the preacher follows the three-year lectionary used by the major church bodies in this country, and if he or she pairs *either* the Gospel *or* the Epistle lesson with the stated Old Testament text, as is intended by that lectionary, the preacher will have occasion to use many texts from the three Isaiahs and Jeremiah. Deutero-Isaiah and Trito-Isaiah especially are quite fully used, many of the passages in Deutero-Isaiah two or three times. Jeremiah is listed less often, and Proto-Isaiah still less, while there are only six passages prescribed from Ezekiel.

The sparse listings from the latter book reflect the difficulty of preaching from Ezekiel, occasioned by the facts that the standard oracular forms have given way in Ezekiel to prose oracles and thirty-two out of its forty-eight chapters are concerned largely with judgment and the destruction of Jerusalem. But the pulpit's neglect of

Ezekiel is partly responsible for the strange apocalyptic interpretations of that book which are appearing in our time: when we in the pulpit neglect some part of the canon, the demons of falsehood and faddism rush in to fill the gap. It therefore would seem wise to use the lectionary with flexibility, following it often but also using other important texts from the Major Prophets, especially when the stated Old Testament reading has been previously used. There is no need to repeat a lesson when such vast treasures from the prophets lie at hand.

Let us now look at some passages that are listed in the lectionary. (For the sake of convenience, I have followed the Lutheran listings.)

For Advent 2B: Isa. 40:1–11. The passage includes the scene in the heavenly council, to which Deutero-Isaiah is privy and in which the heavenly beings are commanded to comfort God's people and to prepare the way on which God will return to Jerusalem (vs. 1–5); the call of the prophet (vs. 6–8); and Deutero-Isaiah's initial preaching (vs. 9–11). Here are but three different announcements from that good news which the preacher might use:

1. "Their warfare is ended" (v. 2). Earlier, through the prophet Jeremiah, Yahweh had declared war against his people's sin and evil. He became their enemy and brought battle and destruction upon them. But now here the battleground is quiet and God pronounces "Peace." In forgiveness and love, he turns from enemy to ally. Has he not done so also in the cross and resurrection of Jesus Christ? "What then shall we say to this? If God is for us, who is against us?" (Rom. 8:31).

2. "All flesh is grass, and all its beauty is like the flower of the field" (v. 6). That is the beginning of the message given to the prophet when he asks, "What shall I preach?" We human beings do have our beauty and glory: We are capable of the deepest loves; we can erect the noblest monuments. But the difficulty is that the grass withers, the flower fades: we die and our greatest achievements turn to dust. One thing remains and does not pass away: the Word of God, which he will fulfill "though heaven and earth pass away." In Deutero-Isaiah's time, God kept his word and Israel was reelected and released from exile. In our time, he will keep his word declared to us in Jesus Christ. (Here let the preacher be very specific.)

3. "Behold your God!" (v. 9). This is the center and climax of the passage. The royal way is prepared (vs. 3–5), and now Yahweh comes upon it. Judah is urged to lift up her eyes and see her God returning to be with her: "Look! There he comes! See him coming to be with

you!" Specifically for Advent, is that not what we await from the birth at Bethlehem? Immanuel? (Matt. 1:23).

For Christmas Day A: Isa. 52:7–10. The passage is based on the ancient Near Eastern practice of sending out runners to announce the enthronement of a new king. The messengers sped forth on foot to announce that "so-and-so has become king!" and that therefore the citizens could expect a new era with new possibilities for good. Thus "how beautiful upon the mountains" were the feet of those speeding messengers! But here it is not the accession of a human king that is announced, but the kingship of God. He reigns over all the world. For the New Testament, he reigns through Jesus Christ. "Hark! the herald angels sing, 'Glory to the newborn King!' "

For Epiphany ABC: Isa. 60:1–6. The lesson is just the beginning of the long oracle of salvation that extends through v. 22. Postexilic Jerusalem, mourning in the dust like a woman grieving over her lost children, is bidden to get up and to be radiant with joy, because all her exiled children will be brought back to her, along with the wealth of the nations (vs. 4–7). But primarily she is to shine forth by reflecting the light of the glory of God, who now dwells in her midst (vs. 1, 19–20). In fellowship with God, she will be righteous and joyful, peaceful and just (vs. 17–18, 21), a beacon light shining forth to the peoples who dwell in darkness (v. 2). So too is the church to be "the light of the world" (Matt. 5:14–16), "a light for the Gentiles" (Acts 13:47), shining "in the midst of a crooked and perverse generation " (Phil. 2:15). The church shines by reflecting the light who is Jesus Christ. She lives in him. She reflects his love and justice, his peace and joy, not her own. And nations are drawn to his light and become members of his people. Surely that is the true work of Epiphany, or "manifestation," of Christ to the world.

For Lent 5A: Ezek. 37:1–14. (Used also for Pentecost B.) The language of this pericope is metaphorical, but it must be interpreted correctly. It does not refer to the death and resurrection of individuals, but to Israel's exile in Babylonia, which meant death to her nationhood and her hope for the future. She has "died" in exile because she has been cut off from the Source of life, the living God. Is that not the story of so many congregations, that they have begun to die or have disappeared because they have lost their relationship as a community with their head, Jesus Christ? The marks of such dying churches are not hard to list: Their worship has turned into subjective concentration on themselves or simply into entertainment. Their social action programs are little more than the application of ethical humanism or attraction to the latest fads. Bible study is nonexistent.

Prayer and disciplined obedience to Christ's commands on the part of the members are lacking. People join the group simply because it is the thing to do, bringing with them their unrepented prides and prejudices. There is little sense among the people of belonging to and caring for one another. There is no lively perception that they are the body of Christ. They are the dead people of God, as Israel was dead in exile, and the question is, "Can these bones live?"

The glad message of the text is that even from such dry bones God can raise up a people for himself, re-creating them as his church, as he created them in the beginning. He poured out his Spirit on the church at its founding. This passage promises that he will pour it out again on any congregation that opens its heart to receive him. Lent, then, marks the renewed dedication of the church to its calling—to be the people of God in Christ through the power of God's promised Spirit.

For Maundy Thursday C: Jer. 31:31–34. (Used also for Lent 5B.) At the last supper before his crucifixion, Jesus offered the cup, after supper, to his disciples, saying, "This cup is the new covenant in my blood" (I Cor. 11:25). He understood his death on the cross as the fulfillment of this promise from Jeremiah. The question then is, What was it that was promised? The passage from Jeremiah is so full that a series of sermons could be preached from it:

1. God here promises to renew his relationship with his people, to restore the covenant fellowship with them that they destroyed by their unfaithfulness. The nature of the relationship is shown by the metaphor for it: God was Israel's loving Husband, she was his wife. That is an astounding statement about the Lord of Hosts! His love for us is the yearning, wooing (cf. Hos. 2:14), intimate love of a faithful husband for his beloved wife. More astounding still is the fact that Israel and we spurn such love and go seeking after other "lovers," who desert us or deceive us or use us.

2. The primary action of God in the new covenant is his forgiveness of us. Despite our unfaithfulness to our divine Husband, he is willing to forgive and forget and take us back. And the sign and seal of that forgiving love is the blood of Christ poured out on the cross. God in Christ cuts the covenant anew. Once again he makes the covenant sacrifice—this time at terrible price to himself and his Son— and he says to us, "You are mine and I am yours."

3. We have no part in that covenant fellowship apart from the people of God, the church. God promised to make the new covenant with his people, not with individuals. That people now is the New Israel in Christ, and if we would enter into relationship with God

through Christ, we must do so as members of his people. Being a Christian implies living in a community of believers. There is no way we can be Christians all by ourselves.

4. But what ensures that we will not prove unfaithful again? In Jeremiah's pictures, obedience will be the result of God's word written upon the heart—the result of an interior, motivating, guiding knowledge and love of God. For the Christian, that inner guidance and motivation are given by Christ's Spirit poured into our hearts, so that it is not we who live, but Christ who lives within us (cf. Gal. 2:20; 4:6–7; 5:22–24). By his Spirit we are enabled to live loving and obedient lives.

For Pentecost 5A: Jer. 20:7–13. What do we do with these "confessions" or, properly, individual laments of Jeremiah's? Three of them are listed in the lectionary, as is his initial call, and these passages are so individual and concrete in their situations and authorship that they seem to defy modern application. We are not prophets. We share neither their direct communication with God nor the newness of their message. Rather, we know God only through the mediation of Jesus Christ, and we preach him crucified and risen, in the long tradition of the church.

Jeremiah has become a "laughingstock" in this passage, because for three years (604–601 B.C.) he has preached God's judgment upon his sinful people (v. 8), and that judgment has not come (cf. 17:15). He is mocked with his own words of doom, "Terror on every side" (20:3, 10; 6:25). Even his friends plot his downfall and death as a false prophet (v. 10). He tries to keep from preaching, but the power of the Word is too great for him and he cannot shut it up inside (v. 9). He therefore accuses God of overpowering him—as a strong man seducing a woman (v. 7)—of deceitfully leading him into a situation of suffering from which there will be no release.

Jeremiah speaks blasphemy, but he utters it where it belongs—in prayer to God. Jeremiah wrestles with the ways of God in the secret place of prayer, as Jesus wrestled with them alone in Gethsemane. Nothing is forbidden in prayer. God sees the heart and mind (v. 12) and the most desperate doubts can be spoken to him.

Certainly every faithful follower of God has come up against Jeremiah's blank wall—the seeming failure of the Word of God to prove true in the world. Like our Lord, we have done God's will and found only a crucifixion at the end of the road.

The Christian who is obedient becomes a laughingstock in this world—make no mistake about it. He is laughed at for suffering an unhappy marriage when divorce would be an easy way out. She is laughed at for refusing to climb the social ladder, when she could afford so easily to do so. He is scorned for the unimportant company he keeps, for not "dressing for success," for insisting on keeping his word, for refusing to ignore the needs of others even though it costs him money. After all, the needs of others cost Jesus his life: the cross is not a good lesson in how to succeed in this world.

"But the LORD is with me as a dread warrior," Jeremiah said (v. 11). Yahweh did bring his judging war on Judah after all. The cross did lead to the resurrection. God does prove true to his Word. With confidence, therefore, we can commit our lives into his hands (vs. 12–13).

For Pentecost 19A: Ezek. 18:25–32. In his book *Whatever Became of Sin?* Karl Menninger pointed out that the central fault of our society today is an unwillingness to accept responsibility. It has ever been so with the human race (cf. Gen. 3:11–13); we always try to pass the blame: " 'They' are at fault"; "my environment has warped me"; "I have a psychological hang-up"; "My parents didn't raise me right"; "I'm not really like that"; "I'm not myself today; it must be the pressure."

So too in this passage, Israel in exile blames someone else for her predicament: "We are suffering for the sins of our fathers," they say, quoting a popular proverb (v. 2). "Therefore it is not just for God to punish us" (vs. 25, 29).

"Not so!" the Word of the Lord comes back. "You suffer for your own transgressions. All souls are mine. The soul that sins shall die, but the wicked person who turns and does what is right shall save his life" (vs. 4, 27).

In short, this passage is proclamation of two facts: (1) Like Israel, we are responsible to God for what we do, because we belong to him, and we cannot escape that responsibility. It is inherent in our creaturehood. (2) But in his incredible mercy, and despite anything we have done in the past, God will forgive and accept us and give us new life if we turn away from evil toward him. "For I have no pleasure in the death of any one, says the Lord GOD; so turn, and live" (v. 32). Far from being a legalistic calculation of our just rewards, this passage is a proclamation of the overriding mercy of God. As Paul put it for us Christians, "For the wages of sin is death, but the free gift of God is eternal life in Christ Jesus our Lord" (Rom. 6:23).

For Pentecost 20A: Isa. 5:1–7. The prophets constantly rehearse God's loving acts toward Israel in the past (cf. Jer. 2:5–7; Ezek. 16:1–14). This parable, put in the form of a folk song sung at the grape harvest, sets forth the care and attention lavished on Israel, here described in the metaphor of God's vineyard (cf. Ps. 80:8–11; Isa. 27:2–6; Mark 12:1–12 and pars.; John 15:1). When we look back on all that God has done in Jesus Christ for the church and for us in our own personal lives, we can identify with the history of love here recounted.

The expectation of farmers who labor over a crop is that it will bear good fruit, just as the expectation of parents who have poured out themselves for their children is that the children will grow up to be good persons. But instead, Israel has produced rotten fruit—injustice and violence in her society. And we children of God, despite all his care for us, have turned out self-centered and sinful. Do we not then deserve God's punishment as Israel deserved it? Jesus announced such judgment on those who bear evil fruit (Matt. 7:16–20).

The prophets used Israel's past history with God in this fashion to show how astounding was Israel's sin as her response to the love of God. More astounding still, however, is God's love that will not let us go, but that took our sin upon itself in the cross of Jesus Christ.

FOR FURTHER READING

Achtemeier, Elizabeth. *The Community and Message of Isaiah 56–66.* Augsburg Publishing House, 1982.

———. *Deuteronomy, Jeremiah.* Proclamation Commentaries. Fortress Press, 1978.

Anderson, Bernhard W. *The Eighth Century Prophets: Amos, Hosea, Isaiah, Micah.* Proclamation Commentaries. Fortress Press, 1978.

Eichrodt, Walther. *Theology of the Old Testament.* Vols. 1 and 2. Tr. J. A. Baker. The Old Testament Library. Westminster Press, 1961, 1967.

Mays, James Luther. *Ezekiel, Second Isaiah.* Proclamation Commentaries. Fortress Press, 1978.

Rad, Gerhard von. *Old Testament Theology,* Vol. 2. Tr. D. M. G. Stalker. Harper & Row, 1965.

8. PREACHING FROM THE MINOR PROPHETS

ERIC C. RUST

When preachers deal with the prophets of the Old Testament, they need to remember that they are dealing with people of their own genre. The prophets were fundamentally preachers, proclaimers, forthtellers. It is true that they possessed unique qualities of insight and understanding and that they filled a distinctive and necessary niche in the historical movement of the divine revelation. Yet they also possessed those personal gifts and distinctive qualities which even today should characterize one who dares to proclaim the Word of the Lord.

THE NATURE AND PLACE OF PROPHECY

Let us note certain characteristic features. The prophet regarded himself as one who had been sent by God and who had shared in the divine counsels. He had a divinely given insight into the mind and purpose of God. He was indeed an extension of the divine personality into history. God had lifted him temporarily into his own immanent presence in the historical scene, so that he became God's mouthpiece. God's Word was enshrined in his words. This meant that the prophet saw and heard more than his fellows. The divine presence lighted up sights like a plumb line for Amos (Amos 7:7–9) with deeper meaning. God lifted human experiences and relationships into his purpose and made them disclosures of his own nature and intention, as in the family relations of Hosea (Hos. 1–3). God sensitized a prophet's senses so that auditions and visions occurred, filled with divine import, as in the hypnagogic visions of Zechariah. Ordinary occurrences carried messages of the divine activity in history, so that, for

Joel, the plague of locusts became the advance guard of the divine judgment (Joel 1:4ff.). We preachers still have the responsibility of awakening our people to the spiritual depth in history and the divine background to their lives. That is possible only if we have such a communion with the unseen Presence that we can trace his ways in life's storms and find his gracious purpose, in judgment and in mercy, within our common life. This was the peculiar gift of the prophets whom we are studying.

These prophets find their focal point in Israel's worship, although many of them were by no means professionals. From the early days of Israel's history, prophetic figures like Samuel, Elijah, and Elisha were associated with prophetic guilds, schools of prophets in which undoubtedly professional traits were developed and characteristic modes of prophesying were practiced. There is every evidence that, in the early days, two forms of prophesying began to develop and ultimately to diverge, although the Hebrew word for prophet, *nābī'*, seems ultimately to have covered all. There was the ecstatic type of prophet who threw himself into a frenzy, manifested highly emotional behavior, and seems often to have prophesied in ecstatic utterances that later had to be turned into rational speech. He might be compared to contemporary charismatics. Dancing and music often accompanied such manifestations. The more rational type was the precursor of the great literary prophets—Isaiah, Jeremiah, Ezekiel, and the twelve prophets now being considered. In these persons, the emotional and ecstatic elements are present, but they are pushed out to the periphery of the consciousness, and the processes of rational judgment and interpretative thought occupy the center of the prophet's consciousness. There is, however, the same preoccupation with mystic vision and the same sense of divine presence. Like Amos, such prophets believed themselves to be called (Amos 7:14f.). They felt themselves to be under such a divine pressure that they had to declare the Word which had come to them. Amos felt this and declared it in one of his great utterances, likening the internal pressure of God's Word to the various daunting pressures of the natural environment such as the lion's roar (Amos 3:3–8). Once the Word of the Lord came to them, they had to declare it, and so these Minor Prophets begin their collections of oracles with the words: "The word of the Lord which came to . . ." (Zeph. 1:1; Hos. 1:1; Hag. 1:1; Zech. 1:1). This should be true of the modern preacher.

Because there was a professional body of prophets, often described by scholars as "cultic prophets," we may expect that such would be included in the group of literary prophets, and it would appear that Nahum was such a person, as also were many of the psalmists. Amos declares that he is not a professional (Amos 7:14). Generally the great prophetic figures like Isaiah and Jeremiah and the so-called Minor Prophets like Amos, Hosea, Micah, and Zephaniah seem to have been laypersons who heard the divine call within their secular vocations. We need to remember, however, that their utterances, like those of the modern preacher, often required the setting of worship.

THE LITERARY FORMS AND COMPOSITION
OF THE PROPHETIC WRITINGS

These utterances took definite forms and all these forms are to be found in the prophetic writings that we are considering. The general content of the prophetic messages can be characterized as either pronouncements of judgment or promises of mercy. Grace and judgment, demands for moral and social righteousness and declarations of divine love, calls for repentance and offers of divine forgiveness—these are focal in the prophetic utterances. The prophet, like the apostle Paul later and as should be true of every modern preacher, called on his hearers to behold both the kindness and the severity of God (Rom. 11:22). Divine wrath and divine grace provided the poles between whose tension the prophetic thought operated. Hence we find oracles of reproach, sometimes beginning with "Woe" (Amos 6:1ff.), and sometimes with the phrase "hear this word" (Amos 4:1–3). Attached to such oracles of reproach we often find an oracle of doom taking the form of a threat. This begins with "therefore" and details the consequences of disobedience (Amos 6:7ff.). Sometimes the oracle of doom or threat follows a statement of such disobedience and is introduced by the word "because." This form appears in the oracles of Amos 1 and 2. In Zeph. 1:2–2:3, we have a series of oracles of doom or judgment. Thirdly, the oracle takes the form of a divine lawsuit, in which God stands over against his people and imagines them before a tribunal at which the forces of nature are often called in as judges (Micah 6:1–8). Fourthly, we find oracles of admonition in which the divine wrath is tempered by mercy and where salvation begins to sound through the message of doom. Here the characteristic introduction is the phrase "hear this word." There follows a call to repent, to turn back to the Lord and so to avoid the approaching judgment (Amos 5:1ff., 14–15; Hos. 14:1ff.). In Zephaniah 3 we have a series of such oracles that begin with threat and finish with promise.

In some sense they belong to this type of oracle, yet there is also present a pure oracle of promise at the end. Finally, we have a form that some scholars characterize as the prophetic *torah,* or law, a statement of moral principle that is grounded in the divine demand. The structure is similar to that of the laws elsewhere, as in the Pentateuch (Micah 6:6–8). Sometimes such *toroth* are combined with oracles of reproach as in Hos. 6:4–6.

The present literary form of the prophetic writings probably finds its origin in the matrix of devoted disciples who gathered and remembered the oracles of their prophetic leaders and committed them to writing. We may conjecture that every prophetic figure had such a group of disciples, and that such a circle would collect and treasure the utterances of their central figure. Such oracles may sometimes have been transmitted orally and committed to writing in a later time. Others may soon have taken literary form, even in the prophet's own lifetime. We know that Isaiah bound up his testimony, a collection of his oracles, among his disciples (Isa. 8:16). Jeremiah certainly committed many of his oracles to writing through Baruch the scribe (Jer. 36), and the contents of this roll can be sorted out from the larger collection that forms his prophecy.

The experience and the memory of the master certainly lie as a focus of inspiration behind the writings that we are considering. In consequence, we find biographical and sometimes autobiographical passages inserted in the collections of oracles, in addition to the historical material often provided at the beginning of the prophetic books. Thus Amos 7:10ff. adds considerably to our knowledge of Amos. Again, Hosea contains a biographical section in ch. 1 and an autobiographical section in ch. 3. We must not assume that the oracles are given in any sequence that corresponds to their actual temporal utterance. When oracles occur within a biographical or an autobiographical section, their position in the prophet's life is easy to place. This is also true when an oracle is prefaced by a specific note that fixes its time and location. More often the oracles are assembled without chronological or topical unity. Sometimes they are grouped together because they have similar themes. They often occur without any preface, and then they may not be identified by reference to adjacent oracles. Sometimes the method of association seems to be the catch-word principle. Thus Amos 7:7–9 is probably connected with Amos 7:10ff. because "Jeroboam" occurs in both v. 9 and v. 10.

Undoubtedly the oracles of such leading figures were remembered and utilized within the public worship of the Temple. Indeed, cultic needs may have contributed to the collection and editing of the prophetic collections. Such oracles would not be merely stored as historical memories but actually recited on appropriate occasions in Israel's worship. This would explain why the oracle on the mountain of the Lord's house occurs in both the Isaianic collection (Isa. 2:2–4) and among the oracles of Micah (4:1–3). This may well have been a detached oracle upon the significance of the postexilic Temple as a center of worship, and thereby found a place in both collections because of its relevance to cultic recitation.

This accounts for how the prophetic oracles that were uttered to a specific historical situation were yet retained in memory and in written form. They were preserved in a worshiping community because they were relevant to the needs and to the changing historical situations of the people. This held true because such oracles contained an eternal Word of God which was relevant to every age. There was a divine activity within the worshiping community which awakened insight into that eternal Word and applied it to a new historical situation. This, of course, is true of us preachers, for we take an oracle uttered between two and three millennia ago and find in it a relevant divine word to our own contemporary conditions. The words of the prophet can still contain a relevant Word of God, and within the worshiping community the divine Spirit awakens insight and understanding in the hearers.

The reference above to editing is a reminder that such prophetic writings were undoubtedly shaped and selected for the needs of the cultus. Hence, at later times, independent oracles were added to the original prophetic collection. Such additions can often be identified because they contain historical references to a time much later than that of the prophet himself. A good example is afforded by the passage at the end of Amos—Amos 9:11ff. The reference to the booth of David *that has fallen* obviously refers to the fall of Solomon's Temple and belongs to the period of the exile. It would be added because it corrected the oracles of doom that dominate the utterances of Amos, and offered an oracle of promise and deliverance.

THE HISTORICAL AND SOCIAL SETTINGS
OF THE MINOR PROPHETS

The minor literary prophets cover a long stretch of Israel's history. Indeed, prophesying was a religious phenomenon in that history from the early beginnings of the Hebrew nation. Moses was the first such prophetic figure and there was a long line of these people until the first literary prophets emerged with Amos, Hosea, Isaiah, and Micah in the eighth century B.C. In this group the towering figure is Isaiah, but we are concerned with the other three.

At the time of this group, the Hebrew people had long been divided into two nations—the southern entity of Judah and the northern entity of Israel. The former centered in Jerusalem and was ruled over by a continuous succession of Davidic kings of varying moral character, religious commitment, and monarchical ability. Israel, on the other hand, was ruled over by a series of kings whose dynasties were short-lived. Samaria was its capital city. The two national groups kept up the hostility that had split them asunder on the death of Solomon, and this foolish state of affairs opened them to the interference of their powerful neighbors.

The Hebrew peoples found themselves wedged between two world powers—Assyria and Egypt. In addition, the smaller nation of Syria, centered in Damascus, was a troublesome neighbor to the north of Israel, bordering directly on the imperial and aggressive Assyria. The three small nations—Israel, Judah, and Syria—rarely agreed among themselves, but they usually lined themselves up to play off Assyria and Egypt. The latter, by the proximity to Judah, was a powerful influence in Jerusalem. Israel and Syria, although often warring with each other, lived in fear of Assyria.

This meant that the political and social life of the Hebrew peoples was subject to external influences and always lived under the threat of invasion and national extinction. In such stirring and eventful days, the prophetic consciousness is stimulated. Faith in the unseen divine activity and hope of a divinely effected deliverance are brought to the surface. It is significant that the prophesying which we are considering flourished until the Babylonian exile of the sixth century B.C., and then began to wane. This waning of the quality and content of the prophetic consciousness is seen as we move through the Minor Prophets until with Haggai, Zechariah, Joel, Obadiah, and Malachi we see the prophetic insight disappearing. No great events were stirring, and apocalyptic arose with its heavy emphasis on the future. This still holds of modern preaching. Our messages can become tame when they are not thrown against the backdrop of political, social, and international movements that are influential in the lives of our hearers. It is not easy to preach to a complacent and indifferent people, who live in a lotus land of ease where no cold wind blows. When people are settling back like wine on the lees, as Jeremiah describes them (Jer. 48:11), or when they are indifferent about the divine activity as Zephaniah pictures them (Zeph. 1:12), they are not open to the searching, judging, and redeeming message of the Christian gospel. We might describe it as the country-club mentality.

Amos and Hosea were prophets to Israel. Micah was a contemporary of Isaiah in Judah. Both Amos and Hosea prophesied to the Northern Kingdom on the reign of Jeroboam II, somewhere in the period around 745 B.C. They were slightly before Isaiah began his ministry, although they overlapped it. They came at a time when Assyria was suffering from internal disruption and dynastic change. Because its power was weakened, both Israel and Judah entered upon a period of unexampled prosperity with all its accompanying corruption. The latter was the stimulating factor in the prophetic consciousness. Amos and Hosea between them provide a picture of the state of affairs—wealth and prosperity contrasted with poverty and oppression, exploitation of the poor (Amos 2:6; 4:1; 5:11; 8:6), rapacious landowners (8:4), a debilitating love of luxury and increasing drunkenness (6:4–6; 3:12, 15; 4:1), false commercial dealing (8:5), and corruption and bribery in the system of justice (5:10, 12). With all of this we find a corruption of religion. Ritual prostitution and naturalistic fertility cults had debased the pure Yahwism of the desert days (2:7). Calf worship and idolatry had replaced the imageless religion of Israel, and Yahweh was even worshiped in the image of a bull, with its fertility associations (Hos. 8:4–6; 10:5; 11:2; 13:2). Add to this, political machinations with the two great imperial powers of Egypt and Assyria, so that Israel and Judah had become the cockpit of the nations. Both Amos and Hosea saw judgment as imminent. Hosea seems to have identified Assyria more clearly as the divine instrument of this. Damascus fell in 732 B.C., and ten years later Samaria followed suit (722 B.C.). Syria and Israel disappeared from the historical scene, and Judah was left alone.

The corruption of Israel as well as its temporary prosperity was felt in Judah, as Isaiah and Micah indicate. Now Assyria was on Judah's doorstep, and we find Micah dealing with this. This prophet faced the covetous absorption of lands (Micah 2:1ff.), the oppression of the poor (3:11), the bribery of judges (7:3), and the corruption of religious leaders (3:9–12). He scathingly attacked prophets who were not willing to become unpopular (3:5ff.)—a warning to us preachers! For him judgment was sure for Jerusalem as well as Samaria (1:5ff., 12).

Judah rested back for a century under political machinations that set Egypt against Assyria and with attempts to buy off the evil day of invasion. With Jeremiah's time, things came to a head, and it is to this period that his lesser contemporary, Zephaniah, belongs. Assyria was in the midst of a convulsive dynastic change at the end of the seventh century B.C. In 612 B.C., Nineveh fell and the Assyrian power passed into the hands of the Babylonians. Babylon now replaced Nineveh, but the same aggressive imperialism was regnant. Nahum celebrates the fall of Nineveh in a long poem that may have been a part of a cultic liturgy. Assyria's weakness allowed marauding Scythian hosts to sweep down from the north. Their invasion stimulated the prophetic consciousness in Jeremiah and probably did the same for Zephaniah. The latter's attack on pagan preachers (Zeph. 1:4–6, 8–9) suggests that he prophesied prior to the Josianic reformation of 621 B.C. Habakkuk also belongs to this period. P. Humbert suggests that this prophetic working may have achieved its present form because it was edited for cultic purposes.

No minor prophet functions across the exilic period (588–538 B.C.). With the return, the dominant power is Persia. Cyrus has overthrown Babylon, and his tolerant policy has allowed the Jews to return from exile and rebuild Jerusalem. Haggai and Zechariah (Zech. 1–8) supported the Jewish prince Zerubbabel when more exiles returned to Jerusalem in 520 B.C. They advocated the rebuilding of the Temple, and based the rising inflation upon the neglect of erecting this center of Jewish faith and worship. Something might be made of Haggai's description of inflation (Hag. 1:5–11). This at least the modern preacher can empathize with!

No great figure or important international event stirred the historical scene between this period and the advent of Alexander the Great in 331 B.C. Both Obadiah and Malachi seem to have been stimulated by a comparatively minor event—the fall of Edom before the Nabatean Arabs (Obad. 1–14; Mal. 1:2–5). Joel is stirred by a plague of locusts that affected the daily sacrifices of the Temple (Joel 1:9, 13). Apocalyptic hopes began to arise. A transcendent divine inbreak replaced the activity of God within the historical process in Joel (3:9–16), and this goes further as Deutero-Zechariah (Zech. 9–14) is stimulated by the approaching invasion of the Greeks under Alexander the Great (especially ch. 12).

THE THEOLOGICAL EMPHASES OF THE MINOR PROPHETS

A close examination of these twelve prophetic writings discloses the same basic faith in the God who had established a covenant relation with the Hebrew people. This is specifically affirmed by Amos (Amos 2:10; 3:1–2) and Hosea (Hos. 2:15ff.; 11:1–4; 13:4f.). God is the electing God. He had chosen the Hebrews for his people, called them, loved them, for he is a God who acts in history. Micah echoes the same theme (Micah 6:4).

But God is not the God of the Hebrew peoples only. He is the God of the whole earth, the Lord of history. In Amos the implicit monotheism of Moses becomes explicit. In a remarkable series of oracles, the prophet arraigns all the neighboring peoples before the divine tribunal. He comes to Judah with words of condemnation and then brings all the fierce powers of his attack to a focus on the Northern Kingdom of Israel (Amos 1 and 2). The skillful build-up, which might cause his hearers to rejoice at the condemnation of their neighbors in Damascus, Edom, Moab, Philistia, Phoenicia, and even the Southern Kingdom of Judah, is suddenly turned on them in scathing accusation (2:6–16). A useful psychological device for the modern preacher who may subtly attack the obvious sins of others, only to bring home the wrongdoings, not so obvious, of his hearers! This thought of God's universal rule is brought home in those prophetic oracles which attack foreign nations in the name of Yahweh. We find Zephaniah attacking Philistia, Moab, Ethiopia, and Assyria (Zeph. 2), for they are subject to God's rule.

These men were not afraid to bring international intrigue and national wrongdoing before the bar of the divine justice, for God ruled over all peoples. Political machinations, social injustice, and economic exploitation among their own people were also under his aegis. They were not afraid to awaken the conscience and sense of guilt among their hearers, though it meant opposition and even persecution. We can learn from them to paint a much broader canvas for our people than a mere gospel of individual salvation would supply. God's saving health and his judgment apply to the complex personal interrelationships of modern society and to international relationships at the economic and political levels. Woe to us if we seek to please and forget the Word of God which should burn within our hearts (Jer. 20:9)!

God is the Lord of history, but he is also Creator and Lord of nature. These prophets lived close to nature, and recognized that its changing seasons and tempestuous movements could serve God's purposes (cf. Amos 4:7–9). Hosea paints a remarkable picture of the way in which, through a chain of psychic response, God would provide for the needs of Jezreel (Hos. 2:21–22). Nature, man, and God can work together in cooperative unity—a useful basis for a sermon on ecology! Amos utters three doxologies in which he announces God as the creator of the constellations of the stars (Amos 5:8), as the Lord of the sun who controls its eclipses (8:9), as the one who forms the mountains and creates the wind (4:13), and as he who calls for the waters of the sea and pours them on the earth (5:8; 9:6). For Joel, a plague of locusts serves as the advance guard of the day of divine judgment (Joel 1:4ff.). The theme is implied that even nature hits back at us when we break our covenant with nature and do not act responsibly before our creator! How relevant this is to one aspect of our contemporary dilemma!

The prophetic vision of God as Lord of history is closely bound up with the understanding of human sin and divine judgment. The characteristic description of the divine character as righteous is central in this understanding. Yahweh is a righteous God because he abides true to himself. His character sets the norm for all human conduct. To enter into a covenant relationship with him means obedience to his righteous will. Hence the Law, the Torah, became a codification of the divine requirements at every level of life. To this process of development prophets, priests, and lawmakers all made their contribution. The prophets were especially sensitive to Yahweh's righteous demands, and were sure that disobedience to and rejection of them brought men under the divine judgment. A vision of Amos sets the plumb line of God's righteousness against man's wayward erections (Amos 7:7ff.). Micah declares what Yahweh requires of us—moral rectitude, kindness to others, humility before God (Micah 6:8). Repeatedly these prophets remind us that the outward cultic ritual and its sacrifices are not sufficient. Moral behavior and steadfast love are what really matter (Hos. 6:6; Amos 5:21–24; Micah 6:6f.). It is no use seeking the shrine if they are not seeking Yahweh (Amos 5:4–6). What an indictment of our civil religion! We need still to remind our hearers that sincerity in worship can only be measured by rectitude of conduct. Religious practice and ethical behavior alike turn upon the inwardness and reality of a person's commitment.

The sin that the prophets attack is most often corporate and social, political and international, concerned more with antisocial conduct than with inner motivation and intention. Amos attacks sin*s*, acts of sin. He describes Israel as in rebellion *(pesha')* against God, but he is not concerned with its inner inclination. The outward expression is what matters, so he speaks of rebellion*s*, transgression*s*, sin*s*, rather than sin (Amos 3:2). It is Hosea who penetrates deeper and describes sin as a spirit of whoredom within (Hos. 4:12; 5:4). Israel's sin permeates their being. Their evildoings have taken away their "heart," and for the Hebrew the heart was the center of volition (4:11). With a weakened will, men become prisoners of their evil desires. In Whittier's words, "habit bound, their feet lack the power to turn." Even their repentance is shallow and goes away like the morning dew (6:4). In such vivid pictures, the prophet is describing our own current dilemma. Here is a basis for preaching on sin and for the relevance of the gospel, the gospel for which Hosea and the other prophets longed and hoped, as they waited for God to fulfill his promise to the fathers and finally establish his kingdom in the day of the Lord. When that day dawned with the coming of Jesus, he emphasized yet more deeply the inwardness of sin and the emptiness of mere outward protestation and behavior (Matt. 15:18–20; 6:1–7; 7:21–23).

So the prophets were, until the exile, prophets of doom. The Minor Prophets who came after the exile speak less of judgment and more of hope. The exile brought new visions, but until that cataclysmic event, the prophets dealt with a people who, heedless of warning, headed into judgment. Perhaps Amos and Zephaniah of all these prophets were messengers of dire judgment. A righteous God must exercise justice. Habakkuk, in a series of "Woes," sees the process of judgment working out in people's lives. Their sin brings its own dire consequences. Sin is self-destructive. A useful emphasis in preaching! What a man builds in his pride comes back on him (Hab. 2:9–11). The cup of evil and suffering which a man forces on his fellows becomes, in the end, a cup he has to drink (2:15–17). Our people need to be reminded that this is a moral universe. The judgment of God is seen in that he allows sin to bring about its own destruction. The prophets saw this and looked upon historical forces like Assyria and Babylon as the instruments of divine judgment. Only the postexilic prophets moved toward apocalyptic and pictured the ultimate judgment as a catastrophic inbreak of God himself, directly intervening.

This emphasis on the Final Judgment is paramount in Amos and Zephaniah. Amos offers little hope for Israel, although he speaks of a remnant that may survive the Final Judgment (Amos 5:15; 9:8). Yahweh is pictured as relenting twice of his judgment at the plea of the prophet, but finally his wrath is unmitigated (7:2–6; 8:2). The final day when God's sovereignty will be made plain, the day of the Lord, will be darkness and not light (5:18–20). Israel must not place reliance solely upon the promise to the fathers. Election and covenant require obedience. Profession without consonant behavior is not sufficient. Church membership, a plot in the burial yard, munificent subscriptions—such artifices are not final qualifying criteria. The prophetic message is so relevant! So, in a key passage, Amos cries that justice should roll down like waters and righteousness like a mighty flood (5:24). Zephaniah portrays the Lord as searching out Jerusalem with lamps when the day of the Lord supervenes in Final Judgment (Zeph. 1:10–13). He points to the imminence of the great day of the Lord in vivid language, so awe-inspiring that it became the inspiration of Dies Irae, the medieval hymn written by Thomas of Celano:

> Day of wrath! O day of mourning!
> See fulfilled the prophets' warning,
> Heaven and earth in ashes burning!

In the light of this, Zephaniah attacks the contemporary corruption (1:14–18). Yet even he promises a salvation beyond the convulsive judgment. For him, Babylon is the final instrument of the day, as Assyria was for Amos. God's finale occurred in the continuity of history and through historical forces. Amos, Zephaniah, and Nahum bring all nations under the divine wrath.

This brings us to the message of hope in these prophetic writings. The prophetic message rested upon the divine covenant which created the Hebrew nation as God's people. Hence underlying their theme of judgment and their call to repentance, there is the continuing conviction that the Lord is a God of mercy and grace. This is manifest in the continuing call to repent. Hosea was a prophet of judgment, but out of his own marriage experience he learned the meaning of divine love in the covenant with Israel. He saw Yahweh as a God of grace. God had loved Israel as a son (Hos. 11:1ff.), and betrothed Israel to him as a wife (ch. 2). The election love that brought them up out of Egypt had remained as covenant love within the covenant. They had rebelled and betrayed his covenant, but he had remained faithful. If only they would repent and keep their covenant obligations, he would display his mercy. Even in the processes of judgment, he was agonizing with them, pleading for repentance and steadfast, covenant love (6:1–6). They might go out into the wilderness, but he would woo them again (2:14ff.). Even the Valley of Achor, of judgment, would be a door of hope. What a theme for a sermon! The last word for a righteous God would be mercy, not judgment (14:1–7). From afar, Hosea caught a glimpse of Calvary, of God as suffering, redeeming love.

Despite the gloomy and dire predictions of the earlier Minor Prophets, we have seen that they hoped that ultimate salvation would come. Amos and Hosea had a larger reference for their hopes, even though the Northern Kingdom vanished from history in 722 B.C. The Minor Prophets were not foretellers but forthtellers. They were not furnished with a crystal ball. But God did disclose to them enough of his redemptive purpose for them to grasp some aspect of it. They were not given the insight into the task of the Suffering Servant, as was Deutero-Isaiah, nor into the cutting of a new covenant, as was Jeremiah, except for Hosea. But they did grasp the truth of a redeemed remnant and painted a glorious future when the day of the Lord had dawned (Amos 5:15; Hos. 2:14ff.; 14:4–7; Micah 2:12f.; 4:6ff.; Zeph. 3:9–20). The hope of a coming Davidic ruler, a Messiah, was a part of the pattern of their hope (Micah 5:1–9—I regard this as authentic Micah). Haggai can describe the Messiah as the Signet (Hag. 2:23), and Proto-Zechariah (Zech. 1–8) describes him as the Branch (3:8; 6:12). Both, coming immediately after the return from the Babylonian exile, tend to see that return as the advent of the final day. In consequence, they identified the Messiah with the governor Zerubbabel, himself a prince of the Davidic line, even though appointed by the Persians. These hopes vanished as Zerubbabel mysteriously disappeared from history. They reappeared as the heaven-sent Son of Man in apocalyptic with its transcendent emphasis.

This movement to apocalyptic and catastrophic divine inbreak is reflected in Joel and Deutero-Zechariah. God now intervenes directly in human affairs and there is a world cataclysm. For Joel the plague of locusts is regarded as the advance guard of the day of the Lord. The latter is portrayed as Yahweh sitting in the "valley of decision" and passing judgment on the nations of the earth. This judgment takes the form of a battle in which the heathen nations are destroyed as God intervenes with cosmic upheaval (Joel 3:9–16). Then comes the "golden age" with Jerusalem exalted, Judah prosperous, and the surrounding nations a desolation. God becomes a tabernacling presence in the holy mountain (vs. 17–21). In all this, the outpouring of the Spirit becomes central accompanied by the democratization of the prophetic consciousness (2:28f.). Preaching sees this actualized at Pentecost and in the church! Obadiah (Obad. 15–21) reflects the eschatological theme in a lesser way.

Here we have universality of judgment, but no hope for the other nations. Amos quite early had proclaimed that God had chosen other nations besides the Hebrews. He had called the Philistines from Caphtor and the Syrians from Kir (Amos 9:7). This universalistic vision is echoed in Deutero-Isaiah's vision of the Suffering Servant. By contrast, in Deutero-Zechariah (Zech. 9–14), we have a developing apocalyptic with a far less universalistic note. Again, we have a direct divine intervention and natural upheavals in which the heathen nations will be overthrown (chs. 12; 14). Yet in the glorious consummation that follows, even the survivors of the heathen nations will share in the worship of Jerusalem, but it will be under threat and duress (14:16ff.).

It remains for The Book of Jonah to sound a more universalistic note, and to this we shall turn in the next section. The Book of Malachi shows narrow exclusiveness in its attitudes to marriages of Jews with foreign wives, and yet it also offers one of the most majestic descriptions of Yahweh as the God whom all people can worship (Mal. 1:11). Another great preaching text with real relevance to our current scene!

HOMILETIC DEVELOPMENTS AND POSSIBILITIES

HABAKKUK 2:1. WHEN GOD'S WAY SEEMS UNEQUAL

Habakkuk, in dialogue with Yahweh, raises the issue of the triumph of evil and violence (Hab. 1:2ff.). Where is the divine judgment? This issue of the success of evil and the apparent silence of God is still with us. We can still draw modern analogues of the evils the prophet attacks from idolatry to exploitation (2:6–19). The divine answer is to point to the Chaldeans as the instruments of the divine judgment (1:5–11). Again, we need to emphasize the reality of historical judgment today. Communism in Russia was a judgment on the tyrannical czarist regime. It is still a judgment on the West with its abnormal contrast of the haves and have-nots and its economic exploitation. Judgment is writ large on history. In the end, sin destroys itself (2:6–19). Emphasize that man is a moral being and that the created order is moral to the core. (This emphasis would be good also for a sermon on Amos 5:24.)

Again, however, the prophet raises his complaint. The instrument of judgment is itself unjust. The Chaldeans act as ruthlessly as the enemies that they overthrew, and the righteous still go to the wall. This problem, too, confronts us. The innocent suffer with the guilty. The historical forces that execute judgment are no more righteous than the evil powers that they destroy.

The prophet retires to his watchtower and waits on God for an answer (Hab. 2:1). The way of the Lord seems unequal, despite the assurance that God's judgment is at work. The prophet does, in so doing, gain fresh insight.

1. The stand on faithfulness. "The just shall live by faith." The righteous will remain faithful to their vision of God's moral being, whatever be the cost they have to pay. "Faith" in this context means faithfulness. The just must abide faithful to God and moral righteous-

ness, whatever be the consequences. Here they will take their stand, wait on God, and rest upon the assurance of God's righteousness. Such assurance grows, for we know that God stands with us. He is faithful who promised.

2. God's final triumph (Hab. 3). The prophet sees God coming in majestic power to the aid of his people, accompanied by cosmic upheaval. In the end the trust in God's faithfulness and moral righteousness will be vindicated. We have experienced what the prophet did not, the historical beginning of that final triumph, God's coming in judgment and in mercy in Jesus. In our Lord and his cross, the final triumph of the divine righteousness was initiated. Here D-day was fought and V-day will surely come. God has marched from Edom, his garments stained with the blood of Calvary, and the final disclosure of righteousness is also a disclosure of grace.

3. The missing note—the place of redemptive suffering. The prophet's concern with justice missed what the ultimate disclosure in Jesus makes plain—God's triumph is redemptive. Grace means that in a moral universe God's Son bears the judgment himself. This vindication of moral righteousness through redemptive suffering implies that the righteous find their place in that life-style. We are members one of another so that the innocent suffer with the guilty. Habakkuk had not Deutero-Isaiah's vision of the Suffering Servant, actualized in Jesus, that the suffering of the innocent, who share in the judgment of the guilty, has redemptive significance. We, too, must take up our cross, and make up what is lacking in Christ's sufferings.

ZEPHANIAH 1:12f.; 3:12f. THE CHALLENGE OF CYNICAL INDIFFERENCE

The prophet Zephaniah was addressing a generation that was on the edge of doom. Yet it was so unaware of this that it was cynically indifferent to the moral nature of the universe. He likened it to wine which settled on its lees, rested back upon its sediment. It needed to be strained and purified. The people were satisfied with the present state of things. They lived at ease with wickedness in its many forms. They were permissive of evil, for they ignored the presence of any moral standard enthroned in the heavens. God, if he existed, would do no good and would do no evil.

This situation is comparable to our own secular and permissive society, in which people live as if God were not a reality. They live, like the people of Judah, for the passing moment, its pleasures and its possessions. They have a naturalistic attitude that accepts no behavioral imperatives other than social pressures and material value.

The prophet was sure that this is a moral universe. God had his times when his judgment would become evident. Most of all, history was heading for a climacteric time, when his presence would be made plain. Zephaniah looked for that dread day, and painted an awesome picture of this "day of Yahweh." It may well have been a combination of the Scythian raiding parties and the ultimate advent of Babylon. Here was the imminent time of God.

1. Such a time of judgment will be a time of exposure, when sin and wickedness will be exposed. God will search out Jerusalem with lamps. The hidden cancer of Judah will be exposed. The wine will be poured out. Jesus saw a moral necessity in the universe. There is nothing hidden, he declared, that shall not be revealed. Judgment is exposure and unveiling. As Toynbee saw it, society disintegrates and falls apart. Men learn that the wages of sin is death.

2. Such a time is also a time of purging. The wine must be poured from vessel to vessel, freed of its sediment and purified. All is not darkness. There will be left in Israel, after the judgment, a remnant of those who call on the name of the Lord (Zeph. 3:12f.). Beyond the judgment lies redemption. Death always leads to resurrection—that is the pattern of Calvary, and it is always the way of God's grace. The purging will lead to the emergence of a new people of God.

3. Zephaniah's picture was fully actualized when the final day of Yahweh dawned with the life, death, and resurrection of Jesus of Nazareth. Here the cross symbolizes our judgment and the resurrection brings promise of a new people of God, a remnant of those who have been redeemed by God's gracious act in his Son. All prophetic oracles refer to more than just the time when they were uttered. Jesus the Christ is *the* time of all God's times, the climacteric event in which all God's creative, judgmental, and redemptive activity is brought to a focus. It is the final unveiling, when the lamps are replaced by him who is the light of the world.

HOSEA 2:7, 14. GOD'S KIND OF LOVE

Hosea's call appears to have come through his own marriage experience. This is recorded in the biographical ch. 1 and the autobiographical ch. 3. We shall accept the interpretation that the record of the first chapter precedes chronologically the event of the third chapter (for details, see E. C. Rust, *Covenant and Hope*, pp. 58ff., or any contemporary commentary on Hosea). The prophet married a woman, Gomer, who subsequently became a prostitute, possibly associated with a religious shrine since Yahwism had taken on a naturalistic connotation, reflecting the fertility cults of the contemporary world. Hosea had, however, sought her out and redeemed her from her sinful existence. In so doing, he had manifested a suffering and redeeming love which became also a revelation of God's love for Israel.

The key to the movement of revelation lies in the fact that marriage constituted a covenant relationship which was supremely patterned in God's relationship to his people. Such a relationship was characterized by mutual obligations and commitments by the parties involved. It was marked by faithfulness and loyalty, brought to a focus in steadfast or covenant love (see I Sam. 20:12ff.; II Sam. 16:16ff.). Just as Hosea had shown steadfast love to Gomer despite her sin, so Yahweh would abide faithful and manifest love to Israel.

In the words of our text we have almost the picture painted by our Lord in the parable of the prodigal son. Here is the promise of the gospel, pointing to the final disclosure in Jesus.

1. God's moral demands and judgment on sin are a reality.

2. The judgmental situation with its division and frustration produces a yearning for God. You could emphasize here that this is one aspect of the persuasive process of divine love. Even in judgment God's love is at work. The realization of personal bankruptcy, the breakup of relationships, points us back to God. (Hos. 2:6–7.)

3. God's last word is one of forgiveness and mercy. He turns the Valley of Achor, of sin and a guilty conscience, into a door of hope (2:15). Once more Hosea, in bearing his own redemptive cross for Gomer, opens a window into the heart of God. Calvary is the ultimate disclosure of the redemptive, suffering love of God. Sin drives God out of his world onto a cross (Bonhoeffer), but this is the way God wins (Francis Thompson's *The Hound of Heaven*).

JONAH 3:1–2; 4:10–11. JONAH: THE GIFT OF A SECOND CHANCE

It is best to follow the finest biblical scholarship here and to accept The Book of Jonah as a prophetic parable. This avoids the foolish arguments about the big fish and attempts to identify the author with a prophet called Jonah and his historical setting (II Kings 14:25). Taken in this way the book belongs to the period after the exile when Jewish thought was wavering between the pole of exclusiveness, typified in The Book of Esther, and of the outgoing sense of mission to the Gentile world, expressed in many of those who constituted the Dispersion. This is a missionary book, a challenge to Israel to be a missionary people and to believe in a God who would have mercy even on Nineveh. Jonah represents the Jewish people, trying to flee its responsibility. It is called to be God's people and witness even to

Nineveh. It fails Yahweh and is taken into exile, symbolized by the belly of the great fish. It is delivered, and, on its return to Jerusalem, has a second opportunity to witness to alien peoples. Jonah, as the Jewish people, has to learn, in this new situation, the breadth of God's mercy. (See George A. F. Knight, *Ruth and Jonah,* pp. 47–78.) For the identification of Jonah with Israel, look at the meaning of the name Jonah (ibid., pp. 59f.).

1. Exclusiveness brings its own nemesis. Narrow-mindedness in religion carries the seeds of its own destruction. The ghetto mentality that shuts the world out brings its own judgment—the growth of spiritual pride, the loss of a spirit of toleration, the easy narrowing of love and concern with a developing arrogance and consciousness, the rebellion of the younger generation, and the loss of family unity. This is Jonah in the belly of the big fish.

2. Often such judgment opens the door to a second chance. Christians have critically to reassess their calling and message, as they become conscious of their failure and its consequences.

3. In such a situation we come increasingly to realize still more the breadth of God's grace. Jonah had to see it extending to the hated city of Nineveh and even to the gourd. All of us and all nature have a place in God's creative and redemptive mercy. Here you could follow with a sermon on the universality of our religious response (Mal. 1:11) and with one on ecology (Hos. 2:19–22).

FOR FURTHER READING

Buttrick, George A., et al., eds. *The Interpreter's Bible,* Vol. 6. Abingdon Press, 1956.

Rad, Gerhard von. *The Message of the Prophets.* Harper & Row, 1962.

———. *Old Testament Theology,* Vol. 2. Tr. D. M. G. Stalker. Harper & Row, 1965.

Robinson, H. Wheeler. *Two Hebrew Prophets.* London: Lutterworth Press, 1959.

Rust, Eric C. *Covenant and Hope.* Word Books, 1972.

9. PREACHING FROM DANIEL, RUTH, ESTHER, AND THE SONG OF SONGS

WILLIAM P. TUCK

The books of Daniel, Ruth, Esther, and The Song of Songs seem to many preachers to be among the least likely sources for preaching. Yet they offer a rich, seldom tapped source for the preacher who is willing to labor in their treasure. The writers were all addressing people living in a secular world where lives were filled with decision-making, job insecurity, grief, death, love, family, and threats of persecution. They faced problems similar to those many of us live with daily. How can we be loyal to what we believe in such a secular world? Faith in God seems so hard to sustain with so many forces pulling upon our life. How am I to understand my own sexuality and the one I love? Do sex and religion have anything to do with each other?

The writers of these biblical books have each addressed some of these questions. They have chosen a narrative or "poetic" style to share their stories. That might be a lesson to us on how to proclaim their messages today. People delight in hearing stories and singing love songs. Centuries ago others found religious insight in these writings which they believed made them worthy of being in the canon. Individuals can turn to them again for direction in a secular age.

DANIEL

Many preachers have avoided preaching on The Book of Daniel because they have seen it as the happy hunting ground for crafty clairvoyants. Some have seen within its pages the divine plan of the ages; while others have viewed it as a glorified fairy tale. Many recall the adventures of Daniel from childhood Bible studies, but having become adults, they have put aside such childish stories. One of the tragedies of today's church is that the message of this book has been so long ignored except by those who are trying to peer into the future, having used Daniel to provide them with weird charts and graphs to predict the events leading to the end of the world. When the preacher is willing to work through the various complexities of the book, the basic message will be clear and meaningful to proclaim today.

The Book of Daniel has usually been classified as a type of literature called "apocalyptic," meaning "unveiling" or "revelation." Books of this type were often pseudonymous, symbolic, and esoteric. The apocalyptic imitators of Daniel were concerned primarily with the future, whereas the writer of this book was interested in disclosing the power of God for his own day and age. Norman Porteous sees Daniel as a distinctive type of writing that drew upon earlier wisdom and prophetic literature as well as the Psalms to proclaim its own peculiar message.[1] The main concern of Daniel was not the future but the present. He was living in the midst of a pressing crisis and his book was written to address that need.

In about 175 B.C., Antiochus IV seized the throne of Syria and took the title Epiphanes, which meant "the manifestation of God on earth." In the year 169 B.C. he sacked Jerusalem and robbed the Temple of sacred items, including the altar. Two years later he erected a statue of the god Baal Shamem in the Jerusalem Temple, and it was rededicated to Zeus of Olympus. Antiochus IV forbade the Jews to practice their religion, with the threat of death. They were forced to sacrifice to pagan gods; the Book of the Law was burned; and circumcision and other practices of their faith were forbidden. This bloody persecution was a time of personal and national crisis for the Jewish people. Judas Maccabeus took up the sword to set the people free. But his effort was short-lived, and the dark days of persecution continued. The Book of Daniel was written ca. 165 B.C. to offer the people hope in what appeared to be a hopeless situation.

To escape detection by the Syrian authorities, the writer set his story in the time of the Babylonian captivity in the sixth century B.C. He used the name Daniel as a nom de plume, a practice that was customarily done in ancient writings. There are two references to a wise man named Daniel in Ezek. 14:14 and 28:3. There are records of a "Danel," who was very wise, in the Ras Shamra texts. The writer may have based his book on these stories. The prophet Daniel and his three friends faced circumstances that resembled the struggles that the Jews in the second century B.C. were confronting.

The writer hoped to lift the crushed spirits of his people so they could meet their own time of testing with faith and courage. He pictured the Seleucid empire as pale compared to the splendor and might of Nebuchadnezzar. He was "the head of gold" (Dan. 2:38), superior to all the rulers who succeeded him. His image was colossal, and the torture of his fiery furnace made the idols and persecution of Antiochus seem tame. Yet God enabled Daniel and his friends to be victorious during their time of persecution. They placed their trust in God and he sustained them. Their unflinching faith was summarized in the words of Shadrach, Meshach, and Abednego: "If there is a god who is able to save us from the blazing furnace, it is our God whom we serve, and he will save us from your power, O king; but if not, be it known to your majesty that we will neither serve your god nor worship the golden image that you have set up" (3:17–18).

The Book of Daniel is divided into two sections. Chapters 1–6 relate stories about Daniel and his adventures. Chapters 7–12 are composed of visions of Daniel. The book is also written in two languages: Aramaic, 2:4–7:28; Hebrew, 1:1–2:3; 8:1–12:13. It is uncertain whether this indicates several sources for the writer, or that he wrote in one of the languages (probably Aramaic) and subsequently translated part of it into the other. The Hebrew literary quality of chs. 8–12 is inferior to the Aramaic used earlier. Many other suggestions have been offered for the two languages, none of which is completely satisfying.

It was indicated earlier that the book was most likely written ca. 165 B.C. This is the internal evidence for a second-century date: the writer's vague knowledge of the details about the Babylonian and Persian period, his historical inaccuracies of that time, his precise knowledge of the Ptolemy and Seleucid periods, Greek words, the development of its theology, and its advanced angelology. The author was not attempting to write scientific history but to teach a moral and religious lesson about the presence of God during a time of great crisis. The main theme of the book addressed how Israel was to live in a Gentile (secular) world. The author assures them that with loyal obedience to God they will discover that they have the wisdom and resources to match any circumstances. Faith in God will sustain the believers even when God seems to remain silent and hidden. God is still in control of history, and whether one lives or dies, his power ultimately will have dominion.

As you prepare to preach from Daniel, commentaries by Eric Heaton, Norman Porteous, D. S. Russell, Louis Hartman and Alexander Di Lella will prove invaluable, especially as you study the second division on Daniel's visions. Chapter 7 may be the central chapter in the book. It draws together the stories of Daniel when he had been at one time the interpreter of dreams, and now he is the dreamer or visionary. In a word, Daniel's vision relates to him that the four kingdoms, which are symbolized by four beasts, have been arrogantly blasphemous toward God and have persecuted his people; therefore, God will totally destroy them and establish his own rule among nations.

The symbolism of the four beasts in 7:1–8 may be stated briefly as follows: (1) The winged lion is Babylon, and the three tusks are the three Babylonian kings known to the writer. (2) The bear is the Median kingdom (although no historical evidence can be found that the Medes conquered Babylon). (3) A panther or leopard is the Persian Empire, and the four heads and four wings represent the four Persian kings. (4) The horrible and alarming beast stands for the Greek kingdom of Alexander the Great, and his ten horns symbolize successive rulers. The small horn, without a doubt, represents Antiochus IV Epiphanes.

As you study the book, look for some of the underlying theological emphases. The following are a few of many: (1) *The Sovereignty of God*. The God of Israel is the Lord of history (4:22; 5:24–28). (2) *Problem of Injustice and Suffering*. Cries go up to God for help in time of persecution and hostilities (1:1–2; 3:19–30; 8:13–14). (3) *An Affirmation of Faith*. The writer challenged the reader to a faith that will not give way to conformity (1:17–21; 3:19–30; 6:18–24; 11:40–45). (4) *Judgment*. Daniel witnessed to the certainty of judgment as a present reality. He envisioned it as swift and terrible (4:28–37; 5:1–4; 7:19–28; 8:13–14). (5) *History and Time*. The book indicates that the writer is primarily concerned with the crisis caused by Antiochus IV. It is an unfortunate twist to read back into the book our present-day history, or assume that the author is concerned with the unknown future (8:13–14; 8:15–19; 9:1–2). (6) *Angels*. Here in this writing is a highly developed angelology. Daniel is the only book in the Old Testament that refers to angels by name (8:16; 10:13; 12:1). (7) *Son of Man*. This phrase translated from the Hebrew (*ben adam*) means "a human being." There is a clear indication that the figure here is to be interpreted symbolically and in a collective sense—Israel. Later Jesus used this as a favorite term to describe himself (7:13–14). (8) *Ancient of Days*. This phrase literally translated is "advanced in days." Here is a figure of divine judgment (7:9–12). (9) *Resurrection*. Daniel contains the clearest and highest concept of resurrection in the Old Testament (12:1–4).

PREACHING THEMES

The message of The Book of Daniel will be missed if we do not take seriously the specific event that the writer was addressing. Knowing the particularity of the text, we are now forced to see what the message is for today. In a world filled too often with war, injustice, prejudice, religious persecution, pain, suffering, and evil, the cry is often heard, "Where is God?" If he is almighty, why doesn't he help the weak? Why is he so silent while injustice reigns? In a world that is largely secular, how do we live out our faith without being ridiculed? We also have to wonder whether or not we could withstand unjust persecution because of our faith. These questions probe some of the same issues that The Book of Daniel was addressing.

A sermon might be drawn from the first chapter (1:8–16) around the theme "Principles Worth Standing For." Do not get bogged down in the issue of whether or not dietary laws are important religious rules for us today. Daniel and his friends believed that there was something ritually unclean about the food they were asked to eat by the king. They stood by their religious principles. It was a similar issue which Paul had to deal with in a Christian's eating meat that had been offered to idols (I Cor. 10). Paul was concerned with the "weaker" brother. Although all things might be "lawful," all things do not serve the cause of Christ. We might feel that ritual uncleanness is not an issue today. Jesus seemed to put aside such laws. "There is nothing outside a man which by going into him can defile him" (Mark 7:15). Peter's vision in Acts 10:9–16 also seems to confirm this. But the particular issue in Daniel was a demonstration of loyalty to God. The young men involved stood by that principle.

The story of Daniel's three friends in ch. 3 offers a fine passage on radical faith and loyalty in the face of persecution and even death. This story was meant to encourage those who were then suffering under Antiochus IV. Nebuchadnezzar is depicted as a worldly authority who feels that there is no limit to his power. "Who is the god that will deliver you out of my hands?" The famous vs. 17 and 18 affirm a faith in God whether or not he intervenes to save their lives. The three chose death rather than worship the emperor's idol and compromise their faith. James Cox in a sermon on this passage entitled "What Can We Expect from God in a Crisis?" concludes with this strong affirmation: "God does not have to spare us from suffering, pain, rejection, and persecution—if only he be with us in it! God may deny us some things, even life, that he may give us himself and all that the gift of himself includes."[2] Many Christian believers in Eastern Europe, South America, and Africa are confronted by the military power of a totalitarian state. To confess their faith often means economic or political sanctions, imprisonment, and sometimes death. Are Christians to conform to any and all demands of the state, even if they feel that these demands conflict with their religious convictions? The state cannot command our worship, nor prescribe how we should worship. Church and state are not one. We worship God alone. The fourth figure in the furnace is not a reference to Jesus. It is translated "like a son of the gods"—a divine being. Verse 28 refers to the figure as an angel.

The strange story in ch. 4 offers some lessons on the sin of pride. The theme of this chapter is recorded in v. 25, where Nebuchadnezzar is told he will be disciplined until he learns the lesson that "the Most High rules the kingdom of men, and gives it to whom he will." The king's condition may be described as boanthropy. This is a form of insanity (lycanthropy) in which a person imagines that he is literally a wolf or some grass-eating animal. Pride, or *hybris,* is what Reinhold Niebuhr called man's "God almightyness." Even the king had to acknowledge that his power was from God and subordinate to it. The image of the stump that is left after the tree has been cut down (4:15) indicates the possibility of restoration.

The judgment of God is the focus of the feast of Belshazzar and the strange handwriting on the wall in ch. 5. The king had committed sacrilege by using the sacred Temple vessels which had been plundered from Jerusalem by Nebuchadnezzar. This was a coded reference by the writer to the sacrilege of Antiochus IV. He was stating that the sacrilege would bring swift and terrible punishment to the offender. A minor point here, which shows some of the historical problems alluded to earlier, deals with Belshazzar. Although he was a historical person, he was the son of the last Babylonian king, Nabonidus; he was never actually king. He did act as regent on certain occasions. This does not alter the point of the story, however. The writer was convinced of the certain judgment of God. The three fatal words, *menē, tekēl, perēs,* are translated "numbered," "weighed," and "divided." These words probably stood for three kinds of coins or weights. Some have suggested that they may represent different numbers. Nebuchadnezzar was worth a mina; Belshazzar was valued at only half a shekel, and the Medes and Persians were worth half a mina each. You are not worth much, Daniel said. This *mašal,* or parable, affirmed that God's judgment was coming upon Antiochus IV as surely as it came upon Belshazzar. The handwriting was on the wall. God was marching on!

The story of Daniel and the lions' den (6:10–24) reveals a man who believed that the law of the land sometimes had to be superseded by a higher law. He did not break the law in ignorance when he continued to pray, but he believed that that law stood in violation to his command from God. Being a man of integrity, he would not change his normal habits of praying in order to make his praying safe. His religion was not a vague, halfhearted thing. It was vital and real to him. Later the writer of The Letter to the Hebrews would include Daniel in the roll call of the heroes of Israel whose faith enabled them to stop the mouths of lions, etc. (Heb. 11:33f.). The tale does not teach that all will be delivered externally by God. Daniel was. But Stephen was stoned to death. Jesus was crucified. Paul was imprisoned and likely martyred. With Paul it is enough to say that nothing can separate us from God when we are in Christ Jesus (Rom. 8:35–39).

Many other passages offer rich soil for sermon growth. The passage on the resurrection (Dan. 12:1–4) is one of the finest in the Old Testament. The cry of anguish, "How long, O God?" is the cry of many persons (8:13–14). The concept of the "Son of Man" (7:13–14) may not have been a Messianic concept in the mind of the writer of Daniel, though he saw it as a corporate figure representing the kingdom of God; nevertheless, Jesus later seemed to utilize that figure to describe himself. Drawing upon another collective image, "the Suffering Servant," Jesus linked it with the "Son of Man" to express his own awareness of the Messiah. The faithful remnant became focalized in the Messiah. The ministry of "waiting" (12:12) sometimes can be one of the most difficult experiences one must endure. Patience is never easy to practice. But everyone has to learn that lesson, since so much of life is spent in waiting. Daniel was writing to urge the persecuted Jews to wait upon God. Wait with faithfulness, he urged; his presence is assured.

ESTHER AND RUTH

Esther and Ruth, two of the brief books in the Old Testament, are superb examples of the ancient short story, or novella. They were written not only to entertain but to edify. Although they have a nucleus of historical truth on which each story is based, in the present form the two books probably contain fictional dimensions much like a historical novel today. Every element within the story did not have to be historically accurate for the basic theme to be communicated. Esther and Ruth are both included with Song of Songs, Ecclesiastes, and Lamentations in the third Jewish division called the Kethubhim, or Writings. The position in the Writings, along with internal evidence, suggests a late date for these books. Drawing on oral tradition which had transmitted these tales through the years, master storytellers, writing most likely after the exile, gave them their present form.

ESTHER

The Book of Esther was probably written to explain the origin of the Feast of Purim. This festival is not mentioned in the rest of the Bible, and was likely borrowed originally from either Babylonia or Persia. In Esther the festival was established to commemorate the victory of the Jews over their enemies during the time they were dispersed in Persia. This festival is still observed today the 14th and 15th of Adar (about March 1). It is not a religious holiday but a secular celebration filled with feasting, gaiety, and the giving of gifts.

Esther has had a tumultuous time as a part of the canon of Scripture. Martin Luther, along with many others, wanted to exclude it. The book is not referred to in the New Testament, and none of the church fathers wrote an exposition of it. There is no suggestion in the book that faith, prayer, or any religious factors have a role in the events of the story. Lewis Bayles Paton believed that Esther was "so conspicuously lacking in religion that it should never have been included in the Canon of the Old Testament."[3] There is much in the book that is sub-Christian, especially the extreme spirit of revenge which is seen in the last chapters. But the Christian preacher should not dismiss this book so quickly. God may be alluded to more indirectly than directly.

When we read Esther carefully we begin to see more than what appear to be mere coincidences: the king's forgetting to reward Mordecai for saving his life yet keeping a record of it, and, at the "right moment," being reminded of this experience; Haman's being present in the king's court to condemn Mordecai just as the king is prepared to reward Mordecai; and the presence of the gallows in Haman's house which was constructed for Mordecai, but became, ironically, the place where Haman himself was hanged. Behind these suspenseful and surprising coincidences the writer was pointing to the providential power of God, who directed the course of events in the lives of men and women. A process of judgment!

Esther clearly gives an example of what life was like for some of the Jews in exile. Although the Jews depicted in this book were not persecuted openly for their religious views, they suffered then as they have for many centuries for being simply a minority group. Esther and Mordecai were drawn as examples to show that Jews could rise to positions of success and renown even in a Gentile world. This book does not give a plea for particular religious customs to be observed during the time of exile, but it issues a firm conviction of the indestructibility of Israel and the obligation of every Jewish person to aid in this cause no matter what the personal risk might be.

RUTH

Once a year at Shabuot (Pentecost) faithful Jews hear again the story of Ruth, "the gleaner maid." In a concise and compelling tale the unknown author of Ruth has written a narrative that is regarded by many as the finest example of the epics and idylls of the Hebrews. The simple story of the Moabitess heroine and her devotion to Naomi, their flight back to Bethlehem, the quest for food, Ruth's marriage to Boaz, and the birth of a son, who is the ancestor of David, is told in six brief scenes: (1) Three Widows in Moab (1:1–18); (2) The Arrival in Bethlehem (1:19–22); (3) The Harvest Field (ch. 2); (4) The Threshing Floor (ch. 3); (5) The City Gate (4:1–12); (6) The Birth of a Son (4:13–22).

Is the story merely to be enjoyed? Did the author have some clearly defined goal in mind when this short story was written? Scholars have struggled with these issues for years. Some are convinced that the teller of the tale had nothing in mind beyond entertainment. But few are willing to accept this answer. This brief story is far more than a simple love story. Several theological themes are discernible. Five will be noted briefly here.

First, throughout the book God's providence is unmistakable. He is the chief actor. Although he is hidden in the shadows and does not manifest himself by intervention, his control of the events is noted in subtle ways. The author never says, "Notice how all the prayers of Naomi are answered." He does not say, "Observe how often there seem to be coincidences happening where God's guidance is clearly visible." He knew that his reader would be able to see the signposts without his having to point them out. With the art of a master storyteller, the writer noted that Ruth "happened to come to the part of the field belonging to Boaz." She found favor with Boaz before she knew him to be a kinsman, and Naomi blessed him before she knew who he was. The presence of God is sensed behind the advice of

Naomi to Ruth, "Wait . . . until you learn how the matter turns out." After the birth of Obed to Ruth, the women affirmed their recognition of the guiding presence of God when they declared, "Blessed be the LORD." God's providence may be hidden to human eyes, but the author believed that God directs all the events of one's life. Divine intentionality, not luck, directs the human path.

Second, the book advocates tolerance and acceptance of foreigners. Ruth addresses the exclusive practices of those who did not want to permit mixed marriages of a foreigner to an Israelite for fear that they would corrupt the Jewish faith. The author argued through Ruth the Moabitess that not only could foreigners be assimilated into the religious life of the Jews, but they might make an essential contribution. This is especially emphasized in the genealogy at the conclusion of the book, where David is listed as a descendant of Ruth the Moabitess.

A third theme in the book is the strong friendship that existed between Ruth and Naomi. Even the marriage of Ruth to Boaz is subordinated to their trust and commitment to each other. Although the book is entitled Ruth, the story begins and concludes with Naomi. Ruth's words, "Entreat me not to leave you," were a radical decision and commitment to her friend Naomi. Ruth the Moabitess chose Naomi the Judahite, her mother-in-law, as the one through whom she would receive direction and guidance. In Ruth's choice she turned her back on her own country, her familiar world, and her own religion when she decided to go with Naomi. As the plot unfolds and Ruth later marries Boaz and bears a son, the storyteller leads the reader from Naomi's cry of bitterness to her declaration of joy for Ruth, who is better than seven sons (4:15). Many see this story as one of the most remarkable tales of devoted friendship in all of the Bible.

A fourth significant theme in the book is *ḥesed,* translated variously from the Hebrew as "kindness," "loving-kindness," "steadfast love," or "loyalty." *Ḥesed* is seen in Ruth's devotion to Naomi. It is seen in the kind treatment of Ruth by Boaz as she gleans in the field and in the scene at the threshing floor. It is evidenced in the response of Boaz to be the "kinsman redeemer" for Ruth. Throughout the story, one is able to discern the power of "loving-kindness" in the lives of all the characters. Ruth, Naomi, Boaz, and even Orpah interact with each other with a high sense of values. *Ḥesed* is seen as the better way and a more noble way of living. It is more than just human "kindness" or "loyalty"; it is patterned after the undeserved love that one experiences from God.

The fifth theme noted in the book is covenant. The word "covenant" does not occur in the story, but the concept is present. Naomi's complaint and bitterness suggest that she felt that the God of the covenant had let her down. The story draws the concept of covenant down to a day-to-day contact with life, and the responsibility of each covenant believer for another. The covenant community itself shared in one another's lives as evidenced in the scene at the city gate (4:7–11). Boaz is fulfilling his role of "kinsman redeemer" as a part of the covenant community. Ruth's loyalty and fidelity and the "kindness" of Boaz were signs of the intertwining of the human and divine aspects of the covenant. Naomi finds her security through human deeds, yet words such as "to cleave to" (1:14) and "not abandoning" (1:16) are covenant expressions. Naomi finds her security through human deeds, yet this kindness is a picture of the covenant God, who directs the action from behind the scene.

The concept of levirate marriage will need some explanation for today's congregation. According to this custom, a brother-in-law would marry his brother's widow and raise up children to his dead brother so that his name and line might continue. (See Gen. 38 and Deut. 25:5–10.) Boaz was not a brother but a kinsman of the deceased sons of Naomi. In the threshing floor scene Ruth asks Boaz, "Spread your skirt over your maidservant," i.e., "spread your wing" or "cover with your skirt"—a common Near East expression symbolizing protection and marriage.

When you prepare to preach on this book, you need to handle carefully the scene at the threshing floor. It will be a shock for some of your listeners to realize that the writer meant to have the readers struggle with the possibility that Boaz and Ruth might have sexual intercourse. She went, at the advice of Naomi, "prepared like a bride" and the uncovering of Boaz' legs clearly had provocative implications. But the author indicated that, faced with this moral choice, both decided in favor of the righteous way. Ruth had shown her courage in exposing herself to being treated shamefully. Boaz revealed that he too was a person of honor. He conducted himself properly and agreed to be the "kinsman redeemer" and marry Ruth.

PREACHING TEXTS

In both Esther and Ruth, God works in the lives of individuals in a quiet, hidden way. The writers seem to hide God's providence. The narrators spoke of God in only a secular way, and God remained in the shadows. In our modern, secular world these books might be able to address a wide audience who perceive God's presence in the same way. A sermon entitled "God in the Shadows" could explore the providence of God as discerned in our lives. Several biblical texts could be helpful here. The hand of God could be observed in the "chance" coming of Ruth to Boaz' field (Ruth 2:3); in the "accidental" coming to the city gate of Ruth's next of kin while Boaz was present (4:1); in the "coincidences" in Esther, such as the king's insomnia and the reading of the account of Mordecai's earlier deed of saving the king's life which had gone unrewarded (Esth. 6:1–2); and in the whole series of events that lead to Esther's becoming queen, all of which appeared to be only "secular" happenings. The most famous verse in Esther, "And who knows whether you have not come to the kingdom for such a time as this?" (4:14) could be a clear declaration of the hidden God without ever mentioning him.

These two books do not speak much about God, but his presence does brood over the events and is the real force working behind them. Is it not a lesson of the way God continues to work out his purpose in the world today, silently and slowly through the lives of many individuals? Working behind the freedom he has given persons to act, God is steadily advancing his cause even through the lives of those who do not recognize him.

One of the meaningful ways that both of these books could be preached is by retelling the story. Either could be told simply as a story or from the viewpoint of a third person (a monologue) who is observing the events as they unfold, or the story of Esther could be told through the eyes of Mordecai and Ruth from the perspective of Boaz. If you are a woman minister, then the logical approach would be from the viewpoint of Ruth, Naomi, or Orpah, and as for the book of Esther you could tell it from the viewpoint of Esther or one of the other maidens in the king's court. The book *Preaching the Story*, by Edmund Steimle, Morris Niedenthal, and Charles Rice, might be helpful.

As you retell the story, you will have an opportunity to explain difficult customs, such as the levirate marriage practice, the symbol of the shoe at the city gate, and the mysterious meeting on the threshing floor in The Book of Ruth. In both books you can address the hiddenness of God and the secular expressions of communicating. Retelling the story of Esther provides opportunity to deal with some of the customs and moral issues raised by the actions of Esther and Mordecai, especially the killing of the Jewish enemies in the empire. Prepare carefully the details of the story and make clear those parts which you know will raise difficulties for the listeners. Donald Gowan has given an excellent example of how one might retell the story of Ruth.[4]

One of the central themes of Esther is the persecution of the Jews as a minority group in Persia. The Jewish people continue to suffer from this kind of problem in many places today. Our preaching of this book could address this issue and the attitude and role the Christian church has in assisting the Jews and other minority groups. In the book Esther became the symbol of deliverance and Haman was a picture of prejudice and injustice that have often threatened the Jews. Note how he used rumors and accusations to condemn the Jews and how quickly and easily these were accepted without examination by the king. The entire third chapter can serve as a strong textual base for this sermon.

The most famous verse of Esther is 4:14. Mordecai has just explained the peril that faced the Jews, and then he says to Esther: "If you keep silence at such a time as this, relief and deliverance will rise for the Jews from another quarter, but you and your father's house will perish. And who knows whether you have not come to the kingdom for such a time as this?" The opportunity for courageous action lay before Esther. She may have been tempted to be silent and do nothing. This is often the path for the selfish. When evil demands denunciation, many people often maintain a prudential silence. Expediency is the easier path; a courageous word may demand the harder path of rejection, misunderstanding, ridicule, suffering, or even death. But Mordecai is convinced that even if she refuses to act, God will move in another way, through someone else to prevent the extinction of his people. Even if one group fails in its work for God, others will be raised up to carry the work forward. God has many instruments through whom he is working. Every opportunity presents a special call for service. Behind Esther's present opportunity stands God's providential purpose. Will she be equal to the task? As you prepare this sermon, help your listeners to sense the lesson for us today as we face such challenges as war, hunger, disease, racism, nuclear bombs, pollution, and injustice. Are we equal to the tasks before us?

The vengeance of Esther, which is seen in the second slaughter in Susa (9:11–15), reminds us that the Old Testament is incomplete. The Christian preacher would not want to commend the spirit of revenge which is evident in this passage. One might reason that the attitude reflected in Esther was a natural reaction for a people who had experienced so much persecution and hostility from others in this society. The wanton destruction of one's enemies is still on a lower level when measured by the Christian call to love, justice, forgiveness, grace, and mercy. The higher revelation came in Jesus when he declared: "You have heard that it was said, 'You shall love your neighbor and hate your enemy.' But I say to you, Love your enemies and pray for those who persecute you" (Matt. 5:43–44).

The five themes of The Book of Ruth mentioned earlier will offer a number of suggestions for sermons. Ruth's commitment to Naomi (Ruth 1:16–17) can provide the text for a sermon on radical decision-making. Phyllis Trible is convinced that there is no more radical decision in all the memories of Israel than the one made by Ruth. Ruth's decision, she believes, surpasses Abraham in its radicality.[5] Abraham made his decision with a sense of divine call. He was a man, with a wife and many possessions. Ruth's decision was made without a sense of call from God. She had received no promise of protection or assistance from God or any other group. She committed herself to her friend and mother-in-law, Naomi, in a man's world. This commitment had no assurance of blessing but offered instead possible hunger and death. Her decision has come to symbolize the noblest expression of human friendship. Ruth subordinated her will to a higher way of sacrificial love and service. Orpah also loved Naomi, but Ruth loved Naomi to the extent that she resolved to love her God as well.

An exposition of this same text for another sermon might proceed by dealing with it in the following divisions: (1) "For where you go I will go"; (2) "Where you lodge I will lodge"; (3) "Your people shall be my people"; (4) "And your God my God"; (5) "Where you die I will die." Here was a willingness by Ruth to go anywhere, without set conditions, to embrace a nation of people she had once despised, to bow before Yahweh with her religious devotion, and to be buried with Naomi wherever they may be, so that even death would not separate them.

The "kinsman redeemer" image offers an interesting sermon theme. Ruth 4:7–14 could be the text. The verb "to act the part of kinsman" or "to redeem" which is applied to Boaz in this passage is used by other Old Testament writers to depict the redemptive action of God. (See Job 19:25; Isa. 43:1, 14; 44:23; Ps. 78:35; 106:10.) This points the way to the redemptive activity of God which the New Testament sees expressed in the figure of Jesus Christ. The Gospel of Matthew traces the genealogy of Jesus through Ruth and Boaz (Matt. 1:5). The "kinsman redeemer" was a human illustration of "loving-kindness" which pointed to a divine redeemer at work behind the scene. In Jesus Christ the focus of God's divine activity moved from the shadows and became visible. "And the Word became flesh and dwelt among us" (John 1:14). "In him [Jesus Christ] we have redemption through his blood, the forgiveness of our trespasses, according to the riches of his grace which he lavished upon us" (Eph. 1:7).

THE SONG OF SONGS

A person upon first reading The Song of Songs might respond with surprise, asking: "How did that book get in the Bible?" It is very different from the rest of Scripture. There is not one place in the book where a religious sentence is found. And God is not even mentioned. Like Esther, this book had a difficult time finding a place in the canon. Some have seen it as nothing more than a risqué collection of love poems.

The title of the book itself is not clear. The inscription in the first verse has been variously translated: "Which is Solomon's," or "to," "about," "concerning," and "for Solomon." It is unlikely that Solomon was the author. In all probability he was the patron to whom it was dedicated. The book is more accurately called "The Song of Songs," which is a way of saying "the best of songs."

Through the years five basic interpretations have been given to this book. The earliest and the one that has dominated both Hebrew and Christian thought is the allegorical approach. The literal meaning of the words has been ignored and a deeper, hidden meaning was found. In the Jewish tradition the shepherd lover was Yahweh, and the maiden or bride was Israel. In Christian thought the lover and the beloved are ascribed to Jesus Christ and the church. With this view interpreters could draw from the text any sermonic notion that their imagination would warrant. Most Jewish and Christian scholars no longer consider this a worthy interpretation.

Others have seen The Song of Songs as drama. Some—for example, Franz Delitzsch—saw only two characters in dialogue, the maiden and Solomon, who was sometimes described as a shepherd. Some, like H. Ewald and J. F. Jacobi, believed that it was a three-part drama with Solomon, the maiden, and the shepherd as the chief actors. Others, like John L. Patterson, saw it as a lyrical drama with actors and a chorus performed in eight acts. Another approach (Renan, Herder, Budde) understood The Song of Songs to be a series of love poems used in wedding festivities. During their celebration the bride and groom were treated as king and queen.

Others (Erbt, Wetzstein, and Meek) have interpreted the work as having cultic origins. The maiden and the shepherd are figures in the celebration of the fertility of the earth in the spring and fall festivals. Similarities have been drawn between The Song of Songs and the wailings for Tammuz from the Adonis cult. Still others have said that the work should simply be interpreted literally as a collection of secular love poems. Theodore of Mopsuestia (360–429) was one of the first to render this verdict. His views were condemned by the Council of Constantinople. Later Paul Haupt, Eduard Reuss, and others gave this same interpretation.

PREACHING THEMES

What is the value of this book for us today? In the first place, the writing should be acknowledged and enjoyed as a collection of frank romantic and erotic love songs. They may be a type of folk poetry collected from several sources without any particular theme throughout the book other than the joy of sensuous love. If there is a poetic drama within the book, its plot is difficult to ascertain. Both the Hebrew and Christian teachings have seen sex as a beautiful gift from God to be enjoyed. This book is a reminder of God's blessing on marriage, sexual love, and marital fidelity.

In the second place, The Song of Songs does have theological meaning. Since God is the creator of sexual love which exists between a man and a woman, there is a sense in which all love, especially sensuous love between husband and wife, may become a reflection of divine-creative love. God, the creator, has given us the creation to enjoy. The Song of Songs speaks of love and sex in the language of poetry and emotion. There may indeed be dimensions of meaning that go beyond the surface expressions. Without question the allegorical interpretation pressed the images too far. On the other hand, there is a sense in which the human love in this song is a picture of God's love. The enjoyment of human love opens an avenue to God which enables us to understand what his love is like.

As you prepare to preach on this book, you might find it easier to use a thematic approach rather than a verse-by-verse method. This book affords an excellent source for a wedding sermon. You might select 7:10–13 or ch. 2. The sermon, "A Wedding Song," based on ch. 2, might speak of the following lessons: (1) delighting in each other (2:3); (2) sustaining each other (2:5); (3) committed to each other (2:13f.).

In the spring of the year you might select 2:11–13 for a sermon on "The Meaning of Spring." In this sermon you celebrate the passing of the cold, difficult days and welcome the newness of life that is beginning to burst forth. The coming of spring can awaken new possibilities within men and women as well as within nature. Spring ushers in the time of singing. It is a time to celebrate the joy of creation, the gift of life, and to rejoice in the opportunity to begin anew. This sermon should focus on the joy, celebration, and new beginnings that are symbolized in spring in this text. Acknowledge that all of this is rooted in the creative grace of God.

The Song of Songs could serve as a source for a series of sermons on love and marriage. Among various sermon titles, you might consider the following:

1. "The Strength of Love" (Song of Songs 8:6–7). The maiden states that her love is as "strong as death." Death is a point from which one cannot return. Her love is like that. It is sealed so that she cannot return.

2. "The Exclusiveness of Love" (Song of Songs 2:16; 6:3; 7:10). Throughout the book an exclusive love between a particular shepherd and a young maiden is focused upon. They declare their love by saying: "I am yours"; "You are mine." "My beloved is mine and I am his." True love chooses and selects to be with one and only one.

3. "The Superlative of Love" (Song of Songs 1:5–6; 1:9–11; 4:1–15). When lovers express their love for each other, they often use superlatives which may easily overstate each other's modest appearance. In this song they even declare each other to be a king and a queen (1:4; 7:1). And so they are to each other. The language of love is not reluctant to flatter and praise.

4. "The Expressiveness of Love" (Song of Songs 4:1–7; 5:10–16; 6:4–10). This is the sexual dimension of love. Each enjoys the beauty of the other, and they express this passionate joy in each other. Many today are afraid of their own sexuality, or feel they should not talk about it. Here in these passages is a strong witness to the beauty, joy, and wonder of sexual love.

5. "The Faithfulness of Love" (Song of Songs 8:5–10). The maiden and the shepherd commit themselves to each other. Verse 6 refers to the ancient practice of persons carrying a seal on a chain around the neck or on a ring for the purpose of making their signature since many could not write. This was the maiden's way of pressing upon the shepherd her desire that he be faithful to her. The image of the "vineyard" in v. 12 stands for the "body" of the maiden and her chastity. "My vineyard is not for sale. It is only for the one I love." A lasting marriage is built on faithfulness.

NOTES

1. Norman W. Porteous, *Daniel, A Commentary,* The Old Testament Library (Westminster Press, 1965), p. 16.
2. James W. Cox, *Surprised by God* (Broadman Press, 1979), p. 108.
3. Lewis Bayles Paton, *The Book of Esther,* International Critical Commentary (Edinburgh: T. & T. Clark, 1908), p. 97.
4. See Donald E. Gowan, *Reclaiming the Old Testament for the Christian Pulpit* (John Knox Press, 1980), pp. 70–74.
5. Phyllis Trible, *God and the Rhetoric of Sexuality* (Fortress Press, 1978), p. 173.

FOR FURTHER READING

Campbell, Edward F., Jr. *Ruth.* The Anchor Bible, Vol. 7. Doubleday & Co., 1975. Good scholarly treatment. Helpful.
Gowan, Donald E. *Reclaiming the Old Testament for the Christian Pulpit.* John Knox Press, 1980. Offers useful suggestions about preaching on Daniel (chs. 1–6), Esther, and Ruth. Includes a sermon on Ruth.
Hartman, Louis F., and Di Lella, Alexander A. *The Book of Daniel,* Vol. 23. The Anchor Bible. Doubleday & Co., 1978. A fine scholarly source. The section "The Book of Daniel Today" especially useful for preaching.
Pope, Marvin H. *Song of Songs.* The Anchor Bible, Vol. 7C. Doubleday & Co., 1977. Massive work of 743 pp. Very thorough.
Porteous, Norman W. *Daniel, A Commentary.* The Old Testament Library. Westminster Press, 1965. Most helpful and very readable.
Russell, D. S. *Daniel.* The Daily Study Bible Series. Westminster Press, 1981. A popular commentary with many preaching suggestions.
Trible, Phyllis. *God and the Rhetoric of Sexuality.* Fortress Press, 1978. Treats both Song of Songs and Ruth. Her chapter on Ruth is an excellent resource.

10. PREACHING ON THE SYNOPTIC GOSPELS

WILLIAM E. HULL

I. HERMENEUTICAL BACKGROUND

There is no little irony in the fact that our contemporary approach to Matthew, Mark, and Luke—called the "Synoptic" Gospels because they share a similar perspective not found in John—has been shaped not by orthodox theologians working within the church but by scholarly historians working within the university. Some preachers are suspicious that biblical criticism is intent on crippling or even destroying the faith, while many more assume that its findings, although useful for specialists, are of little or no value in the pulpit. In the case of the first three Gospels, however, these negative verdicts are unjustified. During the past 150 years, Synoptic criticism has revolutionized our understanding of these pivotal writings, nowhere more than in their relevance for preaching.

Prior to this rediscovery in the modern era, preachers tended to neglect the Synoptic Gospels because they viewed them only as historical sources for the life of Jesus. Preference was given in sermons to the more "spiritual" Gospel of John and to the weighty theology in the epistles of Paul. But patient scholars have now helped us to see that the Synoptic Gospels were fashioned primarily out of preaching material—which, to be sure, contained reminiscences of the historical Jesus—and that the Evangelists edited this material to convey a theology as profound as any penned by the apostle Paul. Now we know that Matthew, Mark, and Luke, as much as any writings in the New Testament, were written *from* preaching *for* preaching and thus should be prime sources of sermonic fare.

A new appreciation for the kerygmatic character of the Synoptic

Gospels has come through the application of three basic disciplines, each with greater relevance to the preacher than the one before: (1) source criticism, which was refined from 1863 to 1924; (2) form criticism, which was formulated between the two World Wars; and (3) redaction criticism, which has emerged since the Second World War. From these three primary tributaries of Synoptic research have flowed the clarifications that provide us with both methods and insights for preaching from these Gospels. Let us consider each of them, in turn, as we construct an effective hermeneutic for the homiletic task.

1. *Source Criticism.* Based on the work of pioneers such as G. E. Lessing (1784), J. G. Herder (1797), and F. E. D. Schleiermacher (1832), the dominant hypothesis explaining the literary relationships between Matthew, Mark, and Luke was refined by a host of scholars from H. J. Holtzmann (1863) to B. H. Streeter (1924).[1] This solution to the Synoptic problem is usually called the "Two-Document Hypothesis" because it posits the priority of Mark, with its subsequent use by Matthew and Luke, plus the existence of a sayings source (Q) also used by Matthew and Luke but not known to Mark. In recent years, this consensus has been challenged, especially by a reassertion of the earlier Griesbach Hypothesis (1783), which contends for the priority of Matthew as the earliest Gospel later used by Luke, making Mark the latest of the Synoptic Gospels that used them both.[2] As if that were not enough, there is also a contention that Luke was the earliest Gospel, later used by Mark, making Matthew the latest of the three.[3]

Confronted with three alternative theories—which argue the priority of Matthew (Griesbach–Farmer), of Mark (Holtzmann–Streeter), and of Luke (Lindsey)—the preacher may be tempted to throw up his hands in dismay. But when the strengths of all three hypotheses are viewed together in balanced fashion, what they tend to confirm is the insight that *each of the three Evangelists was the first to produce a full-scale written Gospel for his own community.*[4] Even if some or all of them utilized a proto-Gospel or the sources of another Synoptic Gospel in their process of composition, they did so by importing "outside" material from other Christian centers rather than by revising a finished work that had already become accepted and authoritative in the community they served. We may never finally solve the somewhat abstract problem of identifying the earliest Gospel ever to emerge anywhere in Christendom, but we may fairly claim that, for their own local centers, each of the Synoptic Evangelists was probably

> The saint who first found grace to pen
> The life which was the Life of men.[5]

The momentousness of that step can hardly be overestimated. In one sense, the Synoptic Gospels appeared at the most crucial juncture in Christian history after Pentecost. The resurrection of Jesus had become a reality to the first generation of believers, and the Spirit of the risen Christ had energized the expanding church. But the eschatological faith had not yet become fully historicized, because it had not yet passed from one generation to the next. Having survived the death of Jesus on the cross, could the church also survive the death of the first apostles when no one was left who had ever seen Jesus in the flesh? In a nutshell, could an *out*-going missionary movement become an *on*-going historical movement that adjusted to new circumstances without losing its original character?

The answer of the Synoptics was as definitive as it was decisive. Having seen Christianity move at first from the Jesus of history to the Christ of faith, these writings now completed the circle by moving from the Christ of faith back to the Jesus of history. In so doing, they forever anchored the changing pilgrimage of the church in the unchanging ministry of its Lord. Furthermore, by embodying this fusion of faith and history in a book, they provided permanent norms to those successors of the apostles who had never known Jesus after the flesh.[6]

To be sure, the competing hypotheses regarding Synoptic origins cannot all be correct, for they are mutually incompatible in basic assumptions as well as in details. But what all of these theories point to, in arguing for the priority of Matthew, or of Mark, or of Luke, is the high degree of originality shown by all three of the Synoptic Gospels, an originality so great that it seems plausible to view any one of them as having been written first! Probably all of them used multiple sources, as Luke freely admits (Luke 1:1–4), but we cannot now precisely identify any of them, because none have survived in independent form. Nevertheless, all three Evangelists were pioneers of the first rank in defining a new balance between Spirit and flesh in the understanding of Jesus Christ. It is precisely this balance between the Jesus of history and the Christ of faith that the Christian preacher ever strives to maintain.

The originality of each Synoptic Gospel should not, however, disguise the high degree of interdependence among the three. Although we cannot always trace the sequence in which each strand was employed, source criticism does confirm the interlocking character of much of the material. Regardless of which account came first, the Synoptics contain instances of single, double, or triple attestation, as a comparison of parallels will show. This means that any preacher working in Matthew, Mark, or Luke must do so from a "harmony" which exhibits all the evidence in adjoining columns.[7] This is the only method for grasping the varied ways in which a particular event or saying was presented in the several sources lying behind our finished Gospels.

Close attention to patterns of attestation in the Synoptics suggests that at least four clusters of material have contributed to the making of Matthew, Mark, and Luke. At this distance we cannot tell whether these components were unified or fragmentary, but the outlook in each is sufficiently coherent to suggest a high degree of homogeneity. They are usually described by source critics as follows: (*a*) The basic narrative framework of the ministry of Jesus common to all three Synoptic Gospels. Because this material dominates the structure of the Second Gospel, it is often designated as "Mark" by those who affirm the priority of that Gospel among the others (e.g., Streeter). (*b*) A sayings source comprised primarily of teaching material common to Matthew and Luke but absent from Mark, somewhat arbitrarily called "Q" by source critics. (*c*) The material unique to Matthew, called "M." (*d*) The material unique to Luke, called "L." These four blocks are thought to cover all of the gospel story except for the infancy narratives (Matt. 1–2; Luke 1–2) at its beginning and portions of the passion narrative and resurrection appearances at its ending.

Only technically trained scholars are equipped to work with the details of source criticism, but preachers may readily benefit from the results of their findings. For example, Julian Price Love wrote a popular study, *The Gospel and the Gospels*,[8] in which he analyzed the religious themes in each major source. Included are chapters on the theology of the fourfold passion story, the compassionate power of the threefold Marcan account, the ethic of love in the twofold Q, the Jewish–Old Testament interests in M, and the Gentile-universal emphases in L. Unless preachers are aware of each stratum underlying the Synoptics, they may unintentionally omit highlighting each facet in the composite portrait of Christ. With the overview provided by Love, any seminary-trained preacher should be able to prepare several series of sermons that clarify the distinctive thrust of the major Synoptic sources, especially since detailed commentaries are available that treat the Synoptic Gospels in accordance with their sources.[9]

Preachers who work with these several sources long enough to realize that no one Gospel is "original," but that all are the end result of a long process of compilation and revision (again cf. Luke 1:1–4), will avoid a tendency to psychologize the text based on an imagined development found in one account but not the others. Constant use of a synoptic harmony is sufficient to show that no sequence is common to all three Gospels, much less to the Gospel of John. Again and again the same incident will be found in completely different contexts in the various Gospels. Clearly all the Evangelists were much more interested in thematic unity than in chronological order. Far from being a limitation to preaching, however, this insight enables us to forget about historical explanations of usefulness only to biographers and allows us to concentrate instead on the religious affirmations so urgently needed by our contemporary hearers.[10]

2. *Form Criticism.* As soon as the end of the First World War permitted the resumption of scholarly publication, New Testament study in Germany began to focus on the form of the gospel material in its preliterary stage. Determined to push back behind the period of written sources (ca. A.D. 50–70) to the period of oral transmission (ca. A.D. 30–50), scholars made efforts to isolate and analyze each unit of the Synoptic tradition (called a "pericope"). Pioneers were Martin Dibelius (1919), K. L. Schmidt (1919), and Rudolf Bultmann (1921).[11] Eventually the discipline was refined and tempered by British scholars from Vincent Taylor (1935) and R. H. Lightfoot (1935) to C. F. D. Moule (1962).[12] In the process, concern shifted from a description of the *form* of each pericope to an assessment of its *function* in the life of the early church. At first, form criticism seemed entirely too technical and skeptical to be of much use to the preacher, but more recently the discipline has come to have enormous value for anyone who would preach from the Synoptic Gospels.

To begin with, form criticism forces us to honor the integrity of the pericope as the most basic building block of the Synoptic Gospels. For all practical purposes, these pericopes correspond to the individual paragraphs in a modern English version (e.g., RSV, NEB, TEV), which means that the individual paragraph is far and away the most fundamental unit for Synoptic preaching. It is impossible to estimate how much mischief has been done to the cause of balanced interpretation by the use for centuries of a KJV text atomized into separate verse divisions which are a later invention superimposed upon the Gospels as a device wholly foreign to their composition. While there may be a key sentence, phrase, or even word worthy of an entire sermon, such bits and pieces of the text should always be set within the context of the form-critical unit to which they belong and interpreted in accordance with the thrust of the entire pericope.

Once the pericope has been correctly identified, its form should be classified. While it may help in this regard to study one or two of the technical treatments mentioned above (e.g., that by Dibelius), preachers need not be so fastidious in defining their categories as would a scholar primarily interested in comparative studies with first-century Jewish and Hellenistic literature. Some obvious types which preachers will readily recognize with just a bit of training are the parable, the miracle story, the controversy story, the discipleship (i.e., commitment) story, the Christological story, the isolated aphorism, the "woe" or lament, and the eschatological prediction. One value in such classifications is that units of similar form lend themselves to series preaching, as will be illustrated below. In fact, the Evangelists themselves often clustered their material in accordance with this principle. Witness, for example, the cycle of ten miracle stories in Matt. 8:1–9:34; or the twin cycles of controversy stories in Mark 2:1–3:6 and 12:13–44; or the triad of "lost and found" parables in Luke 15.

Moving beyond form to function, perhaps the greatest contribution of form criticism to preachers is its emphasis on the life setting (German *Sitz im Leben*) of each pericope. A basic assumption here is that the very usage of the oral tradition about Jesus in the life of the church influenced the form in which it was cast. Thus, for example, we may infer that liturgical forms (e.g., prayers) were used in a worship context, that didactic forms (e.g., aphorisms) were used in a catechetical context, that controversy stories (e.g., debates) were used in a polemical context, and that testimonia forms (e.g., Old Testament quotations) were used in an apologetic context. The enormous relevance of this approach for preachers should be immediately apparent. Obviously preachers will try to meet a pressing need in their own situations by preaching on a passage that was designed to address that very same need in the early church. Preaching is never as truly "biblical" as when the intention of those who speak for God today is to produce the same equivalent impact on their hearers as the scriptural passage intended to make on its hearers when originally addressed to them in the long ago.[13]

One of the best ways to grasp the revolutionary impact of form criticism on the interpretative process is to compare the treatment of the same passages in commentaries written before, during, and after the development of this discipline. Choose, for example, several key passages in the Gospel of Mark. Begin with their exposition by Henry Barclay Swete,[14] the premier commentator on Mark in the pre-form critical period (1909). Notice how Swete simply assumes that the only purpose of the text is to tell what happened in the historical ministry of Jesus. Despite his vast erudition, we learn nothing about what Mark was trying to accomplish in sharing these particular stories with his own church. Then turn to the massive commentary of Vincent Taylor,[15] which, despite its date (1952), reflects the earlier form-critical period between the two World Wars. Here the material is carefully divided into pericopes and each is properly classified as to form. This analysis leads Taylor to distinguish occasionally between the situation in the ministry of Jesus and that in the time of the Evangelist. But as the exegesis unfolds, very little is really made of the form-critical analysis found in the introduction to that paragraph. It is as if Taylor felt obliged to cite the form critics for the sake of thoroughness without really knowing what to do with their results. Contrast this, finally, with Eduard Schweizer's treatment of Mark from a more mature form-critical perspective (1970).[16] Here we learn what Mark understood about the historical Jesus, but, more important, we learn how he applied that understanding to the church of his own day. What this threefold comparison tends to illustrate is that even the best commentaries on the Synoptic Gospels written before the 1960s are, from the standpoint of form criticism, now badly out of date.

3. *Redaction Criticism.* The English word "redaction" (used here as the closest equivalent to the German word *Redaktion*) refers to the editorial activity by which a writer drafts a composite work in final form. When applied to a discipline of Synoptic study, it focuses on the process by which the Evangelists utilized available sources to produce our present Gospels. Emerging after the Second World War—e.g., in the work of Günther Bornkamm on Matthew (1960), Willi Marxsen on Mark (1956), and Hans Conzelmann on Luke (1954)—redaction criticism has become the most fruitful of all the disciplines of Synoptic study for the preacher.[17] The main reason is that it concentrates on the motives and methods by which certain church leaders deliberately transformed a miscellany of traditional religious materials into distinctive "gospels" directed to the needs of their local communities. That process, of course, is precisely the one that preachers follow week by week as they move from the people to the pulpit to declare the gospel. Our task, like that of the Evangelists, is not so much to create new material, in the sense of novel religious ideas, but to adapt existing resources in creative fashion to meet the challenges of our own time and place.

There are three basic ways in which redaction critics go about their task of discovering the editorial intentions of the Evangelists. First, they look carefully at the linkages that connect the separate oral pericopes—i.e., they examine the string on which the necklace is threaded. In one sense, they analyze most closely those outer layers of each account which the form critics peel away in search of its core. Second, they make careful comparisons of the different ways in which each Evangelist treats the same saying or story. Again, they do so not in order to discover the common source in its most basic form, which would be the goal of source critics, but in order to infer the strategy that caused a particular Evangelist to adapt his source in unique ways. Third, they search for recurring themes in each Gospel which root neither in the oral pericopes (and therefore, presumably, in the ministry of Jesus), nor in the pre-Gospel literary sources (and therefore, presumably, in the life of the early church), but in the editorial linkages discussed above (and therefore, presumably, in the mind of the final author). To oversimplify a bit, the redaction critic is trying to isolate neither the setting in the life of Jesus (*Sitz im Leben Jesu*), nor the setting in the life of the early church (*Sitz im Leben Kirche*), but the setting in the life of a particular book (*Sitz im Leben Buch*).

As is true with the other disciplines of Synoptic study, redaction criticism is too technical and too tedious for the parish preacher to practice on a regular basis. However, in addition to profiting greatly from the monographs and commentaries that reflect the fruits of this approach, the preacher can use one simple exercise which has tremendous value and will lead the preacher away from an excessive dependence upon these secondary sources to a personal engagement with the primary texts. I refer to the careful outlining of an entire Gospel in sufficient detail to show the interrelationships of each section down to the individual paragraphs. Nothing helps to clarify the overall design of a literary work more than to attempt a structural analysis of its contents.[18] Personally prepared outlines based on a thorough study both of current scholarship and of the text itself will enable the preacher to track the mind of the Evangelists and, in the process, will reveal more possibilities for truly biblical sermons than can be discovered in any other way.

To summarize this entire section: Synoptic criticism is exceedingly complex but not, thereby, irrelevant for the preacher. At its simplest, in treating any Synoptic passage source criticism demands that we ask, Does it have parallels and, if so, how are they similar and how are they different? Form criticism demands that we ask, What is the basic unit in which this text was originally transmitted? Redaction criticism demands that we ask, What is the place of this passage in the entire book and how does it contribute to the purpose for which this particular Gospel was written? Only when these three questions have been answered as fully as our training and study will permit are we ready to move from text to sermon.

II. HOMILETICAL STUDIES

Since the Synoptic Gospels have come to us today as finished writings rather than as oral pericopes or as fragmentary sources, preaching from them should be based on their canonical form. Therefore we will here take each Gospel in turn and explore its sermonic potential.

A. *The Gospel of Matthew.* The most conspicuous feature of the First Gospel, especially in contrast to the second, is the insertion of massive blocks of didactic material (from Q and M) into a narrative framework which largely follows Mark.[19] The fact that there are five such discourses alternating with narrative (5:1–7:29; 9:35–11:1; 13:1–53; 18:1–19:1; 24:1–26:1), each of them concluded with a stereotyped formula which marks a major transition (7:28–29; 11:1; 13:53; 19:1; 26:1), suggests that both the number and the arrangement may be deliberate (i.e., redactional). Some scholars have even gone far enough to suggest that Matthew's grand design was to prepare a "New Torah" parallel to the five books of Moses.[20] Regardless of how far the theory of a New Pentateuch is pushed, clearly the most distinctive contribution of Matthew to the preacher will come from the five great teaching sections.

The first of these, traditionally called the Sermon on the Mount, is found in Matthew 5–7. Because it is treated in detail elsewhere in this volume, attention will be devoted to only one possible sermon series from this much-studied and greatly beloved section of Scripture. In addition to specialized series treating each of the eight Beatitudes and each of the six petitions in the Lord's Prayer, on which a rich bibliography abounds, an expository treatment of the entire Sermon on the Mount might be divided into eight messages, as follows:

1. The Keys of the Kingdom (Matthew 5:3–6)

    The first stanza of the Beatitudes on inward righteousness in relation to God, a veritable "plan of salvation" according to Christ.

2. The Creativity of Conflict (Matthew 5:7–10)

The second stanza of the Beatitudes on outward righteousness in relation to others, balancing personal salvation with
courageous social action.

3. Great Expectations (Matthew 5:13–16)

   The twin metaphors of salt and light used to describe the
   paradoxical stance of the kingdom disciple as "in but not of"
   the world.

4. The New Morality (Matthew 5:17–48)

   An introduction and six "antitheses" illustrating how kingdom ethics surpass and thereby supersede Old Testament
   law.

5. The Secret of True Religion (Matthew 6:1–18)

   Three traditional practices of piety (almsgiving, prayer,
   fasting) used to illustrate the radical inwardness of true
   religion.

6. The Priority of the Spiritual (Matthew 6:19–34)

   A proper attitude toward the material realm is essential to
   the conquest of anxiety.

7. The Journey Inward (Matthew 7:1–12)

   The path to spiritual maturity moves from self-centered
   criticism to self-giving generosity.

8. The Great Divide (Matthew 7:13–29)

   The ultimate decision by which we follow Christ as the Way
   of life is both a gift and a demand to which we respond in
   obedience.

The second great discourse, on the mission charge to the Twelve, is
found in Matt. 9:35–11:1. It provides an excellent training manual
with which to equip a church for service in a hostile world. Any
congregation discouraged over meager results will find a bracing
tonic in the sober words of this clarion call to ministry. A comparison
with the other Synoptics suggests that, as a literary composition,
Matthew 10 is composite in character, having pulled together in
topical fashion material that was likely uttered at various stages in the
ministry of Jesus. Therefore, an expository treatment of this chapter
will have a comprehensiveness offered by no other single section of
the Gospels. One possible series of sermons might be organized in this
fashion:

1. Mandate for Mission (Matthew 9:35–10:4)

   The foundations of our calling in the compassion of Christ
   for the multitudes (9:35–36); in the power of prayer to the
   Lord of the harvest (9:37–38); and in the commissioning of
   disciples to minister with Christ's authority (10:1–4).

2. Onward, Christian Soldiers! (Matthew 10:5–15)

   Instructions regarding the scope (10:5–6), the strategy (10:7–8), and the seriousness (10:9–15) of our mission to the lost.

3. Advance Through Storm (Matthew 10:16–39)

   The certainty of persecution (10:16–25), the courage to endure persecution (10:26–33), and the costliness of persecution (10:34–39).

4. Ambassadors for Christ (Matthew 10:40–42)

   The cruciality of representing Christ to others (10:40), the certainty of reward for faithful service (10:41), and the basis of reward in helping the insignificant (10:42).

The third of the Matthean discourses (13:1–52) is a natural for preaching, because it is arranged very symmetrically into a cycle of seven parables on the mystery of the kingdom, interspersed with explanatory comments. Here we will identify those clustered in Matthew 13 as a subgroup worthy of special attention.[21] They include the parables of:

1. The seed and the soils (13:3b–9)
2. The wheat and the weeds (13:24–30)
3. The mustard seed (13:31–32)
4. The leaven (13:33)
5. The treasure hidden in the field (13:44)
6. The pearl of great price (13:45–46)
7. The net (13:47–50)

It is well known that Matthew says more about the church than does any other Gospel, and this ecclesiastical emphasis is concentrated in the fourth discourse of ch. 18, which serves as the nearest thing we have to a "Churchbook" or manual of discipline in the Synoptics. Once again, a highly composite treatment has brought together in topical fashion several of the components essential to the building of Christian fellowship. A series of sermons on "The High Cost of Community" might treat each of these ingredients in turn: (1) childlike humility (18:1–4); (2) perennial concern for insignificant people (18:5–6,10–14); (3) radical resistance to sin (18:7–9); (4) a ministry of reconciliation to the estranged (18:15–20); and (5) the practice of unlimited forgiveness (18:21–35).

The fifth and final discourse in Matthew 24–25 is difficult to expound because of its eschatological imagery, and yet it is especially relevant to the neo-apocalyptic temper of our times. Because of its length and complexity, preachers may wish to group their treatment into two different series of sermons. The first of these would deal with the end of the age, which is described as a drama in three acts: (1) travail (24:4–8); (2) tribulation (24:9–28); and (3) triumph (24:29–41). The second of the series would deal with the urgency of being prepared for the sudden inbreak of eternity. Five parables underscore (1) the need for watchfulness: the thief in the night (24:42–44); (2) the need for faithfulness: the obedient servant (24:45–51); (3) the need for readiness: the ten maidens (25:1–13); (4) the need for resourcefulness: the talents (25:14–30); and (5) the need for mercifulness: the sheep and the goats (25:31–46).

Of course, there are many choice texts unique to Matthew not found in these five distinctive discourses. Such verses will regularly suggest themselves to any preacher who maintains a thorough familiarity with the entire Gospel through personal Bible study and wide reading in the better scholarly literature. Furthermore, as a result of the liturgical and catechetical character of the First Gospel, material found in several of the Synoptic Gospels has often been edited most attractively for preaching by Matthew, as the regular use of a "harmony" will reveal. But the preacher best mediates the most original contribution of this Gospel by close attention to the Q and M material concentrated in the five sections examined above (plus the infancy narrative of chs. 1–2 and the passion-resurrection narrative of chs. 26–28 not considered here because of special treatment elsewhere in this volume).

B. *The Gospel of Mark.* In contrast to the complexity of Matthew's fivefold arrangement, Mark is organized into only two equal parts. The first eight chapters are dominated by the Messianic secret (e.g., Mark 1:34, 44; 3:12; 5:43; 7:36). But at the watershed in Mark 8:27–9:1, the secret is out, namely, that Jesus as Son of Man will suffer and die. Therefore, the last eight chapters are dominated by the Messianic suffering (e.g., Mark 8:31; 9:31; 10:32–34; 14:22–25). In that sense, Mark is a martyrology which defines faith in terms of a cross, i.e., as the willingness to save one's life by losing it (Mark 8:35). This paradoxical approach to Christian commitment is developed throughout the Gospel in three major ways, each of them with rich potential for preaching.[22]

The first is Mark's overarching definition of discipleship in terms of "following" Jesus, an open-ended pilgrimage with One who walks that "New Frontier" where two worlds are in collision. At bottom, what we have here is a root metaphor or archetypal image of how the Gospel actually works. The analogy developed by Mark is that of new life by "following the Leader."

There is enormous relevance to this paradigm, or "model," which anchors salvation firmly in a dynamic understanding of discipleship. For one thing, it conceives of redemption not just as a point but as a process, not only as a New Being but as a New Becoming as well. As such, it delivers Christianity from static Victorian categories and establishes effective contact with that incredible sense of motion which so fascinates the children of Darwin. For another thing, it sets "the company of the committed" (Elton Trueblood) in a forward-facing posture at a time when traditionalism (i.e., conservatism for its own sake) exercises undue influence. Here, in other words, is the experiential basis for a true "theology of hope" (Jürgen Moltmann), for a "pro-active" rather than "re-active" life-style that majors on "feedforward" rather than "feedback" (I. A. Richards). Finally, here is a powerful way to define conversion in personal and relational terms rather than in institutional and transactional terms. There is abroad in our world a weariness with collectivism and bureaucracy, a hunger to move beyond the negativism of the antihero movement and rediscover what can happen when one life interacts authentically with another.

A splendid way to tap into the rich resources of the "discipleship as followship" motif is to preach a series of sermons based on the commitment stories in the Gospel of Mark. Such a series might be organized as follows:

1. "Brave Journey" (Introduction to series)
   Mark 1:17a (cf. John 21:18–22; I Peter 2:21)
2. "Great Expectations" (Making "fishers of men")
   Mark 1:16–20
3. "The Gospel for the Socially Despised" (The call of Levi)
   Mark 2:13–17
4. "The Crux of an Inner Core" (The call of the Twelve)
   Mark 3:13–19a
5. "The Family of God" (The true relatives of Jesus)
   Mark 3:19b–21, 31–35
6. "The Marching Orders of the Master" (The mission of the Twelve)
   Mark 6:7–13
7. "The Crisis of Faith" (The Confession at Caesarea Philippi)
   Mark 8:27–33

8. "The Cost of Discipleship" (The way of the cross)
    Mark 8:34–9:1
9. "The Agony and the Ecstasy" (The transfiguration)
    Mark 9:2–8
10. "Dealing with Divisions" (The strange exorcist)
    Mark 9:38–41
11. "The Impossible Possibility" (The rich young ruler)
    Mark 10:17–31
12. "Go South to Sorrow" (The Journey to Jerusalem)
    Mark 10:32–34
13. "Are Ye Able?" (The request of James and John)
    Mark 10:35–45
14. "The Ultimate Ordeal" (The vigil in Gethsemane)
    Mark 14:32–42
15. "He Goes Before You" (The discovery of the empty tomb)
    Mark 16:1–8

Over against this developmental understanding of discipleship, which pictures faith as a deepening commitment to Christ in the crises of life, stands the stark contrast of conflict and rejection. Mark has given greater prominence to controversy than any other Evangelist both by the amount of polemical material that he included and by its strategic placement within the structure of the Second Gospel. In a profound sense, his entire writing was passion literature which began with the cross and then was written "backwards" (M. Kähler) to expose the antecedents of this tragic denouement.

Outside the passion narrative (chs. 14–16), which is, in itself, one long conflict account, there are fourteen major controversy stories in Mark (but only one in Q, two in M, and five in L). These Marcan episodes contain 115 of the 489 verses (23.5 percent) in 1:14–12:44, which means that almost a quarter of the public ministry is devoted to a description of disputes with the Jewish leadership.

Moreover, the distribution of these accounts within the Second Gospel was calculated to give them greater prominence than any other kind of material. The first major block of five controversy stories was located in 2:1–3:6 immediately following the Prologue (1:1–13) and a brief introduction to the typical pattern of Jesus' Galilean ministry (1:14–45). Clearly the arrangement is topical and theological rather than chronological or geographical, suggesting that from the outset Jesus was a scandal to the religious establishment that eventually masterminded his death. By placing in the forefront these five life-and-death issues that climaxed in a plot to destroy Jesus (3:6),

Mark caused the shadow of the cross to fall over the ministry as soon as it was launched. Implicit in the very nature of Jesus' religion were the seeds of violent conflict with the status quo.

The other major block of five controversy stories was located at the very close of the public ministry in 11:27–12:37. Not only does this unit provide a fitting introduction to the passion narrative but, when viewed with 2:1–3:6, it serves as a closing parenthesis within which the entire public ministry was bracketed. When one stands back to view all of Mark 1–12 as an entity dealing with the public career of Jesus, it is hard to resist the impression that 2:1–3:6 at the beginning and 11:27–12:37 at the ending provided the pivotal foci around which the entire narration was intended to revolve. If so, then the Second Gospel is, indeed, an apologia for the message of the cross, a battle manual on the fine art of losing friends and influencing enemies.

As such, it is a powerful antidote to that pervasive amiability which has blunted the cutting edge of a courageous pulpit by avoiding controversy at any cost. One would never suspect from much sermonic fare today the central fact that the Christian Savior managed to get himself crucified after only a few months of unbearably provocative ministry. One way to recover the forgotten insight that Christianity must fight and win the internal battle for integrity before it is ready to fight the external battle for victory over the powers of darkness is by preaching a series on the controversy stories in Mark. As to specifics, the following framework may prove helpful:

1. "Decisive Issues in Religion" (Introduction to series)
   Mark 1:22; 8:15, 31; 9:31; 10:33–34; 11:18
2. "The Everlasting Mercy" (Conflict over personal vs. cultic forgiveness)
   Mark 2:1–12
3. "Beyond the Religious Ghetto" (Conflict over penetration versus separation from sinners)
   Mark 2:13–17
4. "Surprised by Joy" (Conflict over joyful feasting versus sorrowful fasting)
   Mark 2:18–22
5. "Religion: Servant or Master?" (Conflict over spiritual freedom versus religious observance)
   Mark 2:23–28
6. "In Defense of the Do-Gooders" (Conflict over moral imperatives versus ceremonial requirements)
   Mark 3:1–6

7. "Lord of the Flies" (Conflict over divine versus demonic power)
   Mark 3:22–30
8. "The Place of the Past in Religion" (Conflict over Scripture versus tradition)
   Mark 7:1–13
9. "The Significance of the Supernatural" (Conflict over insight versus sight as religious evidence)
   Mark 8:11–13
10. "Perfect Law and Imperfect Life" (Conflict over divine intention versus legal permission)
    Mark 10:2–12
11. "By What Authority?" (Conflict over heavenly versus human credentials for ministry)
    Mark 11:27–33
12. "The Sacred and the Profane" (Conflict over obligation versus rejection of the secular)
    Mark 12:13–17
13. "The Power and the Glory" (Conflict over the transcendent versus the immanent)
    Mark 12:18–27
14. "First Things First" (Conflict over commitment versus commandment)
    Mark 12:28–34
15. "On Taking Christ Seriously" (Conflict over the new versus the old)
    Mark 12:35–37

As the title of the introductory message suggests, the most important concern of these sermons should be to define the crux of each issue as it emerged between Jesus and his opponents, not only in the historical particularity of first-century Judaism but also in the enduring form by which it continues to manifest itself today. Therefore, sermons in this series should have at least two parts, each of these with two subsections. Regardless of the sequence followed, the preacher must, at some point, determine the religious stance of the original opponents of Jesus in essential categories that clarify the existence of the same mind-set in the religious life of today. Over against this alternative the preacher must also isolate the roots of the distinctive position taken by Jesus so that it becomes possible to explore the implication of applying that approach to the religious conditions of our day.

There is no way to treat in detail these deadly conflicts without asking whether Jesus finally failed in his mission to transform the religion of Israel. But Mark knew from the outset how his story would end, thus he took care to counter the note of tragedy implicit in the controversies of Jesus by scattering throughout his Gospel the note of triumph implicit in the miracles of Jesus. Of the 489 verses in Mark 1:14–12:44 devoted to the public ministry of our Lord, 188 of them (39.4 percent) deal directly with his mighty works. Editorially (i.e., redactionally), these accounts are never an appendage to the sacred story; rather, they are always integral to its basic understanding. Just as the controversies of Jesus from the beginning carried the seeds of his crucifixion, so the miracles from the beginning carried the seeds of his resurrection.

There are fifteen major sections in Mark worthy of separate treatment in a sermon series on the miracles.

1. "It Took a Miracle" (Introduction to series)
   Mark 1:32–34; 3:9–12; 6:53–56
2. "The Taming of the Tongue" (Exorcism of an unclean spirit)
   Mark 1:21–28
3. "Reach Out and Touch" (Cleansing of a leper)
   Mark 1:40–45
4. "Help of the Helpless" (Healing of a paralytic)
   Mark 2:1–12
5. "In the Eye of the Storm" (Stilling of a storm)
   Mark 4:35–41
6. "The High Cost of Compassion" (The Gerasene demoniac)
   Mark 5:1–20
7. "The Touch of the Master's Hand" (The raising of Jairus' daughter)
   Mark 5:21–24, 35–43
8. "A Case of Ultimate Concern" (The woman with a flow of blood)
   Mark 5:25–34
9. "Bread for the World" (The feeding of the five/four thousand)
   Mark 8:14–21 (cf. 6:30–44; 8:1–10)
10. "The Haven of Rest" (Walking on the sea)
    Mark 6:45–52
11. "A Defiant Faith" (A Syrophoenician woman's daughter)
    Mark 7:24–30

12. "Ears That Hear" (The healing of a deaf-mute in the Decapolis)
    Mark 7:31–37
13. "Eyes That See" (Restoring sight to a blind man of Bethsaida)
    Mark 8:22–26
14. "The Faith Beyond Faith" (Driving an unclean spirit from an epileptic child)
    Mark 9:14–29
15. "Out of My Darkness" (The healing of blind Bartimaeus)
    Mark 10:46–52

What is ultimately at stake in the proclamation of the Marcan miracles? The reality of miracle is nothing less than the possibility of the presence of God in an otherwise closed universe. For miracle does not mean the contradiction of the created order by some aberrational phenomenon but the infusing and thereby the transcending of the natural with the supernatural (the two realms being congruent rather than contradictory, because they both derive from the same ultimate Source). To claim a miracle is not to indulge in speculation on the bizarre but to confess the intervention of the divine!

C. *The Gospel of Luke.* In sheer size, the Third Gospel offers a unique challenge to the preacher, its 19,400 words making it the biggest book in the New Testament. The two volumes together, Luke-Acts, comprise 27 percent of the New Testament, more than all the letters of Paul combined. Bulk, however, is equaled by beauty, Luke being universally acclaimed, in the famous words of Renan, as "the most beautiful book in the world." But more, Luke is the only Gospel with a sequel which makes explicit the unfolding of what began in the ministry of Jesus; thus it is also the most balanced of the Synoptics.

The best way for preachers to deal with all three of these distinctive characteristics is to treat Luke thematically. A topical approach will allow us to roam far and wide in search of riches. It will also permit us to exploit to the greatest degree the artistry of the Evangelist, for Luke's aesthetic elegance is seen most clearly in the way he sounds his dominant motifs. Further, it will free us to make creative combinations between Luke and Acts, since the same emphases highlighted in the first volume recur in the second. There are at least a dozen dominant motifs in Luke deserving of sermonic attention.

1. *The Foundations of Christianity in Jewish History.* From the outset, the birth of Christianity (in the birth of John and Jesus) was saturated in Scripture (Luke 1–2). Throughout this Gospel, Old Testament

quotations are introduced to explain the ministry of Jesus (esp. 4:17–21; 18:31; 24:25–27; 24:44–47). Luke also showed how Jesus identified profoundly with both of the leading religious institutions of Judaism, the synagogue (4:15–16; 4:44) and the Temple (2:27; 2:41–51; 19:45–48; 21:37–38).

The Holy City, Jerusalem, where the Temple was found, became the center of Luke's theological geography. The Gospel story began there (1:5ff.; 2:22; 2:41ff.); it returned there in the great final journey of Jesus to his cross (9:31; 9:51–53; 13:22; 13:33–35; 17:11; 18:31; 19:11; 19:28); and it ended there with the resurrection appearances that equipped the disciples for a world mission (24:33, 47–48, 52). Preaching on this theme will help to link the New Testament to the Old Testament.

2. *The Future of Christianity in Church History.* Just as Luke pushed back his Christian perspective of the past, rooting the ministry of Jesus in centuries of Jewish devotion, just so he pushed forward his Christian perspective of the future, viewing the ministry of Jesus from the foreground of the ongoing life of the church as recorded in Acts. In so doing, Luke set the life of Jesus in a more spacious temporal context than his predecessors and thus linked his work to a much vaster heritage and hope.

The Jewish apocalyptic idiom in which elements of Jesus' message had been couched was in danger of being interpreted by Gentiles as implying the end of history rather than its transformation. Luke took care to highlight the way in which that proclamation could be fulfilled *in* history, not just *beyond* it. A very real future still lay ahead, for the history of Jesus was only the "beginning," not the end, of the "things which have been accomplished among us" (1:1–2). Luke saw that history itself could become the bearer of eternal realities as it is interpenetrated by the Holy Spirit, the divine power operative both in Jesus and subsequently in his church.

3. *The Function of Christianity in World History.* Luke alone of all the Evangelists was concerned to connect Jesus with the secular events of his time. Both the birth (2:1–2) and the public ministry (3:1–2) were dated by means of elaborate synchronisms which implied that the coming of Jesus deserved to "make the news" as much as the rule of any Caesar, governor, or high priest.

The very nature of the preface to Luke-Acts, with its impressive dedication to Theophilus, indicates that the two volumes were considered, not private, but published materials for the book markets of Greco-Roman society. Luke was clearly interested in the larger world beyond the church, and he wanted that world to take notice of his faith.

4. *The Universality of Christianity.* If early Christianity was to offer itself to the larger world, it must first purge itself of narrow, provincial elements and then emphasize the unlimited scope of its appeal. Luke consistently carried out this twofold task. The angels announced glad tidings to *all* people (2:14). Simeon saw Jesus as "a light for revelation to the *Gentiles*" (2:32). John the Baptist came to prepare for the day when "*all* flesh shall see the salvation of God" (3:6). The ancestry of Jesus was traced back, not to Abraham as in Matthew, but to *Adam,* the father of mankind (3:38). The inaugural sermon at Nazareth highlighted God's dealings with two Gentiles, the widow of Zarephath and Naaman the Syrian (4:24–27). Jesus sent out Seventy (10:1), the symbolic number for all the nations of the world. The risen Christ interpreted the Scriptures to mean "that repentance and forgiveness of sins should be preached . . . to *all* nations" (24:47).

5. *"The Gospel of the Underdog"* (A. M. Hunter). The universal reach of Christianity was portrayed most vividly by Luke in his description of the ministry of Jesus to social outcasts excluded from the Jewish religion. The Lucan Savior was a "friend of sinners" (5:30; 7:34; 15:1–2), such as the woman who washed his feet with her tears (7:37–39), or the extortioner Zacchaeus (19:7–10), or the repentant thief on the cross (23:42–43). Familiar parables, such as the prodigal son (15:11–24) or the publican at prayer (18:9–14), traced the divine reversal that can transform the most pitiable of lives. A Roman centurion was credited with faith not found in Israel (7:9). Despised Samaritans were defended against the prejudice of the disciples (9:54–55) and two of them were made heroes—one of a parable (10:33), the other of a miracle (17:16).

6. *"The Gospel of Womanhood"* (A. M. Hunter). One special group not ostracized from Judaism but largely denied true religious equality was a particular object of Luke's concern. Our Evangelist delighted to dwell on the place of women in the ministry of Jesus, referring to them thirteen times not paralleled in other Gospels. Their importance was foreshadowed in the introductory episodes describing Elizabeth (1:5–7, 24–25, 41–45), Mary (1:26–38, 46–55), and Anna (2:36–38). Two women, one with a lost coin (15:8–10) and the other with a persistent plea (18:1–8), were the subjects of parables, while another two, the widow of Nain (7:11–17) and the daughter of Abraham, stooped for eighteen years (13:10–17), were the objects of miracles. On two occasions Jesus was supported by women from the

crowd, once to praise his birth (11:27) and again to lament his death (23:27).

Most important, as the story of the sinful women (7:36–50) mentioned earlier implies, and as the familiar story of Martha and Mary (10:38–42) makes explicit, women "healed of evil spirits and infirmities" (8:2) were redeemed for full-fledged discipleship. A large company of such women accompanied Jesus and the Twelve, ministering to them as prototypes of later deaconesses (8:2–3). The fact that so many were listed by name (Mary Magdalene, Joanna the wife of Chuza, Susanna) suggests their continuing importance in the life of the early church (Acts 1:14). For Luke, they played a crucial role as witnesses both of the death (23:49, 55) and of the resurrection (24:1–11, 22–24) of Jesus, despite the fact that the testimony of women was not always given full weight in the ancient world.

7. *"The Compassionate Christ"* (W. R. Bowie). In the language of Titus 3:4, Luke wrote of those days "when the goodness and loving kindness of God our Savior appeared." Jesus' "outreach to the unreached" was based on no lust for popularity (4:24), no infatuation with numbers (12:32), no mass appeal of "religion in general" (7:31–34). Instead, it sprang from the wellsprings of compassion within his Spirit. The raising of the widow of Nain's son was expressly motivated by a mercy without measure (7:13). The turning point in the two most famous Lucan parables came when the Good Samaritan had *compassion* on a roadside victim (10:33) and the father of the prodigal had *compassion* on his wayward son (15:20).

8. *The Severity of Jesus.* This "gentle Jesus" of Luke was not without his more austere aspect, however. Almost two fifths of Luke's special material (L) is polemical in character, a fact that is not always noticed because subtler methods of rebuke, such as parables, often took the place of open attack. Renunciation was demanded by the parables of the tower builder and of the rash king (14:33). Disciples who followed Jesus must "leave everything" (5:11, 28; see 14:26; 18:22) and, putting their hands to the plow, refuse to look back (9:62), even if this took them from their parental home (9:59–60) and left them with nowhere to lay their heads (9:58). For Luke, discipleship demanded a self-denial which involved taking up one's cross *daily* (9:23).

9. *Riches and Poverty.* One particular point at which the tenderness and severity of Jesus meet in Luke is in his dealings with the poor and the rich.

On the one hand, the poor were a special concern throughout the Gospel. Humble shepherds, not rich Magi, greeted Jesus at his birth (2:15–18). His family offered a modest sacrifice when presenting him at the Temple (2:24). The ethic of John the Baptist was directed entirely in this area: the multitudes were to share their food and clothing, tax collectors were to avoid extortion, and soldiers were to eschew robbery and be content with their wages (3:10–14). Jesus enunciated this concern at the outset of his Nazareth "Inaugural": "He has anointed me to preach good news to the *poor*, . . . to set at liberty those who are oppressed" (4:18; see 7:22). The first Beatitude conferred happiness on the poor who possessed the kingdom of God (6:20). Disciples were enjoined to be generous with those forced to beg (6:30), and to exhibit the divine mercifulness (6:36) by giving with "good measure, pressed down, shaken together, running over" (6:38).

On the other hand, the first woe in Luke's Sermon on the Plain was directed against the rich (6:24). Men were to "beware of all covetousness" (12:15) lest they become rich fools with worthless barns (12:16–20). No man could lay up treasure for himself and be rich toward God (12:21). Anxiety about food and clothing was the antithesis of trusting reliance on God (12:22–31). Therefore, giving, not getting, was the fundamental way that we could become like the God whose good pleasure it is to give us the kingdom (12:32–34). Salvation came to the house of the rich Zacchaeus when he determined to give half his goods to the poor (19:8–9), whereas it bypassed the "rich young ruler" who would not "sell all . . . and distribute to the poor" (18:22).

In Luke, the ultimate source of Jesus' encouragement to the poor and his warnings to the rich was not to be found in any proletarian prejudice on his part. Although he may have come from the lower economic classes, Jesus freely associated with the more privileged (7:36; 11:37; 14:1) and attracted some of them to his cause (8:3; 19:1–10; 23:50). Rather, his teachings sprang from a profound conviction regarding the spiritual consequences of wealth. So obviously inequitable were the fortunes of men, so frequently did a disparity exist between their material and spiritual resources, that Jesus was certain of a great reversal which would "fill the hungry with good things and send the rich away empty" (1:53). Divine judgment is neither impressed with early achievement nor scornful of earthly poverty, as the rich man and Lazarus both learned beyond the great divide (16:19–31).

10. *The Importance of Prayer.* Unable or unwilling to depend upon earthly influence, the "poor" must instead rely upon the power of prayer. Jesus himself set the example in this regard. On at least ten important occasions, Luke alone portrayed the prayer life of the

Lord: at his baptism (3:21); in the midst of struggles with both bodily infirmities and spiritual enemies (5:16); before choosing the Twelve (6:12); before seeking the faith of his disciples and announcing to them his impending passion (9:18); at the transfiguration (9:29); before teaching the Lord's Prayer (11:1); before Gethsemane, that Peter's faith not fail (22:32); at his crucifixion (23:34); at his death (23:46); and with his disciples at a meal in Emmaus (24:30).

Moreover, Luke alone mentioned Jesus' entreaty to all the disciples in Gethsemane that they pray (22:40). Only in the Third Gospel do we have the three familiar parables on prayer: the friend at midnight (11:5–8), the persistent widow (18:1–8), and the Pharisee and the publican (18:9–14). Only here, in addition to the Lord's Prayer, are we given the four prayer hymns of the infancy narrative: the Magnificat (1:46–55), the Benedictus (1:68–79), the Gloria (2:14), and the Nunc Dimittis (2:29–32). This same section also emphasizes the place of prayer in the lives of the Temple worshipers (1:10), of Zechariah (1:13), and of Anna (2:37). Scattered throughout the Gospel are many teachings on the importance of prayer when persecuted (6:28), when witnessing (10:2), and when watching in time of tribulation (21:36), such as in Gethsemane (22:40, 46).

11. *The Power of the Spirit.* Prayer can open an effective channel of divine power which comes through the presence of the Holy Spirit in the world. Luke's Gospel contains more references to the Spirit than does any other, and this theme is given even greater emphasis in Acts. From the outset, in the infancy narratives, the power of the Spirit is prominent. John the Baptist would be "filled with the Holy Spirit" (1:15; see 1:80), as was his mother, Elizabeth (1:41), and his father, Zechariah (1:67). Jesus was conceived by the Holy Spirit (1:35) and "confirmed" by the Spirit-inspired Simeon (2:25–27). The Holy Spirit descended upon him "in bodily form" at his baptism (3:22), that he might baptize others "with the Holy Spirit" as John predicted (3:16). From the Jordan, Jesus came forth "full of the Holy Spirit" (4:1) both to conquer Satan in the wilderness (4:1ff.) and to begin his work in Galilee (4:14). The very first words of the Scripture chosen for his Nazareth "Inaugural" provide the basic category by which to understand his entire ministry: "The *Spirit* of the Lord is upon me" (4:18).

12. *The Gospel of Gladness.* Doxology is the theme song of the Third Gospel. This motif is closely linked with prayer (the four poems in the infancy narratives being both prayers and hymns) and with the power of the Spirit (Jesus "*rejoiced* in the Holy Spirit," 10:21). The mood which this motif reflects was shaped primarily by the character of the Gospel as "good news." The mood was also shaped by the context of

worship in which the entire book was set, for the story both began (1:8–9) and ended 24:52–53) in the Temple precincts.

More than any other, the Third Gospel is calculated to convey the note of cheer, exultation, even ecstasy, that belongs to the adoration of God by the redeemed. This is seen in the prominence that Luke gave to the concepts of joy, peace, glory, blessedness, and happiness, all of which were emphasized more than a dozen times in the Gospel. In a secondary way, Luke reinforced this theme by accenting the ideas of gladness, exultation, praise, laughter, and leaping. Only the preacher's patient work with a concordance will reveal how deeply this cluster of concepts was woven into the very fabric of the Third Gospel.

There is no space here to develop specific homiletical suggestions regarding each of the twelve themes just analyzed. However, regular use of theological wordbooks will quickly supply useful categories around which to organize the fruits of this thematic approach. Topical sermons have always been popular because they treat a single subject, while at the same time being suspect because they so easily stray from biblical ways of thinking. One great value of majoring on Lucan motifs is that one may be both topical and biblical at the same time.

NOTES

1. For a history of these developments, written to challenge the scholarly consensus, see William R. Farmer, *The Synoptic Problem* (Macmillan Co., 1964).

2. For a strong challenge to the hypothesis of the priority of Mark, which lies at the bedrock of Streeterian critical orthodoxy, see Hans-Herbert Stoldt, *History and Criticism of the Marcan Hypothesis,* tr. by Donald L. Niewyk (Mercer University Press, 1980). Mercer University Press has also reprinted Farmer's *The Synoptic Problem* (1976) and has published John Bernard Orchard's *A Synopsis of the Four Gospels* (1982), which is designed to illustrate the "Owen-Griesbach Hypothesis" or the "Two-Gospel Hypothesis" as it is sometimes called. On the Griesbach Hypothesis in historical perspective, see Bernard Orchard and Thomas R. W. Longstaff (eds.), *J. J. Griesbach: Synoptic and Text-Critical Studies 1776–1976* (Cambridge University Press, 1979).

3. The Priority of Luke is advocated, primarily on linguistic grounds, by the Hebraist, Robert L. Lindsey, in "A Modified Two-Document Theory of the Synoptic Dependence and Interdependence," *Novum Testamentum,* Vol. 6 (1963), pp. 239–263; and in *A Hebrew Translation of the Gospel of Mark* (Jerusalem: Dugith Publishers, 1969), pp. 1–84.

4. Several paragraphs in this section and elsewhere recast my "Preaching the Gospel According to Mark," *Review and Expositor,* Vol. 75 (Fall 1978), p. 489.

5. L. Housman, *Songs of Praise,* no. 228, quoted by A. M. Hunter, *The Gospel According to St. Mark* (London: SCM Press, 1949), p. 15.

6. On this theme, see the now neglected but still useful study by E. F. Scott, *The Purpose of the Gospels* (Charles Scribner's Sons, 1949).

7. The standard harmony for Synoptic study was designed by Albert Huck in 1892. The latest Greek edition (13th) is edited by Heinrich Greeven, *Synopse der drei ersten Evangelien* (Tübingen: J. C. B. Mohr [Paul Siebeck], 1981). The latest (4th) English (RSV) edition is edited by Burton H. Throckmorton, *Gospel Parallels: A Synopsis of the First Three Gospels* (Thomas Nelson, 1979). Also valuable is the Greek-English edition edited by Kurt Aland, *Synopsis of the Four Gospels* (United Bible Societies, 1972).

8. Julian Price Love, *The Gospel and the Gospels* (Abingdon Press, 1953).

9. Probably the best known of these is the work by H. D. A. Major, T. W. Manson, and C. J. Wright, *The Mission and Message of Jesus* (E. P. Dutton & Co., 1938), in which the work by Manson on "The Sayings of Jesus" (pp. 299–639) is superior. Of less homiletical value is the guide to Huck's *Synopsis* by F. W. Beare, *The Earliest Records of Jesus* (Abingdon Press, 1962).

10. Useful comments on this issue may be found in D. Moody Smith, *Interpreting the Gospels for Preaching* (Fortress Press, 1980), pp. 8–11.

11. For a brief history of this ground-breaking stage, together with full bibliographical references, see Vincent Taylor, *The Formation of the Gospel Tradition* (London: Macmillan & Co., 1935), pp. 1–21; E. Basil Redlich, *Form Criticism: Its Value and Limitations* (London: Gerald Duckworth & Co., 1939).

12. For Taylor, see *The Formation of the Gospel Tradition.* For R. H. Lightfoot, see especially *History and Interpretation in the Gospels* (London: Hodder & Stoughton, 1935). For C. F. D. Moule, see his richly suggestive *The Birth of the New Testament* (London: Adam & Charles Black, 1962).

13. The hermeneutical implications of this approach are worked out in William E. Hull, "The Relevance of the New Testament," *Review and Expositor,* Vol. 62 (Spring 1965), pp. 187–200.

14. Henry Barclay Swete, *The Gospel According to St. Mark,* 3d ed. (London: Macmillan, 1909).

15. Vincent Taylor, *The Gospel According to St. Mark* (London: Macmillan & Co., 1952).

16. Eduard Schweizer, *The Good News According to Mark* (John Knox Press, 1970).

17. The dates given above are for the original German works. English translations are Günther Bornkamm, Gerhard Barth, and Heinz Joachim Held, *Tradition and Interpretation in Matthew* (Westminster Press, 1963); Willi Marxsen, *Mark the Evangelist* (Abingdon Press, 1969); Hans Conzelmann, *The Theology of St. Luke* (Harper & Brothers, 1960). The basic research report on early redaction criticism is Joachim Rohde, *Rediscovering the Teaching of the*

Evangelists, tr. by Dorothea M. Barton (Westminster Press, 1969). A briefer, popular introduction is Norman Perrin, *What Is Redaction Criticism?* (Fortress Press, 1969).

18. I have attempted such structural analyses, together with explanatory introductions, in "A Teaching Outline of the Gospel of Matthew," *Review and Expositor,* Vol. 59 (Oct. 1962), pp. 433–444; "A Structural Analysis of the Gospel of Luke," *Review and Expositor,* Vol. 64 (Fall 1967), pp. 421–432; and "A Teaching Outline of the Gospel of John," *Review and Expositor,* Vol. 62 (Fall 1965), pp. 405–416.

19. Note the perceptive comments on this development by William Manson, *Jesus the Messiah* (London: Hodder & Stoughton, 1943), pp. 51–55.

20. A key contender for this understanding is B. W. Bacon, *Studies in Matthew* (Henry Holt, 1930), pp. xiv–xvii, 80–82, 265–335. An alternate approach is by Jack Dean Kingsbury, *Matthew: Structure, Christology, Kingdom* (Fortress Press, 1975); a popular summary is his *Matthew,* Proclamation Commentaries (Fortress Press, 1977), pp. 1–29; and his "Form and Message of Matthew," *Interpretation,* Vol. 29 (Jan. 1975), pp. 13–23. For a judicious evaluation, see W. D. Davies, *The Setting of the Sermon on the Mount* (Cambridge University Press, 1964), pp. 14–25.

21. For such a study, see Jack Dean Kingsbury, *The Parables of Jesus in Matthew 13* (London: S.P.C.K., 1976).

22. Here I return to material developed more fully in my "Preaching the Gospel According to Mark," loc. cit., pp. 491–501.

FOR FURTHER READING

The literature on preaching from the Synoptic Gospels is not great in either quantity or quality. In addition to the references cited in the notes, one may wish to consult the following:

Beasley-Murray, G. R. *Preaching the Gospel from the Gospels.* Judson Press, 1956.

Craddock, Fred B. *The Gospels.* Interpreting Biblical Texts. Abingdon Press, 1981.

Fuller, Reginald H. *The Use of the Bible in Preaching.* Fortress Press, 1981.

Keck, Leander E. *The Bible in the Pulpit.* Abingdon Press, 1978.

Mays, James Luther, ed. *Interpreting the Gospels.* Fortress Press, 1981.

Smith, D. Moody. *Interpreting the Gospels for Preaching.* Fortress Press, 1980.

11. PREACHING ON THE BIRTH OF JESUS
LEO SANDS, C.S.B.

> We need much care, dearly beloved, much vigilance so as to be able to plumb the depths of sacred Scripture. It is not possible to discover its meaning merely incidentally, or while we are asleep, but we have need of careful scrutiny, and of earnest prayer as well, that we may be able to penetrate a little the sanctuary of the sacred mysteries.

In this way John Chrysostom introduces one of his homilies.[1] Such diligence seems to be particularly urgent in the case of the Gospel passages concerning the birth of Jesus, the infancy narratives: Matthew 1–2 and Luke 1–2. This is so because contemporary exegetes have posed fundamental questions about them that cannot be overlooked. Is their content historical, they ask, and should the answer to that question affect the way in which we preach about them? In preaching generally, is there much use being made of historical-critical exegesis, particularly at Christmastide?[2] If not, is it because preachers are not familiar with exegetes' views? Is it because preachers are unsure as to the trustworthiness of the claims being made? Or is it because they worry about presenting to congregations something controversial on such a beloved subject as the Christmas mystery? What if I were to say on the last Sunday of Advent that we don't know whether Mary actually learned from an angel that she was to become the mother of Jesus? Or what if I were to go farther on the Epiphany and say that it is highly unlikely that three men from the east guided by a star went to Bethlehem? Would my parishioners be scandalized? Would I be doing them a disservice? These are questions I would like to consider in the first part of this chapter, relative to the more

195

fundamental question: What purpose in the Gospels do these narratives serve? In the second part, I wish to examine some major sections
of the narratives, in their context in the new lectionary now being
used by many of the churches. What can be made of the readings not
only in themselves but also in their relationship to the biblical passages
with which they are wedded on the feasts of Christmastide?

I. HERMENEUTICAL BACKGROUND:
THE INFANCY NARRATIVES

Probably the vast majority of preachers throughout the ages have
spoken about the events recounted surrounding Jesus' birth as if they
were historical facts. Let us look, for example, at four sermons
preached by Augustine, Martin Luther, John Henry Newman, and
Ronald A. Knox.

Augustine's sermon for the Epiphany is centered on a contrast
between the Jews who rejected Christ and the Gentiles who accepted
him.[3] It was the Magi from the east at his birth and Pilate from the
west at his death, not the chosen people, who bore witness to Jesus as
the King of the Jews. In the course of his sermon, Augustine takes it
for granted that the Magi came from the east to Bethlehem. He treats
Jesus' trial before Pilate and the star over Bethlehem as historical facts
of equal veracity.

Martin Luther, in "A Sermon on the Afternoon of Christmas
Day,"[4] on Luke 2:1–14, makes the same supposition of historicity. He
sets out to convince his congregation that Jesus is their personal Lord
and Savior. He wants them to believe in their hearts, "to *you* is born
this day . . . a Savior" (Luke 2:11). To trust in this way is to have
authentic faith—second faith, as he calls it. Although Luther, like
Augustine, neither dwells at length on the infancy narratives themselves nor embellishes them with imagery of his own, he still assumes
that angels announce to shepherds the good news of salvation, and
that they went to the manger to pay homage to the newborn king. He
gives no indication that he has any doubt about this.

Similar is John Henry Newman's Anglican sermon "Christ Hidden
from the World,"[5] based on a verse from John's Prologue: "The light
shineth in darkness; and the darkness comprehended it not" (John
1:5). Newman is demonstrating the principle that "true religion is a
hidden life in the heart."[6] This he illustrates primarily from the life of
Christ, a life shrouded in obscurity. Would we recognize Jesus today if
he were our next-door neighbor? Probably not. Although Newman,

like Augustine and Luther, says relatively little about the infancy narratives themselves, he still uses the detail in them to support his theme.

> What were the actual circumstances of his coming? His mother is a poor woman; she comes to Bethlehem to be taxed, travelling, when her choice would have been to remain at home. She finds there is no room in the inn; she is obliged to take herself to a stable; she brings forth her first born son, and lays him in a manger.[7]

Newman speaks as if these are historical events.

Ronald A. Knox, in a sermon preached on the BBC radio on Christmas Day 1950, does likewise.[8] Building his address around two views of the Christmas crib, he speaks eloquently of the paradox of the incarnation. If our first view of it is genuine, we realize that Jesus' birth was like that of any other human being. But then when we take a second view of the crib, we realize that the first was incomplete; this is a birthday without parallel, the birthday of the elder brother of every member of the human race, whose life brings restoration of lost innocence and supernatural life to all. Like the other three preachers we have seen, Knox emphasizes not the details of Luke's account of Jesus' birth but its significance in salvation history. He uses them to verify his exposition, in this case of Christ's humanity; there is Mary's pregnancy in Nazareth, a cave in Bethlehem with shepherds and angels in adoration. These are all accepted as fact.

Would it be wise in the light of contemporary exegesis not to do so? First of all, is there little historicity in the birth narratives? Perhaps the most fundamental principle of biblical form criticism is that in the Gospels many things are not presented in the historical context of Jesus' life, but in a catechetical or theological form which brings the reader closer to the life of the early church at the time at which the Gospel was written than it does to the earlier time of which it speaks. "In context and shape, in form and function, they [the Gospels] represent the interests and emphases of early Christian churches, and indeed of early Christian preaching."[9] Fred Craddock makes the same point while encouraging preachers to continue in the difficult task of interpreting the Scriptures. He suggests that most of the New Testament itself can be viewed as "interpretations or reinterpretations of the tradition in the light of new situations found on the mission fields of a vigorous and growing church."[10] Thus preachers are engaged in a task truly biblical in nature. Redaction criticism reinforces this contention that the Gospels were not written as historical documents, by comparing them to one another, emphasizing the distinctive characteristics of each, and thus the insuperable obstacles one faces in attempting to harmonize them in order to produce a composite account of Jesus' ministry and character. "The state of the sources makes it impossible to write a biography."[11]

These arguments take on a special importance in the case of the infancy narratives, for in them it is least likely that the writers of the Gospels had the intention of recounting a series of actual happenings. Let me cite two reasons for this. First, as Raymond Brown in his book *The Birth of the Messiah* puts it: The "infancy material has an origin and an historical quality quite different from that of the rest of the Gospels."[12] Whereas "the stories of the ministry depend, in part at least, on traditions that have come down from the disciples of Jesus . . . we have no reliable source of the infancy material."[13] Before the beginning of Jesus' public ministry there were no disciples present to pass on information about those years. Secondly, the accounts of Matthew and Luke are very different. None of the events, for instance, described in Matthew 2 are mentioned or even alluded to in Luke 1–2. "Such differences are more drastic than anywhere in the canonical gospels—the Synoptic *versus* the Fourth Gospel included."[14] Although this does not mean for a moment that there is no historical basis to the narratives, what precisely is it? Franz Kamphaus cites these facts: "Mary gave birth to Jesus, she was espoused to Joseph who belonged to the house of David, their home was in Nazareth, Bethlehem was the place where Jesus was born, and the conception of Jesus was caused by the Spirit."[15] This may not seem to be claiming much, but it is far more than would those who look upon the narratives as folklore unworthy of serious attention. Such certainly is not the case with exegetes like Brown, Krister Stendahl, Carroll Stuhlmueller, Brian M. Nolan, and George M. Soares Prabhu,[16] all of whom deserve a preacher's careful study. They assert that even though the narratives are not intended as history, they have a historical basis, are an inspired part of the canon of Scripture, and are of immense importance to both the Gospels of which they form an integral part and to the preaching of the word. Still, is Kamphaus' choice of historical facts correct? Is he claiming too much? Surely a preacher who is intending to uphold the ancient creeds of the church could not deny that Jesus' birth was from the Holy Spirit and the Virgin Mary,[17] but must the preacher also insist, for instance, that the birth took place in Bethlehem or that Jesus had physical descent from David? C. H. Dodd comments:

> Symbols and images cluster thickly . . . visits of angels, prophetic dreams, the marvellous star in the east, the miraculous birth greeted with songs from the heavenly choir, all the appealing incidents so familiar in the appropriate setting of Christmas carol and nativity play. That there is a basis of fact somewhere behind it all need not be doubted, but he would be a bold man who should presume to draw a firm line between fact and symbol.[18]

If Matthew and Luke did not write their infancy narratives primarily to supply readers with historical data, why then did they write them? What should be the underlying theme of our preaching from them? They are, above all, gospels—proclamations of the good news that Jesus is Lord. They are the early church's public statement that Jesus was not only a man but also Messiah, and Son of God, acting for the salvation of the human race even from his birth. According to this way of viewing them, they have a distinctive kerygmatic purpose. Underlying the importance of this intention is the repetition of the kerygma in the various scenes in Luke 1–2. Is this not what prompted the Evangelist to put them in the literary form that he did, rather than through them to pursue the development of an idea? Through having angels speak to Mary (1:32–36), then to the shepherds (2:11), through the prophecies of Simeon and Anna (2:27–32, 38), and finally through Jesus' own response to Mary and Joseph in the Temple (2:49), Luke returned to the same point: though as a result of his utter humanity, it is hidden even from his parents, Jesus is nonetheless Son of the Most High; he is Christ the Lord, the Messianic deliverer of the chosen people, absolutely independent of creatures as one sent by the Father. From this we can see that the intent of the church at the time of Matthew and Luke (and also when Christmas was first being celebrated as a feast sometime prior to A.D. 336)[19] was to make Jesus' birth a new proclamation of the paschal mystery.

Should preachers also speak specifically about the narratives' historicity? It seems to be that they might. Would it not help them, in giving their reasons for concentrating upon the essentials of the feast? Its kerygmatic purpose might seem more reasonable to listeners if they realized that the various narratives were perhaps conceived by the Evangelists so as to bring the kerygma to life. Are our fellow Christians so easily scandalized that they cannot bear to hear this? Although we do not tell a child of four the truth about Santa Claus, we do not have the same scruple with adults. We, like C. H. Dodd, may be unwilling to "draw a firm line between fact and symbol." Could we not lovingly and prudently say so to our listeners? Could we not share with them a degree of uncertainty, when it is intended not to weaken their faith but to awaken in them a more realistic and thus deeper appreciation of a mystery which after many years they would surely like to approach with their adult eyes rather than as they did when brought before the crib by their parents? If the interpretation of a scriptural passage is disputed, it is surely doubtful whether we should deal with it either by insisting upon an uncertain interpretation or by putting the whole issue to one side hoping that "George will do it." I would query Adrian Nocent's view. He admits the value of recent literature on Luke's objectivity, but points out that he is not citing it in his biblico-liturgical reflections on Christmastide because "it has nothing to do with Luke's attitude of faith and the Church's attitude of faith at the moment of celebration."[20] What can he mean? If these studies are able to lead to a fuller understanding of the meaning of Luke's Gospel, do they not also speak to the content of Luke's and the church's faith? How can we both use and not use the results of research to uncover the meaning of the text in the course of the homily? We may feel that by doing so we are challenging the importance or sacredness of the incarnation. But are we not in fact enhancing the event's greatness by revealing its genuine significance?

II. HOMILETICAL EXAMPLES: PREACHING AT CHRISTMASTIDE

A. THE FOURTH SUNDAY OF ADVENT

Many people in a congregation may be hoping that their preacher will help them make sense of what they are busy doing during the week before Christmas. They are often quite generous (if not extravagant): parents buying presents for their children, mothers preparing Christmas dinner for their families. Many are engaged in thinking of others far and near while writing Christmas cards. At the same time, there are problems. Some people may be feeling lonely if they cannot foresee an opportunity to celebrate with others. Alcoholics Anonymous urges members to be specially vigilant at this time in order to safeguard their sobriety. It is essential for preachers to address the spoken and unspoken needs of their people.

> Every pastor knows that even with carefully guarded study hours behind locked doors, the people stand round his desk and whisper "Remember me!" They are not intruders; it was in order to be with them that he locked the door.[21]

How can one best be with them on the Sunday before Christmas? The Gospel texts given in the lectionary lead us to preach on the same theme as has been proposed for all the infancy narratives. The readings for all three cycles proclaim and give thanks that the child to be born will even from that time be Immanuel and Son of God. They are a clear call to the Christian community to put all the extra business of Christmas, the parties and the pain, into perspective. The approaching feast is about one thing—God becomes a human being, the most incredible event ever to take place in the created order. This must occupy the center of the community's attention. The Fourth Sunday is a day to break through those fixed patterns, those annual automatic responses, to help listeners hear the familiar Scripture passages anew, lines so well known to them that they often fail to grasp what is being said.

The Annunciation to Joseph: Matthew 1:18–25 (Cycle A). This passage follows upon Matthew's genealogy of Jesus which is concerned with his descent from the recipients of the Messianic promise, Abraham and particularly David. Jesus is Son of David. The Evangelist moves on to a deeper revelation of who Jesus is and how his birth was possible.[22] Jesus is not only Son of David but Son of God, and this was accomplished by God through Jesus' virginal conception. Although Joseph's legal paternity is essential to the narrative, and is stressed by Joseph's taking Mary to his home and naming the child (both of which indicate legal parentage), this is not a sufficient answer to Jesus' question to the Pharisees: "What is your opinion about the Christ? Whose son is he?" (Matt. 22:42). Simon Peter's response is required. "You are the Christ, the son of the living God" (Matt. 16:17). Although Matthew does not use the term "Son of God" as such in the annunciation to Joseph, it is implied. Jesus is begotten not of Joseph but *through the Holy Spirit* (Mary's virginity being important not in itself but for what it contributes to divine Sonship). This surprise assertion, repeated twice (Matt. 1:18, 20), is the key to the passage. Even the traditional order of the narratives is broken so that the reader is made aware of the virgin birth even before Joseph is. All else in the passage can be seen as supporting the proclamation of Jesus' origin: Mary's virginity with Joseph's legal paternity whereby the two parents play a harmonious role in making Jesus who he is; one begets him of the Holy Spirit and the other as legal son of David. The two names he is given also support his Sonship. They are Messianic titles—Jesus, or Joshua, "Yahweh is salvation," and Immanuel, "God is with us." Both emphasize that this is definitely the birth to which the

Old Covenant has looked forward. But these titles are not the headline news in the passage. They were to be expected. What remains paramount and totally unexpected is *Jesus' conception by the Holy Spirit and the virginity of Mary.*

The choice of Isa. 7:10–14 as the Old Testament lesson is a natural one, since it contains the verse that Matthew appropriates, "the maiden [virgin?] is with child and will soon give birth to a son whom she will call Immanuel" (v. 14). Matthew uses the Septuagint reading of the text: *parthenos* (virgin), rather than the Hebrew *almah* (young girl), perhaps thereby to highlight in another way the importance of virginity to his theme. By using the Matthean "the virgin will conceive" as its title for the Isaiah reading, the composers of the lectionary stress the text's fulfillment in Mary. The psalm is the 23d (24th), an antiphonal song of praise for entry into the sanctuary, heralding in the liturgy the coming of the Messiah King announced in Isaiah and the Gospel. The second reading is also appropriate because it contains one of Paul's Christological statements that whereas Jesus by birth was a descendant of David, only through the resurrection was he designated Son of God (Rom. 1:1–7). Could a homily not be built around a comparison of the second reading and Gospel, so as to bring out the distinctive Christological material in the latter?

The Annunciation to Mary: Luke 1:26–38 (Cycle B). Luke seems to have structured this narrative to parallel the annunciation to Zacharias of John the Baptist's birth (Luke 1:5–25), and by the comparison to show the far greater significance of that of Jesus. Both Zacharias and Mary are visited by angels and receive similar messages announcing these extraordinary births. But there are important differences between the two. Whereas John, from his mother's womb, will be filled with the Holy Spirit, Jesus will be actually begotten by the power of the Spirit. Whereas Zacharias' reply to his visitor is flawed with doubt, Mary's is characterized by complete trust and obedience. But as it was in the annunciation to Joseph in Matthew's Gospel, so in this narrative the center of attention is Christ, the subject of the angel's message. Thus the primary theme for preaching is again kerygmatic. What is it we are preparing to celebrate on Christmas Day? For whose coming do we long? The child we greet is *the one unique Son of God.* Luke has Gabriel proclaim Jesus to be Messiah, and so he records the Jewish ancestry that is required for it (vs. 31–33). Then in v. 35 he cites the Jewish expectations again but this time reinterpreted in a dramatically new way, "because the power of the Most High comes not upon the Davidic king but his mother."[23] Jewish expectation knew nothing of a Messiah who would be God's son by conception without a male parent through God's creative Spirit. Is this not the Christological good news, the glory of this famous passage which has inspired so much art and poetry?

The theme is reinforced in the first reading (II Sam. 7:1–16), which takes the form of a promise. God assures Nathan, his prophet, that the house and sovereignty of David will stand secure and established forever. God assures Nathan that he will treat David's descendants as a father does his son, correcting them after the fashion of mankind. The key text is v. 14: "I will be a father to him and he a son to me." This reading is followed by a selection from Psalm 88 (89) in which David sings forever of the Lord's love and faithfulness to the very covenant just announced to Nathan. A further doxology follows in the second reading, which is the conclusion of the letter to the Romans (16:25–27). Paul speaks here of the mystery of wisdom, hidden from endless ages, now revealed in the cross of Jesus through which all things are restored. As in Cycle A, the preacher could show that in the Gospel the revelation of the mystery has been pushed back from Easter to the incarnation; it is neither Jesus' death nor resurrection that bestows on him a new sonship, for they make manifest openly to the world what has already been since his birth. This is the primary theme of Luke's annunciation to Mary.

Is there not a secondary theme which in preaching might well become primary (without neglecting the first upon which it rests)? Since the radiance of God's favor is hers because of Jesus, Mary is not the center of the narrative. She does nonetheless receive considerable attention, and is presented as a model of response to the mystery of Jesus' birth. Mary's attitude is what Israel's and the Christian community's ought to be. She stands for the people of God of the old and new covenants; the angel's message is addressed in her to those who are also especially beloved by the Most High, and it is the cause of great joy in both. They take to themselves the words of Paul: "God chose what is low and despised in the world, even things that are not, to bring to nothing things that are, so that no human being might boast in the presence of God" (I Cor. 1:28–29). They praise and thank God for the inestimable gift of his Son, which is the very reason for their being addressed as "highly favored" in Luke 1:28 (a translation preferable to "full of grace"). This passage of Luke's, particularly vs. 28 and 38, may lead the preacher to speak of joy, the mood of the church in these last days before Christmas. Should the community not try to do the shopping, cooking, and all the rest in that spirit? Luke pictures Mary as being true to Jesus' comment about her

during his ministry, that she and his brothers are among those who
"hear God's word and do it" (Luke 8:21). Her reply, "Let it happen to
me according to your word" (Luke 1:38), is consistent with that spirit
of obedience. But it implies more: her strong desire to do God's will,
accompanied by her joy at being given the opportunity to do it. It is
"the 'Amen' of humanity to God's offer of a Savior . . . an uncondi-
tional affirmation of complete willingness to accept, humbly and
thankfully, God's unmerited offer of redeeming grace."[24] As joy and
obedience are one in Mary, so in the church, where its happiness does
not spring from the gaiety of festivities, but from the fullness of its
obedience to God's word. One might also include in a sermon, since it
is intrinsic to Christian joy, a reminder of the importance of *reconciliation* as preparation for the approaching feast.

The Visitation: Luke 1:39–45 (Cycle C). Thankful praise is even more
prominent in this Gospel passage, sometimes called the annunciation
to Elizabeth, than it is in that to Mary. Both Elizabeth's canticle and
Mary's Magnificat praise God for his gift.[25] With Elizabeth and Mary
coming together, there is reinforced the surpassing greatness of Jesus
over John the Baptist, and what God has done for Mary over
Zacharias and Elizabeth. Elizabeth's "Blessed art thou among women,
and blessed is the fruit of thy womb" (Luke 1:42) is the beginning of
an early liturgical hymn in honor of Mary, providing an explanation
for the use of the verb "cry aloud" to introduce the verses.[26] Such
blessings of other women would have been familiar to the early Jewish
Christians. But whereas Jael (Judg. 5:24) and Judith (Judith 13:18)
were proclaimed blessed because they had killed the enemies of
Israel, Mary is blessed because of the fruit of her womb, the most
fundamental reason for praise. Still, as in the annunciation to Mary,
she is also blessed because of her personal response to God's word—
her faith that God would do as he had promised. As it contrasts with
Zacharias' lack of faith, it is deserving of a beatitude: "Fortunate is she
who believed that the Lord's words to her would find fulfillment" (v.
45).

To evoke further the community's response to Jesus' birth, the
preacher might also incorporate the second reading in this liturgy
(Heb. 10:5–10). In it we are told that the sacrifices of the old law were
not salvific. It required Jesus' sacrifice on the cross to regain for
humanity access to the presence of God. But this sacrifice arose from
his life of faith, his total offer of obedience to the Father. It is his
obedience, not his blood itself, upon which our salvation rests. The
church paradoxically learns at the foot of the cross from imitating

Christ present there what it means to celebrate the mystery of his birth.

B. CHRISTMAS DAY (LUKE 2:1–14)

There are few feasts or holidays that mean as much to Christian people. Christmas is looked forward to, planned for, and traveled to, beyond compare. With the possible exception of Easter Sunday, there are also more Christians in attendance at church. None of the liturgical or other changes seem to have affected the large numbers at Midnight Mass. Extra chairs continue to be brought in for the occasion, and many are still left standing at the rear of the church. This is common in parishes where on a normal Sunday there would not be that many people present at all the celebrations of Eucharist combined. Moreover, people are often better disposed to hear God's Word at Christmas than at other times, because of the extraordinary feelings of sacredness, goodness, and familial generosity associated with it, all of which may well be accompanied by greater trust and openness to preaching. Some have been making a special effort to return to the practice of their faith, including seeking forgiveness and reconciliation before reception of the Eucharist. At the same time, a large number come without any intention of returning to worship until Easter or the next Christmas. For them the Midnight Mass is part of their cultural, familial Christmas practice, somewhat akin to a Christmas tree, or turkey and plum pudding for dinner. The holiday just wouldn't be the same without it. But the significance of Jesus is limited to the crib, to thoughts about the Christmas story, and reminiscences of their own childhood. They have what Luther called first faith, which is, he said, all that Christmas means to most people. What they should have is second faith, by which a person believes the child to be his own personal Savior, someone to whom he has turned over the whole of his life. First faith stops at the narrative itself. What the story means, the transformation of personal and corporate life, is not grasped. And if preachers concentrate on the narrative itself, are they not giving the impression that this is as it should be? This, unfortunately, is the kind of preaching Franz Kamphaus discovered in his survey, "sermons intended to produce the same effect as Christmas plays . . . to induce a Christmas mood . . . a dream . . . to cast our minds back to the joys of the past, whereas anamnesis affects the present . . . summons us to a fresh awareness of the presence of the Christos Kyrios."[27] If our people were only to realize how little their Christmas ought to stay focused on the imagery used by the Evangelists, and how much more upon the risen Christ, who has died that they might have eternal life, Christmas would be for many an occasion of commitment to genuine renewed discipleship.

Christmas is one of the preacher's best opportunities for evangelization—the listeners are in need of it and the liturgical texts, we shall suggest, contain it. Must we preachers not be on guard against being ourselves overcome with Christmas euphoria and neglecting the needs of our people? Do the observations of Jacques Ellul not apply to us: "The effects of de-christianization are evident. . . . Individuals have no interest any more in the questions put to them by Jesus Christ; the questions are regarded as irrelevant and the Christian faith and truth are considered to be completely ineffective for transforming man's situation"?[28]

The Gospel reading for the Mass at Midnight is the account in Luke 2 of Jesus' birth. The selection ends at v. 14 in order that vs. 15–20 may be used for the Mass at Dawn (the Shepherds' Mass), but the more natural ending to the story line is v. 20. Then the passage can be simply divided into three sections: the setting and birth (vs. 1–7), the annunciation to the shepherds (vs. 8–14), and the shepherds' reactions (vs. 15–20). The central verse is the angel's announcement: "To you this day is born in the city of David a Savior, who is Messiah and Lord" (v. 11). The main point of the narrative is here—*the royal proclamation of the angels that Jesus is Savior, Messiah, and Lord.* Because he carries these titles, the angels' announcement about him is "of great joy, a joy to be shared by the whole people" (v. 10). The choice of Isa. 9:1–3, 5–6 as the first reading is an important one, because it is essential to an understanding of the Gospel. It is a beautiful promise to Israel, one of the major Messianic passages, and seems to have been a liturgical hymn of thanksgiving taken from the ceremony of royal accession. It was used, however, not in praise of a particular Davidic king, but of the ideal one. He is the child proclaimed the adopted son of God who would possess all the greatness ascribed to his people: the wisdom of Solomon, the courage of David, and the religious virtues of the patriarchs and Moses. Luke takes this context of Isaiah and within it substitutes new titles. In place of "Wonderful Counsellor, Mighty God, Eternal Father, Prince of Peace" (Isa. 9:6), he inserts, Savior, Messiah (Christ), and Lord. They are the great kerygmatic titles, the three that Paul uses when referring to the Parousia. "For us, our homeland is in heaven, and from heaven comes the Savior we are waiting for, the Lord Jesus Christ" (Phil. 3:20). Luke takes them and applies them to Jesus' birth. The transposition is intensified by noting a similar parallel between the Gloria of Luke 2:14 and the disciples' hymn of praise in Luke at the moment of Jesus' entry into Jerusalem:

"Peace in heaven and glory in the highest!" (19:38). Brown suggests that Luke intended a comparison here, i.e., "the angels of heaven recognized at the beginning of Jesus' life what the disciples came to know only at the end, namely the presence of the Messiah King who comes in the name of the Lord."[29]

As important as the kerygmatic titles in v. 11 are, their challenge to faith can be better understood by combining them with the second part of the angelic proclamation. "And here is a sign for you: you will find a baby wrapped in swaddling clothes and lying in a manger" (v. 12). Here lies a basis for evangelical address, the need of which we discussed above. What does v. 12 imply? Of what is a baby, wrapped in strips of cloth and laid down in a manger, a sign? These are not signs of the kingship of Caesar Augustus or Quirinius; they are signs that will be disputed (Luke 2:34). Like many others in the New Testament they depend "on their ability to condense the gospel message *(de leur densité kérygmatique)*, on their power to pierce the heart."[30] Jesus' totally unexpected human condition, the complete absence of signs of royalty, is the sign to us of the character of his kingship, and of the cross, that appalling means he will use to conquer the world, which is the most unacceptable sign of all. This insane situation is made even worse by bringing in shepherds, who were in Jesus' time usually considered dishonest, excluded from court, neither pious nor humble—totally undeserving of the honor that was theirs. This is the challenge of Christmas to the dechristianization of society. Augustus' power seems redemptive, but it is not. The most glittering things of this world without God are hopelessly empty. They will not answer our ultimate questions, our search for meaning. It is this mother's child who is, in fact, anything but helpless. He is the Savior of the world, "a Savior born to *you*"; he is not merely a good man whose kindness and justice we commemorate by celebrating his birthday.

Further implications for address to the "unchurched" are also to be found in the second reading, Titus 2:11–14. Described there are the consequences to Christians of the revelation of God's grace—to give up everything that does not lead to God, and lead good, religious lives, waiting in hope for Christ's appearing in glory. For this he died on the cross and to this he calls us this very night. There is a strong emotional appeal in the Christmas texts, and a preacher might well decide to use it. People in need of evangelization sometimes know theoretically what it means to live a Christian life, but there is a gap between knowledge and practice. A preacher may have to arouse their feelings, perhaps of fear or of benevolence, moving "their minds, not that they may know what is to be done, but that they may do what they already know should be done."[31] The preacher may want the "unchurched" to ask themselves seriously: "What are the consequences of my indifference to, or continual rejection of, God's gift of faith, again made manifest to me at this celebration? What am I saying to God, who sent his Son into the world in this way for my liberation, when I don't rouse myself to join the community in worship from one Christmas to the next? The baby in the manger is again being raised up as a sign for me. Is it possible that I have been blind, these many years, to its real meaning for my life?"

C. The Epiphany (Matthew 2:1–12)

Because of their discernible pattern, the two infancy narratives have been called "the essential gospel in miniature."[32] This title provides an approach to understanding Matthew's visit of the Magi, the Gospel selection for today. It is appropriate for the following reason. In the church's preaching after Jesus' resurrection and earlier at his baptism, the proclamation of the good news was followed by reactions of acceptance and rejection. This same device is used in the birth stories. In both, we find revelations of Jesus' birth, angelic announcements of it to shepherds or Magi who believe in him, while there lurk in the background those who reject him. In Luke there are those who Simeon predicts will contradict the sign, and more clearly in Matthew, Herod and indeed the whole of Jerusalem who seek to kill the child but are foiled by his flight into Egypt. These are the common elements in Luke and Matthew prompting the title "the gospel in miniature." Each Evangelist has his own emphasis in this context; it is from Matthew's that we discover a theme central to the Epiphany—the child Jesus is king, not only of Israel but of the world, and this is patently manifest in his rejection by the Jews and acceptance by the Gentiles. The newborn child which the Magi thought to be king of the Jews is in reality their king. Matthew, writing during the last third of the century, may have been hoping to make sense of the fact, well known in the Christian communities of the time, that it was Gentiles for the most part and not Jews who were becoming Christian. His reply is that the gospel's universal appeal is just what one might expect. "Many will come from east and west and sit at table with Abraham, Isaac, and Jacob in the kingdom of heaven" (Matt. 8:11), and the Magi are all of a piece with this conception. "They stood for all those who will continue to come from 'the east and west' to be made disciples . . . until the end of time"[33]

The other readings in the liturgy repeat the same theme: Isa. 60:1–6, the prophetic vision of the nations approaching Zion, Psalm 71 (72) with the antiphon, "All nations shall fall prostrate before you, O Lord" (v. 11), and Eph. 3:2–6, Paul's announcement that pagans now share the same inheritance (and) are parts of the same body as Israel. As on Christmas Day, we find in the Epiphany readings another call to conversion. They address today's world, not only the time at which they were written. Are we among those who reject or accept Christ? Do we realize, moreover, that the Christian faith has a dynamically universal appeal if it is not distorted by being tied to a particular language, race, social class, or viewpoint? This is what Epiphany seems to be about, and it will not do to get sidetracked in our preaching by describing the Magi in detail, their color and character, the hardships of their journey, and the symbolism of the gifts.[34] None of it is related to the point of the narrative.

NOTES

1. John Chrysostom, Homily 21 on John.

2. Cf. Franz Kamphaus, *The Gospels for Preachers and Teachers,* tr. by David Bourke (London: Sheed & Ward, 1974), p. 310. The writer has analyzed 1500 sermons preached recently, and concludes that there is little use made of modern biblical criticism.

3. *Selected Sermons of St. Augustine,* tr. and ed. by Quincy Howe, Jr. (Holt, Rinehart & Winston, 1966), pp. 53–56.

4. Martin Luther, *Luther's Works,* ed. and tr. by John W. Doberstein (Muhlenberg Press, 1959), Vol. 51, pp. 5, 209–218.

5. John Henry Newman, *Parochial and Plain Sermons* (London: Longmans, 1902), pp. 4, 239–252.

6. Ibid., p. 243.

7. Ibid., p. 240.

8. Ronald A. Knox, *The Pastoral Sermons,* ed. by Philip Caraman (Sheed & Ward, 1960), p. 20.

9. D. Moody Smith, *Interpreting the Gospels for Preaching* (Fortress Press, 1980), p. 20.

10. Fred B. Craddock, *As One Without Authority,* 3d ed. (Abingdon Press, 1979), p. 120.

11. Walter Kasper, *Jesus the Christ* (London: Burns & Oates, 1976), p. 65. Cf. also Myles M. Bourke, "The Literary Genus of Matthew 1–2," *Catholic Biblical Quarterly*, Vol. 22 (1960), pp. 160–175.

12. Raymond E. Brown, *The Birth of the Messiah* (Doubleday & Co., 1977), p. 33, where he also raises the question of Mary being a source of Lucan material. He considers it unlikely. For a contrary view, cf. John McHugh, *The Mother of Jesus in the New Testament* (London: Darton, Longman & Todd, 1975), pp. 145–149.

13. Brown, op. cit., p. 33. Cf. also J. D. M. Derrett, "Further Light on the Narratives of the Nativity," in *Novum Testamentum*, Vol. 17 (1975), pp. 81–108.

14. Krister Stendahl, "Quis et Unde? An Analysis of Matthew 1–2," in *Judentum, Urchristentum, Kirche*, ed. W. Eltester (1964), p. 96.

15. Kamphaus, op. cit., p. 258.

16. E.g., George M. Soares Prabhu, *The Formula Quotations in the Infancy Narrative of Matthew* (Rome: Biblical Institute Press, 1976), particularly pp. 294–300.

17. Cf. J. N. D. Kelly, *Early Christian Creeds*, 2d ed. (London: Longmans, Green & Co., 1960), pp. 144–149.

18. C. H. Dodd, *The Founder of Christianity* (London: William Collins Sons & Co., 1971), p. 31.

19. Adrian Nocent, *The Liturgical Year* (Liturgical Press, 1977), I, p. 187.

20. Ibid., p. 237.

21. Craddock, op. cit., p. 130.

22. There is an interesting difference of opinion between Raymond E. Brown and Krister Stendahl on the basic purposes of Matthew in 1–2. Cf. Brown, op. cit., pp. 133–143, and Stendahl, op. cit.

23. Brown, op. cit., p. 312.

24. McHugh, op. cit., p. 67. Cf. also Hilda Graef, *Mary: A History of Doctrine and Devotion* (London: Sheed & Ward, 1963), pp. 1, 6–10, who also describes the various theories that have been proposed concerning Mary's virginity during her betrothal.

25. Since the two canticles form a literary unity and are part of the same narrative, it might be preferable to have both of them in the Gospel selection for this cycle.

26. McHugh, op. cit., p. 72.

27. Kamphaus, op. cit., pp. 279ff.

28. Jacques Ellul, *The New Demons* (Seabury Press, 1975), p. 76.

29. Brown, op. cit., p. 427.

30. McHugh, op. cit., p. 88.

31. St. Augustine, *On Christian Doctrine*, IV. xii.

32. Brown, op. cit., p. 8.

33. Prabhu, op. cit., p. 330. Cf. also Brian Nolan, *The Royal Son of God: The Christology of Matthew 1–2 in the Setting of the Gospel* (Fribourg: Editions Universitaires, 1979), pp. 131–134.

34. Kamphaus, op. cit., p. 298.

FOR FURTHER READING

Brown, Raymond E. *The Birth of the Messiah*. Doubleday & Co., 1977. An extraordinarily thorough exegetical study of Matthew's and Luke's infancy narratives.

Danielou, Jean. *The Infancy Narratives*. Herder & Herder, 1968. Theological-biblical reflections on each of the infancy narratives.

Kamphaus, Franz. *The Gospels for Preachers and Teachers*. Tr. David Bourke. London: Sheed & Ward, 1974. Principles and suggestions on the content of preaching, for the Easter, miracle, and infancy narratives.

McHugh, John. *The Mother of Jesus in the New Testament*. London: Darton, Longman & Todd, 1975. A biblical, theological Marian study.

Nocent, Adrian. "The Christmas Mystery," *The Liturgical Year*. Liturgical Press, 1977. A study of the liturgical readings for Christmastide.

12. PREACHING FROM THE SERMON ON THE MOUNT

FRANK STAGG

Is the Sermon on the Mount (hereafter SM) really a sermon? Is it preaching, teaching, or both? Matthew calls it teaching (Matt. 5:2; 7:28f.). It is instruction throughout, every sentence loaded with teaching. It interprets Scripture, tradition, human behavior, the will of God, and life in varied expressions. It is addressed to "the crowds" (5:1; 7:28), with special reference to "his disciples" (5:1). Disciples are learners brought under the discipline of instruction. It is Jesus' authority in "teaching" which is contrasted with that of "the scribes." The SM is teaching, explicitly and emphatically.

Is this also a sermon? Unmistakably so! It has thematic coherence and movement. A sermon does not have to be poured into one particular form—e.g., three points and a poem. It calls the hearer to decision and commitment, prime marks of preaching. It intends to bring the hearer into the presence of God in an encounter conducive to worship, a new self-understanding, a new awareness of the needs and rights of other people, a respect for but wholesome independence of the material/physical world, and a new and radical commitment to God. This is preaching, not just a lecture. This is a model sermon, where teaching and preaching are blended, both instructing the hearer and calling the hearer to decision and commitment.

Is this an actual sermon from Jesus or is it a Matthean arrangement? Probably something of both. That Matthew selected and shaped his materials to meet the needs of his readers is recognized by all competent scholars. Standard commentaries demonstrate Matthew's use of sources and his own redactional hand in shaping his materials. Granting this, the voice heard in the SM is that of Jesus.

The radicality, including an authority asserted over scribes and Scriptures, is not community creation. The church has never proven equal to hearing this sermon, much less producing it. On critical grounds, the SM in essence comes from Jesus. The real question has to do with our willingness to hear him.

I. CONTENT ANALYSIS

From beginning to end, the SM is concerned with human existence under God. It does not play games in a theological or religious sandbox. It deals with identity questions: Who are you? Whose are you? To what are you called? From what are you called? How can you be both free and responsible? What is true righteousness? How does motive determine piety as authentic or phony? What is the proper place for the material? By what tests do we ultimately stand or fall? What really matters?

THE BEATITUDES (MATT. 5:3–12)

Happiness is what? Modern cartoons answer variously. Jesus taught that happiness is in the quality of one's personal being, not in the fluctuations of outward circumstance. It derives from one's proper relationship with God. There is nothing blessed as such in poverty, hunger, thirst, or persecution; but blessedness is possible even under such circumstances. The Beatitudes stand the world's notion of happiness on its head. The world calls miserable those whom Jesus calls happy. Even much religion rejects the Beatitudes, allowing no place for "failure" to faith or piety. The popular electronic church promises worldly triumphalism. Macho displaces meekness.

Jesus identifies with "the crowds" (5:1; 7:28), for they are the ones addressed, the little people whom the world despises. He affirms their blessedness now and their ultimate vindication under God. The Beatitudes are consistent with Jesus' principle, found throughout the Gospels, that a person lives by dying, receives by giving, and rules by serving.

SALT AND LIGHT (MATT. 5:13–16)

"You are!" Jesus did not say, "You should become" or "You may become." He declared this to "the crowds," not to an elite minority or self-styled moral majority. This is the identity question: Who are you? Hearers are called to a new understanding of themselves. There is nothing about God's having to be paid or appeased. God's word is creative, and authority is in God himself. Hearers are called to decision and commitment, chiefly to accept God's affirmation as to who they really are. Decay and darkness do not represent who we really are; such are misdirections of our humanity. "Salt and Light" model our true identity. This is who we are.

The crowds needed no lecture on the nature of salt or light. Salt and light "do their thing" simply because they are salt and light. Salt preserves and seasons. Light shines. A city built upon a hill cannot be hidden. Function follows from the nature of salt and light. Being has priority over saying and doing; but, if genuine, what a person is will be expressed in what that person says and does. Jesus did not say, "People should not light a lamp and then hide it." They don't! You are salt, light, a city built upon a hill. Be what you are! Live in open goodness to the service of people and the glory of God.

Tension appears between 5:16 and 6:1–18. How can a person have it both ways: with good works done openly before men, yet in the secrecy of the closet? Logically it seems that these passages clash. Actually they are compatible. The solution is in motive and maturity. One can live openly in transparent goodness and yet escape ostentation and display. It depends upon where the center is, in self or in God and other people. In our best moments, as in a crisis, we could not care less whether our deeds are seen or not seen. Our visibility becomes a nonissue. Maturity in servanthood turns these rare moments into a pattern in life.

True Righteousness (Matt. 5:17–48)

Legalism and license are constant threats to authentic religion. Legalism is law for its own sake, life reduced to rules. License is permissiveness, freedom confused with a permit to do as we please. Religion tends to become either legalistic or libertine, all demand or all gift. True religion is both gift and demand, held in creative tension. "You are!" is God's gift. "Be what you are!" is God's demand. The SM keeps gift and demand in tension.

The Theme (Matt. 5:17–20). Matthew 5:17–20 is thematic, bringing into sharp focus the rival threats of legalism and libertinism, with the offer of a *tertium quid,* an escape from both by way of a true righteousness transcending both. Many Pharisees (some were different) were legalists who measured piety by compliance with such rules as those for Sabbath, fasting, kosher food, and ritual purification. They saw Jesus as undercutting the Bible (the Law and the Prophets). Their opposites, the libertines, asserted their freedom from the law, stressing salvation as God's free gift. They confused liberty with license, making grace cheap, a gift without demand.

Jesus called for fulfillment of the Law and the Prophets in a way beyond legalism and permissiveness. Contextually, there is no reference to "fulfillment" as carrying out prophecies. Jesus intended fulfillment in another sense. He fulfilled the Law and the Prophets by rescuing their soul or heart, the intention and essence. Also, he incarnated the intention of the Law and the Prophets. True righteousness is embodying the intention of the Bible. Creeds, worship forms, activities, and the like, may or may not be meaningful. The acid test is in how human existence is affected. In six areas Jesus illustrated what he meant by the true righteousness that fulfills the Law and the Prophets.

Six Areas for Testing Righteousness (Matt. 5:21–28). Matthew 5:21–28 probes six areas in which the intention of the Scriptures is clarified. In each case, Jesus shows that sin occurs first within the heart. It is not enough to refrain from such overt acts as murder or adultery; one must be free from the intentions that lead to the overt acts. Jesus is not saying that it is as bad to hate as to kill or that it is as bad to lust as to commit an overt act of adultery. Obviously it is more damaging to the victim to be killed than just hated, or raped than just ogled. The evil is considered here from the side of the offender, not the offended. Jesus internalized good and evil, without obscuring the fact that the farther one goes with evil impulse, the more damaging it is to all concerned.

1. Murder (Matt. 5:21–26). Caution must be exercised against pressing each verse, lest one fall back into the trap of legalism. Jesus spoke graphically, not in abstractions. He drew upon familiar life situations, as when one is brought before different levels of the court system. He shows how far uncontrolled anger can go, hurting offender and offended. He shows that our true relationship with God is linked with how we relate to other people. A person cannot shove aside others on the way to the altar of God's presence. To despise another as worthless (*raca* was a term of contempt for one's intelligence; *more* expressed contempt for one's character) is in essence to murder that person. Such reductionism of another is a form of murder.

2. Adultery (Matt. 5:27–30). Again, sin occurs first within, whether also outwardly or not. Reducing another to a mere sex object is a form of adultery. This is not to confuse temptation with sin, for Jesus himself was tempted in every way that we are, "yet without sin" (Heb. 4:15). Sin is in what we do with temptation. One should not feel guilty simply because one is human in a world like this. On the other hand, one should not feel innocent simply for not having "gone all the way." The further evil is carried out, the more damaging it is to all. The point here is that sin begins deep within us in terms of feeling, impulse, and intention.

Easily missed is the fact that Jesus taught that adultery could be committed against a woman. Culture and religion largely considered adultery as a violation of a husband's rights. It was largely a man's world, and if a married man had a sexual act with a single woman, it was not termed adultery. Jesus rejected this double standard and affirmed the full rights and responsibilities of a woman.

Jesus did not dismiss the sexual drive as easy to control. The strong analogy of plucking out an eye or cutting off a hand reflects his recognition of how hard it is to escape evil, including abuse of sexuality. To literalize the parables of eye and hand is a form of legalism and is totally ineffective, for even with loss of both eyes and hands one may yet live in lust. Scripture is to be taken seriously, not literally.

3. Divorce (Matt. 5:31–32). If the question is simply about God's will for marriage, the answer is loud and clear. He wills that marriage be a union of a man and a woman (not two of the same sex) and that it be unbroken except by death. If this were accepted, many broken marriages and much divorce would be avoided. There are further questions as to God's provision where brokenness has occurred. Those questions are pursued elsewhere in the Bible in terms of redemption. God is in the business of reclaiming and renewing, whatever the failure. But the concern here is more limited. It is concern for the integrity of marriage and its preservation. There is no support here for the modern idea that marriage need not be a life commitment, only an arrangement for one in a series of life chapters. Much must be said for redemption, but this passage focuses on the proper character of marriage.

Again, Jesus affirms the rights and responsibilities of woman. A Jewish woman could not divorce her husband, although she could ask a court to compel her husband to divorce her. Jesus rejected this double standard. A woman has rights, and adultery can be committed *against her.* A woman has responsibility, and she can commit adultery *against the man.* In this context the "except clause" is valid, for the case of a guilty wife is not under consideration here.

4. Oaths (Matt 5:33–37). The issue here is casuistry, not oaths as such. An honest person does not require an oath; but a court may require it. What Jesus protests is casuistry, a legal fiction by which one intends to circumvent the law. It is like taking advantage of "the fine print" understood only by the advantaged. In the casuistry of Jesus' time, the legalists had it that to swear by the altar was not binding but to swear by the gold on the altar was. This is purely arbitrary. It favors the one who knows the fine points of the law and enables such a one intentionally to deceive yet remain "within the law." Jesus cut behind all such fiction, holding that one simply is honest or is not. For the honest, oaths are redundant.

5. *Retaliation (Matt. 5:38–42).* Jesus not only rejected the law of retaliation but replaced it with the obligation to return good for evil: turn the cheek, give more than is asked, go the second mile. Is this unrealistic? Could the world operate this way? Obviously it would have to become a different kind of world. That is precisely what Jesus called for. It took him to the cross, and he promised nothing less for his followers. Jesus practiced what he preached. The church has never been comfortable with Jesus' teaching or his way. It is not convincing that we really accept his way as an ideal, much less as our practice.

6. *Love for Enemies (Matt. 5:43–48).* Love seeks to give and to serve, whatever the other person's merit. Jesus prescribes lavish and indiscriminate giving, rejecting the profit motive. Pagans give to receive. Again, we struggle to accept Jesus' teaching as an ideal, much less as our practice. Verse 48 need not be explained away, for its intention is to be taken at face value. Perfection is God's standard for himself and for us. He accepts us as we are, warts and all; he calls us to perfection. Inclusion in God's family is pure gift; but in that family we come under absolute demand. The tension remains unresolved. The legalist seeks escape from the tension by reducing demand to attainable rules. The libertine seeks escape by waiving the demands in the name of grace. To be a disciple is to live in the unresolved tension: accepted as we are and called to perfection.

MOTIVE AND PIETY (MATT. 6:1–18)

This section continues the probing of true righteousness, with special attention to motive. Religious expression as performance for reward is sham and is futile. To give alms, pray, or fast to be seen gains no reward other than being seen. We can perform for God, for others, or for self—even in the secret chamber. Jesus expected us to give alms, pray, and fast; but he pointed to motive as validating or invalidating such experiences.

Distinct strata in the growth of this section are easily discerned. If vs. 7–15 are omitted, three carefully balanced stanzas appear on almsgiving, prayer, and fasting. They all deal with the threat of hypocrisy, and they are stylistically alike. At v. 7 a new problem is introduced, the pagan misunderstanding of the purpose of prayer, not the problem of selfish motive. The model prayer illustrates the motives, concerns, and manner proper to prayer. The unit vs. 7–15 is placed here because it belongs to the theme of prayer already in the trilogy on almsgiving, prayer, and fasting.

FREEDOM FROM MATERIALISM (MATT. 6:19–34)

This section is made up of many parts, the continuity not always apparent. One theme does seem to tie it all together, a proper disposition toward the material. Perishable treasure cannot sustain us in this life and we cannot take it with us. It has its place, but we perish with the perishable if we bury our hearts in it. In biblical usage the "single eye" stands for generosity (see Rom. 12:8; II Cor. 8:2; 9:11, 13; James 1:5). The "evil eye" stands for stinginess (see Matt. 20:15; Deut. 15:9; Prov. 23:6). The selfish live in darkness; the generous live in light. It is striking that Jesus warned that we cannot belong to God and Mammon (hoarded money) rather than God and Satan. Anxiety for things is unnecessary, futile, and evil. The material is not meaningless, but its meaning is to be secondary to God's kingdom and his righteousness.

JUDGING AND BEING JUDGED (MATT. 7:1–27)

Reducing this material to a tight outline would be forced, yet the basic movement is traceable. The demands here are like walking a narrow pathway, with perils on each side.

Judging Others (Matt. 7:1–6). Forming judgments is inescapable to a normal mind, for the mind functions that way. Expressing judgments can be controlled. We are fallible, vulnerable to inadequate information, misinformation, and bias. The parable of the mote and the beam is a cartoon, designed to show how ridiculous it is for fallible people to pose as judges of others. The point is not indifference to another's problems. The principle is first to come under judgment for one's own faults and then to help the other person in trouble. Verse 6 is problematic, but probably it means that there are situations where there is no openness to ministry. It is right to be accessible to others, but help cannot be imposed upon the unwilling.

Ask, Seek, Knock (Matt. 7:7–12). This does not mean that all we have to do is ask and we will get. Just try it! Jesus means that where there is openness to God, God responds. It may or may not be what we had in mind. God knows how to give, but we need to learn how to receive.

The Golden Rule assumes discipleship, for among the wicked it would be a disaster to do to others what one would want done to oneself. A gangster would want his enemies wiped out. Again, what is to be sought in a text is intention, not literalism.

The Narrow Gate (Matt. 7:13–14). This is neither legalism nor libertinism. Life calls for focus, decision, commitment, and discipline. There are many wrong answers and wrong ways; finding the way leading to life comes only by striving and commitment.

A Tree and Its Fruit (Matt. 7:15–20). Religion is best tested by what it produces. The familiar tests of orthodoxy, ritual purity, conformity to cultural mores, etc., are superficial. A mean spirit or rotten heart can hide underneath all such external appearance. Fruit is not the same as results. Fruit grows from the tree and is of the same kind. Results can be manipulated. Galatians 5:22 indicates what is meant by fruit produced in a godly life.

Doing God's Will (Matt. 7:21–23). We are not saved by our goodness, but God's will is to be obeyed. We acknowledge God's authority not by reciting pledges but by obedience. True piety is more than words, even if the words are "Lord! Lord!"

Two Foundations (Matt. 7:24–27). This parable extends the call for right fruit and for obedience. Nothing short of compliance with the heard word of God is sufficient. The SM is not just for admiration; it is to be obeyed. The word is to be incarnated.

II. PREACHING THE TEXT

An introductory sermon could deal with the primary question as to how the SM is to be heard. Are we just to take it as it is? Who does? A few have tried to take it literally, even to cutting off an offending hand. Probably nobody has really tried to take it all literally. Those who say, "The SM is all the Bible I need," must never have read it. Not one of us comes even close to conforming to the demands of the sermon: purity of the heart, turning the other cheek, giving away all we have to anyone asking, going the second mile, loving our enemies, and being perfect as God is perfect!

Probably the best approach is to see the SM as both gift and demand, leaving us in an unresolved tension between being accepted as we are yet called to perfection. Salvation is God's gift, absolutely free. It is also absolute demand. It's like target practice for a soldier; the bull's-eye is the only proper target, however much or often it is missed. The soldier dare not shoot for anything except perfection but is accepted though short of perfection. There is no contradiction between perfection as goal and acceptance as we are. The SM can be preached this way, and such preaching will be true to the SM and to the tension in every normal life. Thus the preacher does not have to explain it away or water it down or pretend that we actually measure up to it. It is a call; not an accomplishment. But the call is an earnest call, not a game.

The Beatitudes (Matt. 5:3–12). There is some progression in the Beatitudes, and they may be preached that way, as done by Alexander Maclaren in his *Expositions*. Recognition of our spiritual poverty leads properly to mourning over our sins, meekness before God, hunger and thirst for righteousness, and a new and redemptive relationship to others, and some form of persecution in the world. This approach can be overdone, and it can obscure the intention of each Beatitude. In preaching, it is probably best to take each Beatitude separately and in its own right. Chiefly, the Beatitudes reverse the world's values, as well as the values of much that passes for religious piety. In the world and in much religion, the prizes go to the self-assertive persons who press their advantage over others. The Beatitudes affirm and assure the "little people" in the world that under God's rule there are mighty reversals. True happiness is found in who we are and what we are, and the basic traits for such are presented.

Salt and Light (Matt. 5:13–16). These parables deal with identity. Who are you? Whose are you? What is your mission? Many people have a low self-image. Many reject themselves, seeing no worth in themselves. Many think they must earn the right to be. Jesus says, *"You are* the salt of the earth. . . . You are the light of the world." Jesus means *you are* "a city set upon a hill." Preaching here can *assure* people of their worth, and it can call them to their mission. Also, *being* comes properly before doing and saying. See John A. T. Robinson, *On Being the Church in the World* (London: SCM Press, 1960). This puts it all in right perspective. You are! Be what you are! Further, being determines function. Salt behaves as it does (preserving and seasoning) because it is salt. Light shines because it is light.

The Law and the Prophets (Matt. 5:17–20). This passage has to do with the Bible. Jesus' critics accused him of destroying the Bible, the Law (Torah) and the Prophets (Naviim), the two older strata of the Hebrew Bible. In truth, the Bible is negated by the legalism that reduces it to a set of rules and regulations or by the libertinism that wants all gift and no demand. Jesus rejects both fallacies. Preach here on a *tertium quid* (a third option). The only way to honor the Bible is to seek its underlying intention and then incorporate this into personhood and life.

This is what Jesus meant by not destroying but rather fulfilling the Law and the Prophets. A sermon here could be against the background of theological controversy, as in the so-called "battle of the Bible." The Bible does not need to be defended; it needs to be heard and obeyed. To literalize is to trivialize. The Bible is to be taken seriously, not literally. In your sermon, illustrations can be drawn from the four Gospels, where Jesus was often censured by religious persons who thought that they were upholding the law but were really obscuring it. The sermon should not be negative, just refuting something. It should be positive, capturing Jesus' position about the true righteousness that goes beyond legalism and libertinism, as made clear in the balance of the SM.

How to Deal with Anger (Matt. 5:21–26). Anger is universal. God gets angry. A baby gets angry. Even when suppressed, anger is there. Uncontrolled anger can damage or destroy both subject and object. Anger only suppressed can destroy. It is not the fact of anger but what we do with it that matters. In your sermon, don't get bogged down in all the details of the paragraph, lest only a new legalism emerge. The intention is clear enough: To despise or hate another is to murder that person. The target of such anger may or may not know about it or may or may not suffer actual damage from it; but the one harboring such anger is guilty and is damaged. A sermon may deal with creative possibilities in anger. We should be angry at hunger, disease, and injustice. When anger makes us sensitive to what we feel to be wrong, we can let that anger occasion an effort in reform and reconciliation. A sermon could show how Jesus warned against the idea that we can be right with God but hostile or indifferent toward people.

Adultery (Matt. 5:27–30). There is something as certain as death and taxes—humanity's preoccupation with sex! "The oldest profession" is still here, because there is a ready market for prostitution. Pornography prospers as a proxy for sexuality which seems never to be satisfied. Probably more people "lust in their hearts" than confess it. This passage goes far in putting the matter of sex in proper focus. It does not imply that sexuality is evil; its concern is in what is done with sexual desire. The sexual drive is deeply embedded by nature in all of life. A person need not, and should not, feel guilty for being normal. Jesus' protest is against making the overt act of adultery the only wrong. Here as everywhere, Jesus internalizes good and evil. This does not mean that overt expressions of good and evil are insignificant. The overt is significant, but good and evil are not inherent in the overt as such. The overt takes on the character of good or evil in terms of the intention behind what is said or done. Plucking out an eye or cutting off a hand in a literal sense would not solve the problem of lust, but the illustrations do imply the seriousness of the matter. Bringing sex under control is not easy, but it can be done.

Since we have a growing awareness of the rights of women, this would be a good passage for dealing with both their rights and their responsibilities. No person is to be reduced to just a sex object. Adultery can be committed against a woman, not just against the property rights of a husband. A woman can abuse her rights and responsibilities just as a man can.

Divorce (Matt. 5:31–32). This increasingly critical matter calls for at least two responses: a strong affirmation of the intention of God as to marriage and a redemptive word for those who already have experienced divorce. These two ministries need not be competitive. If the question is about God's will, the biblical answer is clear. From the beginning, God willed marriage as a union between a man and a woman (not two of a kind), separable only by death. Anything short of this falls short of God's intention. Sermons need to make this clear to people *before* marriage is undertaken or abandoned. But there is the fact of divorce. Jesus abandoned nobody. Where there is brokenness, what remains is the need for redemption. Once there is divorce, the remaining question is what is the best option out of what remains. This text recognizes equal rights and responsibilities for men and women.

There is a lot of muddled thinking today on the subject of marriage and divorce. One such example is the saying, "Well, you have to give people the right to fail." Life is not fail-safe, and people are to be affirmed even when they fail and probably especially when they fail. However, there is a difference between failing and indifference to failure. The physician may fail to save his or her patient, but does not dare to fail or be indifferent to failure. The pilot may fail to land the passengers safely, but the pilot dare not plan to crash the plane. A marriage may fail, but it is a different matter to choose to fail. A sermon could distinguish between the risk of failure and consent to failure.

Integrity in Word (Matt 5:33–37). The question of oaths is of little importance in itself, although this passage has made it an issue for some persons who feel it wrong to take an oath. These persons should be helped to see the difference between meeting a reasonable requirement of the courts and a personal integrity which requires no oath. Jesus was protesting casuistry, finding the legal loophole to escape what appeared to be a firm commitment. The principle universally valid is that of integrity. A sermon on honesty is desperately needed. In some ways, this is the most basic of all virtues. Without honesty there is no foundation upon which to build in marriage, business, government, sports, or otherwise. Sermons should explore various levels and forms of dishonesty, individual and corporate.

Meeting Evil with Good (Matt. 5:38–42). There are really only two basic approaches to life, for self or for others. Retaliation intends to be self-serving, though actually it serves neither self nor others. Jesus rejected this approach to life. The other way is servanthood, seeking the good of the other. Jesus taught and embodied that way. That is what is at stake in this passage. It is radical. It seems impractical or even potentially harmful. Just give way to the demands of others? Give everything one has on to anyone asking for a single garment? Won't that encourage evil in others? In preaching on this, one must show that Jesus' primary concern is to free a person from all disposition to base relationships upon the self-serving principle. Jesus calls for radical servanthood, at whatever cost to oneself. Of course, it is proper at the right time to consider how a person helps another, by giving or withholding. That is a "must" question, but it is not the one under consideration here. No biblical passage "covers the waterfront." Even Jesus, to make a point, could risk an "overkill." Once we have learned to live out of sacrificial, serving love we can go the next step of asking how this may best be implemented for the good of other people.

Love Your Enemy (Matt. 5:43–48). This passage really restates the lesson above, applying it in another direction. Does love prefer friend to foe? If so, is it really the love that seeks the good of the other, or is it a false "love" that is only self-seeking? A pagan seeks a bargain, befriending those who will respond in kind. Jesus teaches the love that serves apart from any self-seeking. God is the indiscriminate giver. Of course, God's highest gifts must be accepted; they cannot be imposed. God can give sunshine and rain to the good and the evil. Eternal life can only be offered, not imposed.

Motive as Validating Piety (Matt. 6:1–18). This total unit may serve as the basis for a sermon on motive, or it may be treated in at least three sermons. If religious practice is self-serving, it is invalid, mere pretense and sham. Some ego-needs may be met in such phony practice, but the returns are strictly limited to that. One can turn religion into show business and make a showing, but God does not bless such sham. If one gives alms, prays, or fasts to be seen—whether seen by other people, self, or God—one may easily succeed in being seen, but that is the total reward. Authentic religion is that of servanthood, committed to the service of God and of other people. Of course, in such authentic religion one is truly rewarded. The real rewards in religion come to those not seeking rewards. The reward motive does appear here, and the sermon should demonstrate the difference between the self-serving desire for reward over against the principle that goodness embodies its own reward.

This passage is not simple, and simple sermons cannot do it justice. How can we be the salt of the earth or the light of the world and yet remain unnoticed? How can we let our good works be seen to the glory of God and at the same time escape the self-serving motive? The key is in the matter of motive. More precisely, the key is in so escaping the self-serving motive that we neither seek nor shun being seen by others in our religious practice. As long as we are afraid that our religious practice may be seen as self-serving, we are still "hung up" with ourselves. When a person is so completely absorbed in trying to serve other people to the glory of God, the whole matter of seeking the limelight, or avoiding it, fades out of the picture. A sermon here needs to spell out three approaches: the invalid concern to seek attention, the immature concern to run from attention, and the proper concern which frees one from concern for gaining or avoiding attention.

Almsgiving is a rewarding subject for a sermon on stewardship. Jesus assumed that we would give alms. Of course, stewardship calls for more than alms for the poor. Motive is the central concern here, but a sermon could show that when servanthood and not self-serving motivates one's giving, the giving will be generous, tuned to the needs of others, and the whole of oneself and one's possessions will be subject to responsible stewardship. (See, for this, Paul L. Stagg, "An Interpretation of Christian Stewardship," in *What Is the Church,* ed. by Duke K. McCall.)

In preaching on prayer, the sharp line between vs. 5–6 and vs. 7–15 should be observed. As a part of the trilogy on almsgiving, prayer, and fasting, vs. 5–6 deal only with overcoming the self-serving motive. At v. 7 a new problem is considered, the pagan misunderstanding of the purpose of prayer. The problem here is not sham but a misunderstanding of prayer because of a misunderstanding of God. If in praying we feel that we must assume the burden of informing God as to our needs and winning his favor, we misunderstand both God and prayer. God is better informed as to our needs than we are. God is more interested in us than even we are in ourselves. God is ready to relate to us redemptively and supportively. Then why pray at all? There are many reasons for praying. Prayer does not change God; it changes us. God is too wise and loving just to dump upon us all that he already wants us to have. The meaning of a gift depends upon the receiver as well as the giver. Some gifts, like the sunshine and the rain, can be given indiscriminately; but God's highest gifts must be received, not just bestowed. Praying prepares us to receive what God already wants to give. But praying is more than asking (the English word "prayer" means "asking"). Prayer is worship, thanksgiving, petition, intercession, and much more. The model prayer is just that, an example for understanding something of the nature, purpose, and motive in praying.

Fasting is a neglected area in preaching. Jesus fasted and assumed that we would. What he rejected was both the dictation of a religious calendar and the sham of fasting to gain attention. There are many proper motives for fasting that sermons may explore. The world today consists largely of the weight-watchers and the hungry. The church today is more identified with the former than the latter. Many of us need to fast for health, for we eat too much. Care of one's body belongs to Christian stewardship. Sometimes fasting can be a deliberate way of closing doors of escape, for some persons eat just as others drink to escape themselves, their problems, their responsibilities, or God himself. Of course, massive hunger in the world is reason to fast on occasion, both to sensitize ourselves and others as to world need and to set a pattern for a better distribution of the short supply of food for a hungry world. We may have a shortage of preaching here, but there is no shortage of biblical directive in this area.

The Material and Us (Matt. 6:19–34). Although the units are diverse and seemingly disjointed, there is a continuity here. Throughout, the passage is concerned with what the material does to us. Elsewhere in the Gospels, Jesus gave urgent attention to what we should do with the material, putting it to the service of other people. In this long section he deals with the problem the material poses for us. Given the wrong place in our goals, values, or priorities, the material can destroy us. Jesus does not teach that the material is bad, for it is not. He does not imply that we have no material needs; the passage recognizes that we do. It is when the material owns us that it destroys us. A sermon here could demonstrate how we may be possessed by what we think we possess, as in the case of the rich farmer (Luke 12:13–21). To live chiefly for what perishes is to perish with the perishable. In the analogy of the "single eye" and the "evil eye" Jesus was not teaching anatomy; he was characterizing the generous life and the stingy life. A sermon here can both warn and challenge.

Money can become Mammon, a person's God. Ultimate commitment cannot be both to God and to the material. Serious struggle with the demands of life is proper, but there is an anxiety that is neither necessary nor productive and that actually may be evil. The Greek word for "anxious" may best be rendered here "distracted."

Judging Others (Matt. 7:1–6). A sermon here should show that it is not the act of judging but the spirit and intention in judging that is exposed in this text. The process of judging is universal and inescapable wherever there is an active mind. We constantly weigh, measure, evaluate, and approve or disapprove almost everything around us. Such judging may be deliberate or not. There is no meaningful life without judging. Even here, a kind of judging is being judged. What is ludicrous is for one of us to denounce another for failures less serious than ones in ourselves that we ignore. In the sermon, show that Jesus employed a verbal cartoon here in his picture of a person with a beam stuck through his eye trying to remove a speck from another person's eye. A common trick is for us to try to build up our own egos by tearing down another person for even lesser faults. Show that this passage does not exclude the ministry of redemption or correction but rather makes it explicit that it is one's duty to remove the speck from another's eye. Important is the sequence: first submission to judgment and correction for oneself, and then the offer of help to the other.

Verse 6 is problematic. Probably the parables of pearls offered swine and what is holy offered to dogs were proverbial and not to be taken as a slur at anyone. These proverb/parables warn the "do-gooder" that our good cannot be imposed upon unwilling persons. It is one thing to stand ready to help remove the speck from another's eye, but it is another thing to be the self-appointed guardian of people who choose not to accept our help. It is not possible for us to have too much concern for the well-being of others, but our zeal can outrun its productivity or become counterproductive. Sometimes the attitude of the other person is such, or the atmosphere such, that we can only keep silence and await some opening before we offer our pearls or that which is holy to the other.

Asking and Receiving (Matt. 7:7–12). Here is a subject in great need of clarification. The electronic church is winning millions of followers and millions of dollars by exploiting the idea that faith need only ask to get. This text can be so interpreted, but only as isolated from the Bible as a whole and from Jesus in particular. Prayer is no magic ring or lamp with power to gain for those who rub it whatever they want. This is fortunate, for we are neither wise enough nor good enough to be empowered with prayer so understood. Just imagine how chaotic it would be if just anyone with sufficient faith could name a desire and get it. Besides, Jesus calls us away from the self-serving principle of "getting" to the Christian stance of giving and serving. What this passage teaches is that God knows how to give if we know how to receive. Where there is openness (asking, seeking, knocking), God can and will respond. God does not always give us what we desire, but he will give us what we require. Not all that is desired is desirable, but God knows the difference. The Golden Rule puts it in right perspective: seek for others the good that we wish for ourselves. To literalize v. 12 is a disaster, for its principle presupposes goodness and wisdom, not simply the universalizing of just any human desire.

The Narrow Gate (Matt. 7:13–14). This passage rejects permissiveness without playing into the hands of legalism. It calls for decision and commitment, but it does not imply life simply governed by rules and regulations. The heaviest demands upon us come not from codes but from such claims as love, trust, acceptance, and commitment. This is to be understood contextually, as a call to discipleship under Christ. Discipleship and discipline are cognates. To become a disciple (learner) of Jesus is also to come under his discipline (lordship). He is not our Savior except in becoming our Lord. A sermon here could well deal with the chaos today that results from a revolt against discipline. On one side, the revolt is proper if against arbitrary rules and regulations. On the other side, it is wrong and fatal if a rejection of "claim." Meaningful life is lived under the claim of God, the claim of family and community, the claim of one's own true self, the claim of truth and right, all this and much more. A sermon here might deal with the paradox of being free yet bound (see F. Stagg, *Polarities of Man's Existence in Biblical Perspective,* Ch. 5).

Fruit (Matt. 7:15–20). The proof of the pudding is in the eating. Religion is best tested by what it produces in terms of the quality of life (cf. James 1:27). Fruit is not the same as results. Fruit is a part of the tree, growing out of the tree and determined as to kind by the nature of the tree. Results may be only superficially related to the agent bringing them about. Applied to religion, such results as creeds, rituals, structures, programs, and crowds can be produced by techniques and energy. Results can be produced, measured, and manipulated. What Jesus meant by fruit is something akin to the person from whom it comes. Galatians 5:22 helps us understand what is intended by "fruit." A sermon here need not denounce "results" as of no value, but it should expose the difference between fruit and results, showing the limits of the latter and the primacy of the former. The sermon could tie in here the reality that in *being* Christian or in *being* the church, we minister best to the world. What we are validates or invalidates what we do and say.

Doing God's Will (Matt. 7:21–23). A sermon here could expose the fallacy of barren orthodoxy or empty piety. It is not enough to say, "Lord! Lord!" Jesus' lordship is acknowledged in obedience, not in mere confession, even "orthodox" creedal confession. The church has squandered much of its time and energy in such contrived issues as "the battle of the Bible." The point in this passage builds upon the preceding unit. The passage in not teaching that we are saved by our good works; we show our faith by our works. The passage itself gives illustrations of both doing and saying which are ineffective and inauthentic. Don't miss the warning that many will reach the final judgment mistakenly holding that their busywork in religion is what God wants.

Two Foundations (Matt. 7:24–29). How is the SM to be heard? In an earlier sermon suggestion, this question was faced. Is this only for clergy but not for laity? Is it only for sacred but not for secular life? Is it an impossible ethic? Is it an interim ethic? Is it reserved for a supposedly future "dispensation," a kingdom age, but irrelevant to the present "church" age? Is it none of the above? We had better believe from this concluding parable that the SM is for here and now and for all of us all the time. *These words* are to be obeyed now. The SM is not for auditors; it is for students subject to examination and all course requirements. This parable says, "Put up or shut up!" Of course, no one of us measures up to the demands of this sermon; but we all can submit to its claims as proper and right. A steward is judged by faithfulness, not by achievement. A true disciple may fall woefully short of this high demand, but there is no authentic discipleship apart from honest commitment to the claims of this Sermon on the Mount.

FOR FURTHER READING

Bonhoeffer, Dietrich. *The Cost of Discipleship.* Tr. R. H. Fuller. Macmillan Co., 1956.

Davis, W. D. *The Setting of the Sermon on the Mount.* Cambridge University Press, 1964. Difficult but nearest to a definitive study of the Sermon on the Mount.

———. *The Sermon on the Mount.* Cambridge University Press, 1966. A brief and simplified version of the massive book above.

Hunter, A. M. *A Pattern for Life: An Exposition of the Sermon on the Mount.* Rev. ed. Westminster Press, 1966.

Martin, Hugh. *The Beatitudes.* Harper & Brothers, 1953.

Schweizer, Eduard. *The Good News According to Matthew.* Tr. David E. Green. John Knox Press, 1975. One of the best commentaries on Matthew.

Stagg, Frank. *Matthew.* The Broadman Bible Commentary, Vol. 8. Broadman Press, 1969. Approach parallels this chapter but gives more attention to exegetical detail.

13. PREACHING FROM
THE MIRACLE STORIES
OF THE GOSPELS

ERIC C. RUST

Anyone who preaches from the miracle stories of the New Testament must face issues that arise from many fronts. From the biblical side we must face the results of the contemporary historical study of the Gospels. From the scientific side, we must consider the newer attitude to "scientific law" and its implications for the nature of miracle. From the theological point of view, we must see what a "miraculous event" means, since it and religious faith are correlative.

I. CONTEMPORARY BIBLICAL STUDY
ON THE NATURE OF MIRACLE

Let us examine the results of contemporary biblical study. The source of study of the Gospels was, first of all, succeeded by the form-critical study of the material in the sources, and now it has moved to a study of the way in which the redactions have been motivated by theological perspectives. With the form critics, we have been taught to look at the structural forms manifested in these sources and to realize how much the life and worship of the early Christian community shaped and molded its stored-up memories of the Lord. In consequence, the preaching and healing mission of the primitive church has become very evident in the material content of the Gospels. The present-day preacher is dealing with material that reflects the preaching of those early days. We find ourselves dealing with "pronouncement stories" or sermon illustrations, with memorable sayings or logia of our Lord and his apposite parables, and with the passion story and its accompanying events, for the church preached Christ and him crucified. Within such groupings fall the miracle stories with their own distinctive structure—diagnosis, cure, result. They may well have been associated with healing missions, used in preaching and testimony to point to the Christ as one who was concerned with people's whole bodiliness, their physical as well as their spiritual well-being, and also as being the Lord of all the created order.

These data constituted traditions, at first oral and then committed to writing. They reflected the peculiar concerns and selective memories of the different important centers of early Christian activity—such as Jerusalem, Caesarea, Antioch, Rome—and might well be associated with some dominant Christian leader who had particular ties to such a community. Hence the editing of the four Gospels reflects the theological concern of the particular redactors. Memories, selective traditions shaped by Christian usage, were finally subjected to theological formulation in the minds of the four great Evangelists—Mark early, Luke, Matthew, and finally John, the identification of the last two named being debatable. Thus each of the four Gospels has its own theological emphasis, and the very widened theological structure of the Fourth Gospel must not lead us to dismiss the other three Gospels as free of theological redaction. This kind of editing has to be taken into account in dealing with the accounts of the miracles in the Gospels, especially in the Fourth Gospel, where the miracles fit into the author's theological patterns and are regarded as "signs."

There was a time in biblical studies when scholars rejoiced if they could trace material, in context and structure, to sources in the cultural and social milieu of the ancient world. Thus the miracle stories were traced to the presence of wonder-workers and magi in the Hellenistic background of the early church. They were told, even fabricated, to make Jesus a wonder-worker with more power to work wonders than those others of whom extraordinary wonders were recorded. This stage is now past, but we still must face the veracity of the accounts of the Gospel miracles in the light of scientific skepticism. Every preacher must face this issue in order really to address the average listener.

First of all, we must recognize the process through which the miracle stories of the Gospels have passed in the passage from the actual event with its eyewitnesses, through the preaching and witnessing of the believing community, to the final form as it passed through the theological alembic of the mind of the redactor. Undoubtedly elements might be dropped or omitted in passage, other aspects appearing in the final narrative might be added, and the nature of the original incident might have been transformed. We can, of course, cite the presence of the Holy Spirit within the minds and memories of a believing community, and we may also remember that, in the early days, there would have been eyewitnesses enough to exercise restraint on distortion and imaginative transformation. But we must make allowance for the presence of "original sin." God has been pleased to work with people, and even his saints are *being* redeemed. Hence it may well be that the story of the cursing of the fig tree (Mark 11:12–25) originated in a parable (e.g., the barren fig tree in Luke 13:6–9) which was transformed into a miracle. Or, again, the "sign" of the turning of the water into wine (John 2:1–11) may have been a saying like that of new wine in old wineskins transformed into a miracle, although here the details would seem to point to some kind of incident.

In the second place, the preacher needs to remember the uniqueness of the supreme event with which the miracle stories are associated—the incarnate and saving presence of God in the man Christ Jesus. This faith claim places Jesus in a position that requires a very special assessment of the miracles by believers. They will place more credibility in such narratives than will unbelievers. Because they believe in the extraordinary birth and the incredible resurrection of their Lord, believers will not cavil at any other inexplicable events associated with this unique personal being.

Clearly this view dominates the Gospel records. Our Lord's mighty acts were always associated with his Messianic task, with the presence and activity of the kingdom of God in his own person. They were *dunameis,* mighty acts, manifestations of the presence of the kingdom in the midst of history. When Jesus, by the finger of God, cast out demons, then the kingdom of God had come among men (Luke 11:20). The power (*dunamis*) of the Lord was present in Jesus to heal (Luke 5:17). In the Synoptic Gospels, therefore, the miracles are described as mighty acts, disclosing God's presence and power in Jesus.

The unique distinction from workers of wonders and makers of charms appears in miracles where Jesus performs mighty acts by his Word. In this way, he cures blind Bartimaeus (Mark 10:52), calms the storm (Mark 4:39), heals the man with the withered arm (Mark 3:5), and casts out demons (Mark 1:25; 5:8). He thus shares in the creative power of God, who creates all things by his Word and upholds all things by the Word of his power. Here his uniqueness shines through. He was no wonder-worker of marvels who sought to attract the credulous. His mighty acts, like his words, had revelatory impact. They were disclosure situations in which men met God in his person.

Indeed, as the Hebrew word for "word" (*dabhar*) implies, God's word could be a deed as well as an utterance. Jesus claims an authority (*exousia*) which is the direct gift of God (Matt. 9:6–8) and even the winds obey him (Mark 4:41). His healing ministry as well as his preaching was a manifestation of the activity of the kingdom in his Person. Both alike were demonstrations to the disciples of John the Baptist that Jesus was the Coming One (Luke 7:18–23).

Preachers must therefore examine the biblical evidence carefully. They will make allowance for the long process of oral and written tradition, worship and preaching, and also admit human fallibility. But they will emphasize the presence of the divine Spirit inspiring and guiding the process. Most of all, preachers will be biased by the affirmation of faith, confirmed in their own experience, that this is the Christ, the Chosen One of God. In him, the new age dawned and the kingdom of God became manifestly and savingly present. Hence one should not be surprised at the unexpected and untoward. The promised events of the end time when the normal behavior of nature and history would be superseded had already become a reality in the midst of history. This present evil age might continue, but the age to come had already begun and was present in the midst. The powers of that age had been released in Jesus, his words and his mighty acts, and in the greatest miracle of all, his resurrection.

II. THE IMPACT OF SCIENCE ON THE NATURE AND VALIDITY OF MIRACLE

Yet the preacher must still meet the challenge of the contemporary secular culture with its scientific skepticism. With the advent of modern natural science, miracle achieved a new definition. Until this scientific era had dawned, miracle was, in the eyes of general humanity, an unexpected and inexplicable incident within the normal and accepted regularities of nature and the expected processes of human existence—healing from a deadly or incurable disease, a phenomenal escape from what appeared to be inevitable disaster, and so on. But natural science brought with it the unbreakable rule of a causative process, the inevitable linkage of cause and effect. With the Newtonian world view, men were ushered into a realm of scientific law where causality ruled supreme. The universe became a vast mechanism bound by "laws which never should be broken." Between the Creator and his world there was erected a barrier of law which governed the whole universe and which the Creator himself had ordained. Within this system man with his freedom and his spiritual values was a kind of inexplicable super-added presence. Miracles too became a break in this wall of scientific causation. They stood for God breaking into his world and suspending, for his purpose, the laws that he had ordained. In a world dedicated to scientific explanation, such an event seemed incomprehensible.

In the past two centuries, this skepticism has survived. The mechanistic viewpoint has spread from physics and chemistry to biology and psychology. A naturalistic interpretation of the evolutionary process and a Freudian or a Skinnerian understanding of the human mind have completed the picture. Even man has become a product of natural forces, and God has been banished from his universe until, in a secular society, men behave as if God were dead.

In the process of the centuries, however, the mechanistic universe of Newton has given place to the relativistic universe of Einstein and the quantized realm of atomic physics. Thanks to the philosophical quests of Hume and Kant, we have learned not to be dogmatic about our scientific structures. We have come to see that, at best, science is only providing a model for the universe and individual models which may help us to explain, control, and understand the phenomena of nature. We are no longer doctrinaire about our scientific laws, for we know that they are no longer to be regarded as regulative, but rather as descriptive. Nature does have chance and contingency and randomness in its structure, both in the process of evolution and down at the basis of matter where indeterminacy and probability are grounded in our understanding of physical energy in the forms of matter and radiation. Nature does, of course, manifest its regularities, and the whole structure of our world and of human existence depends on this fact. Yet scientific law is statistical, like the life expectancy tables of an insurance company. It describes and points to the regularity in nature, but it does not rule supreme.

We expect regularity. Experience demands it. Hume made a special attack upon the evidence for miracle and argued that such evidence must be overwhelmingly strong for us to accept any break in the accustomed regularity of the natural process. Hume did help us to see that scientific laws are descriptive and not regulative, but his empiricism had a religious bias. His deism isolated God from his world in transcendental majesty and thus would tend to bar miraculous intervention.

In the two centuries since Hume, religious deism has given place to naturalism and secular humanism. Men are even more skeptical about miracle, for they now would dismiss such a category along with the God whom it presupposes. Yet the new attitude to scientific law helps us to reestablish a relationship between the Christian under-standing of God and the natural process. No longer are we to think of an unbreakable chain of causal laws as interposed between man and his Creator. Rather, we may think of the established regularities of the natural order and the created process as expressions of his sustaining will, expressions of his consistency, his overall purpose. Because even science sees its laws positivistically as descriptive and statistical, patterns of high probability, nature is open to expressions of the divine will which may heighten the divine presence for a specific purpose and bring the divine intention to a focus in some special activity.

Once more we can return to the biblical world, except that the scientific disciplines have made us very aware of the secondary causes of which the biblical men were barely aware. They leaned their world back directly, at every point, upon the divine activity. We are very aware of the intricate network of natural forces and agencies that mediate the sustaining and creative activity of God. But we may also see such a world as open to some unexpected divine activity, although we should not expect this to be a frequent occurrence. God is a God of consistency and order.

Miracle then becomes, as it was for the Bible men, more of that divine presence which is everywhere active. As the present writer has written elsewhere: "If God be a God of order, it should not surprise us that he works through order or that what appears to us to be statistical order, arising from probability and randomness, should yet manifest order and directiveness in the eyes of faith" (E. C. Rust, *Science and Faith*, p. 294). Miracle is indeed a religious category, pointing beyond the material subject of scientific inquiry to the depth which is God. It becomes a disclosure event, a divinely ordered situation which becomes revelatory. A miracle is an event in which God makes himself more manifest for the fulfillment of his saving purpose.

III. MIRACLE AS A RELIGIOUS CATEGORY— DISCLOSURE AND FAITH

A disclosure event always requires a human participant as well as a divine presence. Hence the miracles of our Lord were always associat-ed with faith. We are told that he could not work miracles in Nazareth because of the unbelief of the people (Mark 6:5–6). The parables were significant for those who had eyes to see. So also were the miracles. The emphasis on faith occurs twice in the healing of the epileptic boy. Not only was faith demanded of the father before our Lord proceeded to heal. Earlier the disciples, having failed to heal the boy, were rebuked for their lack of faith. Such faith would have enabled them to draw upon the divine power (*dunamis*) which operated in Jesus. The distracted cry of the father, "I believe; help thou my unbelief," opened the door for the healing power to become effective (Mark 9:14–29). Faith makes it possible for one "to share in the Kingdom of God which has drawn near in Jesus and to experience the *dunamis* which is present in Him" (E. C. Rust, *Nature and Man in Biblical Thought,* p. 180).

The preacher could take this incident and remind his hearers that there is always a hiddenness about God's presence and activity which is open only to faith. Remember that faith has here Christological content. It is not belief that Jesus is a kind of wonder-worker. It means relating oneself to Jesus as Savior. It is a recognition that the divine kingdom is present in his Person and that he is the healer-Savior. He can and does make persons whole, physically and spiritually. Without this insight of faith, a miracle would cease to be a miracle and become a mere cause of astonishment. What differentiated the disciples, prior to that dramatic miracle of the resurrection, when their eyes were fully opened, was their spiritual receptivity to the divine disclosure in the person and deeds of their Master. He was not just a wonder-worker possessing magical powers. His miracles were disclosure situations in which they discerned his secret, his Messiahship, the presence and activity of the kingdom. His miracles had Christological import to faith. Jesus was and is, in himself, the power and presence of God.

The Fourth Gospel would seem to suggest that, rather than the performances of miracle requiring faith on the part of the participant, it evoked such faith. John calls the miracles "signs" instead of the description "mighty acts" in the other three Gospels. The word points to the hiddenness. The miracles possessed an inner significance evident only to those who believed. Such faith is, however, not aroused by the miraculous incident. Rather, it is itself a part of the miracle. The mighty act, the sign, brings the faith and insight with it. Hence John can record that, despite Jesus' many signs, men did not believe in him (John 12:37). He suggests, also, that men followed him because they benefited by his signs without realizing their true import (John 6:26). Thus they were filled with perishable bread, without receiving the final satisfaction—the insight into the imperishable bread which the Son of Man would give them. A sign was not an incident standing in isolation. It was a disclosure event, and the insight and response of faith might be part of the divine activity in that disclosure. John was quite sure that faith is a divine gift. God might work through the sign to awaken faith in men.

This discussion is very relevant to our own preaching task, for preachers know that their words only become "the Word" as God makes clear his hidden presence and opens some blind eyes to see and some deaf ears to hear. Such faith is his gift. The preacher's own verbal expression may attract and awaken interest, but faith results from God's lifting that interest into a disclosure situation. It is a miracle. The miracle of the healing of the man born blind brings this truth home (John 9). The preacher could use this! There is a Marcan story of the healing of a blind man (Mark 8:22–26) which parallels John's story. This story is preceded by a reference to the blindness and ignorance of the disciples. Evidently this miracle had Christological import. The healing of the blind man was a sign of our Lord's Messiahship and of his gift of spiritual sight to those who believe in him. The Johannine miracle story is concerned with the same theme. The healing of the man born blind is a sign of the gift of faith. The fact that the man was born blind brings to the disclosure situation an insight into the nature of faith. Faith, the opening of man's spiritual eyes, is something utterly new. He is not born with it. It is God's gift. The healing of the man born blind was a manifestation of our Lord's compassion, but, deeper than this, it disclosed that divine power alone can open men's blinded spirits and release them from the darkness of sin. Here is a sermon in the making!

The present writer has expressed this in these words: "God is active in his world, but even his miraculous disclosures are such only to those with spiritual receptivity. In such a disclosure faith itself may be awakened, yet not by the shock of an unusual material event, rather because the event is so transparent to the divine activity that through it God awakens faith in the one to whom the miracle is directed. Thus the revelation will not be merely in the lifting up of the natural order into the divine activity, but also in the work of God in the heart of the human recipient. . . . Faith is as much a miracle in the recipient as is the corresponding happening in nature. Both together constitute the miracle and the disclosure" (E. C. Rust, *Science and Faith*, p. 292).

IV. THE GOSPEL MIRACLES AND THEIR CHRISTOLOGICAL IMPORT

We must now examine the miracles of our Lord and seek their inner meaning, for that inner meaning is the significant issue for our own preaching. Although our Lord was moved by compassion, yet, as with his teaching, his miracles were signs, manifestations of the presence of the kingdom in his Person. His miracles were "signs." Always they had deeper import than the mere healing which they controlled. Undoubtedly the love of the Lord for men was central, but then the power of the kingdom is the power of redeeming love. And it was this saving power in the fullest sense that was the hidden meaning of the "mighty acts" of Jesus. The typical Hebrew understanding of man in his psychosomatic wholeness characterizes the New Testament witness. Our Lord's query, "Wilt thou be made whole?" is a reminder of this. To forgive sins is also bound up with physical restoration. Man's inner and outer dimensions of being belong together. Even survival beyond death in biblical thought is not Greek immortality but bodily resurrection. Our Lord's own resurrection, the "miracle of miracles," is a reminder of this. Hence the miracles were signs of his saving power, the redemptive presence of the kingdom, just as much as his words proclaimed the same reality. When we preach from the miracles, we need to emphasize his Christological dimension.

A. The Healing Miracles

We need to note that the Gospel miracles fall into two groups—the healing miracles and the nature miracles. The former are the more numerous and are full of preaching significance. We shall deal with these first. The preacher needs to remember that our Lord was, as the incarnation implies, a typical man of his time. He shared our common humanity to the point where he taught in the forms and categories of his contemporary culture. This was one aspect of that divine accommodation and self-emptying whereby the eternal Son accepted the limitation of our human existence and "pitched his tent" among us (John 1:14f. and Phil. 2:5ff.). This means that mental and bodily ills could often be ascribed to demon possession, where modern psychotherapy can offer a more satisfying diagnosis. What matters immediately is that we recognize the presence of evil distortions and misdirection in human life, both physically and mentally, which our Lord put right, however they be described. He had and has the power to make men whole. The evil forces and distortions are present, however we describe them, and the Christ still has power to deal with them.

Another point that the modern preacher must note is that the Jews of our Lord's time associated all suffering with sin, so that disease was a punishment for one's own sin or that of one's ancestors. Thus a Jew would understand how our Lord's healings were often accompanied by the injunction: "Your sins are forgiven." Quite apart from the fact that the strict Jews at that time had no place for the practice of medicine, such a saying of Jesus was scandalous because only a priest could *pronounce* a person whole. Even then, only God had the power to make whole—the priest could not. Thus our Lord's declaration of sins forgiven had indirect Christological implications. We can then understand the queries of religious leaders as to the identity and authority of One who did such things (Luke 7:49; Mark 11:28). Probably the Fourth Gospel tells how some felt: "If this man were not from God, he could do nothing" (John 9:33).

We may presume that Jesus did not accept such a philosophy, although he does not openly reject it. In the story of the man born blind (John 9), in answer to the question why the man was born blind, our Lord declares: "It was not that this man sinned, or his parents, but that the works of God might be made manifest in him." In any case, Jesus made it clear that his saving mission involved the whole person. He recognized, as does modern medicine, that mental illness has physical repercussions and vice versa. Furthermore, when people are out of relation to God, their bodily wholeness suffers. Reconciliation and forgiveness involve the whole person, and one's bodily well-being is bound up with spiritual rightness. In preaching from the healing miracles this is a necessary emphasis.

The healing of the paralytic (Mark 2:1–12) brings to a focus this issue of healing and the forgiveness of sins. There is no reason to dismiss vs. 5b–10 as a later incursion. Undoubtedly, the question of our Lord's authority to forgive sins and to associate this with his healing power was a real issue. In this story Jesus confronts the scribes. He declares that the paralytic's sins are forgiven, and the sick man confirms his word by taking up his pallet and walking off before the onlookers. He thus raises the Christological issue in their minds. They associated sickness with sin, and they knew that only God could forgive sin. Here was One whose authority to forgive sins was affirmed by his power to heal. The scribes faced this paradox. The faith in the healer-Savior that led the paralytic and his bearers to overcome all obstacles in bringing the sick man to Jesus gave them an insight which the cynical scribes did not possess—a vision of his Messianic power.

Again, the preacher should remember that the opening of the eyes of the blind and the unstopping of the ears of the deaf were associated by the prophets with the coming Day of the Lord, the advent of the kingdom (see Isa. 29:18; 32:3f.; 35:5; 42:7; Ezek. 24:27). Mark records three miracles that may well have such an eschatological promise in their background—the healing of the deaf-mute (7:31–37), the miracle of the blind man of Bethsaida (Mark 8:22–26), and the mighty act that restored sight to the blind Bartimaeus (10:46–52). Mark's setting of these stories may help us to see how they were used in the preaching and instruction of the early church. The Evangelist is concerned with the blindness of the disciples, and it is within this setting that the miracles are recorded. The first two stories both follow incidents of miraculous feeding (6:30–44; 8:11–21), in which the disciples have failed to grasp the Messianic identity of Jesus and, at best, were astonished at what they saw. So, in both these healings Jesus points more clearly to his inner secret. After the first, their confession points to the prophetic promises: "He has done all things well; he even makes the deaf hear and the dumb speak" (7:37). Thus both miracles have Christological import. They manifest the compassion of Jesus, but they also point to his Messianic identity as the presence of the kingdom. But then that kingdom is redemptive love! Immediately after the healing of the blind man, there comes the stumbling confession of Peter at Caesarea Philippi—"You are the Messiah." The gospel has been unveiled to those who have eyes to see. Another sermon in the making! "To open the eyes of the blind man is a sign of the disclosure of divine truth to those who have the eyes to see" (E. C. Rust, *Nature and Man in Biblical Thought*, p. 178).

The healing of those suffering from leprosy presents another fact which the preacher may grasp. Mark records the healing of the leper (Mark 1:40–45). The modern preacher needs to remember that leprosy was regarded as a form of religious uncleanness. In the Jewish law it was categorized as a judgment on sin, so that a leper was a sinner (e.g., Num. 12:9–12). The leper was indeed a social outcast, but the basis of such exclusion was not just the contagiousness of the disease; the leper was excluded on the basis of religious law. Jesus stretched forth his hand and touched the leper. This act had symbolic significance. It was a sign that Jesus was identifying himself with the leper and stretching out his hand to deliver him. The Messiah was here the suffering servant of prophecy bearing the sin of many. It is not enough to emphasize the compassion that moved Jesus to act, nor to point out the contact with a contagious disease, a contact that was not regarded as serious if only occasional. The latter meant identification. His was a Christological act in which he brought Messianic salvation and wholeness to the leper. It is not just fanciful to note that the restored man was now enjoined to make the sacrifices required by the law under which he had hitherto been treated as an outcast, condemned to a living death. Commentators sometimes suggest that he could now approach God in the Messiah's identification with him or, as Paul would put it, in Christ. A sermon begins to take shape!

The same thought of Messianic identification underlies the healing of the woman with an issue of blood (Mark 5:25–34). This woman's trouble was another case of ritual uncleanness. She alone, among the many around Jesus, had eyes to see his true nature as Messianic sin bearer. Aware of her uncleanness, she yet dared to believe that he would make his saving power available to her. So she sought for that physical contact which, for her, meant recognition of his identification with a sinner like her and which, for us, symbolizes the Christ's concern with sinful men. Our Lord therefore pointed to her faith as the true bond of identification which had made his healing power available.

We shall look at the miracles of psychological healing and restoration from death in the specific sermonic studies.

B. THE NATURE MIRACLES

Under the heading of nature miracles are grouped the various accounts of the feeding of the multitudes (Mark 6:30–44; 8:1–9; John 6:4–13), the stilling of the tempest (Mark 4:35–41), and the walking on the water (Mark 6:45–52). The miraculous feedings will be dealt with under the sermon section. The other two miracles are bound up with the cosmic significance of the Christological nature of Jesus.

We must not regard such Christological import as imposed upon the material by early Christian interpreters. We can see that the church, in its preaching, and the Gospel redactors did enlarge on the implications of our Lord's mighty acts. But the symbolic significance would seem to have been present from the very beginning. The stories were not "preached" merely to show Jesus' compassion. They always had theological significance, for the Messianic claims are bedded in Jesus' own historical being. The only person that history reveals is an eschatological figure.

This holds of the two sea miracles. Both point to the cosmic dimension of that Christological secret which was hidden in the humanity of Jesus. Jesus shared in the power of the Creator over his creation. If we believe in the divine self-emptying by which Jesus is also the eternal Word or Son of God, then we should not discount these miracles as incredible. It is, of course, in this skeptical age, easier to say that Jesus did not address the words "Peace, be still" to the tempestuous waves but to the fearful disciples; and to say that he was really walking on the surf at the edge of sea. But then we should eliminate the miraculous element, and, knowing the *dunamis* of the Lord, we should tread here very warily.

These miracles were signs that pointed from the power of God over nature to his saving power in the spiritual realm. In the Old Testament, God is the God of the storms, for was he not the covenant God of Horeb? Therefore Jesus, as the manifest presence of God's sovereign power, must also reveal his power over that medium. Furthermore, would not such power be a sign of his power to still the spiritual tempests by which his followers would be beset? His power over the physical storms was his sign to them to take courage as they faced the future. The Jew was always afraid of the sea and likened its depths to the meaningless abyss out of which the Creator called forth order (Gen. 1:1); it was the sea of the story of Jonah. Here our Lord shows himself as the one who deals with the chaotic aspect which underlies the existence of man and his world, both at the physical and the spiritual levels. The psalmist could put side by side, "God's stilling of the roaring of the seas and of the madness of the peoples" (Ps. 65:7). Jesus, grounded in the Hebrew Scriptures, must have been aware of such thoughts in his own mighty act. Later, in its own preaching of such nature miracles, the early church saw these deeper Christological implications. These mighty acts were concerned with nature. They offered a cosmic vision of the Christ's saving activity. But they also were significant for the human existence and spiritual well-being of his followers in the troublesome seas of life. We can still ask, "Who is this, that the winds and the waves obey him?" He can still the tempests of our troubled lives and help us tread their billowy waves. In these miracles Jesus' claims about himself and his mission are so embedded in the tradition that it is difficult to doubt that he himself made them. He is, as John saw, the Word through whom all things were created, in human form. This is a clue to some good sermons.

V. SOME SERMON SUGGESTIONS

A. LIBERATED FOR WHOLENESS (MARK 5:2–20)

The story of the demoniac of Gadara has been so bound up with the Gadarene swine that its true import has been missed. It has also been dismissed because of its emphasis on demons. Remember that demons and their evil inhabitants of the spirit world were ingredients in the contemporary culture. Today, with the impact of modern psychology and psychiatry, we use different categories, but we are describing the same phenomena. Possession by demons was their way of describing the hidden psychic forces that rise out of our unconscious life, and that, partly inherited and partly caused by our own past failings, are battling within our personal being. Neurosis and psychosis are modern ways of describing the reality of the demonic in our lives. The word "demonic" is still very applicable to such forces. They are evil, compulsive, very often uncontrollable. They are demonries with which we still wrestle.

Our Lord, as the creative power of the universe in human form, did battle with all the evil which befalls the creation–sin and evil in all their demonic significance. On Calvary, Jesus dealt with all the demonic forces and triumphed over them in the resurrection. In this story we are given a Christological insight into that ultimate triumph. It is not sufficient to describe Jesus as a superb psychologist. He did understand man, but more is involved than human skill and understanding. The redemptive and re-creative power of the kingdom was present in him.

1. *An Imprisoned Spirit.* The Gadarene demoniac was so torn by demonic forces—biological urges, irrational forces, instinctual urges, uncontrollable desires— that he could call himself "Mob" or "Legion." The word is used here in the sense of "men." He was not a single person. He had many conflicting personalities, like Stevenson's famous duality of Jekyll and Hyde. He was an imprisoned spirit.

He had been treated with the cruelty that often accompanied such cases. Chaining him had failed (v. 4), and he was left to make his home with the dead. Given to violence, he could here do no harm in a graveyard except self-injury (v. 5). He is a picture of a tempestuous sea such as Jesus had just stilled. Today more humane treatment would put him in an institution for the insane.

Our listeners will not be in this position, but many are torn asunder by confronting forces and need to be made whole. They too are in prison.

2. *The Redemptive Act.* The demoniac manifested a struggle between his rational self and his fragmented demonic urges. Thus he recognized the inner secret of Jesus (v. 7). The giving of his own name as "Mob" was equivalent to self-disclosure. He was opening himself up to Jesus and to the immediate response of our Lord. We all need that word, "Come out of the man," the word that overcomes our conflicting urges and sets us free to become whole persons.

3. *The Ambiguous Response.* The bystanders at first rejoiced, but then the merchants began to measure the damage. The awesome power displayed in the healing of the tempestuous demoniac had set

the swine in flight, probably frightened by the gesticulations and shrieks which preceded the healing word. The owners of the livestock saw their livelihood gone. Material values can easily drown the divine presence and activity in many minds.

The demoniac himself, made whole, would have joined himself to Jesus' following. But he was told to go back to ordinary life and take it up again. He must fulfill his Messianic testimony where its witness could be effective—in the marketplace.

B. THE RESURRECTION AND THE LIFE (JOHN 11:1–44)

The miracle of the raising of Lazarus must be put alongside the Synoptic miracle stories of the widow's son of Nain (Luke 7:11–17) and the raising of Jairus' daughter (Mark 5:21–43). All three constitute the Messianic sign of the raising of the dead. The two Synoptic stories should warn against the rejection of the Lazarus story, although there is little doubt that the Fourth Evangelist has exaggerated the details. Indeed, we see a progress—Jairus' daughter had just died, but the widow's son was on the way to the burial, while Lazarus had been dead for four days (John 11:39). The story must not be dismissed, however. The two Synoptic stories indicate that such mighty acts were a part of the tradition. The vividness of the story in John's Gospel, the description of the *dramatis personae*, down to such details as the emotional upset of Jesus himself—all point to a historical basis for the miracle. Something tremendous did happen at Bethany, and this seems to give the most reasonable explanation of the tremendous enthusiasm that greeted our Lord on his triumphal entry into Jerusalem. The Synoptics described this enthusiasm but did not account for it. John gave the clue.

1. Lazarus stands as a type of our humanity, just as does the man born blind or the impotent man. See him as a symbol of the whole human race and link his resurrection with Paul's picture of Christian experience as following the pattern of death and resurrection. Begin with humanity as dead in trespasses and sins—the meaninglessness of human existence without God.

2. Emphasize the place of faith in the resurrection of Lazarus. The sisters believed in the Messianic power and nature of Jesus.

3. Bring out resurrection as a present reality. We do not have to wait for physical death to experience newness of life—resurrection life in Christ is a restoration to new wholeness.

4. This story promises life that physical death cannot destroy. It was a sign of that power which raised Jesus from the dead and points to the Christian hope.

C. The True Bread from Heaven (Mark 6:33–44; 8:1–9; John
   6:1–14; 6:32)

The miracles connected with the feeding of the multitudes were
signs, Messianic acts. Had not Moses, the first great prophet and
lawgiver given the people bread from heaven in the desert? Had not
Elisha, the bearer of Elijah's mantle, fed a hundred men with twenty
loaves (II Kings 4:42–44)? And were not Moses and Elijah fitting
forerunners of Him who was to fulfill the Law and the Prophets?
Indeed, they appeared with Jesus on the Mount of Transfiguration.
These acts of Jesus were thus Christological.

They may not be dismissed as later fabrications. Mark's two
narratives may not be repetitions but refer to two separate occasions.
John's record indicates that the story was present in many traditions
and Christian centers.

Preachers should beware of rationalizing by suggesting that the
sacrificial example of the small boy was contagious, and so on. We
should tread warily if Jesus be truly what his acts and our faith
declare.

The feedings of the multitudes were signs that Jesus is the bread of
life, the giver of spiritual sustenance. They pointed to the Eucharist,
to the bread and the cup in the upper room, symbols of his broken
body and outpoured blood. Appropriate texts for the Communion
meditation! John brings this out (John 6:32; 51–59). This is why the
feeding of the five thousand is the only "mighty act" to appear in all
four Gospels.

1. Phrases in these stories parallel those used in the Last Supper in
the blessing and breaking of the loaves (Mark 6:41). In 8:6, "give
thanks" occurs, as in the story of the upper room (Mark 14:23). These
miracles point to the Bread of Life which was broken for us.

2. Of the two stories in Mark, one, the feeding of the four
thousand, was concerned with a Galilean, and thus a Jewish crowd,
whereas the other, the feeding of the five thousand, occurred in the
area of Decapolis, on the southeast of the Sea of Galilee, and would be
a Gentile crowd. There was a universal note here—the bread of life
was for all.

3. Remember the significance of the fishes in these stories. The
original group of disciples came from among the fishermen of
Galilee. Bread, as the staff of life, and fish, as the product of the area's
most important industry, were the common things by which Jesus
unveiled his Messianic meaning. The fish became later an important
early Christian symbol, and was so used along with bread for the
Lord's Supper.

4. The blindness of the disciples to the inner meaning of these miracles (Mark 6:52; 8:17–21) parallels the blindness of those who do not discern the body and blood of the Lord (see I Cor. 11:23–34). This suggests the development of the theme of real participation in the Lord's Supper and an attack on any idea of *ex opere operato.* We must discern the inner and symbolic meaning.

FOR FURTHER READING

Cairns, David. *The Faith That Rebels.* 6th ed. Harper & Brothers, 1954.

Lewis, C. S. *Miracles.* Macmillan Co., 1947.

Richardson, Alan. *Christian Apologetics.* Harper & Brothers, 1947.

————. *The Miracle-Stories of the Gospels.* Harper & Brothers, 1942.

Rust, Eric C. *Nature and Man in Biblical Thought.* London: Lutterworth Press, 1953.

————. *Salvation History.* John Knox Press, 1963.

————. *Science and Faith.* Oxford University Press, 1967.

14. PREACHING ON THE PARABLES

EDUARD SCHWEIZER

I. HERMENEUTICAL BACKGROUND

Some years ago, Ernst Fuchs declared that the only important discovery that New Testament scholars had made within the last fifty years was the fact that Jesus had spoken in parables. Of course, even a schoolboy who has received a minimum of religious instruction would know that. What Ernst Fuchs wants to point to is the discovery of the importance of that way of speaking. In the wake of Adolf Jülicher's basic work, the parables have usually been understood as illustrations of Jesus' teaching. As a schoolmaster would choose an image, if his pupils did not understand what he wanted to teach them, so Jesus would make use of a parable to explain his statements. The schoolmaster may explain the working of a steam engine by referring to the boiling water in the coffee percolator. Or, if his students do not understand that eight divided by four is two, he might tell them: If there are eight apples and there are four of you, how many apples do each of you get? Two, of course, for eight divided by four is two. In the same way, Jesus would, according to Jülicher, have told about the work of the sower in order to illustrate how the kingdom of God comes to life.

Jülicher is certainly correct in his main thesis that Jesus' parables are intended to help the hearers to understand his message, not to obscure it. Yet they are not simply illustrations of a truth that could and should be understood without the helping image; for, with few exceptions (which are, very probably, even secondary additions to the original parable of Jesus himself), we never find this direct statement of the truth that the parable is allegedly to illustrate. At school, the pupils may forget the illustration, the eight apples, as soon as they have understood the formula "Eight divided by four is two." With Jesus, it is not so. There is never a time in which we could dispense with the parable and merely retain a doctrinal sentence as the gist of the story that Jesus has told us. On the contrary, the parable may speak today differently from what it told us yesterday, and we shall see this in the two interpretations given in the second section. This means that there is, obviously, a kind of truth expressed in the parables that cannot be communicated equally well in direct language.

Why is this so? When we look at the parables of Jesus, as we find them in the first three Gospels, they seem to speak of very ordinary and simple happenings that everyone could understand. They speak of a farmer who sows, a woman who bakes, a growing plant. Nothing absolutely extraordinary, nothing really miraculous seems to happen in them. Yet appearances are deceiving. There is always a most surprising point in them; something takes place that is certainly not impossible, but is at least amazing. What lord would praise such a dishonest manager as the one in Luke 16:1–8? What farmer would, like the one in Mark 4:27, just "sleep and rise" after having sown his seed, without harrowing and weeding and putting up scarecrows? What mustard grain would grow to become "a tree" (Luke 13:19)? What woman would bake bread for at least one hundred persons, as did the one in Luke 13:21? What landlord would let the tenants kill his servants and again and again simply send others to be killed, even finally his son, as we read in Mark 12:1–12? What king would, like the one in Matt. 22:9–10, invite to the wedding feast of his son just everybody at random, "the bad and the good"?

These and many other surprising features of the stories show that Jesus' parables do not simply tell of something that is always and everywhere true, but they tell of an amazing event that surprises everybody and is of a unique quality, without surpassing the limits of real life, without becoming a fairy tale full of miracles that do not happen in reality. This means that we should not expect to find in the parables of Jesus a general truth, a kind of religious or moral law true in all centuries and in all parts of the world. We should expect to find in them the report of an astonishing act that happened, not in a wonderland where all the natural laws do not exist, but in our world, and that is therefore as well understandable as the act of the farmer and his wife, though it will surprise us beyond all expectations. Or to put it positively: we should expect that the parables speak of God who is, in the very parables of Jesus, coming in a surprisingly new and unique way to turn his love toward the hearers of Jesus. Thus, the mystery of the parables is the mystery of Jesus himself.

What, then, is the characteristic of parabolic speech? I have occasionally used the example of an American novel translated into German, in which "honey" (in the sense of "darling") has been translated literally—which makes exactly as much sense in German as if we said in English: "Oh, jam, how sweet you are, let's go dancing." This silly example just shows that as soon as we come to imagery, be it as simple as "honey," we can no longer deal mechanically with language. A computer cannot decide whether that word means the product of the bees or my sweetheart. Only a human heart that gets involved can understand what this (parabolic) word means. Even if we could build a computer that would be able to distintuish the two meanings by means of the context, it would still not be able to feel what "honey" really means. The girl in the shop may ask: "What can I do for you, honey?" and it means nothing beyond some ordinary politeness. The adolescent boy may say, for the first time, to his girl: "Honey!" and the world of first love lies in that one word, whose message only a heart that is able to respond to it understands.

Hence, it is not our free choice whether we speak in direct or in parabolic language. There is a kind of truth that we can express only in imagery. It is clearly so with love. Direct language could point to some facts: the heart beats faster, and I could even count the throbs per minute; the temperature of the body rises, and I could even indicate it exactly in centigrades. All this would not tell the other person what my love for him or her really is. To do this, I can only take refuge in some parabolic language, in a language that reminds the other person of experiences that he or she has had. This starts a process in which the person gets personally involved. When I speak of my ardent love, it may awaken the memory of once having touched a hot plate on the stove and may lead my partner to remember the almost unendurable "heat" of his or her first, unanswered love. Therefore I cannot define by any accepted standard of definition my love to another person, but I can start a process of thinking and feeling and responding within my partner. Somebody who has never experienced love, actively or passively, will never understand what I mean. If, however, I succeed in awakening some reminiscences of earlier experiences, I can certainly lead the other person beyond what he or she has already experienced. My words may raise some memory of what the person felt years ago; at the same time, they also show the differences. It is, for instance, no longer a fifteen-year-old boy, it is now a fully grown man who knows about the responsibilities that he has to take over or about the law that love should never kill the personality of the partner, etc.

When Jesus taught in parables, he knew that he could not simply offer a new dogmatic definition of God that his hearers could reject or accept and, in this case, carry home, so as to possess forever the correct understanding of God. He knew that he had to lead them into a new kind of life in which they would encounter God time and again, and ever again in a surprisingly unexpected way. He knew that it was important to start the process of this encounter by getting his hearers involved, not only intellectually but also in their wills, their feelings, their subconscious lives. He told them parables, because "a parable gives absolutely no information until the hearer has entered into it and experienced it from inside itself" (John Dominic Crossan, *In Parables*, p. 13). He knew that, strictly speaking, he could not teach God, since God cannot be taught, but that he could open hearts, awaken some movement, remind his hearers of certain experiences that might help them to detect some analogies on a higher level—be it their own experiences or those of others, perhaps biblical persons—so that God would prove himself, since he can be experienced.

In the Johannine speeches this becomes even clearer. Strictly speaking, they are not parables. Jesus does not declare that he is like a vine, but that he is *the* true vine (John 15:1); not like a light, but *the* true light (1:9); not like bread, but *the* true bread of life (6:32, 35); not like a shepherd, but *the* good shepherd. According to the Greek text, Jesus does not answer the question "Who are you?" but rather "What is real bread, real life, real light?" Therefore, the "I" is stressed in the original text: "It is I, Jesus, that you are looking for when you want to find true life, light for your way, bread for all your hunger, and water for all your thirst." This says that what we know as bread and water, as light and life is but a weak "parable" of the *true* life which is to be found only in Jesus himself. Thus, the saying "I am the true vine" is not a definition of Jesus by some item known to us. It says that what we experience when eating the fruit of the vine, or being hungry and getting bread, or thirsty and finding water is a weak analogy of what Jesus means for us. It is an experience that may, at least, point in the direction where the much greater experience of meeting Jesus waits for us (E. Schweizer, *EGO EIMI*).

Even modern science understands, more and more, that all language that goes beyond some symbols fixed at random for a technical understanding (like the mathematical language of $a^2 + b^2 = c^2$) participates in the process that I have outlined above. It is a modern scientist who states: "We are forced to speak in images and parables which do not exactly hit off what we really mean. We cannot avoid occasional contradictions either, but we can approach the real facts by these images in some way" (W. Heisenberg, in Hans Weder, *Die Gleichnisse Jesu als Metaphern,* p. 5, my translation), and he speaks of extremely scientific definitions. If this is true for science, how much more will it be true for theology. Thus, it is of an enormous importance for our way of preaching. More than any other literary genre, the parables teach us that we are never the ones who possess the truth, so that the only, or at least the main, problem would be how to transfer this truth to our hearers. We neither possess the truth, for the truth is the living God whom we shall never possess, nor are we able to hand it over to our hearers, since it comes to them only when and where God himself decides to encounter them in our words, or rather in the living process that is started by the words. Thus, we cannot preach except in the attitude of the one who waits, from the first word of our sermon up to the last one, for God's own word. Preaching means expecting God who butts in—into our human words and sentences and paragraphs (which are all only images of the truth). If the congregation gets the impression that its pastor is an expert in religious problems and delivers almost perfect sermons, then the sermon is, probably, a rhetorically good and theologically bad one. The first message that a parable conveys to its hearers is the insight into the fact that we shall never have God in our own hands, that we shall always depend on his own initiative. Therefore, something of the awkwardness of every preacher, who cannot but wait for a stronger One who will come to his rescue, should express itself in every sermon, especially in a sermon on a parable.

How shall we reach this goal? How shall we translate a parable into our situation? To translate means to transfer something verbatim from one area to another one, from one shore to the other one. As with good, old wine, any such transfer damages it and it needs a process of some weeks or months for the original taste to be totally restored. Yet we have to try. To use another image, water can be distilled, but if it is totally pure water, it no longer quenches our thirst. It must, necessarily, contain some minerals of the soil out of which it comes—some mud, if you please. Likewise, preachers cannot distill a pure doctrinal statement out of a parable. But they can and must substitute the "minerals" and even the "mud" of the twentieth century in the United States (or wherever they are preaching) for that of the Palestinian soil of the first century. How shall we preachers do that?

Should we create a new parable in contemporary imagery? Why not, if we are one of the really great poets? Otherwise it is probably wiser to trust in the effectiveness of the original parable of Jesus, even if it may need some explication for people living in our century and, perhaps, in a city in which the imagery of farmers and shepherds seems to be rather farfetched. However, all this is not the pivotal point.

The main problem is the fact that we are not Jesus. He could speak with authority, because his whole existence, his life, and, later on, his death and resurrection interpreted his parables and gave them meaning and sense. We cannot speak with such authority, but we can witness to it. Thus, differently from Jesus himself and even from the Evangelists who embedded the parable in the whole witness of their Gospels, we have to say explicitly in what way the life, death, and resurrection of Jesus is the innermost truth of the parable (cf. section II). There is even more in it. The parable was originally told in a specific situation to which it offered a challenge and/or an answer. This situation was, most probably, different from the one in which our congregations listen to our sermons. On the whole, it will not be necessary to force our audience to bring itself back to the historic situation of the first preaching of the particular parable of Jesus. Though containing basically the same message as originally, the parable may contain another message for us today. Therefore we should help our hearers to see their situation and its problems. They are not, at least for the most part, so ready to speak up as those hearers probably were when Jesus spoke this parable for the first time. We even have to go one step farther. When the Galilean farmers returned to their homes after having listened, they probably discussed among themselves what they had heard and, by doing so, helped one another to detect the implications of what Jesus had said. When preaching, we should not only tell the parable and witness to what Jesus' total ministry means for the understanding, we should also accompany our hearers on their way home. We may make a number of comments, replying to indignant questions as well as helping their attempts to draw concrete consequences out of the words of Jesus. This does not mean that we should give the answers for our hearers and thus relieve them of personal responsibility. It should be quite clear that God alone can tell them what it means for everyone in the church, and that, at best, we can open their hearts to his answer by suggesting some possibilities and thus pointing to some areas in which God may wait for their response.

II. HOMILETICAL STUDIES

1. An analysis of *Mark 4:1–34* (see E. Schweizer, "Mark 4:1–20," in *Review and Expositor,* Spring 1975) shows some problems. In vs. 1–2 Jesus spseaks to the multitude, in vs. 10–13 to his disciples, in v. 33 again to the people, without any note of a changed situation. In v. 36, Jesus seems still to be sitting in the boat of v. 1, though in between he was alone with his disciples (v. 10). According to this verse, "those who were about him with the twelve" ask him about the parables, though he has not told more than one. And who are they? A group "around him" and besides "the twelve"? Verse 11 declares that "those outside" this group should not understand, vs. 33–34, that Jesus spoke "as they were able to hear," namely, in parables. Moreover, vs. 14–20 are written in a different language which we find, outside these verses, only in the letters, not in the Gospels. This shows that we have to distinguish: *(a)* the original parable of Jesus, vs. 3–9; *(b)* its interpretation in the language of the later church, vs. 14–20; *(c)* a theory of the parables as means to hide the truth from outsiders, vs. 10–12; *(d)* Mark's redaction, introducing the situation in vs. 1–2, adding the twelve to v. 10 and the whole of v. 13, which eliminates the separation between out- and insiders: even the disciples cannot understand, short of the miracle of the grace of God. We might preach a first sermon on vs. 1–9, a second one on vs. 12–20, finally, if we dare to do so, a third one on vs. 10–13, perhaps together with vs. 33–34.

Verses 3–9 seem to be a very simple story that every Galilean farmer could follow step by step. This is exactly what happens to him, and it is only the last sentence ("He who has ears to hear let him hear") that starts him thinking. Obviously, Jesus wants to tell him something more than that, and as this preacher speaks so much of the kingdom of God, it says supposedly something about this kingdom. As soon as we understand this we see that the story does not actually go as straightforwardly as it seems to do. No Galilean farmer would get a hundredfold harvest. It is not totally impossible that, on the most fertile soil and with the best weather, one grain may produce a hundred grains, but it would be most extraordinary. Thus, what will happen to the kingdom of God will be extraordinary, not to be expected. Even besides this point the story is strange. Three quarters of it tells of the failure of the sower. Would any normal farmer do that, except when he was furious about his bad soil, and then without adding the last sentence?

What is the difference between the first three quarters of the parable and the last one? Obviously the difference of time between sowing and harvesting. In the first period, one sees only the crows that devour, the thorns that choke, the sun that burns the seed on the rocks. No miracle happens, no cramp paralyzes the open mouth of the bird, no fire consumes the thorns, no earthquake opens the hard rock. This is what we see in the world in which the seed of the kingdom of God is sown. It is eaten up and choked and burned, and no miracle happens. It is the failures that we mostly see. Yet, even now, the real life is in the seed, though the tiny grains hidden in the earth are scarcely visible. Yet, they are, even now, the truly living parts of the picture, though this will be evident only in the future harvest.

Is it of any importance who it was that told this parable? If it had been a Marxist, he might totally agree with the pessimistic view of the present world, in which the living seed is still hidden, and with the expectation of a new world, in which all will have changed. But this change takes place when the good grains will have fought against and overcome their enemies. He would tell about the revolution that takes place when the grains would suffocate the birds, choke the thorns, and pierce the rocks. Jesus tells it differently. A typically religious man, whether a Pharisee of the times of Jesus or an average believer of any contemporary religion, would also agree with the pessimistic view of this world and the expectation of a better one. But he would tell of a stupendous miracle and would emphasize the reward of the true believer and martyr as well as the punishment of the enemies of God. He would tell of medals of honor for the faithfully growing grains and of the killing of the crows, the burning of the thorns, the blowing up of the rocks. Again, Jesus tells it differently. Therefore, he, Jesus, is the interpreter of the parable. He goes his way, sowing the seed, but his words and deeds are rejected everywhere. The kingdom of God is present, but is suffering violence, as Matt. 11:12 puts it. The seed seem to be annihilated totally. Jesus may, on his cross, still say two or three sentences about that kingdom, but only for a few more hours, then it will be ended, and ended forever. What one sees are the triumphant enemies who have destroyed the seed. And just so, God vindicated Jesus and his way of life, in which rejection and failure seemed to dominate totally: he resurrected him. Since then, we know that the real life may be hidden under suffering and breakdown, that God may justify what all our friends and even we ourselves call failure. Since then, we know that God will be the final victor, not his enemies nor his faithful band of disciples. Therefore, we cannot believe in our reward or in the punishment of others, but in his grace alone.

When the church retold the parable of Jesus some thirty years later, the misunderstanding was almost unavoidable. Was Jesus not right? The crows, the scribes fighting against him; the thorns, the Jerusalemites who wanted to choke his seed; the hard rocks, the heathen atheists—all failed, and the seed brought fruit, a hundredfold: twelve disciples then, more than 1,200 church members in one city now. Therefore, the church had to reinterpret the parable, because the enemies were now not those outside, but those inside the church. Therefore Jesus had to continue speaking to them through his parable, for it is the parable of the living seed. Even if one had once detected the growing seed, he could not bring it home and put it under glass and think that he now possessed it forever. Just so, it dies. Thus the church had to ask: where are the crows, the thorns, the rocks today, and did so in its interpretation of Matt. 11:14–20. Thus it is also through the interpretation of the church that the original parable will help us to detect the dangers for the seed today. Especially in these verses we may help people today to do so by giving some examples of where dangers may lurk with us. We should do so in a stimulating way that starts their own reflections, not in a final way that stops them.

The difficult vs. 10–13 emphasize the mystery character of the kingdom of God. They try to circumscribe what revelation means. The choice of parabolic language by Jesus shows that there is no direct language that could catch hold of God, could "circumscribe" him, literally: go around him with human words and sentences and nail him down to a definite place within this circle, as a mathematical or scientific definition would try to do. Thus, the parables prove indeed that we are not able to understand though having ears to hear the words. As an outsider, one may hear the parable word for word, may be able to repeat it exactly as it was told, but still without understanding it. Who is this outsider? Certainly the officials who want to kill Jesus (Mark 3:6); certainly his fellow citizens who cannot overcome the stumbling block of God meeting them in an ordinary man without a proving miracle (6:1–6); certainly also the disciples themselves who, having eyes to see, do not see and, having ears to hear, do not hear (8:14–21, always at the end of a paragraph of Mark's Gospel). They even misunderstand him while calling him the Messiah (8:29). This is what Mark also expresses in 4:13: Nobody, not even the disciples who have left their homes and offices to follow Jesus, can understand God and his kingdom. What then? Mark tells us that when Jesus had died with a loud cry, the Roman officer exclaimed: "This was truly the son of God" (15:39). It is only through the death and the resurrection of Jesus himself that we learn to understand in a new way, overcome by the same Spirit of God who fulfilled the life and death and resurrection of Jesus and is still working in people who hear his message. It is not like our understanding of a mathematical formula, which we possess forever once we have understood it. It is an understanding in which we let ourselves be taken on this way of Jesus, so that we learn to understand him and his heavenly Father in the course of following him. This is the mystery of the kingdom which lives and works in all the positive or negative experiences of a life of discipleship. In 10:32, Mark tells of the disciples following Jesus on his way to Jerusalem. In 10:46–52, he tells of a blind man whose eyes were opened by the miracle of Jesus, so that be became able to follow Jesus "on the way." This is the last sentence before the story of the passion of Jesus starts. Nothing short of the miracle of the grace of God can open our blind eyes so that we become able to follow Jesus and to understand in the course of that experience the mystery of the kingdom of God.

2. The unit in which the parable of the prodigal son, *Luke 15:11– 32,* is reported is ch. 15. According to vs. 1–3, the three parables have been told to Pharisees and scribes. A new unit begins with 16:1, introducing the disciples as the addressees. Thus, in the view of Luke, these parables are spoken against those who reproach Jesus for his openness to "all the publicans and sinners." Is this the original point in Jesus' preaching or rather the view of the Evangelist?

The first of these parables, the one on the lost sheep, is also reported in Matt. 18:12–14. That whole chapter speaks of the responsibility of the members of the church for their fellow members. It is stressed in v. 10 just before and again in vs. 15–20 after that passage. Thus, Matthew understands the parable as a summons to his hearers to care for one another, to go after the ones who are in danger of getting lost, and to bring them back to the church. This was, in the time of Matthew, certainly a good way of listening to this story; no doubt we also may learn something from it. However, it is scarcely what Jesus wanted to say when he created it. The image of the shepherd itself suggests the many Old Testament passages about the Lord God or his messiah as the shepherd of the flock of Israel (Gen. 48:15; 49:24; Ps. 23:1; 80:1; Isa. 40:11; Jer. 31:10; Ezek. 34:12, 23; 37:24; Sirach 18:13). Also the motif of the joy of the shepherd in Matt. 18:13 seems to point to God's joy over the sinner, lost and found again. This seems to be the root of the parable. Thus, the understanding of Matthew is, probably, not the oldest interpretation of the parable.

What about Luke's view? To be sure, there is something of a polemical tone in the parable. The shepherd leaves the ninety-nine (Luke 15:4, as Matt. 18:12) and his joy over the one sheep found again is greater than that over the other ones (Luke 15:7 and Matt. 18:13), and Luke 15:11–32 ends with the open question whether or not the righteous elder son will enter the banquet hall of the father, in which the sinner is already sitting and enjoying himself. Thus, this is a point in the parable, and it is not wrong to stress it in a situation in which it is necessary to listen to this warning. But is it the original situation in the life of Jesus? We cannot be sure about that, for, just a little later, in 16:14–15, Luke introduces again the Pharisees who "justify themselves" as the addressees of words of Jesus (16:14 and 16–17), which, according to Matt. 6:24 and 11:12–13, have been spoken in a much more general way to all the people. Moreover, in the second parable, that of the lost coin, neither the joy of the woman nor that of the angels of God is compared with the lesser joy over the coins that have not been lost or over the righteous people. Thus, any connotation of polemics against the "not-losts" is lacking here. Even more important is another reflection. What is the really surprising point in these parables? Certainly not the fact that the object found again is, for the moment, the center of interest and the basis for the joy of the finder. This goes without saying. Really amazing is the way in which this joy is described. Once in a Sunday school class that I was leading, a boy argued that this must have been a very silly woman to invite all her friends and to spend more for coffee and cakes than the coin was worth. He was quite right. Would a normal woman really express her joy in such an exaggerated way? The same is true for the shepherd of Luke 15:6 and even more for the father of vs. 22–23. Does this not indicate that the emphasis was, first of all, more on the joy of God over the lost and found, and on the invitation to accept this surprising fact by trusting in him and thus causing him to rejoice, than on the rejection of those who opposed such teaching? This is true for other parables of Jesus also. They are open to all hearers. To some they may carry more of a warning; to some, more of a comforting message; but for all of them they are "good news," invitation to the surprising and almost incredible love of God and to unexpected joy.

When we now turn to vs. 11–32, the structure of this parable reveals an important clue to its meaning. It starts with the father, it ends with the father. Only the father appears in both its parts. The younger son is, at least, mentioned also in the second part, but the elder is not in the first. Thus the father seems to be the only important person, certainly not the elder son. When we ask where the unexpected, surprising points are, we see that it is again not with the two sons. They act as we should expect them to act. Surprising are only the acts of the father, from the beginning to the end of the parable.

The younger son acts so much according to the usual pattern that he could serve as a typical example in a handbook of psychology of adolescence. He wants the share that he will inherit after his father's death. This was, in the time of Jesus, unheard of. Even if the inheritance was divided up prematurely, the whole estate still belonged to the father. If a child sold something of it, the buyer could, according to Jewish law, enter upon it only after the death of the father. Thus, the younger son acts as if the father were already dead. It is the well-known Oedipus complex that drives him to "kill" the father, to get rid of him. Therefore he also goes to "a far country," away from the dominating father and his shadow. There he lives in a silly way, not in a bad way, squandering his money. It is not his fault that a famine comes up. Thus the emphasis is not at all on morally wrong conduct, but on the separation from the father. Not moral weakness, but the son's strong will to live without the father is the main point in the story. This drives him to look for a substitute for his father: "he joins himself to one of the citizens of that country." But this is a hard "father," who lets him starve. In this difficulty it is the memory of his father and of all the food in his house that brings the son to his senses. There seems to be only one solution: to subject himself totally to the mighty father, to abandon all striving for independence and freedom—in short, to go back to his former status and to remain infantile. Something like that happens to all of us as we grow up. It also happens in our religious lives. We grow out of the faith of our childhood to a more mature faith; problems and doubts arise in such periods. Will the solution be a total subjection that destroys all independent thinking and represses all questions?

Much the same is true with the elder son. He remains with the father and does not break away from him, so it seems. But it is the father, not as he is, but as the son thinks he should be. Thus, the real father is also dead for him, perhaps more than for the younger son who still keeps some recollection of his father's home. Unlike this one, he can no longer call him "father" (vs. 12, 18, 21, 29), nor can he call his brother "brother" (v. 30). Although only two or three feet from the father, he has separated himself actually more than the younger son. Again, there seems to be but one alternative: either he leaves his home forever, or he subjects himself to that tyrant of a father, who does not even give him a goat to make merry. And again, this is part of the life of each of us, even of our religious experiences. We may, in our understanding, be very close to our heavenly Father and yet be far from him, because we are living with a God of our imagination, a God as *we* think he should be. Will the solution be a total subjection to the image that, for instance, our denomination teaches us, whether we can make it really our own or not?

These thoughts may open us for the message of the parable. They have a double function. On the one hand, they help us to see ourselves "inside of the parable." It would be a mistake to paint the two brothers as extreme types of a sinful or a self-righteous life. It is only the elder son who speaks about whores (v. 30), perhaps because this is what he himself dreams of. The story itself does not say so. And the elder son is really a good, industrious, hardworking young man. Is it not unavoidable that questions rise in us, as unavoidable as the growing up of a youth and his breaking away from his parents? It would be wrong, if we simply stayed unshattered on an infantile level of faith. How bitterly a Jeremiah argued with his God, because he wanted to get free from him (15:17–18), or a Job, because he could not understand his rule (9:21–23, etc.)! On the other hand, these thoughts warn us: we may get farther and farther from our father in our unending questioning or in our cozy religion in which we take for granted that God is exactly as we imagine him. In both functions they invite us to meet the real father as he comes to us in the parable of Jesus. Therefore, we simply reread it, focusing on the father.

If there ever was a permissive, anti-authoritarian father, it is this one. Is he not almighty? Could he not say: "You just wait until I am dead, as I had to wait," or "Well, if you need a bit more pocket money, let's say a fiver more from next Sabbath," or a hundred other things? But this father is actually powerless from the very beginning, because he has decided in favor of love, once for all. He knows that he will lose his son if he does not comply with his son's plans. Again, when this one is starving in the far country, is the father not almighty? Could he not travel to that city and fetch his son or send a friend to do so or phone Interpol to get him home by police escort? Indeed, he could do all this and could be even more enterprising. But again, he is powerless because he has decided in favor of love, and knows that he would lose the love of his son forever if he now forced him to return. Then, this one comes home of his own free will and starts his confession and thinks of a total subjection in which he just becomes a "slave," a mere object, part of the father's property. But now, the father butts in and cuts off his speech, so that just this part of that well-prepared address is never spoken. This father does not want to have infantile sons, he wants them to become free and independent persons, bound to him only by mutual love. Therefore there is no sermon, neither one on repentance nor one on grace. In an almost sacramental way, he accepts his son merely by embracing him and by speaking to others, ordering roast beef, wine, and music.

Is this the image of our heavenly Father? That Father at the head of the table with his son at his right hand and all the servants around, distributing food and drink out of a fullness almost incredible to the starving son, surrounded by music and dance and joy? To be sure, this is a good image of our Father in heaven; but there are no snapshots of him to glue in our albums so that we possess his image forever. Five minutes later, the picture has totally changed. Who is in the banquet hall? That ne'er-do-well younger son. And where is the father? Out in the dark with his rebellious son, where he could catch pneumonia. But is he not still the almighty one? Could he not simply whistle, so that four of his servants would come and drag that rebellious son into the banquet hall? Again, he is actually powerless, because he has decided in favor of love and knows that he would lose his elder son forever if he acted in this way. Therefore he stays—at the end of the parable of Jesus—out in the dark and has nothing but a heart burning with love and some poor words in which to express it. And again, there is no sermon—neither a reproaching one nor a gracious one; there is only the statement that his son, who can no longer say "father," is actually with him and that all that belongs to the father also belongs to him. There is nothing but the invitation to unlimited joy. Both sons act as we would expect them to act, because we are indeed living very much like them. But the father butts in; he acts in a totally unexpected, amazing way; therefore the ways of these sons which seemed so usual and so close to all our experiences did not end in a mere subjection in which the sons would have ceased to be persons in their own right, but in the invitation to total joy.

Has this anything to do with Jesus? He does not appear as a separate figure in the parable. But he is the one who tells it. And he did not merely tell it, he lived it. Perhaps only days or weeks later, he is exactly where the father of his parable is at its end, out in the darkness where the sons rebel against him. Jesus is hanging on a cross. Is he the almighty one? Could he not appeal to his Father, and God would at once send him more than twelve legions of angels (Matt. 26:53)? But the crucified is totally powerless, because he has decided in favor of love, once for all. He is so powerless that he cannot even move his hands one inch. He is so powerless that he has not a square foot of earth on which to stand. He has nothing but a heart burning with love and some poor words to express it: "Forgive them, for they do not know what they do"—"Today you will be with me in Paradise"—"It is fulfilled." They sneer at him and scoff at him: "Descend, and we shall believe"—and do not understand that exactly such a miracle would make love impossible, because love can never be forced upon us. We certainly can tell our son: "Johnny, when your aunt comes today, I do not want to have that spectacle repeated; you just kiss her, or you will learn it the hard way," and if we are authoritarian enough, Johnny will comply. But this is not love; on the contrary, he will probably be blocked against loving his aunt all his life, because he was once forced to kiss her against his will. Therefore, Jesus does not pray for the twelve legions of angels to free him, but is hanging on his cross, seemingly powerless. When they cry: "Where now is your God?" God is closer to them than ever before, though they do not see him. He may often be very close to us when we ask the same question and cannot understand his ways.

Thus, the parable of Jesus is, from its first to its last verse, a flaming appeal and a stirring invitation to joy—to real, eternal joy—because it is an interpretation of that God who acted in the totality of the life and death and resurrection of Jesus. Or, the reverse is true: the life and death and resurrection of Jesus interpret his words. Therefore, preaching is actually a very simple act. We have nothing to do except to go along these sentences of Jesus, trying to see ourselves and our congregation inside this story. It is not necessary at all that our sermon be a rhetorically brilliant performance; perhaps, on the contrary, if this is not so, it becomes even clearer that when we are preaching we are at the same time praying that Another will make our word powerful. Since the words of our text are no "mere words," but have been lived in the ministry of their speaker, up to his cross, why should we not trustfully expect them to become powerful, to ourselves and to those who will listen to our sermon?

FOR FURTHER READING

The Basic Work on Parables
Jülicher, Adolf. *Die Gleichnisreden Jesu.* Darmstadt: Wissenschaftliche Buchgesellschaft, 1963. Earlier editions were published in Freiburg in 1886 and 1889. This is a reprint of the 1910 edition.

On John
Schweizer, Eduard. *EGO EIMI*. Göttingen: Vandenhoeck & Ruprecht, 1939; 2d ed., 1958.

The New Approach
Crossan, John Dominic. *In Parables*. Harper & Row, 1973.
Fuchs, Ernst. *Hermeneutik*. 2d ed. Bad Canstatt: R. Mullerschon Verlag, 1958.
Funk, Robert W. *Language, Hermeneutic, and Word of God*. Harper & Row, 1966.
Perrin, Norman. *Jesus and the Language of the Kingdom*. Fortress Press, 1976.
Via, Dan O., Jr. *The Parables*. Fortress Press, 1967.
Weder, Hans. *Die Gleichnisse Jesu als Metaphern*. Göttingen: Vandenhoeck & Ruprecht, 1978.
Wilder, Amos N. *Early Christian Rhetoric: The Language of the Gospel*. Harvard University Press, 1971.

One Practical Example
Schweizer, Eduard. "From the New Testament Text to the Sermon: Mark 4:1–20," *Review and Expositor*, Vol. 72 (Spring 1975), pp. 181–185. See also Eduard Schweizer, *The Good News According to Mark*, tr. by Donald H. Madvig (John Knox Press, 1970).

15. PREACHING FROM THE PASSION AND RESURRECTION NARRATIVES

DWIGHT E. STEVENSON

Why would anyone want to kill Jesus of Nazareth, "who went about doing good?" Even Pilate, who finally ordered his execution, wondered, "Why, what evil has he done?" (Matt. 27:23).

To answer, we need to look at the political and religious situation in which Jesus lived. In common with most of the Mediterranean and Near Eastern world, the Jews lived under the Roman peace, the Pax Romana. In Galilee this meant that Herod Antipas held his throne by direct appointment of the Roman emperor and that Roman soldiers policed his kingdom. In Judea (which included Samaria) Roman rule was direct, for Judea was a province of the Empire, with a procurator, or governor, appointed by Caesar. The Tenth Legion occupied the land. (Throughout the Empire, there were twenty-five such occupying armies.)

The Romans' constant fear was insurrection. And nowhere was insurrection more likely than in Palestine. Seldom free throughout their long history, the Jews nevertheless burned with a fierce longing to be free. Always rebellion seethed just beneath the surface. To guard against its outbreak, Rome granted as much authority to the Jewish council (Sanhedrin) and local courts as possible, honored local customs and laws, tried valiantly to be just, and mounted an unwavering vigilance. As deterrent to rebellion, Rome threatened the gruesome penalty of execution by crucifixion. This was reserved for non-Roman slaves and foreigners convicted of brigandage or insurrection.

Nevertheless, rebellion did boil beneath the surface. On occasion it broke out briefly, displaying its volcanic intent. There were Sicarri (assassins; literally, "dagger men"), whose slogan was, "The sword and not sparingly; no king but Yahweh!" Beyond these was a larger company of "Zealots" who wanted open, armed rebellion, such as that reported by Gamaliel in Acts 5:36–37. A generation later this growing unrest erupted in the Jewish war against Rome, A.D. 66–70.

The accusation against Jesus before Pilate, accordingly, if proved, would assuredly carry the death penalty. So reasoned Jesus' accusers. And so they charged: "We found this man perverting our nation, and forbidding us to give tribute to Caesar, and saying that he himself is Christ a king" (Luke 23:2–3). It was, of course, a trumped-up charge, cleverly devised to take advantage of the Roman fear of rebellion and of Pilate's known weaknesses. The real reasons were not so clear-cut or so singularly simple. Here are the real reasons as summarized by F. C. Grant in a luminous paragraph:

> The forces arrayed against him were powerful: the scribes, jealous of his influence with the people and resentful of his independent exposition of the Scriptures, and of their methods and their traditions; the Pharisees, stung by his riddling exposure of their weaknesses and failures; Herod Antipas, suspicious of Jesus' possible connection with the Zealots or with John the Baptist; the Sadducees, equally suspicious, and roused to fury by his interference with the routine of temple worship; the Romans, concerned only with peace and security; and Pilate, concerned chiefly over his own waning popularity with the Jews. . . . Hence it was not surprising that Jesus faced the possibility, even the probability of death at their hands.[1]

Death under such circumstance, it could be confidently predicted, would be by crucifixion. After nearly two thousand years of Christian history, even though we know that there were three crosses on Calvary, the single cross of Jesus alone "towers o'er the wrecks of time." It does so by sheer moral grandeur. But within the historical moment of its occurrence, the crucifixion of Jesus was one small statistic lost in a blizzard of execution statistics. Crosses with men dying in agony upon them in public places and along well-traveled highways were familiar sights throughout the Empire.

Rebel disorders broke out in Palestine after the death of Herod the Great in 4 B.C. Then Varus, governor of Syria, marched down with his legions to restore peace and punish the rebels. This he did by crucifying two thousand men. So Jerusalem had seen crucifixions aplenty before. And it was to see them in multitudes yet again. During the Jewish war against Rome in A.D. 66–70 the Roman general, Titus, crucified as many as five hundred Jews daily outside the walls in plain view of the city. This consumed so many crosses that the Mount of Olives was denuded of timber to supply them.

Take one more example, this one from Italy itself in 71 B.C. From 68 B.C. until 71 B.C. the slave-gladiator Spartacus led 100,000 runaway slaves in open rebellion against the Roman legions. When they finally lost their struggle, no less than six thousand of them were crucified on crosses strung along the Via Appia for 132 miles from Rome to Capua. As shown in an authentic painting by Louis S. Glanzman, legionnaires planted crude T-shaped crosses every few feet on both sides of the neatly paved highway, each bearing a dying victim, bleeding from a merciless beating, and left through long days and nights to rot. One can imagine what it meant to travelers passing between Rome and Capua to see that 132-mile sight of punitive horror.[2]

No symbol of defeat could be more convincing. The crucified were victims, not victors. And the forests of crosses throughout the Empire were a display of Rome's merciless power. Who could assail or withstand it? For the Jews throughout Palestine the cruel deaths brought an added dimension, a dimension of shame, for by their law a man hanged on a tree was more than defeated and discredited; he was accursed by God (Deut. 21:23). The defeat of a man crucified was regarded as an ultimate defeat. And the notion of a crucified Messiah was an ultimate blasphemy.

Such is the background from which we must view the Gospel narratives of the passion.

THE PASSION NARRATIVES

Each of the four Gospels has a passion narrative, similar, even parallel, in some respects, but differing in detail and in atmosphere in others. For these reasons, it is better to read each one as a continuous whole and then to look at the episodes comparatively.

The relevant chapters are Matthew 26–27; Mark 14–15; Luke 22–23; and John 18–19. Among the three Synoptic Gospels, the parallels are most quickly and easily seen in a Harmony of the Gospels or in Gospel Parallels. Corresponding passages from John can then be read "in place," using the following table:

1. The Conspiracy of the Chief Priests (Matt. 26:1–5; Mark 14:1–2; Luke 22:1–2; assumed in John but not related as a separate episode).
2. The Anointing of Jesus (Matt. 26:6–13; Mark 14:3–9; given by Luke, but not in the setting of the passion, Luke 7:36–40; omitted by John).

3. The Plot of Judas and the Rulers (Matt. 26:14–16; Mark 14:10–11; Luke 22:3–6; assumed by John, but not related by him).

4. The Last Supper (Matt. 26:17–29; Mark 14:12–31; Luke 22:7–38; not directly related in John, the scene there is after the supper, the incident of the footwashing and the long discourse of chs. 13–17).

5. The Agony in Gethsemane (Matt. 26:36–46; Mark 14:32–42; Luke 22:39–46; omitted by John).

6. Betrayal and Arrest (Matt. 26:47–56; Mark 14:43–52; Luke 22:47–53; John 18:1–12).

7. The Trial Before the Jewish Authorities (Matt. 26:57–67; Mark 14:53–72; Luke 22:54–71; John 18:13–27). Tucked into this account is Peter's denial (Matt. 26:30–35, 58, 69–75; Mark 14:26–31, 54b–55, 66–72; Luke 22:54b–62; only Luke tells this episode as a continuous whole, John omits it).

8. The Trial Before Pilate (Matt. 27:1–31; Mark 15:1–20; Luke 23:1–25; John 18:28–19:16a). Tucked into this account is Judas' remorseful attempt to return the blood money followed by his suicide (Matt. 27:3–11, only in Matthew). Luke interrupts the trial before Pilate to send Jesus to Herod Antipas for questioning (Luke 23:6–12; only in Luke).

9. The Crucifixion (Matt. 27:32–50; Mark 15:21–41; Luke 23:26–49; John 19:16a–30).

10. Removal from the Cross and Burial (Matt. 27:57–61; Mark 15:42–47; Luke 23:50–56; John 19:31–42).

11. The Watch at the Sepulcher (Matt. 27:3–4; only in Matthew).

LOOMING IN THE BACKGROUND

Jesus came to a people who were expecting a Messiah. They had been expecting him for hundreds of years, and their expectation was never more intense than at the historical moment of Jesus' ministry. Not only did they expect the Messiah, they had his agenda already worked out for him. Conquer the Romans and drive them out of Palestine. Avenge Israel against all her enemies, subduing them with a sword. Establish God's reign over all nations. Destroy the weapons of war and usher in universal peace. Renew nature and bring universal prosperity.

Whatever Isaiah 53 may have meant, their Messiah was not to be a Suffering Servant; and certainly he was not to be crucified. The thought did not even cross their minds.

As we read the New Testament nineteen hundred years later, how do our expectations differ from those of Jesus' contemporaries? Suppose God were to come among us as a fellow human being in this our twentieth century. What would we hope for? What would be our agenda for him? He could start by turning stones into bread to feed the world's hungry. He could unseat dictators, turn the weapons of war into the implements of peace. He could solve the pollution problem—renew nature. He could eliminate cancer. Yes, we would have work for one with all the wisdom and power of God! Any work as a teacher? Well, in view of the "information explosion," why would we need that?

And what of the possibility that we might reject, imprison, and execute him? Would that be on our agenda for him? At that point, like Peter of old, we would protest vigorously, "God forbid, Lord! This shall never happen to you" (Matt. 16:22). We would have no more place for the work of the cross on our agenda for him than the disciples did, or the Jews of the first century.

We have not truly looked at the crucifixion of Christ until we see it as *the great reversal,* the transvaluation of all values. God's agenda, when he comes to earth, is not ours. If we would understand the passion narratives, it is there that we must begin.

THE MESSIANIC SECRET

It was with good reason, then, that Jesus (as recorded in the Synoptics) kept the secret of his Messiahship throughout his ministry. Not until the end was imminent did he disclose it to his disciples (Matt. 16:13–20; Mark 8:27–30; Luke 9:18–21). When he at the same time disclosed the imminence of his crucifixion, they were totally uncomprehending (Matt. 16:21–24; Mark 8:32b–33). Small reason, then, that he immediately pledged them to silence regarding his Messiahship!

His triumphal entry into Jerusalem at the beginning of the last week was a symbolic announcement of his Messiahship to the people at large. Few understood it. It was not until the trial before the high priest and Pilate that it finally came out (Matt. 26:64; Mark 14:62; John 19:7).

The high priest immediately labeled it "blasphemy," for which the Jewish penalty was death by stoning. (Only the presence of the Roman occupation prevented the carrying out of that penalty.) When the Jewish authorities carried their case to Pilate, they could not hope to dispose of Jesus with the charge of blasphemy; so they switched their charge to sedition (Luke 23:2, 5). It was not until the confession of Thomas in John 20:28 that a disciple saw and declared the full Messiahship of the Crucified: "My Lord and my God!" Even for the disciples, the light was slow in dawning.

The Gospel of John does not proceed on the basis of the Messianic secret, but it achieves the same effect through the constant and repeated misunderstanding of the disciples. The theme of the Prologue holds throughout: "He came to his own home, and his own people received him not" (John 1:11). In the insightful words of the Negro spiritual, "we didn't know who he was."

THE CROSS AS THE KEY TO DIVINE POWER

Jesus went to his crucifixion not as victim but as victor. He conquered through suffering. Carried to the extremes of powerlessness, he nevertheless demonstrated "the wisdom of God and the power of God." Fate he turned into destiny. All four Evangelists could have written just as John did: "I lay down my life. . . . No one takes it from me, but I lay it down of my own accord. I have power to lay it down, and I have power to take it again; this charge I have received from my Father" (John 10:17–18). Elevation on the cross was an enthronement. By supreme irony, the witness to Jesus' kingship came from foreigners and enemies (Mark 15:2, 9, 12, 18, 26) who, speaking in derision, declared the truth. The inscription over the cross, written in the principal languages of the civilized world, announced a universal kingdom (John 19:19–22).

In the Fourth Gospel, Jesus' hour of ignominy and shame was the hour of his glorification (John 12:23, 27–30, 32; 17:1–5).

THE RESURRECTION NARRATIVES

THE DISCOVERY OF THE EMPTY TOMB

All four Gospels contain an account of the discovery of the empty tomb (Mark 16:1–8; Matt. 28:1–10; Luke 24:1–12; John 20:1–10). In the oldest manuscripts of Mark, which end with Mark 16:8, there are no resurrection appearances, only the empty tomb with an angel sitting within, whom the "two Marys" see, and who directs them to tell the disciples that their Master will appear to them in Galilee. Most scholars have assumed that the original ending of Mark—containing resurrection appearances—was lost. The longer ending (Mark 16:9–20) is generally thought to have been added later. Some scholars now believe that Mark was meant to end with Mark 16:8, with the women fleeing in fear from the empty tomb.

The account of the empty tomb in Matthew is slightly different. Again there are the "two Marys," but they witness an earthquake, the rolling back of the entrance stone by an angel who sits upon it as he speaks to them, directing them to send the disciples to Galilee, where their risen Master will meet them.

Luke's account is slightly different still. Three women come to the tomb—Mary Magdalene, Mary the mother of James, and Joanna. They find the stone rolled away from the door of the tomb, enter to find the body gone but two angels standing within, directing them to send the disciples to Galilee.

In John only Mary Magdalene is at the empty tomb, but John and Peter also enter. There is no mention of an angel. However, special attention is given to the graveclothes, which are not discarded in a heap but neatly folded and laid down within the sepulcher. John, seeing the implication of resurrection, believes.

THE RESURRECTION APPEARANCES

Mark 16:1–8 records none, and in the longer ending (16:9–20) only three: to Mary Magdalene, to two in the country (reminding us of the meeting with the two disciples on the road to Emmaus), and to the Eleven in Jerusalem.

Matthew had two appearances: the first to the "two Marys" returning from the tomb, the second to the Eleven on a mountain in Galilee.

Luke presents two appearances: the first to two disciples (not belonging to the Twelve) on the way to Emmaus, the second to the Eleven in Jerusalem. Luke also reports that there had been an independent appearance to Simon (Luke 24:34).

John (with ch. 21, which is an appendix) has four appearances: to Mary Magdalene (20:11–18); to the ten disciples, with Thomas absent (20:19–23); to the Eleven, Thomas present (20:26–29); and to seven of the disciples who have returned to their fishing at the Sea of Galilee (21:1–23). All appearances, except the one to Mary, reported in ch. 20 are in Jerusalem.

Unlike the passion narratives which unfold sequentially by episodes, the resurrection narratives have no discernible sequence in time or in place, and no clear time frame. It is clear that we are dealing here with something more than a reanimated corpse, unlike the case of the raising of Lazarus, who would die yet a second and final time. Death "no longer has dominion" over the risen Christ

(Rom. 6:9). As both Luke and John show, Christ's resurrection body had tangibility; it was no mere ghost. But neither was it a mortal body.

The apostle Paul understood the resurrection of Christ in terms of Christ's appearance to him on the road to Damascus, which he placed in the same category with Christ's earlier appearances. "He appeared to Cephas, then to the twelve. Then he appeared to more than five hundred brethern at one time, most of whom are still alive, though some have fallen asleep. Then he appeared to James, then to all the apostles. Last of all, as to one untimely born, he appeared also to me" (I Cor. 15:5–8). Paul's explanation? "There are celestial bodies and there are terrestrial bodies; but the glory of the celestial is one, and the glory of the terresterial is another" (I Cor. 15:40).

As written records go, of course, Paul's is much earlier than any of the four Gospels. And, interestingly enough, it lists appearances not given there: to James (the brother of Jesus), and to five hundred brethren in one assembly.

We are helped also by Paul's understanding of the firm connection between Christ's death and resurrection and our new life in Christ: "For if we have been united with him in a death like his, we shall certainly be united with him in a resurrection like his" (Rom. 6:5). The strongest witness to the resurrection, therefore, is existential, not merely historically factual in the antiquarian sense, and certainly not circumstantial and speculative. The early Christians experienced and lived it, as have their successors and heirs down the centuries.

Not only do Christians experience the resurrection through their own new life, they also experience it through Christ's Great Commission. All four Gospels give it, in slightly different words: Matt. 28:19; Mark 16:15 (in the longer ending); Luke 24:47; and John 20:21. So resurrection is not only something that happened to Jesus; it is also something that changes us and something for us to do as Christ's command falls upon us in the succession of the apostles.

SOME HERMENEUTICAL GUIDELINES

1. The public reading of the passion and resurrection narratives.
Liturgical usage through the Christian centuries has divided Scripture into convenient, bite-size pericopes. Each can form the basis of a sermon. If, however, nothing longer than a single pericope is read in public worship, the passion story will be chopped into fragments and the powerful sense of the whole will be lost. At least once a year every

congregation should hear the whole story, read as a continuous whole from one of the four Gospels: all of chs. 14–16 in Mark; or all of Matthew 26–28; or Luke 22–24; or John 18–21.

The reading of Scripture, when well done, can be an exciting experience. The best possible public reader should be chosen to do it, and that person should rehearse carefully. Or the reading may be done by a cast of lay readers representing the various personalities of the passion, plus a narrator. The sermon may then be drawn from a single pericope, from several, or from the whole.

Time can easily be obtained for such an extended reading by eliminating some of the usual features of the liturgy. At least once a year it ought to be done.

2. The basic literary forms of the passion and resurrection narratives.

This is salvation history, but it also contains liturgical formulas, and commands, such as the Great Commission and those from the Last Supper, which are to be *done,* not merely understood. Salvation history is a witness to faith; its appeal is to faith and faith surrender in the present. The reader-hearer is not allowed the luxury of becoming a detached observer of events from antiquity. That person is actually in the passage.

Consider what happens in a good story: We are drawn on by the suspense of the plot: "What will happen next?" We are involved in the conflict (of person with person, or person with self, of person with circumstances). We identify with the characters, sometimes positively, sometimes negatively. And through the vividness, concreteness, and immediacy of the action, "we are there." The clue is *conflict* and *characters.* We take our place in the story by "actualizing" both the conflict and the personalities involved in the struggle.

3. Interpreting the resurrection.

All Gospel miracles point toward and find their fulfillment in the miracle of the resurrection. Miracles are recognized only by the eyes of faith. From this it follows that the interpreting of the miracle of the resurrection does not lie in answering the question: "How do you explain it?" The hope back of that question is the hope of remaining outside the miracle, objective and judging, uninvolved. The uninvolved are also the uncomprehending. There is a better question: "What does it mean?" Better still: "What does it mean for me?"

4. Interpreting the hearer.

To the extent that the passion and resurrection narratives become channels for the Word of God, they probe the reader or hearer. This is a reversal of the relationship of reader to a book in ordinary terms of knowledge. Ordinarily the reader probes the passage, tries to understand it, judges it, dissects it, analyzes it, and accepts or rejects it. In the reading of Scripture all this is reversed. The passage probes the reader, judges him or her, and calls him or her to repentance and decision. With ordinary books, the reader interprets the text; with the Bible, the text interprets the reader.

PREPARING TO PREACH THE PASSION
AND THE RESURRECTION

1. *Choose a text.* Even if you plan to preach on the passion as a whole, your sermon will be better if you have a particular passage as a text. For instance, Jesus' struggle with the temptation to escape crucifixion, as in Gethsemane, or to "come down from the cross," as in the voices of derision from the crowd and the impenitent thief.

2. *Set the text in context.* (*a*) Set the text against the struggles and expectations of the time, as we have sought to do earlier in this chapter. (*b*) Set it in the light of the whole Gospel from which the text is drawn. For example, Matthew presents his Gospel in five books, making Jesus the new Moses; and John presents his Gospel in two books, the Book of Signs (chs. 1–12) and the Book of Glory (chs. 13–21).

3. *Do your exegesis.* This means consulting good commentaries and studying the passage verse by verse. (See the bibliography at the end of this chapter.)

4. *Ascertain the point at which the text intersects the life of your hearers, and your own life.* That is the ignition point. Scripture always involves audience, and reaudiencing. For example, for the passion narrative there were the original actors in the drama of happening events—before there was a written record. Then there were the first readers of the published Gospel, after the fall of Jerusalem and the destruction of the Temple, and the dispersion of Christians throughout the Mediterranean world. Finally, the story is addressed to us: "Where does this text find us?"

5. *Participate in the movement of the text.* Engage in the struggle, participate in the conflict, identify with the personalities. Consider the text as a transport vehicle which picks you up at the point of intersection (just discussed) and carries you beyond it to an outcome that is active in the passage itself.

A FEW SERMON STARTERS

"The God and Father of Our Lord Jesus Christ"
"Pilate said to them, 'Shall I crucify your king?' The chief priests answered, 'We have no king but Caesar' " (John 19:15).
"The God and Father of our Lord Jesus Christ" (Rom. 15:6).

If Jesus is God's Son, this says something about the nature of God, which the chief priest was not ready to hear. Perhaps we are no more ready to hear it than he. The orthodox image of God is that of an all-powerful being who is also perfectly good, a divine emperor of the universe. Such a God would not only prevent suffering and injustice in his world; he would certainly also save himself from suffering.

Beginning at such a point, it is easy to go on to lose faith in God, even to declare him dead, as Richard L. Rubenstein did after learning of the Jewish holocaust. In *After Auschwitz* he wrote, "If there is a God of history, He is the ultimate author of Auschwitz."[3] If the Judge of all the earth does not do right by preventing Auschwitz and other evils, might it not be for other reasons? The God who allows himself to be shoved out of the world onto a cross is not a heavenly autocrat who coerces and overpowers his subjects.

It is the thought of God in the image of Caesar that caused the cry of derision from the crowd: "If you are the Son of God, come down from the cross" (Matt. 27:40). And the raillery of the impenitent thief on his cross: "Are you not the Christ? Save yourself and us" (Luke 23:39).

Alfred North Whitehead, writing to this theme, said: "When the Western world accepted Christianity, Caesar conquered; and the received text of Western theology was edited by his lawyers. . . . The brief Galilean vision of humility flickered throughout the ages, uncertainly. . . . But the deeper idolatry, of the fashioning of God in the image of the Egyptian, Persian, and Roman imperial rulers, was retained. The Church gave unto God the attributes which belonged exclusively to Caesar. . . .

"There is, however, in the Galilean origin of Christianity yet another suggestion. . . . It does not emphasize the ruling Caesar. . . . It dwells upon the tender elements in the world, which slowly and in quietness operate by love; and it finds its purpose in the present immediacy of a kingdom not of this world."[4]

If God is the Father of the Crucified, how are we to think of him? Perhaps we are overdue for a great reversal in our vision of God, who, Paul said, is "the God and Father of our Lord Jesus Christ."

CROSS ON WHEELS

"And they compelled a passer-by, Simon of Cyrene, who was coming in from the country, the father of Alexander and Rufus, to carry his cross" (Mark 15:21).

"And he said to all, 'If any man would come after me, let him deny himself and take up his cross daily and follow me' " (Luke 9:23).

"Pulling for Jesus" is the headline of a newspaper story about a twenty-six-year-old state government worker who spent the week of his vacation in mid-June last year fasting and helping to carry a 120-pound wooden cross from Louisville to Frankfort, Kentucky.

He and four other men took turns shouldering and pulling the fifteen-foot cross sixty miles along U.S. Route 60 between the two cities. The men started out from Louisville on Monday and arrived in Frankfort on Saturday. The end of the upright stake was mounted on wheels, to ease the drag.

Said the leader of the five on arrival in Frankfort: "I've never felt closer to God over a long, sustained period of time. I really felt I was doing his work."[5]

The truth of the matter, in biblical terms, is that the five zealous men carried neither Christ's cross nor their own. The whole circuslike stunt was a misguided sentimental feat of self-salvation through works righteousness, actually an inversion of Christ's vicarious sacrifice.

Once Simon of Cyrene was drafted to carry Christ's cross to the Hill of the Skull; but that was a single, unrepeatable event. Simon obviously made Christ's cross his own later, as evidenced by the presumed presence of his two sons, Alexander and Rufus, in the church at Rome, where the Gospel of Mark was written. (See also Rom. 16:13.)

No one can carry Christ's cross. Christians are to have their own crosses, and they are not on wheels. (This sermon will go on to show what it means to take up our own crosses daily. The clues will be found in Jesus' own words about true greatness, and in Paul's words about salvation by grace through faith issuing in good works.) "For the love of God controls us, because we are convinced that one has died for all; therefore all have died. And he died for all, that those who live might live no longer for themselves" (II Cor. 5:14–15).

WHO-WHAT-WHO KILLED JESUS

Jesus apeared on trial before Caiaphas, the high priest; before Herod Antipas, tetrarch of Galilee; and before Pilate, governor of Judea. Each contributed to the crucifixion.

Caiaphas. John 18:12–14 says it all: "So the band of soldiers and their captain and the officers of the Jews seized Jesus and bound him. First they led him to Annas; for he was the father-in-law of Caiaphas, who was high priest that year. It was Caiaphas who had given counsel to the Jews that it was expedient that one man should die for the people."

Holding office by appointment of the Roman governor, Caiaphas wanted to retain that office, to keep peace with the Romans, and to safeguard the orderly, ritualistic life of the Temple. In other words, he killed Jesus to save the status quo, the establishment; and his ethics in the matter were supplied by expediency. We might call that the devil's atonement.

Herod Antipas. Luke has the account: "And when he [Pilate] learned that he [Jesus] belonged to Herod's jurisdiction, he sent him over to Herod, who was himself in Jerusalem at that time. When Herod saw Jesus, he was very glad, for he had long desired to see him, . . . and he was hoping to see some sign done by him" (Luke 23:7–11). Herod Antipas could have had no love for Jesus, who had once called him a fox (Luke 13:32). Herod's contribution to Jesus' death was a negative contribution; he did nothing to save him. Herod killed him with his idle curiosity.

Pilate. "So Pilate, wishing to satisfy the crowd, released for them Barabbas; and having scourged Jesus, he delivered him to them to be crucified" (Mark 15:15). Pilate killed him to court popularity with the populace. That took precedence over any consideration of justice.

Pilate, in fact, was a cruel and arrogant man. On at least three occasions, recorded by Josephus but not in the New Testament, he offended the Jews. One occasion was his entering Jerusalem with Roman troops bearing standards with the image of the Roman emperor on them. A second occasion was his raiding of the Temple treasury for funds with which to build an aqueduct. When this provoked public protest, he silenced it by beating the protesters with bludgeons. On yet a third occasion, he ruthlessly put down an uprising among the Samaritans, executing the leaders. Luke mentions yet a different occasion when Pilate "mingled the blood of Galileans with their sacrifices" (Luke 13:1). Pilate had full need to

wash his hands of the blood of Jesus and to protest his innocence!
(Matt. 27:24).

Still, when all is said, the question is not, "Who killed Jesus?" For
the devil's atonement—the sacrifice of people to the defense of the
status quo—still continues. And idle curiosity still makes bystanders of
us. Expediency and the desire for popularity still prevail. The real
question is: "What kills Jesus?" And that translates in every generation into: "Who?" For the expedient, the conniving and the curious go
on "crucifying the Son of God on their own account and holding him
up to contempt." (Heb. 6:6).

GOD'S NONSENSE

"And he began to teach them that the Son of man must suffer . . .
and be killed. . . . And Peter took him, and began to rebuke him. But
turning and seeing his disciples, he rebuked Peter, and said, 'Get
behind me, Satan! For you are not on the side of God, but of men' "
(Mark 8:31–33).

"And behold, one of those who were with Jesus stretched out his
hand and drew his sword, and struck the slave of the high priest, and
cut off his ear. Then Jesus said to him, 'Put your sword back into its
place; for all who take the sword will perish by the sword. Do you
think I cannot appeal to my Father, and he will at once send more
than twelve legions of angels?' " (Matt. 26:51–53).

"All we preach is Christ crucified—a stumbling-block to the Jews
and sheer nonsense to the gentiles, but for those who are called,
whether Jews or Greeks, Christ the power of God and the wisdom of
God. . . . For God's 'foolishness' is wiser than men, and his 'weakness'
is stronger than men" (I Cor. 1:23–25, Phillips).

Peter would certainly have agreed that the crucifixion of Christ was
"a stumbling block" to his faith. To him it looked like "sheer folly" and
"weakness" supreme. When, therefore, Peter took his sword and
struck at the high priest's slave, he was exercising the kind of power
that made sense to him—and to the world.

Jesus had access to that kind of power! All he had to do was to ask
God and he would have twelve legions of angels to defend him—one
legion for every disciple! Twelve times as many legions as Rome had
in its Palestinian army of occupation! When, therefore, Jesus deliberately chose the cross in preference to coercive power, he did so
because God's "folly" is wiser than men's "wisdom" and God's
"weakness" is stronger than man's "power."

In time, Peter came to see that, but he went to Gethsemane and to
the trial at the house of Caiaphas not seeing it. In fact, he lived right

through the crucifixion—hiding in fear and remorse—still blind to it. When we meet him again in the book of Acts, we find a man who has undergone a great reversal, and who would have welcomed the apostle Paul's statement of his new understandings.

The Christian faith and the way of life to which it leads plainly call for an overturning of what most of us most of the time take to be "wisdom" and "power." In his former life as Saul, the Pharisee, Paul had embraced the world's understanding of these forces. In his new life, beginning with his meeting with the risen Christ on the road to Damascus, he repudiated the old understanding and its way of ruthless coercion. Thereafter he himself took the way of the cross, as did all the disciples except Judas.

This dual narrative from the Gospels and from Paul's letters finds the hearer of your sermon (along with you) at the "Before" stage of this contrast. That is where this Scripture intersects our lives. The sermon should carry us, through some demonstration of the power of the crucifixion, to the "After" stage which both Peter and Paul came to know and live by.

THE SHAPE OF THE RESURRECTION NARRATIVES

Citing C. H. Dodd, Raymond E. Brown classifies the resurrection appearances under three headings:

A. *Concise Narratives,* such as the appearance to the women at the tomb (Matt. 28:8–10) and to the Eleven on the mountain in Galilee (Matt. 28:16–20). Concise narratives have five features in common, which could easily form the basis of sermon outlines:

1. A situation is described in which Jesus' followers are bereft of him
2. The appearance of Jesus
3. His greeting to his followers
4. Their recognition of him
5. His word of command or mission

B. *Circumstantial Narratives* in which we are led to reflect upon the meaning of the resurrection, but without clear command, such as the appearance to the two disciples on the road to Emmaus (Luke 24:13–35) and to the disciples on the shores of the Sea of Galilee (John 21:1–14). Both appearances have eucharistic overtones. The central feature is the recognition of Jesus. The purpose is to disclose a meaning.

C. *Mixed Narratives,* combining the features of A and B above, such as the appearance to the Eleven in the appendix of Mark (Mark 16:14–15), to the Eleven and others in Jerusalem (Luke 24:36–49), and to Thomas (John 20:26–29).

Appearances to the eleven usually contain a missionary command. This, providing more than knowledge of Jesus' victory over death, gives the disciples new life in terms of a firm mission to the world and for their future.[6]

BACK TO THE OLD LIFE

The continuity of ministry, crucifixion, and resurrection can be shown in a story-sermon focusing on the role of Peter. Pick up the story at the point where Peter said to six of his fellow disciples, "I am going fishing" (John 21:3a). Tell the story in your own words, except for liberal quotations from Scripture as available. The plot:

EPISODE ONE. Peter and six of his fellow disciples go back to fishing in the Sea of Galilee. They fish all night, but catch nothing (John 21:1–3). Flashbacks (while fishing):
1. Jesus calls Peter and Andrew to discipleship (Matt. 4:18–20).
2. The disciples, now twelve in number, are at Caesarea Philippi. Peter's confession (Mark 8:29).
3. Jesus' prediction of the crucifixion. Peter's remonstrance. Jesus calls Peter "Satan" (Mark 8:31–33).
4. The troubled disciples follow Jesus toward Jerusalem, amazed and fearful (Mark 10:32).
5. At the Last Supper. Jesus' warning to Peter (Luke 22:31–32). Peter's pledge (Luke 22:33).
6. On the way to Gethsemane. Jesus predicts the desertion of the disciples. Peter pledges to remain though all others desert (Mark 14:26–29). Jesus predicts Peter's denial (Mark 14:30–31).
7. In the courtyard of the high priest. Peter's denial (Mark 14:54, 66–72).

EPISODE TWO. Back at the Sea of Galilee. As the seven men fish, a stranger appears on the beach (John 21:4–5). The great catch of fish, 153 fish—suggestive of the nations of the whole world (John 21:6–8).

EPISODE THREE. On the beach. The "stranger" at a campfire, invites the seven to breakfast (John 21:9–13). A eucharistic meal?

EPISODE FOUR. Still on the beach. The threefold restoration of Peter, matching the threefold denial (John 21:15–17). Jesus predicts Peter's martyrdom (John 21:18–19).

CLOSE. The symbol of the Greek word for "fish," *ichthus*, "Jesus Christ, Son of god, Savior," on a crypt in the catacombs beneath the City of Rome during the Neronian persecution.

The apostle Paul could have written Peter's epitaph: "That I may know him and the power of his resurrection, and may share his sufferings, becoming like him in his death, that if possible I may attain the resurrection from the dead" (Phil. 3:10–11).

NOTES

1. F. C. Grant, "Jesus Christ," *The Interpreter's Dictionary of the Bible,* Vol. 2 (Abingdon Press, 1962), p. 893.

2. *National Geographic,* Vol. 159, No. 6 (June 1981), p. 727.

3. Richard L. Rubenstein, *After Auschwitz* (Bobbs-Merrill Co., 1966), p. 204.

4. Alfred North Whitehead, *Process and Reality* (Macmillan Co., 1929), pp. 519–521.

5. *The Morning Herald,* Lexington, Ky. June 18, 1981.

6. Raymond E. Brown, *The Gospel According to John* (xiii–xxi), The Anchor Bible, Vol. 29A (Doubleday & Co., 1970), pp. 972–973.

FOR FURTHER READING

Brown, Raymond E. *The Gospel According to John* (xiii–xxi). The Anchor Bible, Vol. 29A. Doubleday & Co., 1970. A must for the student of the Fourth Gospel.

Ellis, Edward Earle, ed. *The Gospel of Luke.* The Century Bible, New Edition. Thomas Nelson & Sons, 1966.

Green, H. Benedict, ed. *The Gospel According to Matthew in the Revised Standard Version.* New Clarendon Bible. Oxford University Press, 1975.

Kebler, Werner H., ed. *The Passion in Mark.* Fortress Press, 1976.

Meier, John P. *The Vision of Matthew.* Paulist Press, 1979.

16. PREACHING FROM THE FOURTH GOSPEL

REGINALD H. FULLER

I. HERMENEUTICAL BACKGROUND

Every seminary professor who teaches the New Testament must have heard one of his or her former students preaching a sermon some years after graduation. Often it is a shattering experience. The years devoted to the study and practice of exegesis are as though they had never been. The historical-critical method is completely forgotten. Why, one wonders, have the efforts of the professors been such an utter failure? Nowhere is the disaster so apparent as in the use of the Fourth Gospel. How often have we heard "Before Abraham was, I am" used from the pulpit as a proof text for Jesus' consciousness of his own preexistence? How often have we heard the great "I am" sayings expounded as if they were the *ipsissima verba Jesu*, what Jesus actually said?

This, though regrettable, is hardly surprising. For it is with the Fourth Gospel that the problems raised by biblical criticism are most acute. In this Gospel we are farthest removed from the historical Jesus. Of course the difference from the Synoptics is now known to be no more than one of degree. There are authentic historical traditions in the Fourth Gospel, many more than were recognized at the turn of the century, as Maurice Goguel and C. H. Dodd have shown. Archaeology has demonstrated the Fourth Gospel's accuracy about the topography of Jerusalem. The Dead Sea Scrolls have indicated that much specifically Johannine thought, such as the great dualisms of light and darkness, truth and falsehood, life and death, was thoroughly at home in first-century Palestinian Judaism, and is not necessarily late and Hellenistic. Again, form and redaction criticism have shown that there is a greater distance between the historical

Jesus and the finished products of the Synoptic Gospels than the authors of "Lives of Jesus" from Reimarus to Wrede ever dreamed. But in relative terms the distance between the historical Jesus and the Johannine portrait is far greater than in any other of the Gospels. Many more stages of tradition history lie in between. There are authentic sayings of Jesus and authentic memories of his activity. There is the adaptation of this material for oral circulation. There is the collection and further adaptation and development of it for the earliest (narrative) form of the written Gospel. There is the expansion of this early narrative or signs gospel by the addition of the discourse material, and there is the final redaction. At least three earlier stages thus lie between the historical Jesus and the Gospel's final form. Hence, no one, whether scholar, preacher, or simple believer, can take the Fourth Gospel as a photographic record of the original history.

When preaching from a Synoptic text, the pastor has a relatively straightforward choice to make. Take, for instance, the parables, say, the parable of the sower. Nine times out of ten, preachers will opt for preaching it at the level of the Jesus tradition, ignoring the later interpretations, the allegorical exposition, and the difficult Marcan saying about the purpose of parabolic teaching. Or they may opt for different levels on different occasions, depending on the situation in their congregation that they wish to address. With John they rarely seem to have that option. There is a relatively small amount of certainly recoverable authentic Jesus material uncontaminated with and extricable from later interpretations. If we follow some critics, we will be chary of taking the earlier level of the signs gospel, since it was precisely the theology of that stage that the Evangelist was apparently at pains to correct. Normally we will be thrown back to the final two stages, the Evangelist and the redactor. In the case of John, if anywhere, the advocates of canonical exegesis—i.e., of concentrating on the final level(s) of the tradition—seem to be correct. That is probably what our average preacher with his or her naive historicism has dimly grasped. The trouble is that the preacher identifies the final stage in the history of the tradition with the first, and with Paul Ricoeur's "first naiveté" takes the Fourth Gospel's record of the deeds of Jesus as historical reporting and the discourses as a sound recording.

But does that really matter in the long run, so long as the message gets across? Does it matter if our people really think Jesus was conscious of his own preexistence? And if our preacher knows better, is it necessary to disturb the people's faith? Of course, the preacher's own intellectual integrity is involved. We have learned better in seminary, and it is either intellectual inertia that allows us to suppress it or misplaced pastoral concern that causes us to dodge it. No. We must assume that our preacher wishes to avoid the two sins of sloth and dishonesty and is prepared to go into the pulpit knowing full well that there is a long history of tradition behind the Johannine text. The preacher should be aware of this history, precisely in order to be true to the text's intention. For to take it as straightforward reporting is to be untrue to the intention of the Fourth Gospel itself. That is the real discovery of historical-critical exegesis. For the Johannine writer(s) the history of Jesus was something that disclosed the final, ultimate truth of God. Their development of that history was undertaken in order not to leave the history behind, but to penetrate its deepest truth. The Fourth Gospel is perfectly aware of what it is doing. It knows that subsequent memory and subsequent interpretation have played an essential role in the Gospel's composition. We are told as much in the two cases of the triumphal entry (John 12:16) and of the cleansing of the Temple (John 2:22). In both cases the Gospel tells that the disciples did not at first perceive the meaning of these incidents. Only later, after the resurrection, did they remember them, and then they proceeded to use the Old Testament Scriptures in order to interpret them through the prism of their later experiences. These experiences include preeminently the Easter experience itself, but also the subsequent history of the Johannine community down to the time of the final redaction. Thus historical-critical method is employed, not in order to undermine the historical reliability of the Fourth Gospel but to expose its truth as never before. For it is the truth of remembered and interpreted history, rather than the truth of straightforward historical reporting.

We have used the word "truth" in this connection. But how can we be sure that the remembrance and the interpretation have really led to truth? We can give two answers to this question, the one historical and the other theological. The historical answer is that a reconstruction of the historical Jesus' message and ministry from the Synoptic tradition discloses that that message and ministry were of an eschatological character. That is to say, Jesus claimed to be bringing the final, unrepeatable, and definitive offer of salvation to men and women. His person, though not directly the focus of his proclamation, was implicitly featured as the point in which this offer of salvation was made, in his word and activity (see, e.g., Luke 12:8f.; Matt. 9:6 par.; Matt. 12:28). The signs and discourses of the Fourth Gospel bring out explicitly what is implicit in the proclamation of the historical Jesus, for they give sharply focused expression to the claim that Jesus is the definitive revelation of the truth of God and the offer of eternal life. The language has changed: the language of revelation has replaced that of apocalyptic. The means have changed: revelatory discourses are in lieu of parables and aphorisms. But there is a material identity between the two messages.

The theological answer is that advanced by the Fourth Gospel itself. In the Paraclete sayings we hear that the work of the Spirit, who came after Jesus' glorification, is to lead the disciples into all truth (John 14:26). This passage speaks of the Spirit as being at work in the process of "remembering" the tradition of Jesus' words (i.e., aphorisms and parables like those of the Synoptic tradition). We find in the Fourth Gospel, as Dodd has shown, both Synoptic and Synoptic-like aphorisms, and "submerged parables" of the Synoptic type. This Spirit, too, will *teach* the disciples "all things." Is this a new teaching, additional to or even contradictory to the teaching the earthly Jesus had given? The answer is found in another Paraclete saying (John 16:13–14). The subject matter of the new teaching of the Paraclete is not itself new: it is "what is mine" (Jesus'). And Jesus' "mine" is intimately bound up with the Jesus tradition as testified by the original eyewitnesses, as is indicated in yet another Paraclete saying (John 15:26–27).

Thus the Fourth Gospel itself forbids us to drive a theological wedge between its discourse material and the historical Jesus as critically reconstructed from the Synoptic tradition.

This means, then, that the preacher can and must use the texts of the Fourth Gospel with a "second naiveté," that is, not as direct historical reporting, but as remembered and interpreted tradition.

It was the work of the Paraclete constantly to apply the remembered Jesus tradition to each successive situation in the Johannine community, and often thus reshape it. The Paraclete has used successively for this purpose the oral traditioners, the Johannine Evangelist and the Johannine redactor. The preacher who expounds a text in John stands in the same succession. It is our task to take the Johannine text as given to us in the canon and to reapply it to the situation in our own churches and congregations in this present day and age. But just as John (or, if we prefer, each successive "John") believed that he was not saying something new, but saying "that which was from the beginning, which we have seen and heard," submitting to the original witness, so too the preacher must first submit to the discipline of discovering what the text said, before venturing to proclaim it.

II. HOMILETICAL TEXTS

I am a priest (presbyter) of the Protestant Episcopal Church and am therefore accustomed to the use of a lectionary based on the church year, to the combination of Gospel with Old Testament and New Testament readings, and to sermons preached in the context of the eucharistic liturgy. This triple liturgical setting largely predetermines the preaching texts and provides their contextual setting for the congregation. The texts are not selected by the preacher's own self-chosen system (as in the book-by-book preaching of the Reformed tradition), nor is the text chosen on an ad hoc basis because it appears to be relevant to some contemporary situation. We shall therefore select five Johannine texts from the ecumenical three-year lectionary used (in various adaptations) by the Roman Catholic, Lutheran, and Episcopal churches, and available for optional use by the Presbyterian, Methodist, and United Church of Christ churches. The five texts are listed here, together with the liturgical occasion where they are prescribed by the lectionary:

John 1:1–14	Christmas Day IIIA
John 2:1–11	Epiphany 2C
John 11:(1–17) 18–44	Lent 5A
John (18:1–40) 19:1–37	Good Friday ABC
John 15:1–8	Easter 6A

My choice of these texts includes as many different genres from the Johannine material as possible. The Prologue (John 1:1–14) is a liturgical poem or creedal hymn. The wedding at Cana (John 2:1–11) is a sign with no discourse and with a minimum of additional material attached to it. The raising of Lazarus (John 11:1–44) is a sign expanded by discourse material. The passion narrative (John 18–19) belongs to a genre of its own and is an extended haggadic narrative. The allegory of the vine (John 15:1–8) is a submerged parable with an allegorizing interpretation. Also, I have tried to choose incidents from the various seasons of the church year: from Christmas, post-Epiphany ("ordinary time" in Roman parlance), Lent, Passion Week, and the Easter season. Missing only is Advent, which uses no Johannine readings in any year, and post-Pentecost ordinary time, which has only three Sundays in year C in which Johannine material is used, viz., the bread discourse based on the sign of the multiplication of the loaves, a genre already represented.

JOHN 1:1–14

It is commonly thought today that the Prologue is an earlier hymn of the Johannine community which was attached to the Gospel at some later stage of its composition, either by the Evangelist or by the final redactor. Indeed, it has probably been spliced into the original opening of the Gospel, which ran from vs. 6–8 (through v. 15?) to v. 19. This means that the hymn is not the presupposition for the ensuing story but is a confession of faith arising out of the impact of that story. Although it may seem just the opposite, the Johannine Christology is a Christology "from below," not "from above." Having experienced the whole history of Jesus (his "flesh"), the Evangelist confesses that this is the Logos become flesh. The whole life of Jesus is the definitive self-communication of God.

But this communication is not something entirely new. It is, rather, a *recognition* of a God who had already communicated himself in the past—in Israel's history (his previous coming "to his own," though rejected by them), and in the general religious and moral experience of humanity (the light that enlightens everyone, v. 9). More than that, it is the self-communication of the same God who had already communicated himself in the act of creation (v. 3). In fact, it is the very nature of God to go out of himself in the act of self-communication (v. 1).

This interpretation of the Johannine prologue is supported by the accompanying reading of Heb. 1:11–12, where the author similarly links the Christ event to God's prior self-communication: God, who in many and various ways had previously communicated himself through the prophets, has in the last days communicated himself definitively in his Son. But as Heb. 1:3b reminds us, and as the Old Testament reading, Isa. 52:7–10, underlines for us, this self-communication is not just the purveying of information; it is a saving act.

In its context in the church year this reading comes at one of the later services of Christmas: not at the first celebration at midnight, nor at the Mass at dawn, but at the third Eucharist during the day. In some lectionaries it is used a second time on one of the Sundays after Christmas. Thus it is assumed that the Christmas story of the birth of Jesus from Luke 2:1–20 has already been read. The Johannine prologue is a comment upon that story. It prevents us from reading that story as a fairy tale surrounded by the glittering tinsel of a secular celebration of human goodwill or by the romanticizing of poverty. It brings out the full, utter seriousness of the incarnation. And it reminds us that it is not just the Child's birth, but his whole human career culminating in the cross, that Christmas celebrates. Note how many Christmas carols lead from the manger to the cross. Note, too, that the proper celebration of Christmas is precisely the Christ-Mass, the celebration of the Lord's Supper.

And finally, to show that all this has a sound exegetical basis in our text, we note that the same brutal word "flesh" (*sarx*), which occurs in John 1:14, is found later in the eucharistic discourse (6:51–59): "Unless you eat the flesh of the Son of man and drink his blood, you have no life in you; who eats my flesh and drinks my blood has eternal life." "The bread which I shall give for the life of the world is my flesh." Think of "flesh," and we think not only of the incarnation at Bethlehem, when that flesh lay on the hard wood of the crib, but of that flesh mangled and torn on the hard wood of the cross, and that flesh which we sacramentally feed upon in the Holy Communion.

Our task as preachers will be to relate all this to the needs of the congregation. As we learn more about the other religions, we learn that there is more than one way of approaching God, and all ways are equally valid. If Christianity were merely "a" religion, that would be a tenable position. But religions are human things—human responses to divine reality. Christianity begins not with human response but with what God has done in Jesus Christ. And what he has done in Jesus Christ he has done there and nowhere else. That claim is implicit in the eschatological preaching of Jesus. In that, Jesus testifies to something that is happening uniquely then and there and nowhere else at any other time or place and that can never be rendered obsolete, like any other happening, but only consummated in the Parousia. To assert this is not human exclusiveness or parochialism; it resides in the objective quality of the Christ event itself. Only there is the Word made flesh—though the word has been spoken elsewhere in diverse fragmentary ways in those other religions—in the light that enlightens everyone coming into the world.

JOHN 2:1–11

It is difficult to know what historical basis the story of the wedding at Cana has. It is not found in any other Gospel. The miracle is different from most of the Synoptic miracles. They were done out of care and concern for the sick and afflicted, whereas the occasion of this miracle seems shockingly frivolous. Moreover, there is characteristic Oriental exaggeration in the amount of wine involved—120 gallons, enough to lay out the whole village for a week!

That Jesus attended weddings, that he perhaps attended this particular wedding in the village of Cana, which was near Nazareth, we may well accept. It could have happened before he began his public ministry. That he used the imagery of weddings to convey his eschatological message we know already from the Synoptists. These two factors, plus the accretion of some popular tale, would adequately account for the development of this story in the oral tradition. It would then have been taken up into the signs or narrative gospel as one of the seven signs which are told "in order that you may believe that Jesus is the Son of God." This is not quite the later apologetic use of the miracles as "proofs" of Jesus' divinity. Nor does it use the reverse argument that since Jesus was divine he could of course do such a thing. Rather, like the other signs, the Cana wonder was interpreted as a display of Messianic power.

Already the Evangelist (the author of the discourse Gospel) seems to have been dissatisfied with this interpretation. But he has not, as was his normal practice, used this miracle story as the launching pad for an extended discourse or dialogue—which is perhaps an indication of the unfinished character of his work. All the same, he has left a few redactional hints that show the meaning he attached to the story. These are:

Woman

My hour has not yet come

The *Jewish* rites of purification

It has often been noted that Jesus' mother is never named in the Fourth Gospel. She is only "mother," or "Woman," both here and at the foot of the cross. Mary serves a symbolic function in the Fourth Gospel. She is the symbol both of the old community and of the New Israel. She is the new Eve, the mother of the people of God. Here, symbolizing the old Israel, she petitions for the messianic salvation. But that can only come through the "hour" of Jesus, i.e., the hour of his passion. But he agrees to perform a sign of what he will do at his passion. By changing into wine the water that was provided for the Jewish rites of purification he symbolizes the replacement of those rites by the purification to be made by his "blood" (John 1:7, 9).

This reading is appointed for the post-Epiphany season, the reason being that it was one of the traditional events associated with January 6—the others being the visit of the Magi and the baptism of our Lord. These other stories have been read on the two previous liturgical occasions in Year C. So the Cana story is read as the third "epiphany," or manifestation, of the "glory" of the Messiah.

The two other readings that go with the Cana wedding story are Isaiah 62 and I Cor. 12:1–11. The Corinthians reading is following a separate course of continuous readings from that epistle, and it has no connection with the Cana story, as is usually the case in the seasons of ordinary time. The Old Testament reading, however, is deliberately chosen to match the Gospel reading, as is usual in this season. In this reading Israel's restoration after the exile is compared to a wedding. The restoration from Babylon serves as a type of messianic salvation, and both are likened to a marriage.

These readings can be connected with the Holy Communion because the celebration of the Sacrament is also in a very real sense the celebration of a marriage—the eschatological marriage between God, Christ, and his church.

As preachers we have several options here. We can latch on to the epiphany theme and speak of the manifestation of God's glory in the incarnate Son. But this glory is not fully manifested until the cross, when with his blood Jesus replaces the Jewish rites of purification.

We could take a Mariological line, treating Mary as the symbol of the old Israel petitioning for the Messianic redemption and as the mother of the New Israel, brought into being through the "hour" of the Messiah's death.

We could also take up the theme of marriage, as a reality of creation and as a parable of the "mystical marriage betwixt Christ and his church."

JOHN 11:(1–17) 18–44

I remember my teacher Sir Edwyn Hoskyns coming home to Cambridge from Wales one night in the winter of 1936–37. He had just been lecturing on the Fourth Gospel to a clergy conference at Aberystwyth, and had been asked by an old Welsh clergyman whether Lazarus really was raised from the dead. Hoskyns told me that he replied, "That's the kind of question you mustn't ask and cannot answer." The trouble is, we feel compelled to ask it, even if we cannot answer it.

We should avoid answering it on *a priori* grounds—e.g., that for scientific reasons miracles like this cannot happen, or that if Jesus was God, he could certainly raise the dead. It is a purely historical question, and must be answered in purely historical terms. Once again, it has only single attestation. It cannot have played the decisive role in leading to the crucifixion that John attributes to it, for in the Synoptists this role is much more plausibly assigned to the cleansing of the Temple. There are also indications that the shift of that episode to the early part of the ministry is itself part of Johannine redaction. In assigning to the story that decisive role in Jesus' history, John is writing as a theologian rather than as a historian. Jesus was crucified because he offered the gift of eternal life—and in a profound sense that is true.

In an earlier work I tried to extract from this story an original narrative kernel by removing the Johannine discourse addition. Now we actually have an earlier form of this narrative in the Secret Gospel of Mark discovered and published by Morton Smith. It is further interesting that this episode occurs there not during the Jerusalem ministry but before Jesus' entry into Jerusalem—which is where R. Fortna had placed it in his reconstruction of the signs gospel. But all the historian can say is that there was an earlier, simpler story of Jesus' raising from the dead a young man just before the beginning of the Jerusalem ministry. There is a saying of Jesus which if taken literally would indicate that raising of the dead was part of his activity. Beyond that the historian cannot go. This conclusion will satisfy neither the credulous nor the skeptical, but that is all we can honestly say.

Hoskyns was right in insisting that the exegete must concentrate upon the meaning that the Evangelist has given to the sign. That meaning is expressed partly by the place in which it is located (just before the passion), as the decisive event that set it in motion, and partly by the discourse material that has been added. This material finds its climax in the great Johannine pronouncement: "I am the resurrection and the life; he who believes in me, though he die, yet shall he live, and whoever lives and believes in me shall never die" (John 11:25–26). This saying corrects Martha's purely Jewish future eschatology: "I know that he [her brother] will rise again . . . at the last day" (John 11:24). Jesus *is* the resurrection and the life. That really makes the miracle itself unnecessary and ultimately trivial. Nevertheless, the traditional story is reproduced as a symbol of the great truth here enunciated. In response to the revelatory saying Martha confesses her faith in Jesus as the Christ, the Son of God. It is faith, not miracle, that enables us to encounter Jesus as the resurrection and the life and to find them in him already here and now. Of course John does not mean to deny that this life already granted here and now awaits final consummation and completion at the last day. Jesus' pronouncement qualifies Martha's standpoint but does not contradict it.

This reading is appointed for Lent 5, that is during the traditional season of preparation for the Easter baptisms. In an increasing number of parishes the ancient practice of administering baptism to adults on Easter Eve is being revived. In any case, whether there are to be baptisms or not, in the liturgical churches all believers will be invited to renew their baptismal vows at the Easter vigil.

The raising of Lazarus is a symbol of what happens in baptism, where believers die to sin, are raised to newness of life, and anticipate their final destiny at the last day. The baptismal connection of the Lazarus story is also accentuated by the final verse of the reading: "Unbind him, and let him go." The word for "unbind" is the same word as is used elsewhere for the forgiveness (RSV) or remission (KJV) of sins in connection with baptism. "Remission" is a better word, for it suggests that salvation is release not just from guilt but from the power of sin and death, as Lazarus was released from his graveclothes, and set free.

The accompanying readings are Ezekiel 37 (the vision of the dry bones) and selections from Romans 6 or 8. Both of these readings reinforce the baptismal associations of the Lazarus story.

Whether or not the congregation which the preacher serves will be holding adult baptisms at Easter, an Easter vigil with the renewal of baptismal vows, or no such liturgical observance, all Christians are baptized. F. D. Maurice used to say that the one point of contact he had as a preacher with his congregation of old women in a London hospital was the fact that they and he were baptized. The preacher is speaking to persons who in a symbolic, sacramental sense have all undergone, or are about to undergo, the experience of Lazarus. They have been dead in sin, in alienation from the life of God. They have had or will have the call, "Unbind him, and let him go." Therefore, the preacher's task on Lent 5 will be to evoke a remembrance of their baptisms in the faithful to prepare them to experience that moment anew at Easter, and to complete the preparation of those who are to be baptized.

JOHN (18:1–40) 19:1–37

It is still a matter of lively debate among scholars whether John's passion narrative is independent of Mark or whether the difference between the two passion narratives may be credited solely to the Johannine editorial work. Suffice it to say that the present writer is unconvinced by recent renewed attempts to reinstate the latter view, and still thinks, as his teacher C. H. Dodd came to think, that the Johannine passion is basically independent of the Synoptics. Some features of the narrative indeed seem to present a better historical tradition than the Synoptic accounts—e.g., the dating of the Last Supper, the minimizing of the investigation before the Sanhedrin, the role of Annas as the power behind the high priestly throne, and the knowledge of the topography of Jerusalem, may originate in the witness of the Jerusalem or the beloved disciple, who was ostensibly the founder of the Johannine school.

Nevertheless, it is the theological portrait of John's passion that is the focus of our interest. There is very little discourse material here as compared with the earlier parts of the Gospel. The Evangelist is, by and large, content to let the events speak for themselves. The theological significance of the passion is to be sought mainly in the preceding discourses, especially in the farewell discourses at the Last Supper. The only exception is the dialogue on true kingship between Pilate and Jesus, which reinterprets that kingship in terms of witness to the truth (18:36–38). By and large, it is by means of certain dramatic features that the Fourth Gospel brings out the theological significance of the passion. Often, as we shall see, these features are connected to the earlier discourses.

In fact, the whole story is dominated by the theme of kingship, not only in the crucial dialogue with Pilate but also in the numerous dramatic touches. When the soldiery (in John it is a detachment of Roman officers, perhaps one thousand strong!) come to arrest Jesus, they are paralyzed into inaction, and Jesus himself has to initiate the passion by urging them, in effect: "Come and do your stuff." This dramatizes what the Johannine Christ had said earlier: "I have power to lay it [my life] down, and I have power to take it again" (10:18). The disciples do not run away in craven fear as in the Synoptics. Jesus lays down the terms for his arrest: the disciples are to be let free. This dramatizes the petition in the high priestly prayer: "While I was with them, I kept them in thy name, which thou hast given me; I have guarded them, and none of them is lost" (17:12).

As we have seen, it is in the trial scene with Pilate that the kingship theme is openly discussed. Jesus says, "My kingdom is not *from* this world." The usual translation, "of this world," is misleading, suggesting that his kingdom is a purely otherworldly affair. It means, rather, that his authority is conferred upon him not by worldly authorities but by his Father. His kingship consists of his revealing the truth of God in this world. For that he was born, and for that he has come into the world. That truth has been revealed in word in the discourses, and is being actualized in the passion. In the mockery scene Jesus is dressed up as a king, and in that guise Pilate presents him to the crowd with typical Johannine ambivalence: *"Ecce homo"*—"Look at that guy," or, "Here is the Man"—the eschatological Judge and King. Like Caiaphas earlier (11:49–52), Pilate bears unconscious witness to Jesus' claims. In the drama of Pilate's altercation with "the Jews" (who represent the unbelieving world of the Evangelist's day, so that there is nothing anti-Semitic about the term), the crowd finally blurts out, "We have no king but Caesar," the ultimate blasphemy that repudiates a millennium and a half of salvation history.

The title of the cross is written, says John, in Latin, Greek, and Hebrew. Jesus had already said that if he was lifted up, he would draw "all" to himself (12:32). He is lifted up as of the whole world, of the secular world (Greek and Latin) as well as of the religious (Hebrew). On the cross Jesus hangs, not as an isolated sufferer as in Mark, but as king: *"Regnavit a ligno Deus"*—"God is reigning from the tree" (Venantius Fortunatus, c. 530–609; tr. J. M. Neale, 1818–1866; alt.). It is the triumph crucifix that expresses John's theology of the passion: Christ on the cross, clothed and crowned. He thirsts, not because of his weakness, but to fulfill the Scripture. He makes his will by committing his mother to the care of the beloved disciple. This is a saying full of significance for ecclesiology and Mariology. In Mary, the old Israel becomes the new, and she is the new Eve, the mother of believers. Jesus ends with the triumphant cry: "It is accomplished." Drama and irony as the assertion of majestic sovereignty—these are the notes of the Johannine passion.

The accompanying readings support the Gospel. Isaiah 53, the Suffering Servant song, read in conjunction with John's passion will highlight the triumph of the Servant: he is "high and lifted up." He is not so much "despised and rejected," the note that would be highlighted if it accompanied Mark. He is not so much "a man of sorrows and acquainted with grief" as he would be if we were reading Luke's passion. Various passages from Hebrews which provide the New Testament lesson stress the doctrine that Jesus' death is a full and complete sacrifice, thus giving concrete meaning to the triumphant cry, "It is accomplished."

The Good Friday liturgy, with its full-length reading of the passion, is probably little used today, even in liturgical churches aside from the Roman Catholic. More usual is a series of addresses on the "seven last words." Popular though these are, they pose a problem, for as usually treated they lead to harmonization and historicism. These words are not tape recordings from the foot of the cross, as though each Evangelist had gotten hold of a different tape and then all the tapes had been spliced together in a historical order. Rather, these words had best be regarded as traditional or redactional articulations of the original "loud cry" of Mark 15:37. Accordingly, the words from the cross should be expounded for their theology, and we have tried to indicate what the Johannine theology is. See our exegetical remarks above on the three Johannine words, "I thirst," "Woman, behold thy son. Son, behold thy mother," and "It is accomplished." The preacher's task will be to re-create the drama of these Johannine sayings, and involve his or her hearers in the triumph of the cross amid its grim horror as an inspiration for Christian living in these perilous times, threatened as we are, for example, by the cataclysm of a nuclear holocaust.

JOHN 15:1–8

Mark already included one or two sayings spoken by Jesus at the Last Supper in addition to the institution narrative. Luke expanded this tradition by adding further sayings, creating thereby a mini-discourse of table talk. The Fourth Gospel takes this very much farther, giving us no longer a string of originally separate sayings, but typical Johannine meditations revolving around traditional sayings of Jesus. It is probable that two originally distinct meditations have been combined, for 14:26 looks like the conclusion of the first meditation. Perhaps these are two homilies, developed in different years for the Passover haggada of the Johannine community. They are also somewhat similar in function to the Synoptic apocalypse (Mark 13 and pars.), for like the apocalypse, they give an open-ended character to the Gospel. Like the little apocalypse, the farewell discourses speak of what will happen after the Messiah's departure: the restoration of fellowship between Christ and his disciples, the gift of the Spirit, the inauguration of the church's mission through the apostolic witness, the persecution of the missionaries, and the final return of Christ. But all this is transposed into a typically Johannine key, with typically Johannine vocabulary such as life, truth, indwelling, etc., while the coming of the Paraclete is almost a substitute for the Parousia.

Today's pericope is, as we noted earlier, an allegory, consisting of a parable with an allegorical interpretation achieved through one of the great "I am" sayings of the Fourth Gospel. We may surmise that the original parable of the vine would have read something like this: "The kingdom of God may be compared to a vine, which the vinedresser prunes so that it may bring forth more fruit." This original eschatological parable has been transformed into a Christological-ecclesiological allegory. Perhaps the process was assisted by the saying about "the fruit of the vine" already found in the earlier Supper tradition (Mark 14:25 and par.; Luke 22:18). As a result, the image of the vine becomes for John's ecclesiology what the body is for Paul's. The ecclesial dimension of the imagery is already suggested by the Old Testament in which Israel is described as a vine of Yahweh's planting (e.g., Ps. 80:8–18).

Typically, John is speaking at two levels or of two situations. One level is the Last Supper, where the branch that does not bear fruit and is taken away is probably to be equated with Judas. At the second level, the author is perhaps thinking of the situation of the church in his own day, of those Christians who, when the Johannine Christians were expelled from the synagogue at the time of Jamnia, elected to stay in the synagogue rather than throw in their lot with the persecuted minority. The Johannine redactor in turn will be thinking of the "1662 situation" of his own day (cf. I John), when gnosticizing members of the Johannine community left because "they were not of us." As for those who remain, they must be purged in order that they may bring forth "new fruit"—i.e., make new converts. The recent disasters call for a self-evaluation on the part of the community and for a new understanding of its mission.

This is a reading for the Easter season, when we are reminded of the effects of Christ's death and resurrection in the ongoing life of the post-paschal community. In the Easter season the Old Testament lesson is replaced by a reading from Acts. This Sunday we read the beginning of the Gentile mission (Acts 10 or 11). The epistle reading is from I John 4:7–21, which enjoins the love within the Johannine community. This is the response that the author thinks is necessary after the exit of Gnostic members of the community.

Once again, the language of the vine provides a link with the eucharistic cup. There we are nourished once more as branches of the vine, and we abide in him and he in us. F. D. Maurice called the Holy Communion "the sacrament of constant indwelling."

The fact that the vine allegory has been applied to successive situations in the Johannine community entitles us to apply it once more to our own congregations. Most mainline churches today have suffered loss of membership. The reasons are largely sociological and cultural. These lost members are persons whose Christianity was primarily a matter of social convention rather than authentic commitment. They have borne no fruit, and the vinedresser has taken them away. Meanwhile those who have elected to stay must be purged. Part of the purgation will mean that the community that is left must learn really to love one another, to stick together in order to carry out the church's mission relevantly to our own day and age.

FOR FURTHER READING

Brown, Raymond E. *The Gospel According to John.* The Anchor Bible, Vols. 29 and 29A. Doubleday & Co., 1966, 1970. An exhaustive and extremely informative commentary and a mine of exegetical and bibliographical information.

Kysar, Robert. *John the Maverick Gospel.* Biblical Foundations Series. John Knox Press, 1976. An easily read introduction to the background, purpose, and contents of the Fourth Gospel, designed for beginning students.

Martin, J. Louis. *History and Theology in the Fourth Gospel.* 2d ed. Abingdon Press, 1979.

Smith, D. Moody. *John.* Proclamation Commentaries. Fortress Press, 1976.

17. PREACHING FROM LUKE-ACTS

FRANK STAGG

In this chapter the Gospel of Luke and the book of Acts will be studied holistically (Luke-Acts), for they are so related that to be studied competently they must be studied together. The homiletical focus will be upon Acts, because an earlier chapter has thus treated Luke as a member of the Synoptic Gospels. The Gospel of Luke has a "dual alliance," belonging both to the Synoptic Gospels and to Luke-Acts. Both Matthew and Luke seem to have built upon Mark, each weaving a new fabric from Mark and other sources; so Luke must be understood in that relationship. On the other hand, the Gospel of Luke and the book of Acts are not just two volumes by the same author; they are two volumes on the same theme, the things Jesus began to do and teach up to the ascension (Luke) and the things he continued to do as a living and dynamic Presence in the early church (Acts).

LUKE-ACTS LINKAGE

The preface to the Gospel of Luke (1:1-4) and the preface to Acts (1:1-5) seem explicitly to link the two volumes. Both are addressed to "Theophilus." Acts 1:1 looks back to "the first book *(logos)*" concerned with all that Jesus "began to do and teach" up to his ascension. Nothing known to us so fits this as does the Gospel of Luke. Volume two (Acts) shows what the risen Lord Jesus continued to do through his people, moving them from their earliest piety within Judaism to a world movement, transcending barriers of language, geography, ethnic identity, and cultic/ritual distinctions.

The major linkage in Luke-Acts is Jesus. It obscures the matter to call volume one "The Gospel of Christ" and volume two "The Gospel of the Holy Spirit." Not only does this imply a tritheism, dividing God into parts, it obscures the fact that Jesus dominates both volumes. Both Gospel and Acts focus on the crossing of barriers separating people from people. The Gospel of Luke shows Jesus reaching out to groups within his own nation who had been rejected: taxgatherers and "sinners," the blind, the lame, the lepers, the deaf, the poor, the imprisoned, women, as well as Samaritans and Gentiles. Jesus found discrimination within his own nation, and his ministry of liberation began there (see 4:16–30; 7:18–23; 15:1–2; *et passim*). Acts shows the extension of this liberating movement, with special attention to barriers separating Jew from non-Jew: Samaritans, who were half-Jews; God-fearing Gentiles like an Ethiopian eunuch and Cornelius, already under Jewish influence; and finally, pagans like the Philippian jailer, with no previous conditioning in Judaism.

Many purposes are served in Luke-Acts, and any one-factor analysis is too simplistic. On the other hand, Luke-Acts does present Jesus as Savior of the world, not a national deliverer. The breaking down of barriers is a continuing theme. The final word in the Greek text of Luke-Acts is *akōlytōs,* "unhindered." This is also a catchword, appearing at crucial points in the narrative. It epitomizes a major message in Luke-Acts: that Jesus and his gospel must be "unhindered" by such barriers as language, geography, cultic rites, physical impairments seen by the pious as rendering one unholy, and ethnic identity.

Contrary to popular understanding, Acts does not tell us how the gospel got from Jerusalem to Rome. It tells us how Paul reached Rome, in chains and awaiting trial for preaching in a way offensive to an exclusivist piety found both in Judaism and in much of early Christianity (see 11:1–2; 21:17–22, 27–36). We are not told how the gospel reached Damascus, Antioch of Syria, Cyprus, Cyrene, Ephesus, Italy, and many other places. There were Jewish synagogues all over the Roman Empire, and apparently the Christian movement spread rapidly and widely through these channels. For some decades, Christian Jews were able to live within the structures of Judaism, including synagogues and Temple. Acts shows that thousands of Jews followed Jesus, yet remained "faithful to the law" (21:20). What finally separated synagogue and church, Judaism and Christianity, was not Christology as such but ecclesiology. Who is to be received and on what basis?

It was not until new perspectives were introduced by persons like Stephen that the Pharisees entered the picture in Acts as opponents, opposing Stephen's nonprovincial views, for Stephen saw God as never limited to any temple or any one land or people (ch. 7). The persecution led by the Pharisee Saul of Tarsus was directed not toward the Twelve but toward Stephen and his views (8:1). The most divisive issue was not recognition of Jesus as the Christ, for Jews believing that and those not believing it worshiped together in the synagogues for some time (see 13:42–43). It was when uncircumcised persons were considered for salvation and/or fellowship that "the fat was in the fire." It was not only that non-Christian Jews opposed the relaxing of cultic laws; many in the Christian movement, including Peter and the Twelve, resisted the inclusion of uncircumcised persons (see 10:28; 11:1–2; 15:5; Gal. 2:11–14). This is the issue dominating Acts. Must a non-Jew be circumcised (become a Jew) to be saved and to have table fellowship with circumcised persons? Luke-Acts shows the victory for an "unhindered" gospel; but it came at a great cost, the self-exclusion of many from a fellowship that made faith alone the sufficient ground for salvation and fellowship.

Acts traces the struggle against exclusivist barriers, showing both victories and costs. Stephen and Philip (table waiters!) and unnamed disciples from Cyprus and Cyrene (11:19–20) pioneered in championing a gospel for all people, followed by a reluctant Simon Peter (ch. 10) and a traumatically converted Saul of Tarsus. Paul finally stated it boldly: "In Christ there is not any Jew and Greek, bond and free, male and female" (Gal. 3:28). There are such distinctions in the world, but they are irrelevant to all that is meant by being "in Christ," whether salvation, fellowship, or ministry. Jesus himself, according to both Gospel and Acts, was the dynamic in the opening of doors and crossing of barriers.

FROM TEMPLE TO ROMAN JAIL

Although Luke does not tell us how the gospel got from Jerusalem to Rome, he does trace its struggle from at-homeness in the Temple to its being preached "unhindered" from a Roman jail (actually, as a Roman citizen, Paul was under house arrest). The Gospel of Luke begins with a picture of Jewish piety at its best: Elizabeth and Zacharias, Joseph and Mary, Simeon and Anna (Luke 1–2). These are Jews, righteous and "filled with the Holy Spirit," enjoying God's favor, worshiping in the Temple. Luke closes with the scene of Jesus' followers (not yet called "Christians") worshiping at the Temple in Jerusalem. Volume one closes thus: They "were continually in the Temple, praising God" (24:53). This is "Christian Judaism." At this point it would be meaningless to say "Jewish Christianity," for there were no non-Jewish Christians among them. They were at home within the structures of Judaism, with seemingly no impulse to break out into the larger, non-Jewish world.

The story in Acts is anticipated in Luke. Jesus himself was thrown out of his home synagogue in Nazareth (Luke 4:16–30). Luke makes it clear what so threatened this Sabbath assembly. Jesus first impressed the congregation with his words, and then he precipitated their violent opposition by citing what God had done for a Sidonian widow and a Syrian leper through his prophets Elijah and Elisha. From Isaiah, Jesus interpreted his mission as giving release from every kind of bondage: hunger, sickness, prison, alienation, death. This implied ministry to the whole person, at every level of human need. Next, Jesus indicated the outreach of God's care, as far as the inclusion of a widow of Sidon and a leper of Syria. To include such persons is to remove all barriers erected by religion to keep itself "separate" and "clean." This stance is what caused the eruption in the synagogue in Nazareth, Jesus' eviction from the synagogue, and his ultimate rejection and crucifixion. As is true in all four Gospels, Luke points up the tension over the Temple. Jesus did not threaten to destroy the Temple; he worshiped there. He did protest its reduction from "a house of prayer" (it is not clear why Luke drops Mark's "for all peoples") to a "den of robbers" (19:46). Jesus' concern for all people and his consequent conflict with entrenched piety emerged more slowly among his followers, but his stance did surface in Stephen, Philip, and others with the same results.

Acts begins the same as does the Gospel of Luke, with piety in Jerusalem, centered in the Temple. This is Christian Judaism. These Christian Jews worship at the Temple and in the privacy of their homes. What they do is of God as they preach salvation in Jesus, the risen Lord, evidenced by the coming of the Spirit upon them. They are bold, refusing to be silent even when so commanded by the Sadducees. They are ready to suffer public beatings and imprisonment and the threat of death. Ananias and Sapphira mar the fellowship; but otherwise, they live in terms of a beautiful *koinōnia*, freely sharing their possessions. Acts closes not at the Temple but in Rome, capital of the vast Roman Empire, the "world" as known to these people. The chief spokesman has been thrown out of synagogues and Temple, and he now preaches from jail a gospel "unhindered." Luke does not mean hindered by Jews but unhindered by Romans. He means unhindered by falsely seeing the gospel itself as excluding persons on such irrelevant grounds as cultic rite or ethnic identity.

Movement in Acts is that from a close-knit Christian Judaism to a world fellowship in Christ. It did not come in one giant step. Jesus himself had to fight to win inclusion for "publicans and sinners" within Judaism, as well as to win acceptance of the blind, the deaf, the lame, the leper, and even women in terms of full personhood, with dignity, freedom, and responsibility. Jesus likewise took the opening steps toward inclusion of Samaritans and Gentiles. In Acts is traced the gradual inclusion of any who were willing to hear and trust. The first breakthrough was the inclusion of Samaritans through the joyful preaching of Philip (8:4–25). The next barrier was crossed when Philip went to the God-fearing Ethiopian eunuch (8:26–40) and when Peter, with fear and reluctance, went into the home of the God-fearing but uncircumcised Roman soldier Cornelius (10:1–11:18). The final breakthrough is typified when Paul affirmed that a pagan jailer at Philippi could come into salvation in one simple step, that of faith (16:16–40). Overcoming of ancient and stubborn barriers is dramatized when a former "Hebrew of the Hebrews" (Phil. 3:5) accepted table fellowship with a Philippian jailer, just one step out of paganism (Acts 16:34). The triumph over the many barriers is celebrated in the very last word in the Greek text to Luke-Acts, "unhindered!"

For a more detailed study of Luke-Acts, see my two journal articles and two books: "The Purpose and Message of Acts" and "The Unhindered Gospel" in *Review and Expositor; The Book of Acts* and *Studies in Luke's Gospel.* For a more comprehensive study of Acts, see Ernst Haenchen, *The Acts of the Apostles, A Commentary.*

HOMILETICAL STUDIES

To introduce a series of sermons on Acts, you might well take the text from the concluding story in Luke-Acts, Paul's preaching while under house arrest in Rome (Acts 28:17–31). This could be likened to jumping to the conclusion of a novel to see how it comes out; it lessens the suspense but adds to understanding. The text for the sermon could come from the final verses (28:30–31), and the title could be the final word in the Greek text, "Unhindered." The best title probably would be "The Unhindered Gospel."

The sermon could begin by posing the question as to how a movement that was born and cradled in the piety of Judaism became within a few generations a predominantly Gentile movement, developing not only outside the land of its origin but outside the structures of Judaism. You might draw two contrasting pictures: a likely gathering of the earliest Christians at worship, exclusively Jewish and at home in synagogue or Temple, contrasted with a Christian congregation today, probably strictly Gentile and far removed from even the memory of our Jewish origins. How did this come about? What forces, factors, and issues entered into this drastic shift? What does it imply for good or bad?

The movement from Christian Judaism to the present complexion of Christianity might be traced in Acts, showing three major stages: (1) Christian Judaism (chs. 1–5); (2) growing tension within the church as non-Jews (the uncircumcised) are received into the fellowship (chs. 6–15); and (3) the widening gap between Judaism and Christianity (chs. 16–28). If there is time, the anticipation of this may be cited from the Gospel of Luke, with its own movement from Jewish piety (chs. 1–2) to Jesus' eviction from his home synagogue and his judgment upon the Temple, and the closing picture in the Gospel of Luke of devout Jews worshiping God at the Temple.

One major caution should be observed, the avoidance of anything sounding like anti-Semitism. History must be related with integrity, with its negative as well as positive side; but it must be done fairly. All the earliest Christians were Jews, both those who erected barriers to a gospel for all people and those who broke them down. Both Judaism and Christianity have had their prophets and their narrow partisans. The Old Testament clearly distinguishes between those in ancient Israel who recognized God's concern for all nations and those who tried to make JHWH a national God. History is always a painful story when told honestly. Luke-Acts does portray some Jewish power figures in negative roles, but the positive figures also are Jews: Jesus, Stephen, Philip, Peter, Barnabas, Paul, and many others. The story can be told "warts and all" without playing into the hands of bigotry or anti-Semitism. The sermon may warn that all people are potentially good and beautiful but also vulnerable to all that is evil and ugly. Stereotyping is "tarring with the same brush" all the people of a given race, nation, or religion. This is to be avoided.

All sermons need not be of the same style. This proposal of a sermon on "The Unhindered Gospel" may be basically narrative in structure, substance, and style. You have a story to tell, and abiding lessons can be drawn from the story. The gospel must always be free or unhindered. There are endless ways of blunting it or perverting it. Consciously or unconsciously, we tend to "domesticate" Jesus and to make the gospel serve our own cultural values or goals. Faithfulness to the unhindered gospel may result in rejection even in religious circles, privation, or even persecution. The risk is high but the rewards are more than sufficient.

"Filled with the Spirit." This may serve as the title for a sermon rich in exegetical study and relevant to issues in the Christian community today. The text may be found in Acts 2:4, studied against the background of wide usage in Luke-Acts. An alternate title for the sermon could be "True Spirituality." The goal in the sermon would include both negative and positive concerns. There are many false ideas about spirituality that need to be corrected. There is a rich and meaningful understanding of spirituality to be found in Luke-Acts. Any picture of spirituality may be developed by building only on isolated texts, but the theme can be put in proper perspective by reviewing massive evidence in Luke-Acts.

The sermon might begin with a comparison of three related expressions: "baptized in the Spirit" (Luke 3:16; Acts 1:5; see also Mark 1:8; Matt. 3:11); the Spirit "come upon" someone (Acts 1:8; 2:17; Luke 2:25, 27); and "filled with the Holy Spirit" (Acts 2:4; 4:8; 6:5; 11:24; Luke 1:15, 41, 67). It is clear that these are variant expressions for the same thing. It is also clear that Pentecost is not the beginning point for the Spirit's coming. Luke-Acts shows that pre-Christian Jews enjoyed the same outpouring of God's Spirit as did the disciples at Pentecost. The Holy Spirit is not a third God or just one third of God. Just as Jesus Christ is the only God uniquely present in a real human life, so the Holy Spirit is the only God present anytime and anywhere. The Holy Spirit is the same divine presence known to anyone who knows God. Jesus is "JHWH Savior," not just "one out of three." He is Immanuel, "God with us," not just one out of three with us. Likewise, the Holy Spirit is "the Spirit of *God*," not just a part of God. There has never been a time when the Spirit of God was not present in his people, awakening them to faith and empowering them for the life they are called to live. There should be no surprise then that Luke 1–2 so closely parallels Acts 2.

The sermon on "Filled with the Spirit" can draw heavily from Acts to show what happens when one is so filled. Barnabas sold a field and gave the money to feed the hungry. Barnabas also stood by Paul when Paul's acceptance in Jerusalem was cool, and he stood by Mark when Mark needed a friend. Stephen was filled with the Spirit, and he preached with insight and courage in words understandable to all, not in some "unknown tongue." Those who were filled with the Spirit crossed difficult barriers that had separated people from people. To go outside Luke-Acts, what results within a person may be seen from

Gal. 5:22, "the fruit of the Spirit." True spirituality is evidenced by the change within and by how one relates to other people, not by the superficial things often confused with spirituality. For a detailed treatment of this whole area, see my book *The Holy Spirit Today.*

"*Koinōnia:* the Common Life in Christ." In preaching from Acts, one should not neglect what is implied by the Greek word *koinōnia* (Acts 2:42) and its cognate *koinos* (2:44; 4:32). The basic idea in this family of words is "common." It may be used to designate the opposite of kosher, or clean, in the cultic sense (10:14, 28; 11:8), but in ch. 2 it designates the life that we have "in common" in Christ. Community and communion are related ideas. We are a "community" in Christ, a people bound together because each is bound to Christ. In the Lord's Supper the cup is called the "*koinōnia* (communion) of the blood of Christ" and the loaf is called the "*koinōnia* (communion) of the body of Christ" (I Cor. 10:16). We are one body, the body of Christ. We share one life in common, the life we have in Christ. *Koinōnia* means "common" in this sense, not "ordinary" but what we have together in Christ.

The scriptural base for the sermon on "*Koinōnia:* the Common Life in Christ" may include Acts 2:42 and 4:32–37. The term is introduced in 2:42 without explanation as to its meaning, presumably because already the term was familiar in Christian usage. First John 1:1–4 points to *koinōnia* as the goal in proclamation and as joy and fulfillment in the Christian life. This passage traces the horizontal relationship (*koinōnia* with one another) to the vertical (*koinōnia* with the Father and his Son). It is not just any "fellowship" that is meant. It is that particular kinship or common life which we share with one another because first of all we participate in the life or kind of existence that was with the Father and that came down into our world so concretely in Jesus that it could be seen, heard, and touched. This and only this is the *koinōnia* celebrated in Acts.

Koinōnia comes to expression in many ways. It is expressed in walking in light and not darkness (I John 1:6,7). It is expressed in the unity of God's people (Phil. 2:1ff.). It is expressed in the acceptance of one another (Philemon 6, 17). It is expressed in our suffering together (Phil. 3:10; 4:14; I Peter 4:13). In Acts 4:32–37 its reality is found in the sharing of material possessions in a time of need. Ironically, what is known today as "Communism" is an atheistic and materialistic version of this beautiful ideal in Acts. Probably there never would have been this present movement had those calling themselves Christian in Russia and elsewhere in the world practiced the "communism," or *koinōnia,* of the New Testament. What we find in Acts is not materialism, making the material an end in itself or the main or whole concern. On the other hand, the material is something God made; it belongs properly and significantly to human existence under God. Creation affirms the material, for God made it. The incarnation affirms the material, for the eternal Word became flesh in Jesus Christ. Resurrection affirms the material, for that means a risen body and not a naked soul. In a hungry world today, Christians need to recover a biblical understanding of the material; and they need to practice the Christian *koinōnia* which does justice to human need for the material. Paul called the collection that he took to the saints in Jerusalem a *koinōnia* (Rom. 15:26). Paul postponed a mission to Spain in order to take an offering of money from Gentile churches to the saints in Jerusalem, hoping thus both to meet material needs and to bind Gentile and Jewish Christians together in a stronger *koinōnia* (see I Cor. 16:1–4; II Cor. 8–9; Rom. 15:22–33; Acts 24:17).

A sermon on *koinōnia* could have three movements: its nature, the common life; its source, God's kind of existence; and its expressions, and these are many.

"The Ministry of the Word and Waiting Tables." What about this as a sermon topic based on Acts 6:1–7? The Twelve protest that it is not fitting for them to "abandon the word of God" (that is not too strong a translation) "to serve tables." Ironically, Acts goes on to show that Stephen excelled in his penetrating insights into the ways of God and in his courage in preaching truth which piety was not yet prepared to receive. Also, Acts shows how Philip went freely and joyfully to Samaritans and an Ethiopian eunuch, while Peter and the Twelve were slow in accepting uncircumcised persons like Cornelius. Stephen and Philip were among those chosen to "wait tables," while the Twelve were to remain free for "spiritual" matters. Is there a lesson for us here? Certainly prayer and preaching are primary in the scale of Christian values, but is it dangerous to make too sharp a distinction between the ministry of the Word and the ministry of tables? Love is concerned for human need at whatever level. Some things are more important than others, but love responds to each need as though that need were primary. Better stated, life is to be seen holistically, not fragmented. Further, our passage may be a warning against making too sharp a distinction between "clergy" and "laypersons." From Stephen and Philip we may learn that those most sensitive to human need at the material/physical level may be in the best position to sense the deeper meaning of the gospel.

"Closed Doors." Dramatic acts sometimes tell the whole story. There is a needed sermon in the dramatic story found in Acts 21:27–

36. Accusing Paul of taking uncircumcised men into the Temple, men of piety threw Paul out of the Temple and closed its doors! Does God dwell behind closed doors? Can a true sanctuary have doors designed to exclude rather than for entrance? Is not a lockout at the Temple an anomaly? There was zeal behind the eviction of Paul and the closing of the doors, but was it sound? Was it zeal without knowledge? Worse yet, was it zeal without love? A sermon here could first present the scene and message in Acts and then examine the "closed doors" today in religion presuming to represent Jesus Christ. This study in "Closed Doors" can be underscored by the closing line in Luke 4:16–30. Jesus was evicted from his home synagogue, its doors thus shut to him; but although rejected by "piety," Jesus "kept on going" (v. 30)! Piety may build walls and lock doors, but Jesus moves on!

My allotted space is used up, and much of Acts remains untouched. From the conference in Acts 15, there is a sermon on "Much Ado About What?" From Acts 20:20, there is a sermon on "The Full Gospel." Just compare Paul's "full gospel" with what passes for the same today! Contextually, what Paul did not "hold back" was the "unhindered" gospel, assaulting every barrier between persons and God, and persons and persons. Sermons lurk in every chapter of Acts.

FOR FURTHER READING

"The Book of Acts," *Review and Expositor*, Vol. 71 (Fall 1974).

Haenchen, Ernst. *The Acts of the Apostles, A Commentary.* Tr. R. McL. Wilson et al. Westminster Press, 1971. The most prestigious commentary on Acts.

Smith, T. C. *Acts.* The Broadman Bible Commentary, Vol. 10. Broadman Press, 1970.

Stagg, Frank. *The Book of Acts: The Early Struggle for an Unhindered Gospel.* Broadman Press, 1955.

———. *The Holy Spirit Today.* Broadman Press, 1973.

———. "The Purpose and Message of Acts," *Review and Expositor*, Vol. 44 (Jan. 1947).

———. *Studies in Luke's Gospel.* Convention Press, 1967.

———. "The Unhindered Gospel," *Review and Expositor*, Vol. 71 (Fall 1974).

Tolbert, Malcolm O. *Luke.* The Broadman Bible Commentary, Vol. 9. Broadman Press, 1970.

18. PREACHING FROM THE PAULINE EPISTLES

KRISTER STENDAHL

I. HERMENEUTICAL BACKGROUND

Paul would be much surprised by the very idea of preachers using his letters as texts for sermons. To be sure, Paul had a rather high estimation of his authority and of his call to be the Apostle to the Gentiles. To be sure, he would like his followers and co-workers to quote him and to expand on his ideas. But that his often quickly dictated letters—including the private one to Philemon—would make it into the Bible was neither his intention nor his dream.

That is not to say we are wrong in preaching on Pauline texts. But we should know what we are doing. It is as letters to specific churches, written in answer to specific churches, and written in answer to specific situations that these writings form part of the Bible. As a matter of fact, the Muratorian Canon (perhaps from the late second century) struggles with the question: How can letters written to specific churches with specific problems speak to all churches?

That question is worth remembering as we seek guidance and insight toward good preaching on Pauline texts. For the power of biblical preaching grows out of a grasp of the specifics of the text. And temptations are considerable to grab hold of so-called Pauline themes and get ever more general in our repeating the obvious. I would even argue that the Pauline and biblical authority in and behind our preaching has its highest density where the message is closest to Paul's original intention and most analogous to the situation to which he addressed himself in the first place.

Fred B. Craddock has pointed out how this principle of distance— as over against hasty relevance—is absolutely essential for effective communication.

> For the message, distance preserves its objectivity as history, its
> continuity as tradition, and its integrity as a word that has
> existence prior to and apart from me as a listener. In other words,
> the distance between the message and the listener conveys the
> sense of the substantive nature and independence of the message,
> qualities that add to rather than detract from the persuasive and
> attention-drawing power of the message. I am much more
> inclined toward a message that has its own intrinsic life and force
> and that was prepared with no *apparent* awareness of me, than
> toward a message that obviously did not come into being until I as
> a listener appeared. (*Overhearing the Gospel*, pp. 121–122)

Thus preachers should not *make* the text relevant. They should get
deeply enough into the text and its original situation and intentions to
find its relevance. By a keen sense for an intelligent analysis of the now
situation—in the world, in society, in the community, in the church, in
the congregation, in the souls and minds of people, both others and
themselves—the preachers are to perceive the analogies between what
Paul said and what he might say to us. Such analogies are only
analogies, they are never one hundred percent identical with the
original. But their power and helpfulness depend exactly on the
depth of understanding of the specificity of the *then* and the specificities of the *now*.

The search for the points of analogy is a risky task. This is so since
there can be no total identity. History never repeats itself completely.
There is always something that is different, and woe unto those who
do not know that. Their overidentifications engender false teaching
and false use of biblical authority.

Thus preaching is a creative art. It is not a cool application but a
creative vision for analogies. Risky it is, and that is why the preacher
must seek the guidance of the Spirit as the sermon grows out of study
and meditation.

We are all familiar with two words of Jesus: "The one who is not
with me is against me" (Matt. 12:30; Luke 11:23) and "The one who is
not against us is for us" (Mark 9:40; Luke 9:50). How do we know
when to quote the one saying or the other, especially since at least the
first of them may well have circulated without context prior to the Q
source and to our Gospels? Even so, we are helped by their contexts.
The first sums up Jesus' sharp critique of the entrenched establishment who accused him of using black magic; the second is a word to
overzealous disciples who did not rejoice in the progress of the
kingdom through people who "do not follow us." It is out of such an
analysis that we seek and find analogies: the difficulties of the

establishment to welcome the kingdom when it comes in new forms by new agents, and the anxious narrowness of Christians who know they are the right ones. Or something like that. I have used this example because it is so simple and so obvious, and because it makes clear that we cannot handle great sayings just by applying them according to our mood. The specifics of the *then* deepen and enliven our capacity to see specific situations in the *now*. The principle of biblical preaching is: from specifics to specifics, not from generalities to ever grander generalities, nor from uncontrolled generalities to haphazardly chosen specifics. The power of biblical preaching lies in the specifics at both ends. I guess that is what could be called incarnational preaching.

In the search for an analogous situation it sometimes happens that we become more struck by contrasts than by similarities between Paul's *then* and our *now*. The problems that agitated him do not seem to agitate us, and the other way around. This contrast has its own analogue in Paul's very correspondence. The Corinthians are agitated by questions that Paul considers trivial, and what they consider trivial he considers crucial. Think about Paul's heavy theological argument about not waiting for the latecomers to the meals, a matter which the Corinthians saw as very minor (I Cor. 11:29–34).

But there are also the texts where both Paul and his addressees are absorbed in problems that seem to have little direct relevance to us, such as questions bearing on the role of Jewish Christians (Galatians), or the fact that most meat sold in the Corinthian marketplace came from the temple sacrifice (I Cor. 8 and 10). To be sure, we could find analogies, but there may be times when it is wiser to spell out the differences, as Luther once said about a passage concerning David: "It is God's word, all right, but not for me." The Bible is for the whole church through time and space. Who said that everything is "for me"? Applications and analogues should be reasonable, not contrived. The contrived application mocks the Bible, like those sermons which grab hold of Luke 5:4: "Put out into the deep and let down your nets . . ," for a sermon on the necessity of a deeper faith or something similar.

In some ways Pauline texts are easier to analyze as to their original intention than most other passages. For the undisputed Pauline letters are addressed to specific congregations and we have some knowledge about their respective geographical and cultural conditions. Sometimes, and especially in I Corinthians, Paul states the question to which he is addressing himself (e.g., I Cor. 7:1; 8:1; 10:25; 12:1; I Thess. 4:13; etc.).

Much of the common picture of Paul comes not from his letters but from the book of Acts. Its account of Paul's call to apostleship, his speeches, his missionary methods and journeys blend happily into our reading of his letters, and vice versa. In the Acts of the Apostles (with Peter and Paul as the two chief figures), Luke is one of the first to *interpret* the Pauline phenomenon. He does so in his own impressive way. In order for us to understand Paul's own writings it is important that we sharpen our eyes for what is Paul himself and what is the Acts interpretation of Paul.

To read about Paul's journeys seems natural and innocent enough. But Luke's account is part of an overall scheme: From Jerusalem to Rome (cf. Acts 1:8). And we remember that Luke structures his Gospel in the same manner by placing the bulk of Jesus' teaching during Jesus' travels from Galilee to Jerusalem (Luke 9:51–18:41). That is Lucan style and within such a scheme Paul functions as the carrier of the gospel to Rome. Hence Luke's surprising lack of interest in the outcome of the trial—if there was one—in Rome (Acts 28:30–31). It is "from Jerusalem to Rome" that interests Luke, and consequently the change of the name from Saul to Paul takes place when he for the first time meets a Roman official, i.e., when the focus shifts to Rome. The official's name happens to be Sergius Paulus and Luke says, "Saulus who also [like Sergius] was Paulus . . ." (Acts 13:9). From then on, Luke calls him Paul—except that the Lord and Ananias address him in "Hebrew" as *"Saoul, Saoul . . ."* (in chs. 22 and 26, as in 9:4, 17). There goes the scriptural basis for one of the most cherished themes for Pauline preaching: Saul who by his conversion became a new person, Paul. It has no basis in Paul's letters either. His Roman name stands rather for his being God's "cosmopolitan for the Gentiles."

Powerful is Acts' three times repeated description of Paul's call (Acts 9; 22; and 26; in the style of Ezekiel's call). Paul himself speaks in a different manner, without any account (Gal. 1:15, in the style of Jeremiah's call; I Cor. 9:1; perhaps II Cor. 4:6, in the style of the creation story; Rom. 15:16, using sacrificial and priestly language). The "Damascus experience" is Lucan specificity in grand narrative style.

A reference to Damascus in relation to his call occurs in Gal. 1:17. But in Acts 9:26f. Paul goes from Damascus to Jerusalem and is introduced by Barnabas to the apostles. In Galatians it is of great importance to Paul that he did not go to Jerusalem until much later. In Acts it is the Jews who are after his life in Damascus. According to

Paul, it was the Nabatean King Aretas (II Cor. 11:32). (See Ernst Haenchen, *The Acts of the Apostles,* pp. 330–336.)

Paul does call himself a Pharisee as to the law (Phil. 3:6), but the specific reference to his having studied with Gamaliel is from Acts alone (22:3), and we should be careful about building whole structures on it, especially since Gamaliel is Luke's "wise Pharisee" in general (5:34).

That he had persecuted the church is to Paul *the* sin in his life (e.g., I Cor. 15:9), but it is in Acts that we find the colorful accounts of Paul at Stephen's stoning (7:60) and the mission to Damascus (9:2; cf. Gal. 1:17).

In listening to Paul's letters one could get the impression that it was Paul who brought the gospel to the Gentiles, and had it not been for Paul, Christianity would have remained a Jewish sect. So strong is this impression that it has engendered that popular view of early Christian history. In Acts, on the other hand, it is Peter—whom Paul considers "the apostle to the circumcision" (Gal. 2:7)—who is credited with the first mission to Gentiles, and that with putting aside questions of food laws and circumcision according to special revelation in a dream (the Cornelius story, Acts 10 and 11).

In Acts, Paul's missionary strategy is one of beginning his preaching in the synagogues and gathering some converts, both Jews and Gentiles who are associated with the synagogue. But when the synagogue leadership turned on Paul he "went to the Gentiles," having registered the repetition of the rejection of Jesus by the Sanhedrin (Luke 22; Acts 13:27ff.). This pattern of Paul's mission is a consistent theme in Acts, most explicit in the first extensive account (in Pisidian Antioch, Acts 13:14–52; esp. vs. 43 and 47). It is repeated in chs. 14 (Iconium), 17 (Thessalonica, Berea, Athens), 18 and 19 (Corinth, esp. 18:6, and Ephesus), and Rome (28:17, 24).

When we read Paul's letters we hear nothing about his ever addressing Jews or synagogues. His mission is thoroughly consistent with his being the apostle to the Gentiles without any "first try" in the synagogues (the word does not exist in Paul's letters). He seems to honor the principle: Peter for the Jews, Paul for the Gentiles (Gal. 2:7; Rom. 1:5; 15: 16, 18, etc.). Nor does he act on the basis of the so-called apostolic council in Jerusalem as Acts states it (Acts 15). Rather, he has agreed to only one thing: to bring a collection from his Gentile churches to the church in Jerusalem (Gal. 2:10). This collection plays a significant role in Paul's mission (I Cor. 16:1–4; II Cor. 8:1–9:15). It ties his mission to the Gentiles into the sacred history of Israel (Rom.

9:4), the Jewish Christians in Jerusalem being the "remnant" (Rom. 11:5). He must travel east to deliver the collection in person, although he is actually headed west to Spain, via Rome (Rom. 15:24–25). It is for this purpose that he embarks on the fateful journey to Jerusalem (Rom. 15:25–33). According to Acts, he got to Rome all right, but "courtesy" of the Roman police. In Acts the collection has a different setting and function, 11:27–30.

There is also the notice in Acts 16:1–3 that Paul had Timothy circumcised in order not to give offense, a highly surprising attitude when compared with Paul's insistence in his letters that circumcision of Gentiles is wrong. His proud report that in Jerusalem the Jews had not compelled Titus to be circumcised (Gal. 2:3), although there seems to have been some pressure, rhymes poorly with the notice of the circumcision of Timothy in Acts.

Finally, there is a striking contrast between the pious style of Luke in Acts and the crisp style of Paul. In Acts 16:7 "the Spirit of Jesus" does not allow Paul to follow his travel plans; in I Thess. 2:18 it is Satan that thwarts his travel plans (cf. II Cor. 2:12).

We are not listing these discrepancies between Paul and Acts' picture of Paul as an exercise in historical exegesis. Rather, in the interest of that specificity which is necessary for good biblical preaching we must sharpen up the image of what Paul actually says, how he speaks, and how he thinks. Of course, one can minimize the differences and harmonize the texts in many ways. A homogenized image of Paul as it has traditionally been drawn with pieces from Acts and pieces from Paul's letters has its charm. It also serves certain types of apologetics for those who feel the need to "defend the Bible" against contradictions or varieties of theological perception. But such homogenized texts are a doubtful basis for powerful preaching with specificity. Once you have homogenized the milk, you can never make whipped cream. Hence we should rather glory in the specificities than produce sermons that have lost the glow of Paul's unique perception.

If we follow such a principle in Pauline preaching, we come to recognize that even within the Pauline corpus the various epistles address themselves to different situations. The traditional order of the epistles is that of the Vulgate. It is not chronological, but seems to be according to their length. Romans, for example, is the last of the assuredly Pauline epistles, and I Thessalonians the oldest.

During the last two hundred years the authenticity of six of the thirteen Pauline writings has been seriously questioned (on Hebrews, see below, p. 314). In the case of the Pastorals (I and II Timothy, Titus), there is a clear scholarly consensus that they are not written by Paul. In the case of Ephesians and Colossians the opinions are more divided, as also in the case of II Thessalonians. This discussion is rehearsed in all introductions and commentaries. For the purpose of preaching, the matter is both of great importance and relatively easy to handle. The pulpit is hardly the place to lecture on such questions. "Do not read the cookbook—serve the food." Whether these writings are by Paul or not, all scholars agree that they show distinct features in their eschatology, their soteriology, their ecclesiology, etc. These very differences are part of that specificity of the text which we have hailed as the source for good biblical preaching. Thus it is important to increase one's sensitivity to what the text says, without being numbed by theologically timid or psychologically rash homogenization. A few examples may suffice for making the point.

In the assuredly Pauline letters, there is a striking use of tenses when Paul speaks of death and resurrection. We *have* died with Christ and we *shall* rise with Christ. Paul never says that we have risen with Christ. At most, we are to walk in newness of life, we are to *consider* ourselves dead to sin and alive to God in Christ Jesus so that we cannot be ruled by sin (Rom. 6:1–12). "If we have died with Christ, we believe that we also *shall* live with him" who has already been raised (6:8).

This careful use of tenses cannot be accidental. It rhymes well with Paul's consistent use of the forms "we shall be saved" or "we are in the process of being saved"—not "we have been saved."

This lack of symmetry (have died/shall rise) is important to Paul and may well be what he refers to when he criticizes those who "say that there is no resurrection" (I Cor. 15:12), i.e., no *future* resurrection. We know how important it is for Paul that Christians co-groan with the creation, awaiting the full salvation. For it is in hope, not in reality, that we are saved so far (Rom. 8:22–24). Paul is afraid of a piety where the believer already has passed from death to life. We could even say that he is afraid of the consequences of Johannine piety (John 5:24; 11:25). He is afraid of those gnostics who claim that the resurrection has happened already (see II Tim. 2:18, a view well known in the second century, Justin Martyr, Dial. 80).

In Colossians, however, this asymmetry of tenses is not retained. "You were buried with him in baptism, in which you were also raised with him" (Col. 2:12). Here the rhetorical and theological symmetry (buried/raised) has smothered Paul's precious insistence on resurrection as future. So also in 3:1–4: "If you have risen with Christ . . .", but here with a beautiful echo of Paul's sense: "For you have died, and your life *is hidden* with Christ in God. When Christ, our Life, becomes manifest, then also you shall be manifest with him in glory."

A second example: We are all familiar with Paul's image of the church as a body, as the body which is Christ (I Cor. 12:12–27; cf. Rom. 12:4–5). Here the head is just one of the members of the body (I Cor. 12:21) and the point is that all limbs/members have their distinct function and should not boast over against one another in the life of the congregation. But in Eph. 4:1–16 the body expresses a very different ecclesiology (and Christology). Here the head is Christ and "we are to grow up in every way into him who is the head, into Christ, from whom the whole body . . . upbuilds itself in love." Such a use of the image goes well with the speculative and beautifully transcendent view of the church as the bride of Christ (Eph. 5:23–32). The church is now the object of speculation. And the apostles are called "holy apostles" (Eph. 3:5), a term that suggests an author who looks back toward the days of the greats. It is hard to imagine Paul calling himself "holy" in that sense.

It is, of course, not impossible to see that such growth of language and theology is possible in the ministry of Paul, although, all things being equal, it strikes me as more reasonable to see these writings as the first steps on the long way of devoted interpretation of Paul in churches with new challenges and new experiences.

For our preaching it is, however, mandatory that we see the differences and make the most of them for the passage which constitutes our text.

Some people speak about Paul's *epistles* and others about his *letters*. Is that just more dignified versus more contemporary style? Scholars have made a significant distinction. An epistle is a recognized literary form in antiquity. Its intention is to be literature written for public consumption—in the form of a letter. A letter is a real letter to a person or the leaders of a group or a group at large. With this useful distinction in mind, we see that Paul's writings are letters rather than epistles, but with a certain spectrum in which Philemon is most clearly a letter and Romans tends most toward the epistle. Among the disputed writings, Ephesians has the character of an epistle—perhaps originally composed as an introduction to a collection of the Pauline corpus assembled in Ephesus for circulation in the churches. An indication of the epistle/tractate character is that the reference to

Rome and Ephesus is missing in some manuscripts (Rom. 1:7, 15; Eph. 1:1). Hebrews, which came to be associated with Paul (and is so designated in KJV) in spite of doubts already in the second century, is a striking example of an epistle. Origen's statement that "only God knows" who wrote it has been amply verified by all the guesses, ancient and modern, as to its authorship. Its closest theological relative within the New Testament is Stephen's speech in Acts 7.

If one considers some of the thirteen writings attributed to Paul as written or edited by others in his honor and as testaments somewhat analogous to the Testaments of the Twelve Patriarchs (the Pastorals, Ephesians, Colossians, II Thessalonians), then these writings assume the character of epistles, while studiously retaining the form of actual letters (see, e.g., the ending of II Thessalonians).

II. HOMILETICAL TEXTS

But we have spoken long enough about specificity—in rather general terms. Now to some texts. I have chosen what may be considered classical passages, and it may be wise to begin with those which have dominated Western and especially Protestant understandings of Paul, i.e., those where Paul contrasts the Law and the Faith. That theme is not at all as pervasive in Paul's thought as is often believed, but is a theme central to two of his writings, Galatians and Romans.

GALATIANS 3:19–25. WITHOUT BABY-SITTER

What is the situation? What is the problem which so upsets Paul that this is the only one of his letters without the usual greetings expressing thanks and warmth. Galatians begins rather with an anathema (Gal. 1:8f.) against those who deviate from his gospel. This is a hot and angry letter. The beautiful beginnings of the church (4:12–14) are seriously threatened (2:4) in the same way as some of James's people from Jerusalem had intimidated the church in Antioch. There Barnabas had been taken in and Peter had vascillated (2:11–14).

As the apostle to the Gentiles, Paul is fighting for his God-given (1:15ff.) understanding of his mission to the Gentiles. They are children of Abraham not by circumcision (2:3) and food laws (2:12). Gentiles should not be forced to accept Jewish ways; they should not try to be Jews.

That is the issue in Galatians, epitomized in Paul's reprimand to Peter: How come you force Gentiles to accept Jewish life-style (2:14)?

In Galatians the issue is not Judaism, nor is it the pros and cons of a Jewish Christian life-style—but for Gentile Christians to "Judaize," as Paul calls it (2:14), is at issue.

In ch. 3, Paul assembles a series of arguments in defense of his conviction, all based on Scripture, actually on Torah (*the* Law, the Pentateuch). His main argument is simple, and the key is his favorite interpretation of Gen. 15:6 (Gal. 3:6; cf. Rom. 4:3): Abraham believed God's promise and it was counted him as righteousness. That promise was toward all nations (Gal. 3:8, Paul's interpretation of Gen. 18:18) and it was to reach them through Christ (Gal. 3:16)—since the word "seed" in Gen. 12:7 has singular, not plural form. "If you are Christ's, then you are the seed of Abraham, heirs according to the promise" (Gal. 3:29)—*quod est demonstrandum.*

In such a scheme of things the law (i.e., Torah, or Scripture) "proves" that the Law (i.e., the Law given to Moses) has a limited role. It came 430 years after the promise and hence does not annul the promise (3:17). Now Paul piles up a series of observations indicating the "less than fullness" of the Mosaic law: it came as an addition to the Abrahamic covenant, and because of transgression (the golden calf incident? Ex. 32); it was given for a specific time, i.e., until Christ, "the seed"; it was not handed to the people directly but through angels. "Angels" in plural, so that the mediator Moses represents more than one—which for Paul and his time was a sign of imperfection: "One" being perfection, as God is One (Gal. 3:19–20). It all goes to show that the law points beyond itself. This was not a new thought in the Judaism of the time, but Paul gears his argument toward the specific issue of a Gentile Christian life-style.

The law is God's law, and had God wanted to, he could, of course, have given a life-giving law. But God had his eye on the promise, and therefore the law was to preserve the promise intact until there was to be "Gentile time," i.e., until the faith in Jesus Christ was to be offered to the Gentiles. This is now happening in Paul's mission. Seen from such a perspective of the Gentile mission, the law proved to be the firm baby-sitter (the Greek word *paidagōgos* refers not to a teacher and even less to a pedagogue; this is a servant charged with watching children, Gal. 3:24–25) who saw to it that the Children of Israel did not raid "the refrigerator before the big party" when people would come from east and west and sit at "the table with Abraham, Isaac, and Jacob in the kingdom of heaven" (Matt. 8:11). But once that faith is a live option for Gentiles, the duty of the baby-sitter has been fulfilled (Gal. 3:23–29).

The argument is crystal clear, even though we may find Paul's exegesis of Genesis and Exodus strange. To be sure, it is special pleading from the perspective of his mission.

Before we ask what analogous situations come to our minds, we should note two things.

1. "Faith" as Paul speaks of it here is not the attitude of faith versus the attitude of obedience to commandments. Paul does not say: The trouble with the people of Israel was their attitude of legalism. Had they only had faith instead. . . . No, faith here means the opportunity that came with Christ to be his. Note how Paul uses "faith" as if it said Christ: before the coming of the Faith (Gal. 3:23); once the Faith has come (v. 25). The difference is the object of Faith, not a new or deeper or warmer attitude.

2. In striking contrast to his similar thoughts in Romans, where Paul reflects on the relationship between Gentile Christians and the people of Israel (especially Rom. 9–11), in Galatians, Paul is totally absorbed by the problem at hand: Gentiles shall not try to be Jews.

1. The first analogue for our preaching is not an analogue. The most obvious response to Paul's message should be an expression of exuberant gratitude on the part of us Gentiles—that we have been invited to be children of Abraham; that Israel's riches of wisdom and insight and understanding of how God is One, and yet not crushing but loving—have been extended to us Gentiles since the gospel came to us, making us "children of God" through Sarah and Abraham in Jesus Christ. In a very special sense, we affirm that Israel is a light to the Gentiles (Isa. 49:6), a special sense celebrated in the Song of Simeon about the Christ (Luke 2:32). We must regret deeply that Christian history lost sight of the second half of that verse: "and for the glory of thy people Israel." For Paul, the Gentile mission as he sees it according to the Scriptures is part of the glory of Israel.

Yet this is an analogue of sorts, for Galatians is based on Paul's joy as a Jew that his heritage is now shared with the Gentile world. The polemics of the letter should not overshadow that joy. It is exactly that joy which makes Paul angry with those Jewish Christians who try to limit God's generosity.

2. This is *not* the text for reflections on the glories of Christianity versus Judaism. That is not the focus of Paul's thought. His only aim is to chart the course of, and defend his views on, the Gentile mission. It was in his letter to the Romans that he was to come to grips with the relationship between the Gentile church and the Jewish people. In Romans 9–11 he is addressing what he sees as pride and condescen-

sion of Christians toward Israel, and his message is clear: I'll tell you a secret, a mystery, lest you be conceited (11:25). And that mystery is that the church and Israel are to live side by side. Somehow Israel will be saved, apparently not by "conversion of Jews" (vs. 25–32). Thus Paul ends this part of Romans with a doxology to God's glorious mysteries (vs. 33–36), the only doxology to God without reference to Christ.

3. Then there is the striking analogy between the Galatian situation and the phenomenon of "overconversion." The serious Christian has the desire to go the whole way, and because of our fallen nature it is easier to feel serious by accepting or constructing absolute rules and clear barriers. The Galatians felt good about doing things right— circumcision and all. The gate can be made narrow in many ways, theologically and ethically. That feels serious, but is it "giving life" (Gal. 3:21)? What follows in vs. 26–29 about slavery and sexism reminds us of the way in which the church fell short of the Pauline vision—even Paul himself was not yet clear on the radical implications of his theological vision when the pressures of society pressed in on him.

4. When Paul defends the new Christians who live as Gentiles in a world different from the one in which Jesus and his disciples moved within Judaism, we easily come to think about the task facing Christians far from Western culture. Their witness makes us see how often we have identified Christianity with Western culture and ideologies. Christians are now the children of Abraham's promise, questioning our theological and cultural baby-sitting. . . . But once faith came, the job of the baby-sitter was done.

ROMANS 7:7–25. THE LAW IS FOR LIFE AND YOU KNOW IT

Romans and Galatians have much in common. Much of the vocabulary is the same: faith, law, justification, promise, etc. The quote from Hab. 2:4 is a decisive one in both Gal. 3:12 and Rom. 1:17. And that is the case in only these two letters. It is in these letters only that Abraham's faith is a key to the argument (Gal. 3; Rom. 4). In Romans as in Galatians the point is made that Moses does not change things that much (Gal. 3:17–20; Rom. 5:14). The arch of fundamental importance in Galatians is from Abraham to Christ (3:6 to v. 16 and on to v. 29); in Romans it spans from Adam to Christ (5:12 to v. 15, and on to v. 21). In both cases Paul practices a "bypassing of Moses." The references to Moses in II Corinthians 3 are quite different. There the style of Moses' ministry is contrasted to the style of the ministry of Paul—not to that of Christ's.

Yet there are striking differences of focus. In Galatians, as we saw, the focus is on the evil of Gentiles "trying to live as Jews." In Romans there is no attention to Judaizers or Judaizing. Rather, Paul reflects on how his apostolic mission to the Gentiles fits into God's total plan. He takes stock now when his ministry to the east is completed and he is ready to go west via Rome (Rom. 15:14–24). He has come to recognize that the Jesus movement on the whole is to become a Gentile movement (Rom. 11:11ff., 25ff.)—as we know, it actually did. How could that be? Romans is Paul's reflection on this mystery. Using the same and similar thoughts as in Galatians, he now applies them to a grand vision of the *missio Dei,* the *missio Christi,* and the *missio ecclesiae.* It is the first fundamental document on Christian missiology, not just by implication. That is Paul's overt intention. Hence the climax of the epistle is Romans 9–11. While Galatians had its specificity in the problem of Judaizers, Romans has its focus on real Jews and real Gentiles according to God's economy.

With such a perspective we turn to the classical text, Rom. 7:7–25, which has lived its life in the church pretty much oblivious of that overall context. And that for obvious reasons, for it is here we have those catchy words about a most existential and general human predicament: "For what I want to do, I do not—but what I hate, that I do" (v. 15), and: "The good I want to do I do not, but the evil I do not want to do, that I do" (v. 19).

A study—or just a careful, commonsense reading—of this passage serves as a good lesson in exegesis for preaching, a lesson that is especially useful when we deal with well-known passages. First, close your eyes and visualize, or try to remember, the text, and then read the text and see if there is something that is different from what you remembered. Chances are that it is exactly in such differences you will find the keys to a fresh and new grasp—and the ideas that enliven your sermon.

Two things may strike you immediately. (1) People often quote those words in v. 19, "The good I want to do . . ." with the shivering conclusion: "Wretched person that I am, who is to deliver me from this body of death?" (Note that it says "death," not "sin," v. 24). But quite a few verses separate them. (2) Not only that, but what Paul gets out of his observation of the predicament is far from the sentiment of v. 24a. To him that predicament proves that thus "I agree with the law that it is good" (v. 16) or "then it is not I who do it. . . . I rejoice in the law of God" (vs. 20 and 22). No blues there. How come?

It is quite clear what Paul's question is. He has proven to his satisfaction that the law is holy, and the commandment holy, just, and good (v. 12). Now he asks: Did the good produce death for me (v. 13)? Yes it did, but don't blame God's holy law. Rather blame sin.

Paul has already given a mini-sermon on the old story where the serpent tricks the first couple by twisting the commandment that was for life (Gen. 3:3; Rom. 7:10). "So sin tricked me by using the commandment [for life] as pretext" (Rom. 7:11).

The famous passage 7:13–25 is Paul's attempt at exonerating the law by putting the blame where it belongs, i.e., on sin and flesh, lest Christians think of God's law as something negative, inferior, or even evil. That is Paul's point. That is important to him. Is it important to us? Our well-known incapacity to do what we want to do proves to Paul that deep down, in our true self *(autos egō)*, we agree, rejoice with, and serve the law of God (vs. 16, 22, 25). To be sure, we are miserably trapped, since we are caught in the flesh, but that is not our true self. In ch. 8, the great chapter on life, Paul will show how God solved this dilemma by the incarnation, how he came "in the likeness of sinful flesh" and how thereby the intention of the law was restored with its intention toward life (8:3–4). But in ch. 7 his concern is to use our impasse not for making us feel guilty or depraved, but quite to the contrary, in order to show that our true self is on the side of God's good law.

Thus the main theme of our sermon could be something like: "The Law Is for Life and You Know It—As Did Eve." Or we could reflect on the ways in which God's good law has been twisted through the ages. We could come to see more clearly (7:13) how good commandments became deadly weapons of oppression in the hands of sinful people. For it is true that the real evil in the world was and is done by people who claim to do good. The crusades are the prototypes, but the analogies are legion. "For Satan masquerades as an angel of Light" (II Cor. 11:14; Lucifer, cf. Isa. 14:12 LXX/Vulgate). God's law unmasks that sham, and we know it deep down, but our true self is on God's side. And God has sent help—but that is not in ch. 7 but in ch. 8. In ch. 7 the human predicament is seen from its positive side. We do, in spite of it all, stand on God's side—we rejoice in the law.

II Corinthians 12:1–10. Against the Secularization of the Gospel

If we were to continue our study of Romans and move farther into ch. 8, we would hear Paul getting high on the glories of the Spirit who gives life to the Christian, in ways analogous to the Spirit by whom God raised Jesus Christ (Rom. 8:11; cf. the traditional formula used by Paul in 1:4). In that Spirit, Christians cry "Abba! Father!" (8:15). For Paul, "Father" is not an expression of God's nature, but of our being heirs, co-heirs with Christ (8:17). Remember that Romans is about how Gentiles became adopted into God's people—"engrafted," as Paul says in Rom. 11:19f.

But right there in Rom. 8:17 comes the typically Pauline shift: "that is, if we co-suffer [with Christ] in order to be co-glorified [with him]." As always, Paul is afraid of overstating the degree of savedness. He goes on to rub in how we are co-suffering, co-groaning with the creation (v. 23). Even with the Spirit as a downpayment on our inheritance (cf. II Cor. 1:22; 5:5) we long and hope for—rather than see and own—our salvation (Rom. 8:24). So weak are we that we do not even know how to pray, but the Spirit intercedes for us by inarticulate groans—perhaps a reference to glossolalia as a sign of our weakness rather than a sign of spiritual accomplishment (8:26–27).

This weakness motif—what Luther identified as the Theology of the Cross over against theologies of glory—is one of the most striking features of Paul's thought. He can make use of it in many ways, but we are in the happy position that his writings allow us to trace its roots to traumatic and hard experiences in his apostolic ministry. The clearest picture is in II Corinthians 12.

Traditional interpretation of Paul identifies Paul's speaking of weakness with the idea of being a sinner. Not so Paul himself. At no point does Paul feel guilty for his weakness. Only once, in a general theological context, does he see an analogy between sin and weakness (Rom. 5:6, 8). The analogy to his weakness is rather in the Christ "crucified in weakness" (II Cor. 13:4). Weakness has to do with the way God acts—and hence the style of ministry.

Second Corinthians may well be a document composed from different pieces of Paul's correspondence with Corinth over the years. In any case, there are distinct sections with different themes and distinct tones. Chapter 1:1–2:13 and 7:5–16 may be from a conciliatory letter (cf. 2:5–11 with I Cor. 5). Chapter 2:14–7:4 is a defense for Paul's type and style of ministry. Chapters 8 and 9 are about the big collection for Jerusalem (cf. Rom. 15:25–33). And chs. 10–13 have been called the Letter of Tears, perhaps referred to in 2:4.

Here Paul is locked in a verbal battle with competing missionaries who claim much authority and spectacular results. Nowhere else is Paul as scathing (11:13–15), and his weapon is irony (e.g., 10:1, 12; 11:1, 7; 11:19–21; 12:13). These "superlative apostles" (11:5; 12:11) have made an inroad in Corinth and they or the Corinthians describe

Paul as writing strong letters but "his bodily presence is weak" (10:9, 10; cf. 10:1).

It seems that the superlative apostles impressed people with their credentials, their letters of recommendation (cf. 3:2). Paul counters with a list of hardships—and rounds it off with the laughable picture of being lowered in a rope basket and fleeing (11:33). It seems the superlative apostles referred to their visions and revelations. Paul counters with describing his own—but with studied notes of uncertainty and stress on what he does not know, only God knows (12:1–4). Thereby he minimizes his right to be proud of the experience, although he could (vs. 5–6).

The main point comes in what follows. The tough lesson that Paul has slowly learned has to do with his health. God has sent an angel of Satan (cf. "Satan hindered us," I Thess. 2:18), a sharp thorn in the flesh. He is a handicapped apostle. That was hard for him who wanted to be fully fit for travel and work. After all, he was *the* apostle to the Gentiles, and one could expect Christ to keep him healthy. Three times he had gone on retreat, perhaps on a prayer fast in the wilderness, beseeching the Lord to do just that. Now he had come to understand that God could use him better when the power of Christ was shining through his weakness.

We know about how Paul's illness interfered with his travels. Actually the mission to the Galatians was a fruit thereof, and he praises them for not having taken offense at his weakness (Gal. 4:13–15). A sick apostle was not a good recommendation for the healing power of the gospel—perhaps the superlative apostles had made that point. Paul himself can use the argument of sickness and death against people (I Cor. 11:30).

In II Cor. 4:1—again after speaking of wonderful revelatory experience—Paul says: "But this treasure we have in clay pots in order that the abundance of power be God's and not as of ourselves." He carries around in his body that very dying which also was Jesus' burden (4:10).

This traumatic experience of Paul's is the root of his understanding of weakness. We do not know what his physical problem was. Epilepsy is as good a guess as any, if we want to picture it without knowing for sure.

And the analogies in our situations? We had best begin with the contrasts between what we tend to hear and what Paul says. For him the weaknesses came from without, were laid upon him. Hence this passage is not on the sin-guilt axis of the human condition. It is, rather, a deep insight into the conditions and the style of ministry and the conditions of the church in this world. Paul sees the superlative apostles as "secularizing" the gospel and the church (II Cor. 11:18; cf. 10:2–3, where RSV rightly translates *kata sarka* with "worldly"). The same point in a somewhat different context is made in I Cor. 3:1.

A somewhat vulgar and overly catchy title for a sermon on II Corinthians 12 would be: "One Does Not Sell Jesus as One Sells Toothpaste." Here is yet another mystery in God's way of working, in the *missio Dei,* mentioned earlier. That mystery is God's fear of triumphalism, of selling the gospel as a success story. Billy Graham, chastened by "the Jerries come lately" of the electronic church, put it well: It is hard for media evangelism not to fall into triumphalism.

Paul was horrified by the developments in Corinth. The obvious success of his impressive opponents saddened him. He saw their achievements as the secularization of the faith. As we may perceive it, when churches fall for Madison Avenue techniques, then they have become secularized, however "biblical" their message may be.

Such analogues to Paul's argument with his opponents in Corinth capture the thrust of II Corinthians 10–13 in its specificity. But such specificity implies limitations. I believe Paul's insights are true and important, and they call for sermons as specific as Paul's letter, sermons that withstand the temptation to generalize, or broaden the theme into all the kinds of things we come to think about when we hear the word "weakness."

Yet one warning is in order. Paul addresses a congregation tempted to measure the church's ministry by success in numbers and acclaim. And he was no mean achiever in his own missionary work. He is fighting with his own temptations, his sense of importance and even arrogance—which were considerable.

But many of us are too timid to ever be so tempted. Our problem is not triumphalism. Our timidity does not deserve to be dignified by the word "weakness" as Paul uses it. His words are not an excuse for self-made humility. True humility comes from trying hard and being slapped down. It comes from without, it cannot be produced from within. So also the weakness that Paul learned about requires a burning zeal for the Lord and the kingdom.

I CORINTHIANS 13. LOVE ALLOWS TENSION AND CONFLICT

Not only a classical but a most beloved Pauline text, often used at weddings. It is so used, since it speaks about love. Actually there are many features in this chapter that do not fit very well in the context of weddings, unless one give a different meaning to "speaking with tongues." And what about "prophecy," and "gnosis/knowledge" (13:2, 8)?

The key to the Pauline Ode to Love is perhaps in I Cor. 8:1: "Gnosis/knowledge puffs up, but love builds up." I Corinthians is about the tension between various factions and fractions in the congregation, and on the whole it is Paul's most irenic and "ecumenical" letter. He tries his utmost to find ways by which the tensions between various teachers and life-styles—all apparently Gentile Christian—can coexist. For the church is a garden, and a body—not a fight between various schools of thought, as is that of the philosophers (I Cor. 3). He is even willing to await God's final judgment as to what is good teaching and what is bad teaching, and also the bad teachers will be saved (vs. 12–15). Perhaps he is opting for "pluralism" in order to be allowed to stay in the picture—he pleads with the Corinthians not to settle these matters: "Do not judge prematurely, before the Lord comes" (4:5). In the advice he gives he is anxious not to claim more authority than he has; he distinguishes carefully between cases where he has a commandment from the Lord (7:10–11) and where he gives advice on his own (7:6, 12, 25), even if he thinks that he also—and not only others—has the Spirit of God (7:40).

Here is a fascinating image of a Paul of strong conviction who is sure he is right (4:4), nevertheless willing, or forced, to accept the pluralism of the Corinthian church. He is still hoping—II Corinthians 10–13 sounds sadly different.

One special issue in Corinth is that of "charismata," those spectacular gifts of healing, of glossolalia, of secret knowledge which apparently the Corinthians thought of and sought as signs of true spirituality—perhaps the kind of gifts in which the superlative apostles in II Corinthians 10–13 excelled. Paul is not against it—as a matter of fact, he claims to be more into glossolalia than anyone (I Cor. 14:18; cf. Rom. 8:26). But his overarching criterion is "what builds up the church" (14:3, 4, 5, 12, 17, 26). As he said about matters concerning meat that originated in the temples: All may be permissible—but not everything builds up (10:23).

In I Corinthians 12, Paul argues that all gifts—spectacular and less spectacular—are gifts of the Spirit, and they are all needed (even administration, 12:28). Different gifts are given to different members—for the building up of the whole body.

Then comes the Ode to Love, by which Paul wants to "show the superior way" (12:31). It is worth noting that there is no reference to God's or Christ's love, not even implicitly. Love is thought of as a style of action along with, and above faith and hope (13:13). Why above?

Because of its capacity to accept diversity and handle tension. And without that kind of love even the great gifts of the Spirit—glossolalia, revelatory knowledge, prophecy, the perseverance in martyrdom—become divisive instead of upbuilding. Hence, compared with love the other gifts and qualities prove to be partial and preliminary (13:8–12).

Colossians has a striking formulation, similar to Paul's thought. After a list of virtues it says: "Over all those [virtues, put on] love, which is the bond that holds it all together perfectly" (3:14). Without that bond, that belt, one trips on the flowing robe of virtues.

Here we hardly need to seek analogues. They are so shockingly close at hand. A marvelous opportunity to free much of our love language from romantic and emotional overgrowth. For it is clear that when Paul sees love as the way to handle tension, he does not intimate that love "feels good." It is not measured in degrees of warmth. Rather, it is measured by how much tension and diversity it can take. It is measured by its elasticity, its capacity "not to insist on its own way"—as does knowledge, and other things when they become touchstones of true spirituality. Love is different. That is why love builds up. That is why it is the one thing without which none of the others will last.

But the church has often missed that point. Christians know that they are supposed to have love. And by that they mean "having warm feelings for and relations to others." Therefore it is considered shameful or improper to have tensions or conflicts in the church. And the easiest way to avoid such is to gather like-minded, like-looking, likable people. Then we feel loving.

Paul's point is the opposite. The gift of love makes diversity, tension, even conflict possible, without rupturing the church. For "love does not insist on its own way."

In a way, Paul's Ode to Love is part of his theology of weakness. For in Corinth he was not in command. He has to plead for love so that they allow him to remain in the picture as one among others. As it is in this world: We understand love when we need it, not when we dispense it out of our safe superiority.

Once we see Paul's Ode to Love in its specific context, and understand it as a prescription for the building up of the church in its fullness, there is hope for new vitality in the body of Christ. Then the church can become the space in which we can experiment with new ways of thought and action about which Christians can and must disagree. Then the world will say: Look at those Christians; what a capacity they have for sticking together although they are so different in ideology, cultural values, tradition, piety, theology. And we shall answer with Paul: It is quite a strain, but that is our holy experiment. If you think of faith as knowledge, it puffs up—but love can take it— and so it builds us up into a fuller richness.

A reader of this chapter on Pauline preaching may by now be puzzled by the fact that it all seems to be about the church, its mission, its problem, opportunities, weakness, and glories. So little is about "religious" questions, for we usually think of them in individual terms. That is not my fault, not even by arbitrary selectivity. For that is what Paul wrote about. After all, that was his job as an apostle. His letters are letters to churches, not theological tractates or spiritual meditations.

It is exactly as letters to churches that his writings exude theological and spiritual power. They do so best when we hear them in their congregational setting and when they speak to the churches of our times. For Paul saw his mission as a builder of communities. Toward that end he wrote. In that spirit he is best heard.

FOR FURTHER READING

An excellent source for working with Pauline material is Wayne A. Meeks (ed.), *The Writings of St. Paul* (W. W. Norton & Co., 1972). Here we have in one paperback volume the essential texts for the whole development from the ancient church to the present as to the understanding of Paul's writings.

For questions of introduction to Pauline writings, the data are available in the standard Introductions. The most extensive, also reporting on a wide spectrum of views, is Paul Feine and Johannes Behm, *Introduction to the New Testament*, reedited by Werner Georg Kümmel, tr. by A. J. Mattill, Jr., 14th ed. (Abingdon Press, 1966). Helmut Koester, *Introduction to the New Testament* (Fortress Press, 1982), is a major and stimulating work which gives a good sense of how Paul fits into the full history of early Christianity. It gives data and perspectives which feed well into the approach I have used in this chapter.

For studying the various letters a commentary is indispensable. Of the one-volume commentaries on the whole Bible, I prefer *The Jerome Biblical Commentary*, edited by Raymond E. Brown et al. (Prentice-Hall, 1969), although its judgment tends toward a minimizing of biblical and Pauline variety. Coupled with Koester's Introduction it serves well. For some of the epistles I find some commentaries especially useful. For the rest, the introductions and "Jerome" give ample choice. Here are a few for special mention:

Romans. Two recent commentaries are outstanding: Ernst Käsemann, *Commentary on Romans,* tr. by G. W. Bromiley (Wm. B. Eerdmans Publishing Co., 1980), and C. E. B. Cranfield, *A Critical and Exegetical Commentary on the Epistle to the Romans,* 6th rev. ed., International Critical Commentary (Edinburgh: T. & T. Clark; Vol. 1, 1975; Vol. 2, 1979). While Cranfield carefully spells out all possible alternatives of meaning, Käsemann has more of an overview and drive in his passionate presentation of his image of Paul.

I Corinthians. The outstanding work is Hans Conzelmann's *Commentary* in the Hermeneia series (Fortress Press, 1975). This series also offers a significant commentary on *Galatians* by Hans Dieter Betz (1979).

It is obvious that I have depended on my *Paul Among Jews and Gentiles and Other Essays* (Fortress Press, 1976). Among the general books on Paul, the one by Günther Bornkamm, *Paul* (Harper & Row, 1971), is a dependable classic. The recent work by J. Christiaan Beker, *Paul the Apostle: The Triumph of God in Life and Thought* (Fortress Press, 1980), is a challenging interpretation of Paul, rooted in contemporary scholarly discussion and bringing a distinctly Calvinist perspective to a field often dominated by Lutheran perceptions.

19. PREACHING FROM HEBREWS AND THE GENERAL EPISTLES

JAMES EARL MASSEY

THE EPISTLE TO THE HEBREWS

HISTORICAL AND THEOLOGICAL MATTERS

The Epistle to the Hebrews is one of the most carefully written books in the New Testament. The author was well informed and articulate about the Jewish Scriptures and the message about Jesus Christ.

The writer's extended use of the high priesthood theme would suggest that his readers had a Jewish background, and his appeal to the Old Testament practices and promises supports that judgment. But beyond these considerations nothing more can be affirmed with any certainty about who the first readers of this epistle were.

Nor has the question of who wrote it been settled. From an early period many names have been associated with this epistle: Paul, Apollos, Barnabas, Luke, Silas, Priscilla, Aquila, Philip, Timothy, Clement of Rome, and still others. Origen (A.D. 184–254) considered its teachings Pauline, yet commented, "But who wrote the epistle, in truth God [alone] knows."[1] This writing does lack the apostle's usual identifying mark (see II Thess. 3:17; I Cor. 16:21), but the Eastern church circulated it and canonized it largely because it was associated by tradition with the name of Paul.[2]

Clement of Rome knew The Epistle to the Hebrews and quoted from it many times in his Letter from the Romans to the Corinthians (ca. A.D. 96). This epistle should be dated in the 60s, perhaps as early as A.D. 64.

The writer addressed a distressed and discouraged people (4:14–16; 10:32–36; 12:1–3) who were feeling the strain of tensions fomented by the Neronian order. No deaths had been experienced yet (12:4), however, but the writer sought to stir hope for the best while helping the people get ready for the worst. He used the Old Testament writings, characters, and economy to illustrate the importance of faith and patience to face and handle their circumstances. In many graphic statements the writer explained that "the Old Testament religion was provisional, prophetic, symbolic, premonitory, pointing beyond itself"[3] to what was not available to all in the person and ministry of Jesus Christ.

Thus we have The Epistle to the Hebrews, a confessional writing sent to strengthen faith, inform the will, and renew the hope of impatient, questioning believers who needed to be "looking to Jesus the pioneer and perfecter of our faith, who . . . endured the cross, despising the shame, and is seated at the right hand of the throne of God" (12:2).

The writer knew that his argument carried force and relevance because it gives a statement that faith and experience can verify as the truth. The Epistle to the Hebrews is a needed word for questioning pilgrims caught in the disciplines of history.

HOMILETICAL USES OF THE EPISTLE TO THE HEBREWS

The writer himself classified this epistle as a "statement of exhortation" (13:22, *logos paraklēseōs*), and one can see in it many fundamental traits of a practical sermon. The rhetorical patterns in it reflect considerable experience with gathered assemblies. Some sections are so polished and pointed that they might have been used earlier on preaching occasions, especially 3:1–4:13 and ch. 11 with its many biographical miniatures.

Preachers and readers alike will find this epistle difficult because of its ancient images and involved line of argument. Many texts from Hebrews are often used without any reference to the epistle's background and purpose. But now and again exceptions are located.

The argument and biographical miniatures in Hebrews 11 have been given considerable treatment in pulpit work.

George Arthur Buttrick (1892–1980) used Heb. 11:13 for his sermon on "Frustration and Faith."[4] He applauded the "stark realism of the Bible," pleased that it gives us "no glossing of disappointed hopes, no easy fiction of the happy ending," the writer of the text being "obliged by facts to admit . . . that the promises and hopes of our mortal days are not fulfilled." That preacher underscored the need to see life through the eyes of faith and cleave to that faith while working through the frustrations that life presents. Arthur Leonard Griffith also used Heb. 11:13 for his sermon on "The Pilgrim View of Life."[5]

Arthur John Gossip (1873–1954) used Heb. 11:33–34 in a story-filled, invitational, and evangelical sermon about "The Romance of Religion."[6] Lamenting that for all too many, "religion has lost its romance, has dwindled to a very tame affair," Gossip described true religion and called every hearer to experience it with daring, deeper interest, and the spirit of eager excitement. This was his claim: "There is no life that can make so big a call upon stout-heartedness and courage as that to which Christ leads."

The pulpit use of The Epistle to the Hebrews ought to highlight the meaning of Jesus as the determinative person under God for the salvation and maturity of all who believe on him.

The epistle sets forth five elemental truths about the life and ministry of Jesus: (1) His humanity relates him fully to all humans; (2) his exemplary Sonship is a model and means of hope for all; (3) his life and death are our access to God; (4) he now holds a continuing priesthood; and (5) his present ministry as ascended Savior grants a ready and necessary help to all who call upon him.

Harry Emerson Fosdick (1878–1969) once preached a now-classic Christmas sermon entitled "Christ Himself Is Christianity," based on Heb. 2:8f.[7] The sermon had four points:

1. The coming of Jesus was prophetic.
2. The coming of Jesus was historically influential.
3. The coming of Jesus was personally moving.
4. The coming of Jesus is reassuring fact.

That sermon was a strategic message at a time of postwar disillusionment in America and across the Western world. The preacher knew that Hebrews 2 speaks quite pointedly to those who are confused and fretful about what they see and experience in the world as it is.

Arthur J. Gossip dealt with the same problem and text in his sermon "On the Clue to Life's Enigmas."[8] Calling attention to the context, Gossip began with these words:

> Life was not easy to this writer; and, even with his gloriously valiant faith to help him, he never pretended that it was.

He continued, "There are mysteries that haunt, and enigmas that confuse and shake the soul, and dark, tremendous facts that must be faced and taken into account in our reading of things." There are still persons who are bothered by their "reading of things," and ch. 2 is an excellently worded passage from which to help those who are beset by dark and gray days.

Hebrews is unique among the New Testament writings in describing Jesus as one who also lived by faith: "I will put my trust in [God]" (2:13a). He was "tempted as we are, yet without sinning" (4:15). He offered up "prayers and supplications, with loud cries and tears, to him who was able to save him from death, and he was heard for his godly fear" (5:7). Jesus was tested by life, the writer reminds us, and he handled himself obediently to the glory of God—living by faith while "he learned obedience through what he suffered" (v. 8). Thus this grand declaration: "Being made perfect he became the source of eternal salvation to all who obey him" (v. 9). And this one: "For we have not a high priest who is unable to sympathize with our weaknesses, but one who in every respect has been tempted as we are, yet without sin. Let us then with confidence draw near to the throne of grace, that we may receive mercy and find grace to help in time of need" (4:15–16).

Frederick William Robertson (1816–1853) treated this text and theme in his sermon about "The Sympathy of Christ."[9] The treatment was doctrinal, devotional, pastoral, and was marked by two divisions:

I. The Redeemer's preparation for his priesthood
II. The Redeemer's priestly qualifications
   a. Mercifulness, based on his sympathies
   b. Helpfulness, based on his power to grant us aid

John A. Broadus (1827–1895) sensed the need to help hearers understand the present ministry of the exalted Christ, and he used Heb. 7:25 in a sermon that declared: "He ever liveth to intercede."[10]

Broadus acknowledged, "Perhaps we are accustomed to look too exclusively to the Saviour's atoning death, not dwelling as we should upon the idea of his interceding life." The sermon explained what the believer can expect and experience because the ministry of Jesus continues in his exalted role as intercessor:

1. We have his help to conquer temptation.
2. We have an advocate if we should sin.
3. We have help to attain holiness.
4. We have comfort when in sorrow.
5. We have hope when we die.
6. We have the pledge of a new body like his.

Sermons based on texts from Hebrews should honor the central fact of Jesus' passion and death—how it all happened (12:3), how he handled it (2:9–10; 5:7–8; 12:2–3), and what it effects for us (2:15,

17–18; 3:14; 4:14–16; 5:9; 7:25; 9:26b–28; 10:10, 19–22; 13:12, 20–21).

W. E. Sangster (1900–1960) grappled successfully with Heb. 13:12–13 in his sermon "Bearing His Reproach" (13:13).[11] He advised three things for believers who are abused or ostracized because of their faith and witness.

    I. We must accept the reproach of the gospel
       a. When ostracized socially
       b. When we lose out on professional advancement because of our faith
       c. When we are made the butt of jokes
   II. We must not increase the reproach unnecessarily
       a. By any eccentricities on our part
       b. By being censorious
       c. By breaking fellowship when we shouldn't
  III. We must show an eager willingness to suffer for Christ when we are made to suffer.

All in all, it was a bracing statement about the cost of discipleship—and the blessedness of "thrusting one's shoulder underneath his cross," sharing his lot *and life.*

The picture of Jesus in The Epistle to the Hebrews is one of a Savior fully identified with us by a common humanity and by raw experience. The writer insisted that Jesus must be understood both as religious subject and as religious object, as one who *shows* us faith and *sustains* us in faith. This epistle gives statements, scenes, declarations, and affirmations about Jesus as tested brother, knowing sharer, concerned Savior, and exalted advocate. He is a figure of hope, the "forerunner" *(prodromos)* who has gone ahead in the interest of those still behind. We are still behind, and this epistle can be used to strengthen faith and obedience for going "on to maturity" (6:1).

THE GENERAL EPISTLES
SOME PRELIMINARY OBSERVATIONS

Eusebius of Caesarea (ca. A.D. 260–340) referred in his *Ecclesiastical History* to seven "Epistles called Catholic." The book of James headed his list, and Jude was named as one of the seven.[12] The classification "Catholic" *(katholikos)* Epistles called attention to their lack of address or reference to named congregations. Unlike the Pauline epistles which mention specific audiences and vividly reflect that writer's personality and relation to the addressees, the seven "Catholic Epistles" are more general, and questions about their authorship, date, and exact recipients have never been completely settled in the church. As James Moffatt explained, these letters "are found to be in use throughout the later church in certain quarters; echoes of them in later writers help to prove their period within certain limits, and internal evidence determines their relative order now and then. But beyond this we can seldom go with very much security."[13]

The General Epistles (James, I and II Peter, I, II, and III John, and Jude) have always had a rather minor place in the regard of the church. Donald Guthrie has commented that "with the exception of I Peter and I John the Catholic Epistles have played only a minor part in moulding the thought of the Christian Church and have been largely overshadowed by their more illustrious companion Epistles in the New Testament, notably by the Epistles of Paul. If this is true in the modern Church, it will be no great surprise to find that a similar phenomenon occurred in the ancient Church."[14]

The seven General Epistles gained a comparatively late acceptance across the church (East and West). Since the time of Athanasius (ca. A.D. 297–373), bishop of Alexandria, who first used the word "canon" in connection with the books of the Old and New Testaments, the seven General Epistles have been generally regarded across the church as bearing apostolic authority although the question of apostolic authorship for some of them was never securely settled.

Across the long history of the Christian preaching tradition, the epistles of James, I Peter, and I John have been the most used of the seven. The reasons are rather obvious: The need to know and understand personal faith in its social dimensions (James) is perennial in church life; the need to encourage believers to be steadfast under stress and strain (I Peter) is expected in proper pulpit work; and the colorful affirmations provided in I John about God, Jesus Christ, and the meaning of the Christian life lend themselves readily to the fertile concern of the preacher who reads them with both mind and heart.

It is at those points of church need that the appeal of these three epistles has been sensed and their messages applied. A recent examination of some of the sermons in *Twenty Centuries of Great Preaching*, the most recent and inclusive encyclopedia of preaching now available, showed this.[15] The multivolume set contains 406 sermons representing the pulpit work of 96 pulpit masters who spoke effectively to the issues and needs of their day. Of the 406 sermons, 21 are based on texts from the General Epistles, with 9 texts used from I John, 5 from I Peter, and 2 from James; the other four epistles were used with less frequency (2 texts from II Peter, and 1 text from each of the three books: II John, III John, and Jude). The direction the preachers took in using these texts can be examined by studying the sermons listed below.

Epistle	Text	Preacher and Sermon	Volume and Page Numbers
James	1:2–11	R. W. Dale (1829–1895) "The Gospel of Suffering"	V:188–194
	1:27	Thomas Guthrie (1803–1873) "True Religion"	IV:117–127
I Peter	1:2	G. Campbell Morgan (1863–1945) "Sanctification"	VIII:19–27
	2:9–10	William Temple (1881–1944) "God's Call to the Church"	IX:192–196
	3:4	George A. Buttrick (1892–1980) "The Hidden Man of the Heart"	X:287–291
	4:7–11	Martin Luther (1483–1546) "Soberness and Moderation"	II:12–18
	5:5–11	"Third Sunday After Trinity"	II:19–46
II Peter	3:18	Alexander Maclaren (1826–1910) "Growth"	V:25–32
	3:18	Ralph W. Sockman (1889–1970) "The Tragedy of Not Growing Up"	X:206–209
I John	2:14	Henry Ward Beecher (1813–1887) "A Sermon to Young Men"	IV:304–316
	2:15	Thomas Chalmers (1780–1847) "The Expulsive Power of a New Affection"	III:300–314
	3:13–18	Martin Niemöller (1892–) "Brotherly Love Versus Hatred of the World"	X:233–237
	4:7	Lyman Beecher (1775–1863) "The Native Character of Man"	III:226–237
	4:7	Paul Tillich (1886–1965) "The Truth Will Make You Free"	X:68–74

Epistle	Text	Preacher and Sermon	Volume and Page Numbers
	4:7–8	Rufus M. Jones (1863–1948) "The Two Loves—Agape and Eros"	VII:311–314
	4:8	Theodore Parker (1810–1860) "War" (text combd. w/Ex.15:3)	IV:210–223
	4:8, 16	Paul Scherer (1892–1969) "The Love That God Defines"	X:307–314
	4:20	Samuel Shoemaker (1893–1963) "Another Approach to Conversion"	X:77–81
II John	v. 3	Alexander Maclaren (1826–1910) "Grace, Mercy, and Peace"	V:21–25
III John	v. 2	George Whitefield (1714–1770) "Soul Prosperity"	III:159–168
Jude	v. 24	Robert Murray McCheyne (1813–1843) "Address at the Close of Day"	IV:288–290

The General Epistles offer some of the most striking terms in the language of faith, and some of the most graphic instructions to believers caught in threatening contingencies. These epistles are strategic tracts for our need and use: James, with its call for commitment to a life of responsible faith and strong social impact; I Peter, with its strengthening witness to those being "tried with fire" (1:7); II Peter, with its reassuring message about the shape of things to come— a prophetic reminder that rebukes rank secularism; I, II, and III John, with their tone of intimacy and clear call for careful living; and Jude, with its bracing reminder that "the faith which was once for all delivered to the saints" (v. 3) still has falsifiers and foes who must be confronted and challenged by the faithful. The General Epistles speak readily and strategically to our time and needs.

I. THE EPISTLE OF JAMES

HISTORICAL AND THEOLOGICAL MATTERS

The book of James opens with the words "James, a servant of God and of the Lord Jesus Christ" (1:1). No further description is offered and no additional claim is made, as if the writer was well known and possessed understood authority. The weight of church tradition has been crucial in linking this letter with James the brother of Jesus. Perhaps this explains the absence of additional personal claims on the author's part as he wrote.

The leadership position James held in the Jerusalem church could account for his authoritative manner in writing. Converted after the resurrection of Jesus (I Cor. 15:7 tells us that James experienced a Christophany), James rose to a high post of responsibility, as the book of Acts shows (12:17; 15:13–21). Galatians 2:9 mentions James, Peter, and John as "pillar" leaders *(stuloi)*. This James died in A.D. 62, the victim of a conspiracy by members of the Sanhedrin.[16] The known date of his death suggests that this letter (or substantial sections of it) came rather early. Some scholars consider an early date unlikely for this letter because some statements in it suggest an attempt by the writer to correct an apparent misuse by some persons of Paul's emphasis on faith, with a presumed reference to his letters.

The writer was a teacher (James 3:1) steeped in Old Testament thought, Wisdom expressions, and the teaching tradition from Jesus. Many quotations and allusions in James are related to the tradition of the teachings of Jesus as found in the Sermon on the Mount.[17]

The writer of the book of James called for full adherence to the Christian faith and life. He promoted a thoroughgoing commitment: thus his emphasis on being "doers of the word, and not hearers only" (1:22) and on "religion that is pure and undefiled before God" (1:27).

The book of James is largely filled with admonitions about how to live by the rules. It treats a rather disconnected series of topics that pastors can use in training and guiding their people. These topics include temptation *(peirasmos,* 1:2, 12; *peirazō,* 1:13, 14); a working faith *(pistis,* 1:3, 6; 2:1, 5, 14, 17, 18, 20, 22, 24, 26; 5:15; *pisteuō,* 2:19, 23); wisdom *(sophia,* 1:5; 3:13, 15, 17; *sophos,* 3:13); patience *(makrothumeō,* 5:7, 8; *makrothumia,* 5:10); and prayer *(proseuchomai,* 5:13, 14, 15, 16, 17, 18; *euchē,* 5:15; *deēsis,* 5:16). The rest of the book is filled with Wisdom-like aphoristic statements and admonitions. The many admonitions are forcefully given as imperatives, but the epistle is really a blend of stirring reminders and pastoral encouragement.

HOMILETICAL USES OF THE EPISTLE OF JAMES

Given the paraenetic character of James, with its three brief homilies (2:1–13; 2:14–26; 3:1–12) and grouped sayings on the mentioned themes, this epistle is best treated by attention to distinct sections and single sayings in it.

Dwight E. Stevenson has offered advice on how to convey even the rather scattered message of the book of James in a single sermon.[18] From his study of it, Stevenson sensed that the epistle stresses wholehearted religious living, and using five key verse-sections (1:6b–8, Phillips; 1:22; 2:17; 2:18; 2:8), he developed an outline and title about "The Undivided Life."

Eric W. Hayden, one-time minister of Spurgeon's Tabernacle, London, also dealt with the entire book of James in a single sermon.[19] Using 1:27 as his key text, Hayden titled his sermon "A Description of True Religion." This was his outline:

    I.   Practical love
       a. To see
       b. To sympathize
       c. To succor
   II.   Pure living
       a. Separatedness
       b. Self-watchfulness
       c. Spotlessness

Hayden's treatment, however, was more a textual treatment of his key verse than a book sermon like Stevenson's.

But lacking as it does a strong unifying theme, the book of James is not best treated in a single sermon. More wisdom is shown in seeking to treat its message through single sections or sayings, and, if one is ambitious, in an expository series.

W. A. Criswell did this in seventeen *Expository Sermons on the Epistle of James.* Criswell sometimes needed two sermons to treat a text, as when, using 1:27, he preached about "Real Religion" and "Personal Religion"; when treating 3:1–12, he preached about "The Untamed Tongue" and "Our Words."[20]

One of the ablest contemporary expositions of the book of James was preached on radio by David A. Hubbard, who subtitled his sermon series "Wisdom That Works," and he used the word "wisdom" in the title of all thirteen sermons.[21] He covered the entire book of James, with six to ten verses used as the basis for each message. Hubbard's historical references, skillful outlining, pungent pointing, and contemporary application all mark his sermon series on James as truly outstanding pulpit work.

As for single sections and texts, the trial/temptation (1:2–4, 12–16) passage merits careful study and sensitive use. Every hearer knows the sense of threat while being in trial or under temptation. The preacher can use these verses to share wisdom on how to stand up to life's tests, but more particularly, how to *understand* the awesome feeling of exposed individuality when one experiences some sensed need, personal desire, or some pleasing possibility. The textual passage tells us that failure is not determined by what happens outside us but by what happens within.

As David A. Hubbard's attentive sermon on the temptation theme advised: "Face reality, James was saying—the reality that temptation is *our* responsibility."[22]

Another strategic section in the book of James addresses attitudes toward wealth: the poor are advised against seeking it as an ultimate good (1:9) and the rich against hoarding it as an everlasting boon (vs. 10–11). Some other passages rebuke partiality and privileged treatment because of possessions (2:1–13; 5:1–6).

This word about divisive distinctions between social classes needs to be sounded by the preacher, and believers need to be reminded about the social meanings of religious experience. Class lines should not affect the way members of congregations relate, neither during the times of gathered fellowship nor after the worship services; rich believers should not take (nor be given) authoritative pride of place over the poor. James rebuked such selfishness and unwarranted distinctions. The rich-poor problem is treated at several places (1:9, 10, 11c; 2:1–7, 8–9, 14–17; 5:1–6). Some of these passages in James give a rather radical criticism of wealth and affluence, largely because arrogance seems to follow pride in possessions, and social privilege is often expected because of economic advantage. Wealth can lead one astray, seducing by a false sense of self-importance. The crucial word from James is that Christian faith demands a heart, and that love is proved by its unselfish deeds. A common faith and an open fellowship go together, and true love always seeks to reduce the problems and ills that people suffer.

The section about healing for the sick believer (5:14–16) should also be treated. The passage is very similar to Ecclus. 38:9–15, which links prayer and healing with confession of sin and trust in the one (doctor) who can assist recovery. In the New English Bible rendering, the passage reads: "My son, if you have an illness, do not neglect it, but pray to the Lord, and he will heal you. Renounce your faults, amend your ways, and cleanse your heart from all sin" (38:9–10). The next verse (v. 11) mentions the use of oil, as does James 5:14. And vs. 12–14 advise:

> Then call in the doctor, for the Lord created him;
> do not let him leave you, for you need him.
> There may come a time when your recovery is in their hands;
> then they too will pray to the Lord
> to give them success in relieving pain
> and finding a cure to save their patient's life.

The kinship between the two passages is hardly coincidental. James explained that "elders of the church" are agents of help toward forgiveness and healing. There are times when sin has occasioned sickness, and when prayer and confession aid healing. The pouring of oil on the believer is perhaps a dedicatory action, presenting the sick one to God (as a "living sacrifice"?). Given the kinship between the two passages, James might well have been using or reflecting that section of Ecclesiasticus.

The book of James bids preacher and people to address the great issues of daily life, and to do so in faithful action. Harold S. Songer has aptly written:

> James is concerned with war, the oppression of the poor, unwise conduct, disorders in worship, prejudice in Christian congregations, the authenticity and honesty of Christian conversation, the awareness that our lives are in the hands of God and that our plans should be made accordingly, and the power of prayer. James addresses these issues generally and seems at times to be taking a rather simplistic approach to complex problems. This is not a mark against his intellectual acumen. He is seeking to pose major issues in such a way as to inspire the Christian to respond creatively in terms of relevant action.[23]

The Epistle of James is not thin or deficient; it is a call to action after hearing (1:22–25). It is a clear statement to believers about social regard and social demand in the Christian life.

II. THE EPISTLES OF PETER

HISTORICAL AND THEOLOGICAL MATTERS

I Peter was accepted in the first century as from the noted "Peter, an apostle of Jesus Christ" (1:1a). The writing is addressed "To the exiles of the Dispersion in Pontus, Galatia, Cappadocia, Asia, and Bithynia" (1:1b), which some scholars view as Hebrew Christians living there and others view as Christians in the world at large. The Muratorian Canon does not mention I Peter but its use by Papias (ca. A.D. 60–ca. 130)[24] and Polycarp's (d. A.D. 155) quotes from it in his

Letter to the Philadelphians show its appearance and acceptance at an early period.[25] The theme of suffering suggests that the readers were in distress, and the writer's call to patient endurance suggests that the stress might be prolonged. The writer appealed to his readers' faith, underscored their privileges as the people of God (1:2, 3–12; 2:9–10), encouraged their hope and best behavior (1:13–22; 2:1–3, 11–20; 3:1–16), reminded them of the redemptive ministry of Jesus Christ (2:4–8, 21–25; 3:18–20), the depth meaning of their baptism (3:21–22), and challenged them to remain watchful (ch. 4). In 5:1–11 he gave some instructions to the church leaders and added some final paraenetic statements. In v. 12 Silvanus is mentioned as the secretary, which explains the rather good Greek style of the writing. The writing was done "at Babylon" (v. 13), an expression that was Peter's code name for Rome, where he lived during his last years; Mark was also there with him (v. 13). The writing should be dated perhaps A.D. 62–63, before Peter was put to death at Rome.

I Peter has a distinctly sermonic cast. The emphasis upon Christian experience as a changed life is accented strongly, and the word is given to *show* that difference and to *witness* courageously about it (3:15b).

II Peter also bears a personal salutation, "Simon Peter, a servant and apostle of Jesus Christ" (1:1), plus some autobiographical details in vs. 12–15, 16–18. The first recipients are not stated or known, but some tie between writer and readers is assumed from the warm personal tone throughout, and the writer's reference in 3:1 to a previous letter he had sent them. The eyewitness remarks give strength to the autobiographical references, and the mention in v. 15 of "our beloved brother Paul" suggests his acquaintance with that apostle. Tradition reports that Peter and Paul were in Rome together and that they died there.

The true authorship of II Peter was questioned at an early period partly because it quotes so much from Jude (compare Jude 4–16 and II Peter 2:1–18), and it differs in style from I Peter. Perhaps Peter chose to use the rather graphic language of Jude because it better expressed his point, and it is possible that he used a different secretary when preparing this epistle.

I and II Peter differ in thematic focus. In I Peter the writer appeals for a steadfast faith, an undaunted love, and a contagious witness that would help the growing church offset mounting criticism in a pluralistic and a sometimes hostile environment. The appeal in II Peter is for a renewed faith in God's promises, the sure return of Christ, and the grand future awaiting the true believer (ch. 3).

HOMILETICAL USES OF I AND II PETER

The message in I Peter speaks well to believers who are troubled about why God allows the cruel treatment to which Christians are sometimes subjected in life—especially when doing God's will in the world. The theme of tested faith is always current for use because someone needs an encouraging word by which to *stand* and *understand.*

Paul Scherer (1892–1969) put this epistle to great use while preaching during the crucial years of the Second World War. Speaking to his parishioners and to a radio audience as well, Scherer sought to help them handle the great strain that was upon all. Using I Peter 2:20–21 for the sermon "Do You Find Things Hard?" Scherer used a two-point outline:[26]

    I. We are not here to be "happy" merely.
        a. We should not resent our lot.
        b. We should not try to renounce life.
        c. We should not try merely to endure our lot.
        d. We should regard our lot and face it.
    II. We are called to make something out of our ugly situations.
        a. Jesus did this on Calvary.
        b. Difficulties are part of a plan from God.

During that same preaching series, Scherer used I Peter 2:20 for a second time. He took his title from the text: "If Ye Do Well and Suffer."[27] Again, a two-point outline was used.

    I. This is the kind of world in which people do suffer because of the good in them.
    II. When you suffer for doing good, take it patiently.
        a. Jesus did.
        b. Nothing less than patience is creative enough to be a reasonable response to suffering.

George Arthur Buttrick once picked I Peter 3:4 and developed an illuminating sermon on "The Hidden Man of the Heart."[28] The sermon had four well-illustrated points, and the sermon motif was restated throughout in an ever-expanding way.

    I. Who is this hidden man in us?
        a. It is not the intimate self that loved ones know.
        b. It is not our subconscious self that we alone know.
        c. It is the self that surveys transient life.
    II. Why should our real self be "hidden"?
        a. It is by nature lowly and prefers modesty.
        b. Other aspects of self shield him from ready view.

III. The hidden self needs a reinforcing Ally to bring it forward, and help it against all that subdues.
   a. Christ is that Ally.
   b. The real self is nourished when "hid with Christ in God."
   c. The real self grows by friendship with the Eternal.
IV. The hidden man always needs something other than extravagance and display: he needs simplicity and spirituality.

I Peter 3:1–6 has been put to interesting uses in preaching history. Buttrick knew this and intimated it in his introduction. He reminded one and all that pride is not confined to females; he thus disarmed certain prejudices in order to deal with the deeper issue in that text, namely, the needs and expressions of the real self.

Buttrick's introduction was crucial:

> This began in a discussion of women's fashions, and by a man at that who dared to take issue both with the woman and the fashions. Brave man: almost as brave as if he had faced lions. He was like the old preacher who, when an extravagantly dressed woman asked him if her garb was all right, answered: "Better so. If you have the spirit of vanity, better to hang out the sign, so that people may be warned." Of course men also suffer from this pride: imposing offices and memberships in the clubs. And preachers too: appointments and prestige in the church. It is a human failing to try to play one's own god. But this man suddenly lifts the whole issue into an upper world: "Whose adorning, let it not be . . . plaiting the hair [beauty parlor pride], and of wearing of gold [jewelry store pride], or of putting on of apparel [dress salon pride]; but let it be the hidden man of the heart."

He then probed the problem of pride and the help that Christ offers to all. As always, the accent of the cross was present in his sermon.

Frederick William Robertson used I Peter many times in his pastoral preaching at Brighton. During a series to his people on the meaning of baptism he used I Peter 3:21, a text that explains baptism as an authoritative symbol about salvation as personal deliverance by the grace of God.[29]

Robertson's sermon on "The Preeminence of Charity" was based on I Peter 4:8.[30] His outline, as usual, had two points:

I. What charity is.
   Definition: the desire to give and to bless.
   a. It is fervent.
   b. It is capable of being cultivated.

II.   What charity does: "covers a multitude of sins":
    a. Not by refusing to see faults or barriers,
    b. But by making large allowances for human frailty and
       folly; and
    c. By tolerating uncharitable intolerance.

Interestingly, that sermon reflected the preacher's own experience. When he prepared and preached it (March 1853), Robertson had been uncharitably criticized by some for his theology and ministry. The experience had put that preacher's temper under test and his own charitableness needed strengthening; thus his words about learning how to "tolerate even intolerance."[31]

Paul Scherer used I Peter 4:10 to enlist his people in personal work that could enrich others. The outline is difficult to trace, but the topic was "As Every Man Hath Received."[32] That text lends itself readily to the service theme, especially evangelical endeavors that involve one in sharing one's life and faith with others.

I Peter is filled with evangelistic themes. I have used 1:18–19 to preach about redemption through "The Precious Blood of Christ."[33] The outline included three points.

The blood of Christ is precious because:
   I.   It belongs to a unique person: Jesus.
     a. Descendant of a royal figure (David).
     b. Son of God.
  II.   It is the means of our salvation.
 III.   It has great power to deliver and help us for life.
     a. Delivers from futile ways.
     b. Delivers from personal sin and immoral social influences.

There are some pivotal passages in II Peter which the preacher can use for pulpit work. II Peter 1:3–4 should not be overlooked, because the passage holds before us one of the most pertinent claims of the early church: that those who fully surrender to God's love will share his likeness, and that living life on God's terms lets one increasingly experience life on God's level. This textual passage reminds us that God brings change not only in our *experience* and expectations, but that he distinctively affects our very *being*. The writer's words underscore what the early church understood can happen when one lives *in the affective sphere of* God's promises to us. II Peter 1:3–4 calls attention to the immediacy and potency of full-orbed faith. James W. Cox ably treated this in his sermon "Your Right to God's Promises."[34]

I once used II Peter 1:3–4 as the text for a radio message about "Our Experience of Holiness."[35] The outline had four points:

  I. Our experience of God is *individual.*

  II. Our experience of God is *identifiable*, affecting both character and behavior.

  III. A sustained experience with God is *intelligible.*

  IV. An experience with the holy God is *instrumental*, fitting us for strategic service in the world.

Some leads on handling the Christian growth theme in II Peter 3:18 are seen in the sermons, previously noted, that Alexander Maclaren and Ralph W. Sockman preached on this text.[36] Nine other texts and themes in II Peter have been treated more recently by W. A. Criswell among his twenty-seven *Expository Sermons on the Epistles of Peter.*[37]

This writer once used II Peter 2:15 ("Forsaking the right way they have gone astray") to explain "Why Cults Arise."[38] The occasion was an international radio message not long after that awesome group suicide in Jonestown, Guyana, on November 18, 1978. Aware that so many were questioning how and why that had happened, this writer was stirred by his research into and assessment of the People's Temple cult to explain it all as a sad modern instance of what happens when a group follows the wrong path, having forsaken the right way. The outline had three points: (1) Some cults arise because of confused thought and muddled emotions. (2) Some cults happen because some leaders selfishly forsake the right way. (3) Cults arise because people listen to cult leaders and foolishly follow them.

III. THE JOHANNINE EPISTLES

Historical and Theological Issues

The three epistles of I, II, and III John have been associated traditionally with the apostle John, or as works known first within a "Johannine circle," or "the community of the beloved disciple."[39]

The New Testament has five writings traditionally associated with John as the author, but of them only the Revelation expressly mentions his name as writer (Rev. 1:1, 9–11; 22:8). The Gospel and the three epistles linked with John are actually anonymous writings, but the witness of early church leaders connects these works with John the Apostle, son of Zebedee and Salome (Matt. 4:21; 27:56, with Mark 15:40), and brother of one James (also an apostle, Matt. 10:2).

I John does not mention the author's name, but the salutation in both II and III John carries the description "the elder" *(ho presbuteros).*

Eusebius preserved statements from Papias, who compiled reminiscences from "the elders," and, though a bishop himself, had preferred "elder" as a title, as if it was a common and revered church expression in his time and place.[40]

II and III John are letters indeed, but the character of I John makes it more like a treatise. I John has sections of polemical materials (I John 2:4–5, 18–27; 3:7–10; 4:1–6) which show the situation of the church(es) addressed, but II and III John also reflect church problems: conflict and controversy stirred the writer to produce these Johannine epistles and offer authoritative guidance for dealing with the problems at hand. Those problems were: slanted views and false teachings about Jesus Christ, the incarnate Son of God (I John 1:1–3; 2:22–23; 4:3, 9, 14–15; 5:1, 9–12, 20–21; II John 3, 7, 9–10); division in the church (I John 1:7, 8, 9–10; 2:1–2, 12, 29; 3:1–10, 24; 5:2, 16–18); some needed assurance about salvation (I John 2:24–25, 28–29; 3:1–3, 19–22, 24; 4:12–13, 16–17; 5:13–15); love was needed in the fellowship (I John 2:5, 10; 3:10, 11, 14, 17, 18, 23; 4:7–8, 10–12, 16–21; 5:1–3; II John 3, 5, 6; III John 1, 6); false prophecies needed to be countered (I John 4:1–6); wisdom was needed to deal with backsliders and apostates (I John 5:16–17).

HOMILETICAL USE OF THE JOHANNINE EPISTLES

I John has many sections and texts eminently suited for proclaiming the Christian faith and for the nurture of believers. I John can be used to grant insight into the historical basis of the Christian faith (1:1–3), the nature of God (1:5; 4:8), and the meaning of Christian experience (1:6; 2:1–6; 3:1–3). The preacher can call attention to the social claims of the Christian life (1:10; 3:11–18; 4:7, 11, 20–21) which are answered out of *agapē* love. The Antichrist theme should also be treated, so that the hearers come to grips with the many antithetical irregularities that work against the gospel and the Christian witness. There *are* foes at work against the gospel, and John said so with frankness: "Many antichrists have come" (*antichristoi polloi gegonasin,* I John 2:18). The first epistle also warns about the dangers of worldliness (I John 2:15–17). The promised return *(parousia)* of Jesus Christ is recalled and hope in it restated (I John 2:28; 3:2, *phaneroō*).

The preacher will be wise to treat John's ethical and theological vocabulary, especially the following words: "love" (*agapaō,* I John 2:10; 3:10, 11, 14, 18, 23; 4:7, 8, 11, 12, 19–21; 5:1, 2; II John 5; III John 1; *agapē,* I John 2:5; 3:17; 4:7, 8, 10, 12, 16–18; 5:3; II John 3, 6; III John 6); "sin" (*hamartanō,* I John 1:10; 2:1; 3:6, 8, 9; 5:16, 18;

hamartia, I John 1:7, 8, 9; 2:2, 12; 3:4, 5, 8, 9; 4:10; 5:16, 17); "confess" (*homologeō,* I John 1:9; 2:23; 4:2, 3, 15); "confidence" (*parrēsia,* I John 2:28; 3:21; 4:17; 5:14); and "testimony" (*marturia,* I John 5:9, 10, 11; III John 12; *martureō,* III John 12).

George Arthur Buttrick used some texts from I John in his *Sermons Preached in a University Church.* In the sermon on "Anxiety and Faith," I John 4:18 was used, with Matt. 6:34 as a companion text, but the treatment was marginal. The sermon on "Expiation," based on I John 2:1–2, dealt more centrally with the text and was interestingly handled against a background analysis of Albert Camus's book *The Fall.*[41]

Discussing Jean-Baptiste's life, the main character in the novel, Buttrick described sin as violence of self, vanity of self, and cowardice of self, from which we need deliverance. He used I John 2:1–2 and I John 4:10 to announce that a worthy motive and new power for daily life under God are now possible for us in Jesus Christ. Camus's novel was thus used to show the need for expiation.

Buttrick's introduction began: "I have been reading the Camus novel *The Fall.*" Then this: "That title is the name of a traditional Christian doctrine, the fall of man. . . . The novel itself (it is mono-logue rather than novel, the various characters being seen only by reflection in the monologue) is a study of sin . . . keeps talking about God . . ."

Frederick William Robertson's use of I John 2:15–17 in treating "Worldliness" also offers a most instructive sermon model.[42] The preacher described:

    I. The nature of the forbidden world.
    II. The reason for which it is forbidden:
        a. It is incompatible with the love of God.
        b. It is transitory: "it will pass away," and so will an appetite for it.

In his conclusion Robertson declared, "The love of this world is only unlearned by the love of the Father": *(a)* The cross holds that love before us; *(b)* that love measures our meaning; and *(c)* the cross inspires in us an ambition that is above the world.

Robertson also left an exemplary treatment about the incarnation in his sermon on "The Sinlessness of Christ," preached from I John 3:4–5.[43] The preacher mentioned the heresy against which John wrote, then went on to declare some essential truths about Jesus' life and work. This was the outline:

    I. The sinlessness of his nature.

II. The power that sinlessness gave him to be the Savior of the
world:
    a. The power of faith in what we can be.
    b. The power of hope that we so become.
    c. The power of love to effect our deliverance.

Robertson developed a sermon on I John 5:4–5, which he titled
"The Victory of Faith," still another deeply evangelical statement
inspired by that epistle.[44] That sermon, preached in May 1850,
anticipated much that he preached two years later in the April 1852
sermon on "Worldliness." The following outline was used:
    I. The Christian's enemy, the world.
    II. The victory of faith:
        a. As a motive of action.
        b. Jesus Christ as the object of that action.

A worthy treatment of I John 4:17 closer to our time is seen in John
N. Gladstone's sermon "Confidence for the Day of Judgment," one of
the sermons in *The Twentieth Century Pulpit*.[45] Gladstone did not use
the text to frighten, but to instruct and invite. He underscored the
aspect of the believer's "confidence" (*parrēsia*, openness before God,
freedom in his presence because of obedience and faith) when the
judgment comes. That preacher explained it as a confidence grounded in:
    1. Our belief in Christ (v. 15)
    2. Our union with Christ (v. 16)
    3. Our conformity to Christ (v. 17)
Gladstone's sermon is an excellent example of how to treat one of
John's crucial terms, and with the context in full view.

IV. THE EPISTLE OF JUDE

HISTORICAL AND THEOLOGICAL CONCERNS

The literary relationship between parts of Jude and II Peter is a
well-established fact. Most New Testament scholars agree that Jude
was written first, and that the writer of II Peter borrowed from him—
because Jude's style seems more original. Bo Reicke has suggested,
however, that "the best assumption is that both epistles derive from a
common tradition which may well have been oral rather than written.
Very possibly there was a sermon pattern formulated to resist the
seducers of the church: This would explain both the similarities and
the differences in a satisfactory fashion."[46]

The Epistle of Jude contains only twenty-five verses. The author identifies himself as "Jude, a servant of Jesus Christ and brother of James" (v. 1a). Both tradition and calculation identify the writer as that Jude who was a blood brother of Jesus (Matt. 13:55; Mark 6:3). Perhaps modesty dictated that he identify himself as "a servant *[doulos]* of Jesus Christ" but a "brother *[adelphos]* of James," that same James who held wide influence in the Jerusalem church and throughout Palestinean Jewish Christianity. Paul's reference in I Cor. 9:5 to "other apostles and the brothers of the Lord" might well suggest his acquaintance with both James and Jude as acknowledged believers busy working by ca. A.D. 55 as trusted leaders in the growing church.

The Epistle of Jude should be dated as a first-century work which perhaps circulated after the death of James (A.D. 62) but earlier than A.D. 81. The good Greek style used in it suggests that someone quite accomplished in that language was used to write the epistle in Jude's name.

HOMILETICAL DIRECTIONS IN JUDE

As in treating II Peter, some of which parallels portions of Jude, the preacher can use this writing to deal with errors that hinder the experience and progress of "our common salvation" (Jude 3a). The book warns about threats against "the faith which was once for all delivered to the saints" (v. 3b). Two of those threats were: (1) ungodly ethical views—"perverting the grace of our God into licentiousness" (*aselgeia*, v. 4), meaning that moral standards were wrongfully dismissed as unnecessary for those who are "forever saved"; (2) promotion of erroneous beliefs contrary to the "delivered faith"—mainly a defective and reductionist Christology: "deny our only Master and Lord, Jesus Christ" (v. 4). Jude warns against distorted doctrines and undisciplined behavior, and these are still common threats against true Christianity.

The preacher has a warrant from God to declare the true faith, unmask sin, warn of judgment, and encourage the faithful. In declaring "the faith," the preacher can use Jude's epistle as a pointer to its "once for all-ness," calling attention to the uniqueness of Jesus Christ and the biblical standards for Christian experience. A survey of salvation history deserves periodic treatment in the pulpit, and this epistle is useful to such an end.

Unmasking sin calls for courageous comments about religious error and the characteristic marks of ungodliness. Jude wrote graphically about the iniquitous "way of Cain," and "Balaam's error" and "Korah's rebellion" (v. 11). His vivid picture rebukes unprincipled conduct, the selfish seeking of gain at someone else's expense, and all disregard for promised judgment against sin.

The book of Jude recalls believers to apostolic teaching about Christian experience. It offers a ready rebuke against waywardness, and it issues a stirring call to faithfulness in Christ.

The exhortation in vs. 17–23 is especially tender; it is a call to "remember" *(mnēsthēte)* the truths of the faith—and the persons who brought and voiced those truths. The Epistle of Jude encourages a truly personal hold on faith—"build yourselves up on your most holy faith" (v. 20a)—which leads to a well-integrated self steeped in holiness of life, as the instrumental dative used in that verse surely suggests.

The preacher can treat Jude's call to continue to "pray *[proseuchomenoi]* in the Holy Spirit" (v. 20b), since personal prayer is crucial to Christian development. The preacher might well use the expression ("praying in the Holy Spirit") as an introduction to the New Testament prayer tradition as voiced by Paul in Rom. 8:26; I Cor. 12:3; Gal. 4:6; and Eph. 6:18.

Jude's writing can be used as guidance on how to "keep yourselves in the love of God" (Jude 21a), how to avoid disobedience and backsliding, and how to maintain the hope that trusts God's "mercy . . . unto eternal life" (v. 21b).

While the preacher should deal with Jude's call for steadfastness in faith, his words of concern for the fallen in vs. 22–23 should not be overlooked. The Christian way involves compassion ("And convince some, who doubt; save some, by snatching them out of the fire; on some have mercy with fear, hating even the garment spotted by the flesh.").

Compassion, yes, but a compassion exercised with necessary cautions. Compassionate believers must remain on guard against being corrupted by those whom they seek to restore to faith. The picture is one of attempted rescue. Those who have fallen from faith need to be challenged by a warm and accepting concern. Those who are in error or troubled by doubts need to hear clear and intelligent convincement. Doubt can be handled and false arguments can be effectively countered by those who both *know* and *care.*

Verses 24–25 are a benediction and a wish prayer of great promise. It reminds us that God can be trusted to sustain those who trust him to do so. To be kept from "falling" (literally, from stumbling, *aptaistos*), and for the whole of life, so that one stands at last "before the presence of his glory with rejoicing," this is the joyous concern of the earnest believer, and Jesus Christ is the guarantor of it all. This is an encouraging word for steadiness and a needed sense of security.

One of Robert Murray McCheyne's (1813–1843) most memorable sermons was based on Jude 24. His topic, "Address at the Close of Day,"[47] was treated by a simple structure suggested by that verse:

   I. To keep you from falling.
- a. We ministers (anxious about you) are not able to keep you from falling.
- b. You are not able to keep yourselves from falling.
- c. Our Savior-God is able.

  II. To present you faultless.
- a. Faultless in righteousness.
- b. Faultless in holiness.

 III. To him be glory.

NOTES

1. See Eusebius, *Ecclesiastical History*, VI. xxv. 14.

2. Ibid., VI. xxv. 13.

3. William Manson, *The Epistle to the Hebrews* (London: Hodder & Stoughton, 1951), p. 184.

4. George A. Buttrick, *Sermons Preached in a University Church* (Abingdon Press, 1959), pp. 110–116.

5. A. Leonard Griffith, *What Is a Christian?* (Abingdon Press, 1962), pp. 214–223.

6. A. J. Gossip, *The Hero in Thy Soul* (Charles Scribner's Sons, 1929), pp. 64–76.

7. See G. Paul Butler (ed.), *Best Sermons: 1947–1948* (Harper & Brothers, 1947), pp. 2–7.

8. Gossip, op. cit., pp. 117–129.

9. Frederick W. Robertson, *Sermons Preached at Brighton* (Harper & Brothers, 1947), pp. 88–98.

10. Vernon L. Stanfield (ed.), *Favorite Sermons of John A. Broadus* (Harper & Brothers, 1959), pp. 28–37.

11. See James W. Cox (ed.), *The Twentieth-Century Pulpit* (Abingdon Press, 1978), pp. 180–187.

12. Eusebius, *Ecclesiastical History*, II. xxiii. 25; III. xxv. 3; VI. xiv. 1.

13. James Moffatt, *An Introduction to the Literature of the New Testament* (Charles Scribner's Sons, 1915), p. 316.

14. Donald Guthrie, *New Testament Introduction*, rev. ed. (Inter-Varsity Press, 1970), p. 736.

15. Clyde E. Fant, Jr., and William M. Pinson, Jr. (comps.), *Twenty Centuries of Great Preaching*, 13 vols. (Word Books, 1971).

16. See Flavius Josephus, *Antiquities of the Jews*, Bk. 20, par. 200.

17. See E. H. Plumptre, *The General Epistle of St. James* (Cambridge University Press, 1886), pp. 7–8; James H. Ropes, *A Critical and Exegetical Commentary on the Epistle of St. James* (Charles Scribner's Sons, 1916), pp. 295–301; Donald Guthrie, *New Testament Introduction*, p. 743; Sophie Laws, *A Commentary on the Epistle of James* (Harper & Row, 1980), pp. 12–14.

18. Dwight E. Stevenson, *Preaching on the Books of the New Testament* (Harper & Brothers, 1956), esp. pp. 186–189.

19. Eric W. Hayden, *Preaching Through the Bible* (Zondervan Publishing House, 1964), from the Introduction, n.p.

20. W. A. Criswell, *Expository Sermons on the Epistle of James* (Zondervan Publishing House, 1975), pp. 36–40, 41–47, 62–67, and 68–74, respectively.

21. David A. Hubbard, *The Book of James: Wisdom That Works* (Word Books, 1980).

22. Ibid., p. 29.

23. Harold S. Songer, "The Literary Character of the Book of James," *Review and Expositor*, Vol. 66 (Fall 1969), p. 388.

24. See Eusebius, *Ecclesiastical History*, III. xxxix. 17.

25. Polycarp, disciple of John, wrote his *Letter to the Philadelphians* ca. A.D. 135, and quoted I Peter at 1:3; 2:1–2; 5:3; 7:2; 8:1; 10:1–2. See *The Apostolic Fathers*, tr. by Kirsopp Lake (Harvard University Press, 1952), Vol. 1, pp. 282–301.

26. Paul E. Scherer, *The Place Where Thou Standest* (Harper & Brothers, 1942), pp. 73–78.

27. Ibid., pp. 134–139.

28. In Fant and Pinson, op. cit., Vol. 10, pp. 287–291.

29. Robertson, op. cit., pp. 185–198.

30. Ibid., pp. 776–787.

31. See James R. Blackwood, *The Soul of Frederick W. Robertson: The Brighton Preacher* (Harper & Brothers, 1947), pp. 143–152, 167–180.

32. Scherer, op. cit., pp. 157–162.

33. My radio message published in *Vital Christianity*, Feb. 10, 1980, pp. 15–16.

34. See James W. Cox, *Surprised by God* (Broadman Press, 1979), pp. 31–38.

35. My radio message published in *Vital Christianity*, July 20, 1980, pp. 15–16.

36. See Fant and Pinson, op. cit., Vol. 5, pp. 25–32, and Vol. 10, pp. 206–209, respectively.

37. W. A. Criswell, *Expository Sermons on the Epistles of Peter* (Zondervan Publishing House, 1976).

38. My radio message published in *Vital Christianity*, Aug. 10, 1980, pp. 15–16.

39. See J. H. Houlden, *A Commentary on the Johannine Epistles* (Harper & Row, 1973), pp. 38–42.

40. Eusebius, *Ecclesiastical History,* III. xxxix. 2–7. F. F. Bruce has suggested that Papias, as Irenaeus did later, might have used the word "elder" to indicate a post-apostolic generation person who had known an apostle or immediate follower of Jesus, but admitted, however, that "the coincidence between this designation in the Johannine letters and Papias' mention of 'the elder John' may be a *mere* coincidence, but it may be more." F. F. Bruce, *Peter, Stephen, James and John: Studies in Early Non-Pauline Christianity* (Wm. B. Eerdmans Publishing Co., 1979), pp. 143–144. See also Stephen S. Smalley, *John, Evangelist and Interpreter* (Exeter: Paternoster Press, 1978), pp. 73–75.

41. Buttrick, op. cit., pp. 37–43, 179–186, respectively.

42. Robertson, op. cit., pp. 333–343.

43. Ibid., pp. 680–689.

44. Ibid., pp. 446–455.

45. See James W. Cox and Patricia P. Cox (eds.), *The Twentieth-Century Pulpit,* Vol. 2 (Abingdon Press, 1981), pp. 76–84.

46. Bo Reicke, *The Epistles of James, Peter, and Jude,* The Anchor Bible, Vol. 38 (Doubleday & Co., 1964), p. 190.

47. In Fant and Pinson, op. cit., Vol. 4, pp. 288–290.

20. PREACHING FROM ESCHATOLOGICAL TEXTS

GEORGE BEASLEY-MURRAY

1. INTRODUCTION

The reader should be acquainted at the outset with the scope of this essay. We shall briefly consider the fundamental elements of the eschatology of the Bible, and the language in which it is commonly expressed, and then examine the book of Revelation as the great exemplar of biblical eschatology. This will give us a vantage point from which to view the eschatological drama as it is presented in the book of Revelation, and at the same time set that book in its context within the biblical revelation.

2. BASIC BIBLICAL ESCHATOLOGY

The term "eschatology" denotes thought about the "last" things, the end of history and all that lies "beyond" it. In the Bible all such thought is rooted in what God has done in the past and is doing in the present. The revelation of God is bound up with testimony to the acts of judgment and salvation that God has performed in the past; he is continuing in such activity in the present, and this, in turn, is to culminate in a great consummation of judgment and salvation in the not-distant future.

THE COMING OF GOD

The primary concept in this complex is that of the *coming of God* into the world to achieve his will. God's action for the accomplishment of his purpose takes place in the sphere of this world. He is therefore represented as "coming" from his dwelling place to intervene in this world's affairs. The great model of such intervention is the exodus, the accounts of which include judgments on the oppressor nation, the deliverance of Israel from bondage, their adoption as the covenant people of God at Sinai, and their settlement in the Promised Land as the free people of Yahweh. The earliest employment of this model occurs in the Song of Deborah, Judg. 5:4f., which finds almost precise repetition in Ps. 68:8f.:

> Lord, when you went out from Seir,
> Strode here from Edom's field,
> Then the earth quaked, the heavens dropped,
> Before Yahweh, before him from Sinai.

Jörg Jeremias points out that the fundamental understanding of the nature of theophany, the "coming" of God, occurs here in its simplest form:

> God comes,
> All nature reacts in terror.[1]

The pictorial language of the elements of the universe going into confusion before the appearance of the almighty God is a constant feature of the descriptions of the coming of God. It finds its fullest elaboration in the poem of Habakkuk 3, which links recollection of God's coming at the exodus with expectations of his coming in like power in the future. The language about the shaking of the heavens and the earth at the Lord's appearing has nothing to do with the notion of the breakup of the universe, but is a mode of setting forth the majesty of the Creator when he appears before his creation. Other examples of poetic descriptions of the coming of God at the end of the age may be seen in Isa. 40:9ff.; 59:15ff.; 66:15; Zech. 2:10–12; Mal. 3:1–5.

THE DAY OF THE LORD

Linked with these portrayals of the coming of God are descriptions of the Day of the Lord. These too signify an intervention of God in history, generally in the near future, with emphasis on judgment upon nations that act in defiance of the Lord. Gerhard von Rad suggested that the concept of the Day of the Lord is rooted in the "*days* of the Lord," when God intervened for Israel in her times of war; these were understood as theophanies for Israel's deliverance. It is conceivable that the process by which the days of the Lord in the past became the Day of the Lord in the future is bound up with the concept of the salvation of God as a new exodus, when God will deliver his people from their enemies as in the first exodus, establish a new covenant, and bring his people into the Promised Land of the kingdom of God.[2]

The suggestion is likely to be right. It would explain the imagery that is constantly associated with the Day of the Lord. Its link with the traditional pictures of theophany brought into association the pictures of the confusion of the universe in terror before God. Its link with the days of the Lord in history brought into use images of warfare and slaughter (see, e.g., Isa. 13 and 34; Ezek. 30; Joel 2). The coalescence of these two traditions inevitably involved an overpainting of the picture of the future, sometimes overwhelmingly so. Nevertheless the seers of Israel will have been conscious of their employment of hyperbole, as the representations of the day of the Lord in Zephaniah illustrate (see especially 1:2f. and 3:8f.).

THE KINGDOM OF GOD

Salvation rather than judgment is the ultimate hope of Israel's prophets. Although the expression "kingdom of God" does not appear in the Old Testament, the reality dominates it from beginning to end. Ludwig Köhler affirmed, "The one fundamental statement in the theology of the Old Testament is this: God is the ruling Lord."[3] That statement provides the clue as to what is meant by the kingdom of God in the Hebrew-Christian tradition: primarily it is neither a territory nor a people occupying that territory, but an assertion that God is king, and that he exercises his sovereign power over the nations. By that sovereign power God brought the people of Israel out of Egypt, led them through the Red Sea, made them the people of his covenant, brought them to the Promised Land, and subdued their enemies, so showing that he was Lord of all and Lord of his people in a saving way. The prophets declared that God was to do the same kind of thing again in the future, delivering his people from the forces of oppression and the powers of evil, making a new covenant, and establishing his saving will in the world, so bringing into being the period of universal acknowledgment of his Lordship which we call the kingdom of God.

These elements of eschatological hope are embodied in the great apocalypse of the Old Testament, The Book of Daniel: the coming of God in mighty power is shown in the two cardinal visions of chs. 2 and 7; the coming of the Day of the Lord on the oppressor power is seen both in them and in the other prophetic visions (chs. 8; 9; 10–12); and the hope of the kingdom of God is the real object of the work. These features of expectation of the future are the stuff of the apocalypses which followed Daniel.

The same basic elements are at the heart of the message of Jesus and of the church which followed him, but provided with a new keynote: the hope of the future has moved into the present! Jesus proclaimed that God had come and was present for his saving rule among men (Mark 1:14–15). He revealed that saving sovereignty in action (e.g., Matt. 11:5; 12:28). The apostles similarly declared that God had come in saving grace in Christ to his people, and they echoed their Lord's teaching that he would complete his purpose in creation through his coming at the end of the age (Mark 14:62; cf. the watchword *Maranatha*, I Cor. 16:22). The coming of God in judgment in the cross of Christ and in the end of the times lies at the heart of the teaching of Jesus, alike in the Synoptic tradition (e.g., Luke 12:49f.; Mark 14:22–25 and pars.) and the Johannine (John 12:31f., 47f.), as also in the apostolic teaching (e.g., II Cor. 5:10, 14–21). The presence of the saving sovereignty of God through Christ and its consummation in the future forms the sum and substance of the entire New Testament writings.

3. THE ESCHATOLOGY OF THE BOOK OF REVELATION

It is of first importance to recognize that the same fundamental Christian interpretation of eschatology is presupposed and set forth in the book of Revelation. It is supremely the book about the coming of God in and through Christ, but its delineation of the future manifestation of God in Christ must not blind us to its clear representation that in Christ God has already come. The fulcrum of the book of Revelation lies not in its vision of the parousia at the end but in the vision of God and the Lamb in ch. 5: through the "conquest" of the Lamb by his death and resurrection, authority over the universe has been given to him. The turn of the ages, therefore, lies in the past. Such also is the purport of the highly colored apocalyptic vision of ch. 12: the "dragon" has been thrown out of heaven in virtue of the redemptive death of the Lamb, and the song is sung, "*Now* the salvation and the power and the kingdom of our God and the authority of his Christ have come, for the accuser of our brethren has been thrown down."

The book of Revelation, in fact, presents the deeds of God in Christ in all three tenses: his coming in Christ incarnate in the past, his presence in the here and now, and his "coming" in decisive action in the future. In Christ the future has moved into the present, without destroying the prospect of a future wherein God is "all in all."

4. THE PURPOSE OF THE BOOK OF REVELATION

The traditional belief that Revelation was written near the close of the reign of the Emperor Domitian, about A.D. 96, is likely to be right, though it is not impossible that it was written in the confused period that immediately followed Nero's death in A.D. 68. The date is of less importance than the recognition that the chief feature in the contemporary scene was the emergence of emperor worship, and its challenge to the existence of the church. From Augustus on, the view of kings and rulers in the East, as adopted sons of the gods or actual offspring of deities, was transferred to the Roman emperors. A kind of Messianic hope attached to such a view of kingship: the ruler should bring deliverance from the evils of this world and establish the golden age of peace. Augustus took this view as a means of unifying the sentiment of the peoples who comprised the Empire, but it was taken with greater seriousness by his successors, supremely and ironically by the mad Caligula, by Nero, and by Domitian. Nowhere in the Empire was the adulation of the emperor taken up with such enthusiasm as in Asia Minor. John had been banished to Patmos "on account of the word of God and the testimony of Jesus," i.e., presumably for refusing to acknowledge Caesar as Lord and Savior, and for inciting others to do the same through his proclaiming Christ as Lord and Savior. John sees this situation as a manifestation of the spirit of Antichrist (cf. I John 4:1–3 for a related application of the Antichrist expectation); he writes his book to reveal the end of this process: humanity called to allegiance to the Christ of God or the Antichrist of Satan. In so doing, he betrays no hint of pessimism or doubt as to the outcome of the struggle. He labors rather to make Christians aware of the nature of the conflict, to nerve them for resistance to the forces arrayed against them, and to witness fearlessly for Christ in the situation. E. F. Scott described the book as being a "trumpet call to faith."[4] It is that, and more: it is a call to faith and obedience to the limit, to the last drop of Christian blood, in the knowledge that the issues are in the hands of God.

5. THE STRUCTURE OF THE BOOK OF REVELATION

Despite its visionary nature, no book of the Bible has been more
carefully structured than this one. The plan is simple, but the
outworking is complex. We may divide the book as follows:

1. Ch. 1 — Prologue and Introductory Vision
2. Chs. 2–3 — The Seven Letters to the Churches
3. Chs. 4–5 — The Vision of God and the Lamb
4. Chs. 6–18 — The Messianic Judgments
5. Chs. 19:1– 22:5 — The Coming of the Lord and of the Kingdom of God
6. Ch. 22:6–21 — Epilogue

The long central section, dealing with the Messianic judgments, is
the most complex. The key to its understanding is twofold. First, the
implication of 13:5 (with 11:2–3) that the judgments are confined to a
relatively short period, that of the "three and a half years" of Daniel's
description of tribulation (Dan. 12:6f.; cf. 9:27). Second, the three
series of judgments are not intended to represent three chronologically successive periods of judgment, but three symbolic representations of the one period. Each series appears to conclude with the end
of the age and allusion to the final theophany (8:1–5; 11:15–19;
16:17–21). This is plain in 11:15ff. and 16:17ff., but is equally clearly
intended in the first series of judgments, for the sixth seal (6:12–17)
describes the Day of the Lord immediately prior to the end, just as the
sixth trumpet describes Armageddon immediately preceding the
parousia of the conquering King of Kings (16:12–16; cf. v. 17).

There are, however, three comparatively long sections that perform the function of excursuses to the visions narrated; they serve as
explanatory notes, added at a later point so as not to disturb the flow
of thought. The longest of these is chs. 12–14, inserted between the
second and third series of judgments; it depicts the nature of the
conflict between the church and the antigod empire. The second is
17:1–19:10, which describes the city that rules the world and the
doom that it faces. The third follows the description of the parousia
and kingdom of God, 21:9–22:5, and portrays the City of God. There
can be no doubt that the description of the City of God is intended to
contrast with that of the city which rules the world: the former is the
Bride of the Lamb, the latter a harlot consort of the Antichrist; the
former is from heaven, the latter of hell; the former is destined to

inherit the new creation, the latter is doomed to destruction. The book of Revelation is "a tale of two cities."

6. THE IMAGERY OF THE BOOK OF REVELATION

Our review of basic biblical eschatology makes it clear that in the Bible, eschatological concepts are conveyed in highly pictorial forms. The representations of the coming of God utilize ancient imagery, often stamped with the thought of God as the Lord of the storm, traveling on the clouds and hurling his lightning spears at a terrified universe (cf. Ps. 18). The representations of the collapse of the powers of heaven in the Day of the Lord are of a related nature. None of these portrayals should be taken literally; they resemble the impressionism of a Picasso rather than the details of a photograph.

In its symbolism the book of Revelation has a feature in common with other apocalypses: it utilizes many symbols in a fashion that had become standard among John's contemporaries (and long before). The description of a world political power as a seven-headed sea monster (ch. 13) will have been everywhere recognized in John's day as a kind of cartoon, going back to the ancient story of the war between the evil power of the sea and the powers of heaven, the latter represented by a champion who fought and overcame the sea monster. Thereby the nature of the political power as evil is conveyed, together with its inevitable doom. Significantly the same figure is applied to Satan (ch. 12), the Antichrist (ch. 13), and the Empire (ch. 17); they are all characterized as emerging from the "abyss," i.e., hell.

Although this picture is common among apocalypses, no writing of this kind known to us employs so fully the pictorial mode of representing a message. Jesus conveyed truth through parables that drew on scenes familiar to his hearers. John set forth his message through parabolic visions full of images known to his contemporaries. It is in this sense that the visions should be read and interpreted.

John shares with his fellow apocalyptists yet another characteristic: he freely makes use of the pictorial representations of other writers, adapting them in order to convey the message he has been given. Many of these are drawn from the Old Testament (e.g., the vision of the four horsemen; cf. Zech. 1:7ff.; 6:1ff.), but others appear to have been adapted from current apocalyptic writings. This would explain, for example, the vision of the sealing of the 144,000 from the twelve tribes of Israel in Rev. 7:1ff., which originally is likely to have been a purely Jewish picture, adapted by John to represent the church; the vision of the two witnesses in 11:3ff., which originally depicted Moses and Elijah, but which set forth in symbolic fashion the church as it witnesses to a hostile world in the spirit and power of Moses and Elijah.

In passages of this kind it is necessary to distinguish between the meaning of the original picture and that which John desired to convey, and to recognize that some of the details of the visions are retained as scenic background and are not intended to be applied.

7. EXPOUNDING THE BOOK OF REVELATION

Study Series of the Book

One answer to the question, What should we preach from the book of Revelation? would be, Preach *the whole* book. All preachers are aware of the inroads that are made into the minds of multitudes of Christians by popular preachers who major on doubtful interpretations of the book of Revelation, to say nothing of the sects that present caricatures of the eschatological teaching of the Bible to people on their doorsteps. We owe it to our churches to present them with a guide to Revelation based on sound principles of biblical interpretation. This could be done by a series of studies on the book, treating it in the six sections we defined in dealing with the structure of Revelation, perhaps dividing the fifth one into 19:1–21:8 (Parousia and Kingdom) and 21:9–22:5 (The City of God), so expounding the book in seven sermons (a not inappropriate division of the book of Revelation!). Or one could expand the series to twelve sermons by giving more time to the central section on the Messianic Judgments, treating separately the Seals (6:1–8:5), the Trumpets (8:6–11:19), and the Cups of Wrath (chs. 15–16), with a separate study devoted to the Vision of the Woman and the Dragon in ch. 12 and another to the Harlot City in chs. 17–18.

The Beatitudes of the Book of Revelation

The opening paragraph of the book includes the first of seven beatitudes: "Blessed is he who reads aloud the words of the prophecy, and blessed are those who hear, and who keep what is written therein" (v. 3). The other six are found in 14:13; 16:15; 19:9; 20:6; 22:7, 14. They are a reminder that there is "blessedness" at the heart of this book, despite the judgments that feature in it so prominently, and that its purpose is to inspire faith to experience that happiness now and hereafter. The seven beatitudes provide an unusual angle from which to consider the message of the book.

SOME OUTSTANDING PASSAGES

Of passages in Revelation that particularly call for proclamation one would include the Prologue of 1:1–8, which serves a not dissimilar function in Revelation as the prologues to Mark's Gospel (Mark 1:1–15) and to the Fourth Gospel (John 1:1–18); the Seven Letters; the visions of the 144,000 and of the Countless Multitude in Revelation 7; the Two Witnesses of 11:1–14; the Woman and the Dragon in ch. 12; the Parousia in ch. 19; the City of God in 21:9–22:5; and the Epilogue, 22:6–21.

The Letters to the Churches are the most frequently expounded section of the book of Revelation and have had more attention paid to them than any other area of the work. Since there are so many excellent guides to these chapters, we shall devote our attention to other areas of the book.

A GREETING FROM GOD

In the Prologue the greeting in 1:4–5a and the doxology of 1:5b–6 merit attention. The former is a highly unusual blessing in the name of the Trinity. It is likely that the first two members reflect a Jewish mode of blessing, in terms of the God who revealed himself at the bush (Ex. 3:1–14) and the "Angel of the Presence"; John has, with good reason, interpreted the "spirits before the throne" as the sevenfold Spirit of God, who is the Holy Spirit of the church(es), and then added the reference to Jesus the Christ, hence the unexpected order of persons (Father, Spirit, Son). But while every syllable of the greeting is Jewish, no non-Christian Jew could ever have penned it. The name of Yahweh made known to Moses, "I am who I am," came to be understood among many Jews as "I am he who is and who will be" (so the Septuagint translated it). The Jerusalem Targum expanded it to mean, "I am he who is, and who was, and I am who will be," so defining God as the Lord of time. John gives the name an unexpected twist by replacing the future tense in "who will be," by the phrase "who is to come"; it is thereby represented that God not only transcends the ages, but it is of his nature that he "comes" from the future and works his gracious and powerful will. Of course in Revelation, when we read of God's coming in the future, it is impossible not to think of his coming in Christ's parousia. That is precisely what the parousia signifies: God intervening in history in Christ the Redeemer-Lord for the completion of his will and the blessedness of humanity. All history is embraced in this revelation of the nature of God, with emphasis on its happy outcome. We may look for God to "come" in every conceivable situation—until he brings it all to summation at the happy end.

The description of Jesus in 1:5a will have been deeply significant for the first readers of Revelation. He is "the faithful witness." To our knowledge, this is the first instance in literature of the term "witness" (*martus*) being synonymous with the specialized meaning "martyr," denoting a witness who seals his testimony with his blood. The primitive church constantly remembered that Jesus "made the good confession" before Pilate and the Jewish authorities, and died for it (I Tim. 6:13); it was an inspiration to them as they faced trial for the sake of the name. Its pertinence for suffering Christians in the world at all times is obvious. Jesus is also described as "the first-born of the dead." In Judaism the firstborn in a family had the chief rights in the inheritance; it was natural for the firstborn to be associated with the first place in the inheritance of God's kingdom, and so for the term to connote sovereignty in the kingdom. This was encouraged by Ps. 89:27: "I will make him the first-born, the highest of the kings of the earth." By his resurrection Jesus became the Christ in power, and opened the gates of death as the pioneer of resurrection to glory. And so the risen Lord is also "the ruler of the kings of the earth"—with particular reference, so far as the original readers were concerned, to the rulers of the Roman Empire: the latter viewed themselves as lords of the bodies and souls of men, and of their destinies; they were ignorant that *they* had a Lord of all power in heaven, and that his despised people are to share in the sovereignty of the coming age. *They* did not know it, but the people of the risen Christ are told never to forget it!

ROYAL PRIESTHOOD: CHRIST'S AND OURS

It was a custom of Jewish writers to utter a doxology at every mention of God's name. John does not do that, but it was natural that after pronouncing a benediction which concludes with the name of Jesus, and which reminds John of the redemption Jesus accomplished, he should utter an ascription of praise (Rev. 1:5–6). The doxology is of importance for understanding the whole book, since it represents the redemption of Christ as the second exodus for which the Jews were waiting. The death of Jesus revealed an eternal love (present tense, "loves"; not the past tense!). Through it he "has *freed* us from our sins." The alternative term "washed" is due to a later confusion, through the difficulty of distinguishing in sound between *luō,* to loose or release, and *louō,* to wash. Our earliest manuscripts have the term "freed," and it harmonizes with the typology of

Exodus: the blood of Jesus, God's Passover Lamb, with his resurrection has made possible an emancipation of the whole race from the slavery of sin and the death to which it leads, so that all may enter into the Promised Land of the kingdom of God.

John uses the past tense, for in Jesus the emancipation became actual: in him humanity was liberated, and they who own him as Lord have been made "a kingdom, priests to his God." The language echoes Ex. 19:6; it signifies not "a kingdom of priests," but kings and priests who make up the holy nation, and who have the privilege of exercising priesthood and sovereignty. In the Christian context it means nothing less than the privilege of becoming *kings and priests with Christ,* sharing in his priestly ministry for the world and in his saving sovereignty. The new exodus therefore leads to a world mission. The New Israel shares with its Savior-Lord the task of representing God to the world and of bringing people under that sovereignty which is salvation and life. Old Israel was strangely blind to this element of her vocation; New Israel cannot be so, without denying the foundation of its own existence. The concept of the church as made up of royal priests, serving God and man in the Spirit of Jesus, with dignity and sacrifice, is a striking one that calls for development and application by the preacher.

The God Who Is Lord of All Time

The last sentence of the Prologue describes God as "the Alpha and the Omega." *Alpha* (A) is the first letter of the Greek alphabet, Omega (a long O) is the last letter; so the phrase is the equivalent of "A and Z." The beginning and the end of the alphabet becomes the symbol of the beginning and the end of all things. Such a use of the letters of the alphabet was common in ancient times, and the use was adopted by the Jews. They said, for example, that Adam broke the law from A to Z; but they affirmed that Abraham kept the law from A to Z. There, A and Z meant not only beginning and end, but all that lies between. If that idea was in John's mind, "I am A and Z" would imply "I am the beginning and the end of all things, and Lord of all that lies between."

It is of special interest that in 22:13 the symbol is applied to Jesus. And surprisingly enough, the earliest appearance of the symbol A and the earliest use of the cross as a Christian symbol put the two together, thus A†Ω. It means that the First and the Last is the Man who died on the cross and rose from the dead. We know this through the extraordinary fact that it appears in a Roman word puzzle! This Latin word square has turned up all over the world, but the earliest copies that we know of were found scrawled on walls in the ruins of

Pompeii, which was destroyed by an eruption of the volcano Vesuvius in A.D. 79, a generation before Revelation was written. Here the preacher must use a chalkboard or some other visual aid so as to let his congregation see the word square. Here it is:

```
S A T O R
A R E P O
T E N E T
O P E R A
R O T A S
```

The sentence, it will be seen, reads the same whether read across, or down, or from the bottom right-hand corner backward or upward! The words are quite innocent, meaning, "The reaper Arepo holds with [hard] work the wheels." The significance of the square lies in the letters, and the clue is that in ancient times the letter T was written as a cross, thus †. In the square the cross is central on every side, and it is flanked each time by A and O, the Latin way of writing Alpha and Omega. Astonishingly, the letters taken in a certain arithmetical progression spell out the first two words of the Lord's Prayer, "Our Father," shaped in the form of the cross of him who is Alpha and Omega, like this:

```
                A

                P
                A
                T
                E
                R
    A PATERNOSTER O
                O
                S
                T
                E
                R

                O
```

So, God, the everlasting Lord of all, is made known in the cross of Jesus. In that revelation of love and power we see the A and Z of every alphabet that matters: God in Christ is the A and Z of the alphabet of *creation;* he is the A and Z of the alphabet of *history;* and he is the A

and Z of the alphabet of *salvation*. The book of Revelation shows how
it all comes to pass.

THE SECRET OF THE LAMB OF GOD

No studies of Revelation should omit the Vision of the Scroll and
the Lamb in ch. 5, for its theology controls that of the whole book.
The vision of ch. 4 serves as a kind of introduction. God is therein
described as the Creator who is the Lord of the universe, exalted
above the storms of history, unreachable by the puny antichristian
forces that attempt to resist his will. The chapter concludes with a
song that celebrates his exaltation over creation, which shall yet give
"glory and honor and power" to him, for the Lord "was and is *and is to
come*" (v. 8).

How that will come to pass is the theme of ch. 5. It is as though a
television camera in heaven zoomed in on the scene beside the throne
of God, where are seen a scroll and one who alone can open it. The
scroll sealed with seven seals represents not a book, but a document; it
images either a *contract,* the contents of which are fully described
within and briefly stated on the outside, as was customary in ancient
times, or possibly a *testament.* There is not a great deal of difference in
the significance of the two symbols; the former would indicate the
covenant of God to give humanity the kingdom of salvation, and the
latter would represent the same, bequeathed through a death. Since,
however, the Lamb has "won the right" through his death to open the
scroll and carry out its intention, the contract or the testament entails
the same condition. The Lamb alone has the power to execute the
saving will of God. This he has achieved through his death and
resurrection.

Observe the way the Redeemer is described: he is the Lion of
Judah, the Root of David (the King), the Lamb which has been slain
but stands—alive from the dead. But this is no weak little lamb: he has
seven horns and seven eyes. Horns signify strength; seven horns
immense power. This is the mighty Warrior Lamb of Jewish apocalyptic tradition, the one who leads the flock of God to battle against
the wild beasts of the nations which would tear them to pieces. But he
conquers through sacrifice, for he is God's Passover Lamb, bringing
about an exodus for all the nations of the world into the Promised
Land of the eternal kingdom of God. This is why the symbolism has to
change; Jesus is the Christ of God, the royal Messiah, the Lion of
Judah; but one can never think of a dead lion as achieving deliverance. This can come about only through the Lamb of God; he also has

immense strength, but he renounces it in death, that he may use it in resurrection for the life of the redeemed.

This secret of the Lamb is hidden from earth, but it is known in heaven. When the Lamb takes the scroll from the hand of God, and so receives authority to establish the universal saving rule of God, all heaven goes wild with joy. The supreme angelic powers sing the worth of the Lamb to carry through the purposes of God, for redemption has been achieved, the new Israel of kings and priests has been formed from every nation, and their eternal reign with God has been assured (5:8–10). Their praise is echoed by the multitudes of the heavenly host (vs. 11–12), and then by the entire creation (v. 13). Since the last can happen only at the end, it is evident that the time between the resurrection of Christ and the end of all things has been telescoped into a moment. Though much has yet to unfold, the victory of God in Christ over sin and death, resulting in life and new creation, is *one,* and it has been *won.* History is the unfolding of the meaning of Good Friday and Easter Sunday, and it will be seen in the unveiled glory of the Parousia.

THE CITY OF GOD, REV. 21:9–22:5

In our understanding of the structure of Revelation this passage is in the nature of an excursus, just as is 17:1–19:10. The outpouring of the last two cups of wrath brings Armageddon and the cry from heaven, "It is done" (16:12–21). That is explained in 19:11ff., and is followed by the description of the kingdom of Christ in 20:1–10, the last judgment in 20:11–15, and the unveiling of the new creation in 21:1–8. That completes the drama in its successive stages. But, just as John shows to his reader the doom of the City of Antichrist in chs. 17 and 18, so he shows the glorious City of God in 21:9ff. The book of Revelation, as we earlier remarked, can be viewed as "A Tale of Two Cities," having the subtitle "The Harlot and the Bride."

In 19:7 the Bride is the people of God, who are united with the Bridegroom at his parousia. In 21:9ff. the Bride-City is revealed at the parousia. If the kingdom of Christ in 20:4ff. encompasses history, we have the interesting concept that the City of God is the context of the kingdom of God in this creation and in the new. Ever since Easter the City of God "comes down" from heaven to earth, for Easter signifies the saving rule of Christ in the world and life eternal for humanity. Life in the City, life in the kingdom, life in Christ, life eternal—all represent the same thing. But all that is hidden from the world until the unveiling at Christ's parousia. It should occasion no surprise, therefore, that the whole description of the City in 21:9–

22:5 is capable of application to life in this world, and also to the life of the world to come. God's rule in Christ embraces both—the world of history and that which time cannot measure.

The Bride-City, we are told in 21:11, has the glory of God (cf. 4:3); that we could expect from II Cor. 3:18.

It has a wall (Rev. 21:12), to keep those within safe and those without from entering (cf. 22:15). Its gates and foundations reveal the unity of the one people of God in all ages (vs. 12–14) with the added thought that forever the City of God is built on the bearers of the "testimony of Jesus" (1:2; cf. Eph. 2:19ff.).

The City has the shape of a cube like the Holy of Holies in the Temple (I Kings 6–20). Its measurement is 12,000 stadia each way— 1,500 miles, long, wide, high! The measure is not meant to be translated; clearly it shows that the City embraces the world then known and unifies heaven and earth into one sacred dwelling of God and humankind.

That the nations and kings of the earth bring their glory into the City (Rev. 21:24) is notable, for earlier in the book the nations and the kings offer their wealth and services to the City of Antichrist (chs. 17– 18). The opponents of God and the Lamb render up their swords and bring their willing tribute to God and the Lamb (so George Caird): "Nothing from the old order which has value in the sight of God is debarred from entry into the new. . . . Nowhere in the New Testament do we find a more eloquent statement than this of the all-embracing scope of Christ's redemptive work."[5]

The blessedness of the City is described in 22:1–5 mainly in terms of the imagery of Eden, with clear reminiscences of Ezekiel 47. The dominant thought is that of the abundance of life in the City (the river reminds us of the Milky Way!) and the joyous fellowship of humanity with God, expressed not only as a face-to-face enjoyment of God, but as participation in the eternal reign of God and the Lamb—royal service in the Jesus way!

EPILOGUE

The book ends with a final appeal: to the risen Lord to "come" and fulfill the vision, and to the thirsty to "come" to that same Lord and have thirst forever removed by the river of living water (Rev. 22:17), a notable conjunction of hope and evangelistic appeal. There follows a final promise from the returning Lord: "Assuredly, I am coming soon," and a voicing of the ancient prayer, *Maranatha Jesou,* "Come, Lord Jesus"—(v. 20). Of the promise and the prayer, Adolf Schlatter wrote *(Offenbarung):*

That promise is the sum of all promises.
And that prayer is the sum of all living hopes.[6]

We do well to cherish the promise and pray the prayer, with serenity and confidence in both.

NOTES

1. Jörg Jeremias, *Theophanie. Die Geschichte einer alttestamentlichen Gattung* (Neukirchen-Vluyn: Neukirchener Verlag des Erziehungsvereins, 1965), p. 10.

2. Gerhard von Rad, *Old Testament Theology*, Vol. 2, tr. by D. M. G. Stalker (Harper & Row, 1965), pp. 119–125.

3. Ludwig Köhler, *Old Testament Theology* (Westminster Press, 1957), p. 30.

4. E. F. Scott, *The Book of Revelation* (Charles Scribner's Sons, 1940), p. 174.

5. G. B. Caird, *The Revelation of St. John the Divine*, Harper's New Testament Commentaries (Harper & Row, 1966), pp. 270ff.

6. Adolf Schlatter, *Briefe und Offenbarung des Johannes*, Erläuterungen zum Neuen Testament, Vol. 10 (Stuttgart, 1950), p. 344.

FOR FURTHER READING

Beasley-Murray, George R. *The Book of Revelation.* The New Century Bible Commentary. London: Oliphants, 1974. Now in softcover. Wm. B. Eerdmans Publishing Co., 1981. An attempt to make the book of Revelation understandable in an interesting manner.

Caird, G. B. *The Revelation of St. John the Divine.* Harper's New Testament Commentaries. Harper & Row, 1966. A must for the preacher.

Charles, R. H. *A Critical and Exegetical Commentary on the Revelation of St. John.* 2 vols. International Critical Commentary. Edinburgh: T. & T. Clark, 1920. A work of reference which no serious student of Revelation can afford to ignore.

Ladd, George E. *A Commentary on the Revelation of John.* Wm. B. Eerdmans Publishing Co., 1972. A sober and reliable guide.

Mounce, Robert H. *The Book of Revelation.* The New International Commentary on the New Testament. Wm. B. Eerdmans Publishing Co., 1977. A condensed yet readable commentary that takes into account most of what has been written of importance on Revelation.

Rissi, Mathias. *Time and History: A Study on the Revelation.* Tr. Gordon C. Winsor. John Knox Press, 1966. A valuable discussion of the theology of the book of Revelation.

HOMILETICAL INDEX
OF SCRIPTURAL REFERENCES